Economic Shocks and Authoritarian Stability

Over two billion people still live under authoritarian rule. Moreover, authoritarian regimes around the world command enormous financial and economic resources, rivaling that controlled by advanced democracies. Yet authoritarian regimes as a whole are facing their greatest challenges in the recent two decades due to rebellions and economic stress. Extended periods of hardship have the potential of introducing instability to regimes because members of the existing ruling coalition suffer welfare losses that force them to consider alternatives, while previously quiescent masses may consider collective uprisings a worthwhile gamble in the face of a declining standard of living and possible elite splits.

Economic Shocks and Authoritarian Stability homes in on the economic challenges facing authoritarian regimes through a set of comparative case studies, which include Iran, Iraq under Saddam Hussein, Malaysia, Indonesia, Russia, the Eastern bloc countries, China, and Taiwan, authored by the top experts in these countries. Through these comparative case studies, this volume provides readers with the analytical tools for assessing whether the current round of economic shocks will lead to political instability or even regime change among the world's autocracies. This volume identifies the duration of economic shocks, the regime's control over the financial system, and the strength of the ruling party as key variables to explain whether authoritarian regimes will maintain the status quo, adjust their support coalitions, or fall from power after economic shocks.

Victor C. Shih is Ho Miu Lam Chair in China and Pacific Relations at the School of Global Policy and Strategy, University of California, San Diego.

WEISER CENTER FOR EMERGING DEMOCRACIES

Series Editor
Dan Slater is Professor of Political Science,
Ronald and Eileen Weiser Professor of Emerging Democracies,
and Director of the Weiser Center for Emerging Democracies (WCED)
at the University of Michigan. dnsltr@umich.edu

The Weiser Center for Emerging Democracies (WCED) Series publishes cutting-edge research in the pivotal field of authoritarianism and democratization studies. We live in a historical moment when democracies seem increasingly fragile and authoritarian regimes seem stubbornly resilient across the globe, and these topics continue to be a central part of research in the social sciences. The WCED Series strives to collect a balance of titles on emerging democracies and enduring dictatorships, as one cannot understand the conditions under which democracies live and thrive without comprehending how they die and remain unborn.

The WCED Series is interested in the full range of research being conducted on authoritarianism and democratization, primarily in political science but at times from history, sociology, and anthropology as well. The series encompasses a global geographic reach. We invite works that are primarily qualitative as well as quantitative in approach and are interested in edited volumes as well as solo-authored manuscripts.

The series highlights the leading role of the University of Michigan Press, Weiser Center for Emerging Democracies, and International Institute as premier sites for the research and production of knowledge on the conditions that make democracies emerge and dictatorships endure.

Economic Shocks and Authoritarian Stability: Duration, Financial Control, and Institutions
Victor C. Shih, Editor

Electoral Reform and the Fate of New Democracies: Lessons from the Indonesian Case
Sarah Shair-Rosenfield

Campaigns and Voters in Developing Democracies: Argentina in Comparative Perspective
Noam Lupu, Virginia Oliveros, and Luis Schiumerini, Editors

ECONOMIC SHOCKS AND AUTHORITARIAN STABILITY

Duration, Financial Control, and Institutions

Edited by Victor C. Shih

University of Michigan Press
Ann Arbor

Copyright © 2020 by Victor C. Shih
All rights reserved

This book may not be reproduced, in whole or in part, including illustrations, in any form (beyond that copying permitted by Sections 107 and 108 of the U.S. Copyright Law and except by reviewers for the public press), without written permission from the publisher.

Published in the United States of America by the
University of Michigan Press
Manufactured in the United States of America
Printed on acid-free paper
First published January 2020

A CIP catalog record for this book is available from the British Library.

Library of Congress Cataloging-in-Publication Data

Names: Shih, Victor C., editor.
Title: Economic shocks and authoritarian stability : duration, financial control, and institutions / edited by Victor C. Shih.
Description: Ann Arbor : University of Michigan Press, 2020. | Series: Weiser Center for Emerging Democracies | Includes bibliographical references and index. |
Identifiers: LCCN 2019032123 (print) | LCCN 2019032124 (ebook) |
  ISBN 9780472131778 (hardcover) | ISBN 9780472037674 (paperback) |
  ISBN 9780472126460 (ebook)
Subjects: LCSH: Authoritarianism—Economic aspects—Case studies. | Political stability—Economic aspects—Case studies. | Regime change—Economic aspects—Case studies.
Classification: LCC JC480 .E46 2020 (print) | LCC JC480 (ebook) |
  DDC 320.53—dc23
LC record available at https://lccn.loc.gov/2019032123
LC ebook record available at https://lccn.loc.gov/2019032124

Cover photo by Maria Goff.

Acknowledgments

This project was inspired by events in 2014 and 2015, which saw capital flight and currency volatility in both Russia and China. Although strong growth in the United States and other advanced economies in subsequent years has stabilized most authoritarian regimes, the question remains how dictators managed to stay in power, or lose it, during economic crises. I am extremely grateful to the dedication, patience, and generosity of the contributors to the edited book: Lisa Blaydes, Martin Dimitrov, Kevan Harris, Natalia Lamberova, Tom Pepinsky, Daniel Treisman, Joe Wong, and Sean Yom. Dan Slater deserves a special mention. In addition to authoring a key chapter on Malaysia, Dan also made crucial introductions to the University of Michigan Press, which paved the way to the publication of this manuscript. At the Press, Elizabeth Demers and Danielle Coty patiently answered my questions and helped me navigate the bewildering process of putting an edited book together. This volume would have been impossible without a 2015 workshop, which brought the contributors together with faculty members and graduate students at the University of California, San Diego. I would like to thank my colleagues Karen E. Ferree, Clark Gibson, Christina Schneider, Jesse Driscoll, and Stephan Haggard for providing incisive comments and helpful suggestions. Graduate students Jason Wu, Jack Zhang, Jonghyuk Lee, Yin Yuan, Deborah Seligsohn, Brian Tsay, and Matt Nanes asked smart questions and helped me record the engrossing conversation that day. Susan Shirk, Guang Lei, and Jude Blanchette at the 21st Century China Center provided crucial intellectual and administrative support for the conference. This book would not have materialized without the generosity of everyone mentioned here and doubtless others whom I have neglected to mention.

Contents

Introduction   1
   Victor C. Shih

ONE   The Domestic Political Implications of Economic Sanctions:
   Evidence from Iraq under Saddam Hussein   22
   Lisa Blaydes

TWO   Economic Shocks and Communist Survival and Collapse   41
   Martin K. Dimitrov

THREE   Of Eggs and Stones: Foreign Sanctions and Domestic
   Political Economy in the Islamic Republic of Iran   72
   Kevan Harris

FOUR   Economic Shocks and Authoritarian Responses:
   Putin's Strategy after the Global Financial Crisis of 2008–9   97
   Natalia Lamberova and Daniel Treisman

FIVE   Crises, Coalitions, and Change in Indonesia and Malaysia   119
   Thomas Pepinsky

SIX   Pathways to Stability and Instability in the Midst of
   Prolonged Slowdown: The Case of China   145
   Victor C. Shih

SEVEN   Maladjustment: Economic Shock and Authoritarian
   Dynamics in Malaysia   167
   Dan Slater

EIGHT Authoritarian Durability in East Asia's Developmental States:
Surviving the 1973 Energy Crisis in Taiwan and South Korea   189
Joseph Wong

NINE Bread, Fear, and Coalitional Politics in Jordan:
From Tribal Origins to Neoliberal Narrowing   210
Sean Yom

Conclusion   236
Victor C. Shih

Contributors   247

Index   251

Digital materials related to this title can be found on the Fulcrum platform via the following citable URL: https://doi.org/10.3998/mpub.11354716

Introduction

Victor C. Shih

Well into the second decade of the 20th century, over two billion people still live under authoritarian rule. Moreover, authoritarian regimes around the world command enormous financial and economic resources, rivaling those controlled by advanced democracies. For these compelling reasons, the study of non-democracies has enjoyed a revival in recent years. Yet authoritarian regimes as a whole are facing their greatest challenges in the recent two decades due to rebellions and economic stress. Syria has been mired in a bloody civil war since 2011, while Iran saw its first nationwide protest in years in early 2018, partly due to sanction-induced economic hardships. China's growth has slowed dramatically compared to the first decade of the century and is embroiled in trade tension with the US, while all the oil-producing authoritarian regimes, including Russia and Saudi Arabia, are facing a potentially prolonged period of low oil prices. Regimes subsidized by oil states, such as Jordan and Cuba, likewise face enduring economic hardship. Such extended periods of hardship have the potential of introducing instability to regimes because members of the existing ruling coalition suffer current, and expected future, welfare losses that force them to consider alternatives, while previously quiescent masses may consider collective uprisings a worthwhile gamble in the face of declining standard of living and possible elite splits (O'Donnell, Schmitter, and Whitehead 1986; Acemoglu and Robinson 2006). In response to such stresses, the incumbent regimes will marshal existing institutions, both economic and political ones, to survive the period of hardship (Haggard and Kaufman 1995).

This volume homes in on the economic challenges facing authoritarian regimes through a set of comparative case studies authored by leading comparative politics scholars and also the top experts in these countries. By economic shock, we mean a significant contraction of resources available to the regime due to a wholly or partly external change in the economic environment. Such externally driven shocks include substantial increases or decreases in commodities prices, substantial reduction in portfolio and direct investment flow from Organisation for Economic Co-operation and Development countries, and economic sanctions imposed by another country, especially the United States. Through these comparative case studies, this volume provides readers with the analytical tools for assessing whether the current round of economic shock will lead to political instability or even regime change.

Alternatively, in order to survive, economic shocks may compel authoritarian leaders to radically change their support coalitions. In changing support coalitions, the ruling regime adjusts the flow of benefits and access to power of the existing winning coalitions, whose support is crucial to the survival of the regime (Bueno de Mesquita et al. 2003). Formerly favored constituencies suddenly find themselves with substantially diminished benefits. Other members of ruling coalitions or even those formerly outside of them may obtain greater benefits even after the onset of economic downturns. By adjusting the flow of benefits and power to the support coalitions, authoritarian rulers hope to enhance their ability to survive economic shocks. Of course, if shocks are too severe or if adjusting the coalition fails to galvanize sufficient support for the incumbents, the authoritarian leadership or the entire regime may still fall from power. In brief, this volume has identified the duration of economic shocks, the regime's control over the financial system, and the strength of the ruling party as key variables to explain whether authoritarian regimes maintain the status quo, adjust their support coalitions, or fall from power after economic shocks.

The cases in this volume suggest that regimes with confident control over financial institutions and strong ruling parties very likely will survive short economic shocks and have a good chance of surviving even prolonged shocks, perhaps with some adjustments to the main support coalitions. On the other extreme, regimes with weak control over both their financial and political institutions may well lose power as a result of even short economic shocks and face significant risks of losing power in the midst of a prolonged shock, even if they adjust their main support coalitions. In the meantime, regimes with either strong control over financial institutions or strong ruling parties have a good chance of surviving short economic shocks but need to radically adjust their support coalitions in order to survive prolonged downturns. Even so, these regimes at times still fall from power in persistent downturns. The cases in this volume do not suggest deterministic outcomes, but offer a range of outcomes depending on the duration of the crisis and institutional configurations in the regime.

Is Authoritarian Resilience Purely an Institutional Question?

Since the late 1990s, a thriving literature has focused on the internal institutions of authoritarian regimes as keys to understanding the phenomenon of "authoritarian resilience," the apparent longevity of some authoritarian regimes in the face of modernization and the growth of the middle class (Nathan 2003). The literature has clarified many channels through which institutions have allowed dictators to rule with relatively low costs and high effectiveness. Yet institutions per se may not provide all the answers to regime longevity and how regimes seek to survive. Instead, complex interactions between internal institutions of these regimes and exogenous economic and political shocks may ultimately drive regime longevity, as well as major adjustments in the coalitions supporting these regimes.

In Geddes's (1999) seminal paper on different types of authoritarian regimes, she theorizes that because the authoritarian party provides club goods to the various factions in the regime, upholding the regime still presents a better option for the elite than splitting up the regime, even amid factional conflicts. Thus, she observes empirically that single-party regimes had greater longevity than either monarchies or military dictatorships in the postwar period (Geddes 1999). Svolik's works extend and formalize this insight by specifying a whole host of incentives embedded in the authoritarian ruling party that make regime longevity more likely, from longer time horizon of officials to generating sunk costs for party members to creating more credible power-sharing arrangements (Svolik 2012). The literature on one-party states also dovetails nicely with the rich literature on authoritarian legislatures, which also shows how authoritarian institutions in themselves enhance regime stability and longevity (Svolik and Boix 2007; Gandhi 2008).

A thriving empirical literature has also developed in parallel to theoretical works on one-party regimes. A large scholarship on the Chinese Communist Party shows that the party-instituted cadre evaluation system motivated local officials, especially those in lower tiers of government, to engage in yardstick competition, which produced greater growth for China, presumably beneficial to the regime (Landry, Xiaobo, and Duan 2018; Jia, Kudamatsu, and Seim 2014; Landry 2008; Li and Zhou 2005;

Chen, Li, and Zhou 2005; Edin 2003). Another literature on Latin America and the Middle East shows that authoritarian ruling parties prevented internal splits by distributing spoils to key elite constituencies (Magaloni 2006; Brownlee 2007; Blaydes 2011).

Beyond the ruling party, a host of other institutions and practices are also pinpointed as keys to authoritarian resilience. Slater (2003), for example, finds that Mahathir took advantage of colonial-era institutions, including the courts, economic policy bodies, and the police, to help maintain the status quo of United Malays National Organization (UMNO) dominance. Of course, authoritarian regimes also used secret police and networks of informants to prevent the rise of any credible opposition from outside of the regimes (Dimitrov and Sassoon 2014). The burgeoning literature on censorship and internet control strongly suggests that ruling parties can deploy vast resources and technical know-how to enhance legitimacy and to prevent collective action (King, Pan, and Roberts 2013, 2017). An older literature suggests that regime control over financial and economic institutions may allow some autocracies to grow faster, thus creating greater resources for the regime (Gerschenkron 1962; Haggard 1990).

Despite the torrent of literature on the institutional advantages embedded in authoritarian regimes, which are implicitly or explicitly linked to the larger questions of regime durability and managing key support coalitions, a skeptical view is warranted. At the very least, the literature on authoritarian survival needs to inject another dose of comparative research. That is, while focusing on one or a small handful of durable authoritarian regimes like China may suggest institutions in the ruling party as key causal variables, a broader examination of cases suggests a much more complex causal mechanism. For example, all of the Eastern European communist regimes had Leninist party structures that were touted in the literature as keys to regime longevity and integral components of authoritarian survival strategies. Yet they all collapsed within a short time of one another around 1990. Among Eastern and Central European regimes, the varying degrees of party penetration in society and internal coherence of the ruling parties were not determined by institutional variation. Rather, historical contingencies and Soviet perception of societal opposition in these countries explained the degree of party intrusion in society in these countries (Grzymala-Busse 2001). In any event, for these regimes, the variation in the strength and penetration of the ruling parties did not much explain their longevity, as they nearly all collapsed within two years of each other.

Similarly, although secret police in authoritarian regimes had varying degrees of effectiveness (Dimitrov and Sassoon 2014), this variation did not explain the timing of regime collapse among the best-known cases. Among the Eastern European regimes, the German Democratic Republic (GDR) had the most fearsome and extensive secret police organization (Grzymala-Busse 2001). Yet the GDR was among the first East European communist regimes to collapse. Also, when protests snowballed in the GDR, the regime attempted to stay in power by acceding to the demands of the people who wanted to leave the country, rather than to rely on repressive means at its disposal (Kuran 1991). Saddam Hussein likewise had a loyal and ruthless secret police organ supported by a vast network of informants (Dimitrov and Sassoon 2014; Blaydes 2013). Although it kept him in power through harrowing internal challenges, the ultimate demise of the regime had little to do with the effectiveness of the secret police.

While these various regimes remained in power, institutional strength seemed the obvious explanation for their survival. Yet when they collapsed or had to radically reorient support coalitions, institutions alone often could not explain the outcomes. Ultimately, major exogenous shocks likely impacted both authoritarian institutions, as well as key outcomes such as regime longevity and the composition of key support coalitions (Pepinsky 2014). Institutions still mattered, but there likely were more complex interactions between significant exogenous shocks and existing institutions that paved various pathways toward at least three major outcomes: status quo, a shift in support coalitions, and regime collapse. Through case studies of past and present authoritarian regimes, this volume homes in on the interaction between one type of exogenous shock, economic hardship, and political and financial institutions and how it affected regime longevity and changes in the support coalitions of these regimes. Moreover, the cases in this volume examine authoritarian regimes' survival strategies *over time*, which turns out to be revealing. In essence, as the cases of Malaysia and China show, regime strategies to deal with economic shocks in one period may undermine the effectiveness of institutions in these regimes in subsequent shocks.

We begin with a set of cases that are largely similar to each other in one important dimension. All of the cases are established and institutionalized one-party authoritarian regimes, with the exception of Jordan, which can be classified as a monarchy (Geddes 1999). In other words, most of these regimes had an extensive party structure that answered to the incumbent autocrat. Thus, most of the regimes in this volume enjoyed the advantages of single-party rule discussed in the literature. Also, by the time the economic shock under discussion descended on these regimes, they had been in existence for a decade or more. While this selection still does not control for all institutional and circumstantial factors, it excludes analysis of new or highly volatile authoritarian regimes such as warlord regimes. Thus, this volume mainly homes in on variation among established, institutionalized one-party states.

Authoritarian Survival as a Dynamic Strategy

Contributors to this volume provide nine richly contextualized case studies that provide new insights into how authoritarian regimes survive economic shocks. First, focusing on some of the most established authoritarian regimes, our cases show that although economic shocks slightly elevated the chance of regime collapse, a remarkable number of regimes among our cases survived economic shocks. The cases in this volume further reveal that regimes often changed the composition of the ruling coalitions in response to economic shocks, and that such changes profoundly influenced *how* regimes continued to rule, even if institutions stayed largely static. In some cases, such as Malaysia and China, these changes ultimately affected the sustainability of the regime in the medium term.

This volume focuses on the dynamic challenge of economic shocks and regime responses. First, our cases reveal that the duration of the economic shock plays an important role in the outcome. If the support coalition perceives a short shock, the leadership may not need to change the status quo too much, and the risk of losing power entirely may be small. Existing institutional strength likely has the greatest influence on shorter shocks, because a fiscal surplus, a large deposit base in state-controlled banks, or persistent balance-of-payment surpluses can reassure the elite that a short shock can be made even shorter with fiscal or monetary policies. Even with considerable fiscal or financial resources, however, a prolonged crisis ultimately reduces GDP and tax revenue and produces greater government debt, necessitating that the regime cut current benefits to supporters (Reinhart and Rogoff 2009). Elite actors in such an environment deeply discount the future benefits of the status quo, giving them less of a stake in maintaining it. Authoritarian leaders in turn must respond to the wavering support coalition with new policies, else face the possibility of losing power.

Contrary to the expectation of the existing literature, however, authoritarian leaders in our case studies by and large *did not* respond to diminished resources by enacting institutional changes to credibly signal future payoffs to supporters (Acemoglu and Robinson 2006; Desai, Olofsgård, and Yousef 2009). Jordan in the early 1990s was the only case whereby economic hardship led to liberalization. Even there, Yom's chapter points out, liberalization was quickly reversed once foreign aid became available, again contrary to the expectation of the literature. Instead, authoritarian leaders often reacted to diminished resources by drastically cutting benefits to existing members of the support coalition, thus reducing fiscal outlays. Blaydes's chapter on Iraq in the 1990s shows that Saddam Hussein responded to US economic sanctions by drastically reducing benefits to the Sunnis, especially those based outside of his hometown, Tikrit. Instead of credibly reassuring all members of the existing coalition, a key strategy during an economic shock seemed to be preserving available resources for core priorities, even at the cost of higher levels of dissatisfaction.

Although democracies often enact such coalition change during "hard times" (Gourevitch 1986), it is much more surprising for authoritarian regimes to do so because they presumably already give minimal benefits to ordinary citizens and focus their payoffs on essential regime supporters (Bueno de Mesquita et al. 2003; Acemoglu, Egorov, and Sonin 2008). But if existing coalitions were already the minimum viable assemblage, how could dictators afford to reduce benefits to their coalitions during crises without at least promising future benefits in some credible way? The chapters in this volume suggest that dictators maintained much more complicated coalitions than is suggested by the literature. For example, authoritarian regimes may have maintained surplus coalitions when the economy allowed it to do so (Magaloni 2006). Another possibility is that because a prolonged shock reduced everyone's resources, including that of the opposition, an authoritarian leader could afford to reduce the ruling coalition and still survive. Similarly, during economic shocks, members of the dictator's support coalition knew that the diminution of the flow of benefits was caused by external factors rather than a diversion of resources to increase the dictator's relative power. This knowledge may have maintained political stability (Svolik 2009). Although this volume by no means provides the final word on this issue, it opens up a fruitful avenue for future theoretical and empirical research.

Finally, the cases suggest that regimes' control over their financial systems at the time of these crises constituted another important factor. To be sure, control over the financial system was somewhat related to the occurrence of crises, but in all of our cases, the crises were triggered by external factors, such as sudden increase or collapse of commodities prices or sanctions and monetary policy enacted by external actors. Other medium-term factors drove regime control over the financial system, such as the relationship between major financial conglomerates and the autocrats, external debt, and dependence on the export of commodities. As previous studies show, regimes that relied heavily on the domestic private sector for financing left themselves vulnerable to the sudden withdrawal of support, which often brought about regime change (Haggard and Kaufman 1995; Pepinsky 2009). This volume incorporates this insight by highlighting the role of regime control over the financial sector as a key variable. With firm control over the financial system, such as in China in 2008 and Taiwan in the 1970s, the regime immediately mobilized deposits in the banking system to stabilize the economy, which negated the need for institutional or coalition changes. In contrast, where private businesses were crucial veto players by virtue of their control over key financial institutions, such as in Indonesia, the regimes left themselves highly vulnerable to the withdrawal of financial resources (Haggard and Maxfield 1996; Haggard and Kaufman 1995).

Surprisingly, many regimes, including Russia, East Germany, Bulgaria, Jordan, and Indonesia, allowed themselves to develop reliance on external funding, either through external debt or commodities export. These regimes were perfectly comfortable with developing this vulnerability in order to appease status quo supporters of the regime, which included the defense industry in the case of the Soviet Union and ordinary workers in Eastern Europe (Miller 2016). Perhaps these regimes' control over key financial institutions lulled them into a sense of complacency. This is in sharp contrast to what we expect of farsighted dictators. Authoritarian leaders may have been more shortsighted and confused than the literature expects. Again, this volume opens another avenue for future research by asking why dictators occasionally behaved in such a shortsighted manner.

Interaction between Economic Shocks and Institutions

This volume, which grew out of an intense two-day-long workshop at University of California, San Diego, with the contributors and a small handful of UCSD PhD students, has identified the duration of economic shocks, the regime's control over the financial system, and the strength of the ruling party as key variables to explain whether authoritarian regimes maintain the status quo, adjust their support coalitions, or fall from power after economic shocks. Although this volume falls short of proving causation due to the complexity of the interactions between these variables, it attempts to draw out some possible causal paths toward various outcomes.

The general approach here seeks to inductively highlight potential causal mechanisms ripe for future theory building and to generate new hypotheses for more systematic empirical testing (Mill 1846; Thelen and

Steinmo 1992). Instead of deductively generating and testing hypotheses from a well-specified theory, contributors were asked to think broadly about how a largely exogenous economic shock in their cases interacted with other parameters to produce the outcomes of interest. The editor only sought to narrow the number of possible causal pathways by focusing on the downstream impact of an economic shock. Obviously, an external political shock such as an invasion would interact with existing institutions in very different ways.

Even the outcomes of interest were inductively derived from the cases, as contributors realized that besides status quo and regime collapse, changes in the support coalitions constituted an important departure from the status quo in several of our cases. We thus decided that it was an important outcome to explore. Also, inductively, contributors learned through the comparative cases that the complex interaction between financial institutions, the ruling parties, and the economic downturns had an important impact on the outcomes. The ambition of this volume falls short of making causal inference because of heterogeneity across the cases (Mahoney 2012; King, Keohane, and Verba 1994), but the common empirical patterns witnessed suggest new directions for future theory building and empirical research.

We first focused on economic shocks because major components of these shocks tended to be exogenous, beyond efforts by the dictators or institutions embedded in the regimes. Oil price shocks, both positive and negative, affected the former Eastern bloc countries in the Dimitrov chapter, Russia in the Treisman and Lamberova contribution, Jordan in the Yom chapter, and Taiwan in Wong's chapter. Research has shown that although supply shocks can have a short-lived effect on oil prices, major shifts in the real price of oil tended to be caused by changes in global precautionary demand and cyclical demand (Kilian 2009). Given this finding, medium-term oil prices likely were beyond the control of the dictatorships studied in this volume. An oil price shock also may be longer-lasting than other shocks, and thus regime insiders may quickly come to expect a prolonged period of austerity under the status quo. As discussed, these medium- and long-term shocks may have discounted the utility of regime control over financial institutions.

Traditionally, financial crises have been triggered by the sudden withdrawal of portfolio and even direct investment by investors, who tend to come from advanced countries. This can be the result of a default by an emerging market (EM) country or because of shocks from within developed countries, such as interest rate hikes by the Federal Reserve (Reinhart and Rogoff 2009). Into the 1990s, as capital accumulated in many developing countries, bouts of domestic capital flight also became a mechanism of emerging market financial crises. Among countries studied in this volume, financial crises led to severe capital flight and economic slowdown in Indonesia and Malaysia, Russia, and China. Given the relatively small presence of these countries in the global financial market at the time of these crises, it is doubtful that they had any substantial impact on the crises. The crises, of course, had a major impact on export, capital flows, fiscal expenditures, and growth in these regimes (Haggard 2000b). The impact and duration of financial crises varied depending on external circumstances and internal institutions and reactions. For example, during the 2008–9 crisis, Federal Reserve quantitative easing starting in late 2008 ended the panic on dollar liquidity and inaugurated a period of EM rally in 2009 and 2010. Regime control over financial institutions likely had the greatest impact on the duration of financial crises, relative to crises of other origins. In Malaysia, for example, the UMNO imposed effective capital control, which shortened the period of panic and minimized the impact of the Asian Financial Crisis.

The economic hardship described in Blaydes's chapter on Iraq and Harris's chapter on Iran was caused by US sanctions. To be sure, US-imposed sanctions may be caused by the dictators' own calculus, which led to behavior likely to trigger sanctions. However, given the hardship sanctions imposed on these regimes, the probability and full impact of the sanctions likely were not fully anticipated by the rulers of Iran and Iraq. As the Lacy and Niou model suggests, potential recipients of sanctions often did not fully appreciate the determination of the coercer to carry out the sanctions in the event of noncompliance to the initial threat of sanction (Lacy and Niou 2004). Thus, when sanctions actually were imposed, they were far from fully expected. In those cases, the full impact of sanctions likely constituted an exogenous shock to these regimes. Also, in the case of US-imposed sanctions, a mixture of domestic US politics and international reactions to sanctions determined their duration and severity, creating uncertainties among elite supporters of the targeted regime as to their future payoffs. In this type of economic shock, regime control over financial institutions likely helped regimes avoid an initial panic. In general, however, as the coercer reveals its determination to impose a prolonged and severe sanction, control over financial institutions or even strong party institutions may see their utility decline over time.

When economic shocks put authoritarian regimes under duress, our cases suggest that the interaction between the duration of the shock, regime control over financial institutions, and institutions of the ruling party have an impact on whether these regimes maintain the status quo, change their support coalitions, or fall from power. As table 1 reveals, we are by no means making a deterministic argument. Instead, our cases suggest that the presence or absence of these three crucial variables makes certain outcomes more probable along a continuum. The three variables in question at times interacted to substantially increase or decrease the probability of a coalition change or regime collapse. For example, where the shock was a short one and the regime had both a strong party and strong control over the financial system, status quo was the expected outcome. However, where the crisis persisted or where party institutionalization or control over the financial system was weaker, the likelihood of coalition change increased. To be sure, this volume is missing cases of short shocks where the ruling party was weak, but an instructive case might have been Russia in 1999 just after a relatively short-lived financial crisis. Although Russia was a weak democracy in the late 1990s, an increasingly ill Yeltsin felt that he needed a strong deputy to help him navigate the political maelstrom after the crisis. He thus nominated Putin, a man with well-known KGB ties, to the premiership in 1999, thus fundamentally altering the internal balance of his support coalition (Gessen 2012).

When a regime with little control over its financial system and minimal mobilization capacity confronts a prolonged economic shock, it faces a high likelihood of regime change in the absence of substantial external aid (table 1). To be sure, even at the extremes, our predictions are probabilistic rather than deterministic. For example, even facing prolonged periods of

TABLE 1. The Relationship between the Duration of Shock, Regime Control over the Financial System, Party Institutionalization, and Regime Outcomes

	Strong party / strong control over finance	Strong party / weak control over finance	Weak party / strong control over finance	Weak party / weak control over finance
Short shocks	Status quo (China 2008–9, Taiwan 1973, Malaysia 1998)	Coalition change / regime change (Indonesia 1998)	Status quo / coalition change	Coalition change / regime change
Prolonged shocks	Status quo / coalition change (Iran 1980s, Iraq 1991–2003, Russia post-2014, China post-2015)	Coalition change / regime change (Eastern bloc states 1990, Malaysia post-2010)	Coalition change (Iran post-2006)	Regime change / coalition change (Jordon 1990s)

downturns in oil prices, Jordan, a monarchy without a ruling party, still survived with the help of external aid. Between the extremes, regimes with varying degrees of control over the financial system and party strength manipulated support coalitions in various ways to ensure survival. Not all such effort succeeded, but the cases in this volume reveal that even risky coalition changes, such as the ones enacted by Saddam Hussein or Russia after US sanctions, succeeded in avoiding regime change.

The contributors to the volume recognize that shock duration, regime control over the financial system, and party institutionalization are not orthogonal variables, but each variable has aspects that are exogenously driven. A short shock lasted two or less fiscal cycles, and actors could see an end of the exogenous pressure after one fiscal cycle. As long as key regime supporters anticipated short shocks, they likely would not forgo future benefits by defecting from the regime at the first sign of trouble. Many cases in this volume display this pattern. A prolonged crisis is one that lasted longer than two fiscal cycles, where actors could not see an end to the sharp contraction in regime resources after one fiscal cycle. In this case, supporters of the ruling regime found it worthwhile to explore alternative ruling coalitions due to high discount rates on the future benefits of the status quo. The costs of governance also increased due to rising popular protests, which further discounted expected payoffs of key supporters of the regime. The regime's leaders likewise realized that they had to make some tough choices in a prolonged crisis because the economic resources previously available to the regime had shrunk substantially and no end was in sight. In order to maintain the solvency of the regime, benefits had to be cut from members of the support coalition, or the regime would need new sources of revenue, which could incur its own risks and costs.

When confronted with the harsh reality of drastically reduced benefits and heightened risks of uprisings, some regimes, including Indonesia in 1998 and East Germany and Bulgaria in the late 1980s, just collapsed due to defection by core members of the support coalitions. To be sure, the length of crises was partly determined by regimes' control over the financial system. However, external factors, such as commodities prices, withdrawal of oil aid, and sanctions also drove the duration of the shocks, which determined outcomes.

Control over the financial system included two crucial aspects: the regime's direct control over major financial institutions, and reliance on external funds via external debt, aid, or commodities export. Direct control over major financial institutions meant that authoritarian leaders could order major financial institutions to enact policies detrimental to the interests of major groups in the society or even those of key regime supporters in order to provide these regimes with additional financial resources during economic downturns. This pattern of behavior is similar to the notion of insulated policymaking often considered a key to economic reform (Nelson 1995; Haggard 2000a), except changes enacted by authoritarian regimes often entailed even heavier state intervention in the financial markets.

Control over the financial sector allowed regimes to mitigate the negative impact of economic shocks in two crucial ways. First, regimes could deploy financial resources toward fiscal expenditure to smooth consumption of elite insiders and even the population to minimize discontent (Lardy 1998). As the Shih chapter in the volume reveals, the Chinese Communist Party simply ordered the banks to lend trillions of renminbi to investment projects in late 2008, which brought Chinese growth rates back to double digits by the end of 2009. The massive expenditure immediately ended expectation of "hard times," thus preserving the status quo even amid a global economic recession. Wong's study of Taiwan and Treisman and Lamberova's of Russia display similar patterns. Second, strict control over the financial system also prevented large-scale capital flight, which lessened the likelihood of external defaults, currency devaluation, and high inflation (Reinhart and Rogoff 2009). The Pepinsky contribution in this volume shows that Malaysia's ability to largely stifle capital flight allowed the ruling UMNO government to avoid the worst possible outcome of the crisis. The ability to prevent large-scale capital flight likely increased regimes' ability to survive economic shocks. But again, the state's autonomous control over the financial sector harmed private sector interests, which no doubt would have preferred to move their wealth offshore to safe havens.

However, direct control of domestic financial institutions may not be sufficient if reliance on foreign funds is high on the eve of a shock. If, like East Germany, as described in the Dimitrov chapter, or Jordan in the 1970s, as described in the Yom chapter, the regime relied on external credit for a large part of the state budget and consumption, the sudden withdrawal of such credit causes a sharp contraction in fiscal expenditure, regardless of regime control of key financial institutions (Haggard and Maxfield 1996). The case of the GDR suggests that even where one-party dictatorships control all the major domestic institutions, financial stability is elusive. The Blaydes contribution on Iraq also demonstrates that although the government had firm control over financial institutions, US-imposed sanctions after the First Gulf War drastically reduced the inflow of foreign exchange, which Iraq depended upon to import food.

The reduction in oil revenue immediately necessitated severe rationing, which triggered political instability. In Jordan, as the Yom chapter details, weak control over the financial system due to dependence on external funding forced the regime to reduce benefits to traditional stakeholders of the regime soon after the fall of oil prices.

Regime control over financial institutions likely had differential impact on disparate types of crises. Control over financial institutions likely helped regimes the most during financial crises because such control could minimize the two biggest threats to financial stability, capital flight and a domestic credit crunch. Firm control of financial institutions likely increased the common expectation of a short-duration crisis, which already was common for financial crises (Reinhart and Rogoff 2009). Many cases in this volume displayed this pattern. In contrast, in a longer-duration, exogenous shock, such as a fundamental shift in oil prices or a determined economic sanction, elites may realize, after a while, that the state is increasingly indebted to foreign creditors or that the state will be plagued by persistent deficits and ballooning debt for some time to come. Such persistent shortfalls likely raise elite supporters' willingness to defect from the ruling coalition, which compels the dictators to reduce the size of the winning coalition. Otherwise, elite defection may snowball into a collapse of the regime. In other words, firm control over financial institutions may matter less for long-lasting commodities shocks or determined economic sanctions.

Finally, in accordance to existing literature on authoritarian rule, the cases in the volume suggest that having a credible ruling party helped regimes survive economic shocks. As much of the literature has pointed out, a strong ruling party or governing pact can credibly distribute resources to core members of support coalitions, and the typically pyramidal structure of authoritarian parties provides an incentive for party members to maintain the status quo even when short-term payoffs are reduced (Magaloni and Kricheli 2010; Brownlee 2007; Svolik 2012; Magaloni 2006; Nathan 2003; Geddes 1999; Slater 2010). Our studies of China, Taiwan, and Malaysia show that one-party states or dominant-party states possessed greater capacity to coordinate elite action during crises. More important, the institutionalization of the ruling party allowed regimes to distribute the pain associated with economic shocks without defection from these regimes due to expectation of future payoffs from promotions within the ruling parties. The oil shock in Taiwan demonstrates that the Kuomintang was able to impose costs on state-owned enterprises without too much resistance because senior managers of these SOEs were also party cadres. A strong one-party state often had strong media control, which allowed them to shape popular perception of a crisis via propaganda. China, Malaysia, and Russia shared this pattern. Still, these institutional factors were much more deterministic of outcomes in the cases of short economic shocks than prolonged ones. Prolonged crises led to greater indeterminacy of outcomes as regimes struggled to enact new policies and fashion new coalitions, the failure of which led to regime collapse.

To be sure, a strong one-party dictatorship is associated with regime control over financial institutions, but as the cases of East Germany and Bulgaria show, one-party states can well develop vulnerable financial systems if they have high external debt. If, as the GDR had done, regimes exerted extensive party control over society by borrowing heavily overseas in order to pay for large public sectors, they inevitably developed severe vulnerability to a sudden withdrawal of external credit (Grzymala-Busse 2001). In contrast, Iran, despite having a "diffused" political system, managed to maintain a balance-of-payments surplus through the sanction years, which allowed a not particularly powerful leadership to provide basic necessities to a suffering population. That might have staved off larger-scale unrest.

Cases and Future Research

The chapters in this volume were written by some of the most knowledgeable scholars of comparative politics, including Dan Slater (University of Michigan), Lisa Blaydes (Stanford), Tom Pepinsky (Cornell), Daniel Treisman and Natalia Lamberova (UCLA), Joseph Wong (University of Toronto), Martin Dimitrov (Tulane), Kevan Harris (UCLA), Sean Yom (Temple), and Victor Shih (UCSD). They all have written about countries where they have done extensive research and about which they have accumulated a wellspring of knowledge. Some contributors leverage extensive archival and elite interview sources to provide insights on elite actors' calculus. Given their deep knowledge of these cases, the authors are able to adjudicate the relative weight of the various independent variables and how they interacted to produce outcomes in the countries under examination. Although not conclusive, these potential causal pathways generate new directions for research on authoritarian regimes. In all the cases, the authors provide background information about the broad institutional configuration of these regimes, which shape elite actors' preferences and policy choices. Then a description of the duration and severity of the economic shocks is provided. Finally, the contributors describe some of the short-term and long-term consequences of the interaction of these variables.

As mentioned above, several themes emerge from this collection of cases. First, as table 1 suggests, the interaction between political and financial institutions during an economic crisis may not have received sufficient attention in the extant literature on authoritarian resilience. In Shih's account of China, he describes the extensive financial resources and tight control over the financial sector available to the Chinese Communist Party on the eve of the 2008–9 global economic shock. Despite plunging exports, China quickly counteracted the growth slowdown with a massive stimulus financed by the state-controlled banking sector. Without complete control over all the financial institutions, even a strong ruling party would have had difficulty turning the economy around so quickly. Similarly, the Wong contribution on Taiwan during the 1973 oil embargo suggests that both the party control and control over financial institutions laid the groundwork for a relatively uneventful oil price shock for Taiwan. In addition, the disturbance was a relatively short one, which likely enhanced the effectiveness of party control over firms and financial institutions. In a similar vein, Slater details how the Malaysian UMNO regime was able to mobilize financial and fiscal resources to counteract the damage caused by the Asian Financial Crisis, thus avoiding a political crisis in the short run. In contrast, Pepinsky shows that during this crisis in 1997, the New Order coalition in Indonesia failed to agree on the proper response, which ultimately led to mass defection from the ruling coalition. These cases suggest that additional cross-country data gathering on government control over financial institutions may be a worthwhile exercise to systematically assess the impact of this variable on regime-level outcomes.

Several of the chapters suggest that authoritarian regimes may have been more generous than is theoretically predicted, which created long-term vulnerability. Dimitrov shows that despite having control over financial institutions, the welfarist promises made by East Germany and Bulgaria left them vulnerable to economic shocks by increasing deficits. By the time the Soviet Union withdrew oil aid to East Germany and Bulgaria, they had developed a heavy dependence on Soviet aid to maintain these welfare policies. The collapse of the socialist welfare states led to the collapse of these regimes. In contrast, China was able to time and again compress wages and social services to reduce costs during hardship. Similarly, Harris's chapter focuses on two periods of economic hardship in Iran—the Iran-Iraq War starting in 1980 and the sanctions imposed by the United States from 2011 to 2013. In the first case, a united Iranian leadership for years imposed hardship on regime insiders and the population alike. In the latter case, a much more divided leadership with weaker institutional control felt compelled to negotiate with the United States to end the sanctions after three years. Clearly, regimes, even when faced with similar institutional settings, had varying ability to impose hardships on the population and key supporters during economic downturns. Future work should both further specify the mechanisms that generate this variation and empirically test them.

Two of the chapters in this volume highlight the need to reexamine two core theoretical results in the extant literature. First, the theoretical literature puts a heavy emphasis on the dictator's maintaining only a minimum winning coalition and not giving surplus resources to key supporters (Slantchev and McMahon 2015; Bueno de Mesquita et al. 2003). Yet Blaydes's exhaustively researched study of Iraq under Saddam Hussein shows that his response to the 1990 US sanctions was a deep reduction of subsidies to Sunni areas, leaving untouched only the subsidies to his core supporters based around Tikrit. She shows that it wasn't until 1990 that Hussein reduced his payoffs to supporters to a "minimum" level, as signified by the rising number of actual and rumored assassination attempts against him. This strongly suggests that his payoffs to supporters and the size of his coalition previous to 1990 were not "minimal" and may have been at a surplus level. At the very least, this case demonstrates a need to reframe our understanding of the minimum winning coalition in dictatorships and suggest a need to derive new ways of conceiving dictators' survival calculus.

The Treisman and Lamberova chapter on Russia suggests another potential major turn in the literature. That is, in a world of deep social media penetration and rapidly declining costs of censorship and of saturating social media with pro-government messages, perhaps the traditional ruling party is no longer a necessary ingredient for surviving economic shocks. Focusing on Putin's capacity to censor and direct the media, this chapter points out that despite lacking a grassroots party structure, the Kremlin successfully mobilized support for Putin and minimized the political fallout of economic hardship. Although a wave of scholarly work is now exploring the specific impact of government censorship and positive messaging (King, Pan, and Roberts 2017, 2013), cross-national studies in the future can systematically assess whether, on average, internet control has to some degree substituted for the party organization. If that were the case, it would suggest that authoritarian regimes, like corporations, have taken advantage of technological shocks to reduce the costs of key tasks such as censorship and propaganda (Treisman and Guriev 2015). This is an aspect of "authoritarian resilience" that begs for more theory development and testing.

Finally, an interesting theme that emerges is the long-term consequences of short-term fixes to economic crises. Surprisingly, unlike the farsighted and cost-conscious dictator described in some models (Egorov and Sonin 2011; Bueno de Mesquita et al. 2003), many regimes engaged in unsustainable fiscal and financial maneuvers to stave off the worst impact of the current crisis, planting the seeds for future crises. In Malaysia, for example, the regime's failure to respond to the financial shock of the late 1990s with economic or political reforms has yielded an increasingly corrupt and uncompetitive political economy built on unsustainable fiscal practices and unpopular repression of the growing urban middle class. Similarly, Yom's chapter on Jordan shows a desperate regime, after a period of low oil prices, borrowing more and more from the West through a transnational financial elite, which made its rule more brittle given the ever-increasing cost of its coalitional commitments. The coalitional narrowing that resulted, which replaced popular tribal forces with a new business elite, has replaced the economic overhead of the past with the political uncertainty of new opposition from former supporters. Similarly, the massive stimulus in 2008 and 2009 in China created an unsustainable path of credit expansion that will one-day require painful deleveraging (International Monetary Fund 2017). Future work needs to theorize why authoritarian regimes engaged in such shortsighted policies and examine the medium-term economic and global financial implications of regimes' reactions to economic shocks, especially large-scale international borrowing.

REFERENCES

Acemoglu, Daron, Georgy Egorov, and Konstantin Sonin. 2008. "Coalition Formation in Non-democracies." *Review of Economic Studies* 75 (4): 987–1009.

Acemoglu, Daron, and James A. Robinson. 2006. *Economic Origins of Dictatorship and Democracy*. New York: Cambridge University Press.

Blaydes, Lisa. 2011. *Elections and Distributive Politics in Mubarak's Egypt*. New York: Cambridge University Press.

Blaydes, Lisa. 2013. "Compliance and Resistance in Iraq under Saddam Hussein: Evidence from the Files of the Ba'th Party." Palo Alto: Stanford University.

Brownlee, Jason. 2007. *Authoritarianism in an Age of Democratization*. New York: Cambridge University Press.

Bueno de Mesquita, Bruce, Alastair Smith, Randolph M. Siverson, and James D. Morrow. 2003. *The Logic of Political Survival*. Cambridge, MA: MIT Press.

Chen, Ye, Hongbin Li, and Li-An Zhou. 2005. "Relative Performance Evaluation and the Turnover of Provincial Leaders in China." *Economic Letters* 88 (3): 421–25.

Desai, Raj M., Anders Olofsgård, and Tarik Yousef. 2009. "The Logic of Authoritarian Bargains." *Economics and Politics* 21 (1): 93–125.

Dimitrov, Martin K., and Joseph Sassoon. 2014. "State Security, Information, and Repression: A Comparison of Communist Bulgaria and Ba'thist Iraq." *Journal of Cold War Studies* 16 (2): 3–31.

Edin, Maria. 2003. "State Capacity and Local Agent Control in China: CCP Cadre Management from a Township Perspective." *China Quarterly* 173 (March): 35–52.

Egorov, Georgy, and Konstantin Sonin. 2011. "Dictators and Their Viziers: Endogenizing the Loyalty-Competence Trade-off." *Journal of the European Economic Association* 9 (5): 903–30.

Gandhi, Jennifer. 2008. *Political Institutions under Dictatorship*. New York: Cambridge University Press.

Geddes, Barbara. 1999. "What Do We Know about Democratization after Twenty Years?" *Annual Review of Political Science* 2: 115–44.

Gerschenkron, Alexander. 1962. *Economic Backwardness in Historical Perspective*. Cambridge, MA: Belknap Press of Harvard University Press.

Gessen, Masha. 2012. *The Man without a Face: The Unlikely Rise of Vladimir Putin*. New York: Riverhead Books.

Gourevitch, Peter Alexis. 1986. *Politics in Hard Times: Comparative Responses to International Economic Crises*. Ithaca: Cornell University Press.

Grzymala-Busse, Anna. 2001. "The Organizational Strategies of Communist Parties in East Central Europe, 1945–1989." *East European Politics and Societies* 15 (2): 421–53.

Haggard, Stephan. 1990. *Pathways from the Periphery: The Politics of Growth in the Newly Industrializing Countries*. Ithaca: Cornell University Press.

Haggard, Stephan. 2000a. "Interests, Institutions, and Policy Reform." In *Economic Policy Reform: Second Stage*, ed. Anne O. Krueger. Chicago: University of Chicago Press.

Haggard, Stephan. 2000b. *The Political Economy of the Asian Financial Crisis*. Washington, DC: Institute for International Economics.

Haggard, Stephan, and Robert R. Kaufman. 1995. *The Political Economy of Democratic Transitions*. Princeton: Princeton University Press.

Haggard, Stephan, and Sylvia Maxfield. 1996. "The Political Economy of Financial Internationalization in the Developing World." In *Internationalization and Domestic Politics*, ed. Robert O. Keohane and Helen V. Milner. New York: Cambridge University Press.

International Monetary Fund. 2017. "People's Republic of China: 2017 Article IV Consultation." In *Article IV Consultation*, ed. IMF. Washington, DC: IMF.

Jia, Ruixue, Masayuki Kudamatsu, and David Seim. 2014. "Complementary Roles of Connections and Performance in the Political Selection in China." *Journal of the European Economic Association* 13 (4): 631–68.

Kilian, Lutz. 2009. "Not All Oil Price Shocks Are Alike: Disentangling Demand and Supply Shocks in the Crude Oil Market." *American Economic Review* 99 (3): 1053–69.

King, Gary, Robert O. Keohane, and Sidney Verba. 1994. *Designing Social Inquiry: Scientific Inference in Qualitative Research*. Princeton: Princeton University Press.

King, Gary, Jennifer Pan, and Margaret E. Roberts. 2013. "How Censorship in China Allows Government Criticism but Silences Collective Expression." *American Political Science Review* 2013 (107): 1–18.

King, Gary, Jennifer Pan, and Margaret E. Roberts. 2017. "How the Chinese Government Fabricates Social Media Posts for Strategic Distraction, Not Engaged Argument." *American Political Science Review* 111 (3): 484–501.

Kuran, Timur. 1991. "Now out of Never: The Element of Surprise in the Eastern European Revolution of 1989." *World Politics* 44 (1): 7–48.

Lacy, Dean, and Emerson M. S. Niou. 2004. "A Theory of Economic Sanctions and Issue Linkage: The Roles of Preferences, Information, and Threats." *Journal of Politics* 66 (1): 25–42.

Landry, Pierre F. 2008. *Decentralized Authoritarianism in China: The Communist Party's Control of Local Elites in the Post-Mao Era*. New York: Cambridge University Press.

Landry, Pierre F., Lu Xiaobo, and Haiyan Duan. 2018. "Does Performance Matter? Evaluating Political Selection along the Chinese Administrative Ladder." *Comparative Political Studies* 51 (8): 1074–105.

Lardy, Nicolas. 1998. *China's Unfinished Economic Reform*. Washington, DC: Brookings Institution Press.

Li, Hongbin, and Li-An Zhou. 2005. "Political Turnover and Economic Performance: The Incentive Role of Personnel Control in China." *Journal of Public Economics* 89 (9–10): 1743–62.

Magaloni, Beatriz. 2006. *Voting for Autocracy: Hegemonic Party Survival and Its Demise in Mexico*. New York: Cambridge University Press.

Magaloni, Beatriz, and Ruth Kricheli. 2010. "Political Order and One-Party Rule." *Annual Review of Political Science* 13:123–43.

Mahoney, James. 2012. "The Logic of Process Tracing Tests in the Social Sciences." *Sociological Methods and Research* 41:570–97.

Mill, John Stuart. 1846. *A System of Logic, Ratiocinative and Inductive: Being a Connected View of the Principles of Evidence and the Methods of Scientific Investigation*. New York: Harper.

Miller, Christopher Richard. 2016. *The Struggle to Save the Soviet Economy: Mikhail Gorbachev and the Collapse of the USSR*. Chapel Hill: University of North Carolina Press.

Nathan, Andrew. 2003. "Authoritarian Resilience." *Journal of Democracy* 14 (1): 6–19.

Nelson, Joan. 1995. "Linkages between Politics and Economics." In *Economic Reform and Democracy*, ed. Larry Diamond and Marc F. Plattner. Baltimore: Johns Hopkins University Press.

O'Donnell, Guillermo A., Philippe C. Schmitter, and Laurence Whitehead. 1986. *Transitions from Authoritarian Rule*. Baltimore: Johns Hopkins University Press.

Pepinsky, Thomas B. 2009. *Economic Crises and the Breakdown of Authoritarian Regimes: Indonesia and Malaysia in Comparative Perspective*. New York: Cambridge University Press.

Pepinsky, Thomas B. 2014. "The Institutional Turn in Comparative Authoritarianism." *British Journal of Political Science* 44 (3): 631–53.

Reinhart, Carmen M., and Kenneth S. Rogoff. 2009. *This Time Is Different: Eight Centuries of Financial Folly*. Princeton: Princeton University Press.

Rogoff, Kenneth S., and Carmen Reinhart. 2009. "The Aftermath of Financial Crises." *American Economic Review* 99 (2): 466–72.

Shih, Victor. 2010. "Local Government Debt: Big Rock Candy Mountain." *China Economic Quarterly* 2010 (June): 26–32.

Slantchev, Branislav, and R. Blake McMahon. 2015. "The Guardianship Dilemma: Regime Security through and from the Armed Forces." *American Political Science Review* 109 (2): 297–313.

Slater, Dan. 2003. "Iron Cage in an Iron Fist: Authoritarian Institutions and the Personalization of Power in Malaysia." *Comparative Politics* 35 (1): 81–101.

Slater, Dan. 2010. *Ordering Power: Contentious Politics and Authoritarian Leviathans in Southeast Asia*. New York: Cambridge University Press.

Svolik, Milan. 2009. "Power Sharing and Leadership Dynamics in Authoritarian Regimes." *American Journal of Political Science* 53 (2): 477–94.

Svolik, Milan. 2012. *The Politics of Authoritarian Rule*. New York: Cambridge University Press.

Svolik, Milan, and Carles Boix. 2007. "Non-tyrannical Autocracies." Working paper. Princeton: Princeton University and Champaign: University of Illinois.

Thelen, Kathleen, and Sven Steinmo. 1992. "Historical Institutionalism in Comparative Politics." In *Structuring Politics: Historical Institutionalism in Comparative Analysis*, ed. Sven Steinmo, Kathleen Thelen, and Frank Longstreth. Cambridge: Cambridge University Press.

Treisman, Daniel, and Sergei Guriev. 2015. "How Modern Dictators Survive: An Informational Theory of the New Authoritarianism." NBER Working Paper No. 21136. Cambridge, MA: NBER.

ONE

The Domestic Political Implications of Economic Sanctions

Evidence from Iraq under Saddam Hussein

Lisa Blaydes

How do authoritarian regimes weather the political strain of severe economic sanctions? In 1990, the United Nations Security Council announced an economic embargo on Iraq that was unprecedented in terms of its comprehensiveness. Sanctions affected virtually all Iraqis, creating distress and suffering at every level of society. The sanctions came as a particular shock since Iraqis had enjoyed among the highest per capita food availability ratings in the Middle East prior to imposition of the embargo (Gordon 2010, 33). During the sanctions period, malnutrition became widespread and Iraq saw the rise of both child mortality and childhood stunting. Using data from multiple sources, I provide information about the geographic distribution of human suffering within Iraq, with a special emphasis on the harm sanctions caused to Iraqi children.

The sanctions regime had implications that went beyond the health and well-being of Iraqi citizens, however. In this chapter, I examine the domestic political impact of the massive, prolonged economic shock associated with the international sanctions regime using Iraqi archival sources captured in the wake of the 2003 US invasion of Iraq.[1] On the one hand, the economic embargo strengthened the regime's hand in a number of meaningful ways, particularly through state control of both the rations system and financial opportunities. At the same time, however, sanctions represented a major challenge to the regime, creating vulnerabilities for the Baath Party and Saddam Hussein. I argue that the economic embargo forced a narrowing of the regime's base that created incentives to unseat Hussein through coup d'état and assassination attempts. Many of the most serious threats to Hussein were initiated by fellow Sunnis, including those from western Iraq, a region that was particularly hard-hit by sanctions. While none of the coup or assassination attempts against Saddam Hussein proved successful, his coup risk increased during the sanctions period even as the threat of popular revolt declined.

Iraqi citizens were hard-pressed to engage in public dissent during the sanctions period as a result of a variety of factors. In particular, regime repression made it exceedingly difficult to organize acts of rebellion. Perhaps even more importantly, ordinary Iraqis struggled for everyday survival, reducing the energy available to engage in mobilizational activities. Despite the challenges to popular protest during this period, Iraqis turned to covert forms of political behavior to express their dissatisfaction with the regime. I provide a window into Iraq's "hidden transcript" through an examination of the rumors circulating during the 1990s. Many of these rumors were related to economic grievances, including rumors about how the actions of Saddam Hussein brought harm to the Iraqi people. Taken together, the archival evidence I have collected suggests that sanctions had important political implications that manifested in underground political activities—like coup planning and rumor mongering—that reflected the highly repressive nature of the Baathist regime during this period.

International Sanctions as an Economic Shock

Few countries have been subjected to a negative economic shock on the scale of that experienced by Iraq as a result of UN-imposed sanctions following the Iraqi invasion of Kuwait.[2] The scope of the sanctions was unusual vis-à-vis norms within the international community; unlike sanctions imposed by one country (or set of countries) on another, the sanctions on Iraq were imposed by the United Nations Security Council and, therefore, binding on all UN members (Gordon 2010, 10). Iraq was also highly vulnerable to sanctions as a result of its heavy dependence on oil as a major source of foreign revenue (Graham-Brown 1999, 57), in particular, and trade reliance, more generally (Gordon 2010, 21). In fact, Iraq had been dependent on imports for two-thirds of foodstuffs in the years leading up to the imposition of the embargo (Khoury 2013, 44). While public sector employees saw large losses in terms of income, poor Iraqis suffered most grievously, often forced to sell any personal resource of value to keep their families afloat. In this section, I examine the impact of sanctions on health and well-being, with a particular focus on the effects of sanctions on Iraqi children. I consider two outcome variables with the goal of estimating, in part, the burden of the economic sanctions. In particular, I look at mortality for children under five years old and childhood stunting as proxies for the human cost of sanctions.

Declining Calorie Availability

In order to prevent mass famine as a result of the international economic embargo, the Iraqi government implemented a monthly food-rationing system for items like flour, rice, sugar, cooking oil, tea, and soap (Graham-Brown 1999, 168; Gordon 2010, 128). Despite flaws in its design, the rationing system has been described as essential to saving "the bulk of the population from starving" (Mazaheri 2010, 257).[3] Sassoon (2012, 243) argues that the rationing system needed to be effective since the regime knew that inefficiencies in that program would threaten social stability. While the regime-controlled food rations system has been credited with saving Iraqi lives, the manner in which food rations were distributed made citizens dependent on the regime for subsistence, reluctant to engage in political dissent, and fearful of losing state resources viewed as vital for personal survival. The net result was that the rationing system "strengthened state power vis-à-vis the weakened Iraqi society" (Rohde 2010, 68).

The deteriorating humanitarian conditions in Iraq eventually led the international community to sign on to the "Oil-for-Food" program that permitted Iraq to sell oil in exchange for food and medicine. The program allowed imports of $130 per person per year; prior to Oil-for-Food, Iraqis were importing $20 per person per year during the sanctions period (Gordon 2010, 25). As a result of Oil-for-Food, it was reported that average kilocalories per person per day rose from 1,295 in 1993–95 to 2,030 in 1997–98 (Graham-Brown 1999, 169).[4] Figure 1.1 displays the per capita daily protein (dashed line) and fat (solid line) calorie consumption in Iraq over time. Protein consumption in Iraq halved after the introduction of the embargo and only improved slightly after 1997, while fat consumption rebounded more clearly beginning in 1995.[5]

Iraqi government documents express concerns about food availability and cost. For example, an internal Baath Party study from the early 1990s

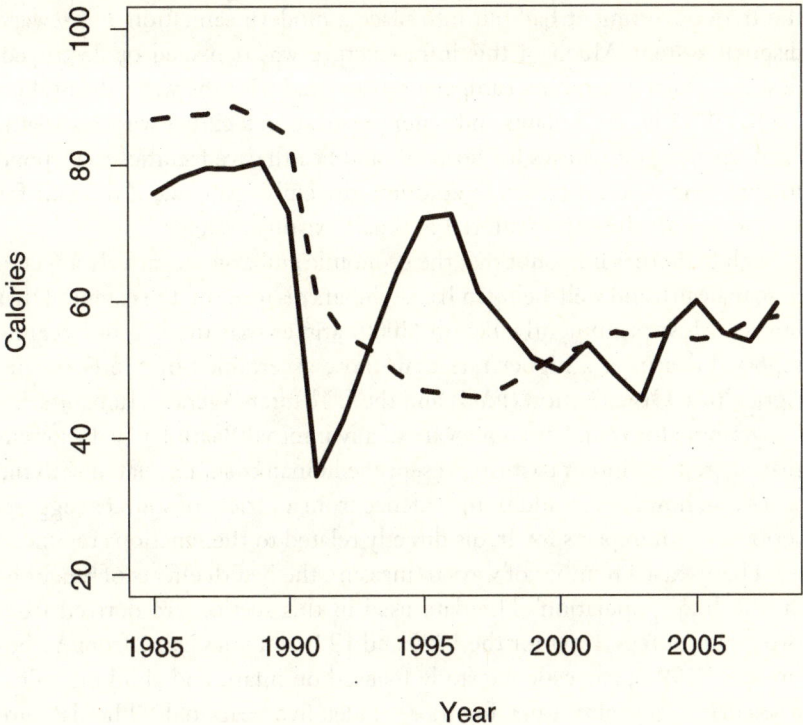

Fig. 1.1. Per Capita Daily Calorie Consumption in Terms of Protein (*dashed line*) and Fat (*solid line*) over Time

describes shortages of grain, cooking oil, meat, fish, sugar, and milk.[6] Many of these items had previously been imported. According to the report, Iraq witnessed major increases in child morality, maternal morality during labor, as well as decreases in newborn birth weights.[7] One Iraqi Ministry of Health report suggested that a number of previously rare illnesses had seen a resurgence since the introduction of sanctions; this included diseases related to vitamin deficiencies, like childhood night blindness and thyroid gland inflammation, but also extended to cholera, rabies, polio, and viral kidney disease.

Sanctions and Child Mortality

Destruction of critical infrastructure during the course of the First Gulf War (1990–91) extended to health, water, and electricity systems that had long provided public goods to Iraqis. For example, during the 1970s the Iraqi government had put into place a modern sanitation and sewage disposal system. Much of this infrastructure was damaged or destroyed, however, during bombing campaigns associated with the war (Al-Jawaheri 2008, 119). Electrical plants and water purification facilities were also damaged, creating difficulties for hospitals and health care facilities to respond to emerging medical crises. In addition, the embargo made it difficult for Iraq to import the parts required to repair existing systems.

While there is no doubt that the economic embargo negatively affected human health and well-being in Iraq, scholars disagree on the extent of that impact. Most prominently, Baram (2000) argues that the Baathist regime reported deaths at a higher rate than those ascertained by the Food and Agriculture Organization (FAO) and the UN Inter-Agency Humanitarian Programme for Iraq. I am not aware of any internal Baath Party document that suggests an intent to misrepresent the human costs associated with the sanctions, however. In addition, evidence from a variety of sources suggests serious health impacts for Iraqis directly related to the sanctions regime.

There exist a number of ways to measure the health effects of sanctions on the Iraqi population. The data used in this section are derived from two main sources. Data for the 1990 and 1991 statistics come from Ascherio et al. (1992), an academic study focused on infant and child mortality, particularly mortality rates for those under five years old.[8] The data are presented at a high level of aggregation (i.e., the regional level) because of shortcomings in the original coding. Data on under-five mortality for 1997 come from the Iraqi census available through the Integrated Public Use Microdata Series (IPUMS).[9] The data are most valid from a cross-sectional perspective, as they were collected by different organizations at particular points in time. I map the data at the level of the governorate, as my primary interest is in understanding the variation across Iraq in terms of the sanctions burden.

Under-five mortality rates are lowest in 1990, increase in 1991, and improve, at least in some areas, by 1997. The first Oil-for-Food shipments arrived in March 1997, so it is unlikely that the 1997 figures reflect improvements as a result of the program. Under-five mortality is lowest in Baghdad throughout the study period, suggesting the existence of better conditions in the capital compared to other parts of the country. In 1991, it also appears that Baghdad and the central parts of Iraq have lower rates of child mortality than the northern and southern regions. By 1997, the Kurdish areas of northern Iraq were autonomous, making it impossible for the Iraqi government to conduct a census there. As a result, the three northern governorates are not included in the data.

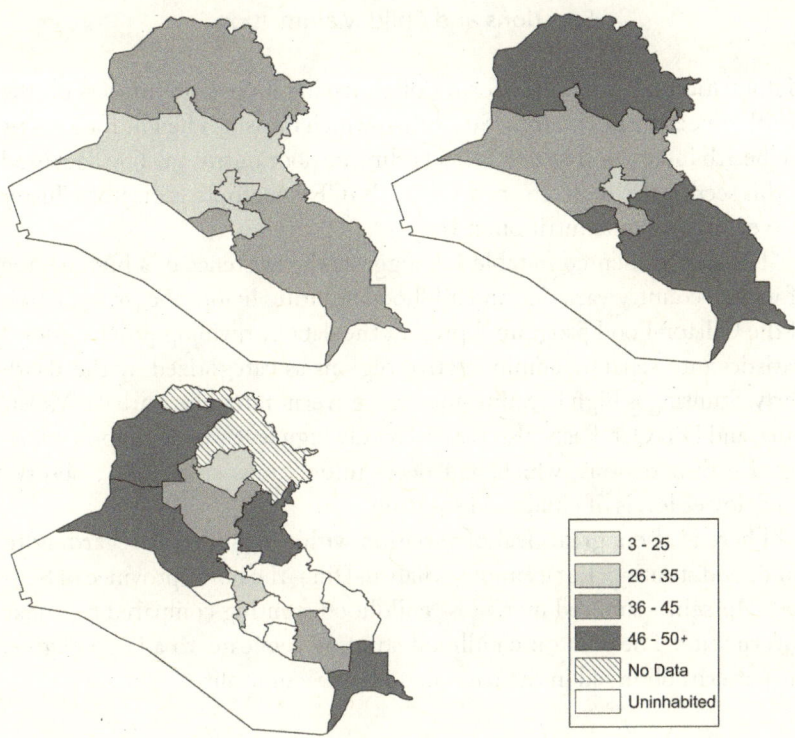

Fig. 1.2. Under-Five Mortality Rates in 1990 (*top left*), 1991 (*top right*), and 1997 (*bottom*)

Cross-sectional variation in under-five mortality in 1997 suggests different regions of Iraq were differentially harmed by the economic embargo. Again, Baghdad performs relatively well compared to other parts of Iraq. Basra governorate, the southernmost governorate in Iraq, on the other hand, has very high rates of child mortality. It is notable that child mortality declined for most Shia areas, other than Basra. Anbar governorate, the major Sunni governorate in western Iraq, saw relatively high levels of child mortality compared to other Sunni areas of the country. This suggests that despite claims that the Baathist regime enjoyed a "Sunni" basis of support, regime backing did not extend to all Sunni regions of the country. Sunni Arabs from Anbar were previously beneficiaries of regime largesse but witnessed declines in economic support during sanctions despite the fact that military officers from Anbar provided assistance to the regime during periods of previous social unrest.

Sanctions and Child Malnutrition

Malnutrition takes multiple forms, often having long-term impacts on the health trajectory of children. Stunting—which measures height for age—is the health indicator that best reflects chronic poor nutrition. The data used in this section are drawn from a 1996 UNICEF Multiple Indicator Cluster Survey on child malnutrition in Iraq.

The data presented in table 1.1 suggests the existence of a high degree of within-country variation in childhood stunting before the introduction of the Oil-for-Food program. I present the data by dividing province-level statistics into separate administrative regions as categorized by the Baath Party. Stunting is high in Shiite-majority governorates like Karbala, Muthanna, and Dhi Qar. Basra also sees relatively high levels of childhood stunting. Kurdish regions, which had been autonomous since 1991, observe much lower levels of childhood stunting.

There is also a great deal of variation within Sunni areas regarding to childhood stunting. For example, Salah al-Din—the home province of Saddam Hussein—suffered much less childhood stunting compared to Anbar governorate. The data on childhood stunting replicate, to a large degree, the patterns observed in the data on under-five mortality.

TABLE 1.1. Childhood Stunting across Iraqi Governorates, 1996

Location	Percentage
Baghdad	31
Central	
Anbar	36
Diyala	21
Salah al-Din	27
Euphrates	
Babil	26
Karbala	39
Muthanna	38
Najaf	34
Qadisiyya	27
Southern	
Basra	33
Dhi Qar	37
Wasit	32
Northern	
Dohuk	27
Erbil	29
Kirkuk	28
Ninewa	32
Sulaymaniyya	24

The Political Implications of Sanctions

The evidence I have presented suggests that sanctions had serious and negative effects on the health and well-being of Iraqis, with a particularly deleterious effect on Iraqi children. These effects persist despite efforts made by the Iraqi state to mitigate political and social harms associated with sanctions. Indeed, sanctions provided an opportunity for the regime to serve a key role through its control of the distribution of rations for basic goods (Al-Jawaheri 2008).[10] State control over the limited financial and nutritional resources within Iraq may have helped to stabilize the regime and extend the levers of control enjoyed by Saddam Hussein over the Iraqi population. The sanctions program and the government's rationing system served as constant reminder of the population's dependence on the state and regime (Mazaheri 2010, 258).

At the same time, however, sanctions created conditions for instability by fostering extreme economic anxiety within the general population and generating economic grievances among members of the elite who saw their access to resources decline. The evidence I have provided in the previous section suggests that regions of Iraq were differentially impacted by sanctions. At a popular level, sanctions were difficult for all Iraqis but may have been particularly harmful for Shiite regions distant from Baghdad as well as for residents of Anbar governorate—a predominantly Sunni governorate. At an elite level, individuals who were close to Hussein's government through family ties were able to benefit from sanctions through privileged access to state resources and opportunities (Mazaheri 2010, 263). For many others, however, sanctions had the effect of widening "the gap between a small number of privileged, who have managed to maintain their living standards or even profit from the crisis, and the majority of the population" (Graham-Brown 1995).

The decline in state revenue available for distribution caused a narrowing of the regime's core coalition, creating opposition to Hussein's rule from within the broader set of elites. This may have particularly been the case for non-Tikriti Sunni co-"ethnics"—constituencies who had been beneficiaries of regime largesse in the pre-sanctions period. In particular, the economic exclusion of western Sunnis, including those from areas like Anbar, may have increased coup risk since these elites had been important to the regime in putting down previous popular uprisings but were no longer receiving high levels of benefit from the regime.

Sanctions impacted multiple aspects of political and coalitional life in Iraq during the 1990s and early 2000s. Yet it is exceedingly difficult to measure levels of political dissatisfaction given the highly repressive nature of the Iraqi regime during this period. As a result, there are limited opportunities to identify and measure dissent on the part of the Iraqi population. This section explores two measures of dissent—one related to popular responses and a second associated with elite behaviors. Given the extreme forms of economic and political stress associated with Iraq in the 1990s, avenues of response were very limited, often emerging in private settings, sometimes to be revealed in a public fashion. At the elite level, I discuss coup attempts against the regime, both those reported in public media sources as well as coup attempts that were reported to have happened but were not confirmed. At a popular level, I examine the proliferation of rumors in Iraq related to economic stress as well as attribution of blame for Iraq's difficult economic conditions.

Public Economic Anxiety

The Baathist regime was highly concerned about public reaction to the sanctions. Indeed, a number of government studies were commissioned to explore these issues. In one case, Saddam Hussein directed the state apparatus to canvas the public in order to determine the overall societal reaction to the embargo.[11] Another report prepared by the Baath Party linked sanctions to a decline in the social values of Iraqi society.[12] The report also pointed to an increase in economically motivated crimes. Women were thought to be particularly harmed by the negative social implications of sanctions.[13]

In high-level meetings between Hussein and his advisers, the Iraqi leadership expressed concerns about the black market and difficulties associated with austerity under sanctions.[14] Skyrocketing inflation was deemed very difficult for Iraqi citizens.[15] Hussein implored members of the Council of Ministers to mitigate the negative societal effects of the embargo since Iraqis were increasingly demoralized as a result of rising food prices.[16]

There are a number of ways to observe public manifestations of economic anxiety during the 1990s. One way that economic anxiety manifested in Iraq's highly repressive society was through the proliferation of rumors. DiFonzo and Bordia (2007, 13) define rumors as "unverified and instrumentally relevant information statements in circulation that arise in contexts of ambiguity, danger, or potential threat that function to help people make sense and manage risk." Some of these rumors provided critical information meant to guide one's activities in the uncertain and stressful period of international sanctions. Yet even rumors intended to assist an individual in day-to-day survival are regime undermining because they break the regime's monopolistic control on relevant information (Blaydes 2018). This interpretation of rumor mongering as a political act connects to existing scholarly work that seeks to document the everyday forms of resistance available to those living under forms of political or economic subordination (Scott 1985; Wedeen 1999). The Iraqi regime collected and cataloged rumors that circulated, many of which were explicitly political in content.[17] In this section, I examine the rumors that were circulating in Iraq during the 1990s.

Rumors that reflected societal economic anxiety were exceedingly common. Many of these rumors dealt with public fear of government expropriation of financial resources under sanctions. According to one rumor, any citizen who took money from the banks to purchase a house or a car would have half of the funds taken by the state.[18] A similar rumor was repeated a week later that suggested that citizens who put money in state banks would not receive the full amount when they sought to withdraw their funds.[19] Another rumor reported that Saddam Hussein was going to expropriate all farmlands and designate his son, Uday, manager of agricultural resources.[20]

Iraqis were also concerned about the possibility of currency manipulation and devaluation of Iraqi coinage. Rumors proliferated about how metal was being painted to resemble gold,[21] and about coin shortages as a result of people melting coins to make keys and other metal goods.[22] Iraqi money was rumored to be rapidly losing its value.[23] Bank runs were reported to be common, with Iraqis withdrawing their savings.[24]

Dozens of rumors focused on the effects of inflation and the withdrawal of various dinar notes and coins from the local market.[25] According to one rumor, the Iraqi government bought five billion dinars from Jordan, all in 25-dinar notes.[26] Another rumor suggested that the state was buying gold from Kurdish agents, paying for it in 25-dinar notes (which were later to be canceled).[27] Currency traders were reported to be taking advantage of the situation by hoarding 25-dinar notes.[28] Around the same time, there were rumors about protests against higher prices, including a large protest that was expected to take place in Baghdad.[29] Price-related protests were also rumored to take place in Dhi Qar and Maysan.[30]

Iraqis were highly concerned about regime intervention in the local economy during the sanctions period.[31] One rumor circulating suggested that high-quality wheat was being distributed in Baghdad whereas lower-quality wheat was going to southern provinces.[32] A second rumor suggested that the reason for the circulation of poor-quality flour was that Uday had a large quantity of wheat for his horses but after that wheat became spoiled, it was given to people in the southern region of Iraq.[33] Other rumors circulating around this same time suggested that the ration share of wheat would be reduced from nine to eight kilograms.[34]

The rumors also reflected fear that the regime would take advantage of the economic crisis. One report suggested that the state turned off electricity to distract the people from economic problems associated with the embargo,[35] while another suggested that power outages were happening because the Iraqi state was exporting electricity to Jordan.[36] Another rumor suggested that Saddam Hussein's wife artificially created a tomato shortage in order to sell more of her tomatoes.[37] It was rumored that Uday sought to sell chickens with hemorrhagic fever.[38] A third rumor suggested that the flour rations were cut with toxic substances, causing injuries and hospitalizations.[39]

In some cases, public anger over the economic situation was directed at Saddam Hussein himself. One rumor suggested that influential merchants were saying that Hussein was building expensive new presidential palaces and that, as a result, food prices would remain high.[40] Other rumors also reflected a sense that the regime was profligate in its spending. It was rumored that Hussein was having a car made of pure gold and that he would show off the car on the occasion of his birthday.[41] A related rumor suggested that during his birthday celebration, Hussein would ride around in a special, imported car that had cost 70 million Iraqi dinars.[42]

Even after the introduction of the Oil-for-Food program, economic anxiety rumors continued.[43] Some rumors suggested a belief that the program would not provide the Iraqi people with the economic benefits that had been promised by the international community. In some cases, the government was blamed for delays in the implementation of the Oil-for-Food program.[44] Other rumors suggested that the food aid coming into Iraq meant for ordinary Iraqis was instead being sold in markets.[45] Another rumor suggested that eggs, meat, and vegetables were being diverted to Syria.[46] A third reported that food was being stockpiled in Ministry of Commerce warehouses but that the state had no intention of distributing those resources.[47] Rumors of this sort continued for a number of weeks.[48]

Narrowing the Elite Base

In the wake of the Iraqi withdrawal from Kuwait, popular uprisings erupted across Iraq, first in southern provinces and later in the Kurdish northern regions. Militarily stretched thin, Hussein found himself fighting a two-front rebellion while simultaneously needing to maintain security in Baghdad. A decision was made to focus the efforts of regime loyalists from the "geographic spine" of the Baath Party—the Sunni heartland—on repressing the southern uprising (Mackey 2002, 289). Audio recordings of a high-level meeting convened at the time suggest Hussein's belief in the crucial loyalty of citizens in Anbar governorate that had remained "clean" in the eyes of the regime (Woods, Palkki, and Stout 2011, 200). While the revolt in the south was successfully subdued, the Kurdish provinces of northern Iraq were able to achieve a degree of political autonomy following the uprisings.

Although the Baathist regime under Saddam Hussein has typically been described as having a Sunni basis, the relative standing of various Sunni tribal and regional groupings varied over time. In particular, political rule during the 1990s came to increasingly rely on four major clans—the Bakr, Talfah, al-Majid, and Ibrahim—from in and around his hometown of Tikrit (Bengio 2000, 97). Coveted positions were filled by individuals drawn overwhelmingly from loyalists who hailed from the provincial towns neighboring Tikrit (Marr 2004, 264). The reliance on Iraqis from Tikrit represented a decrease in political importance for those from western towns, like Ana and Ramadi, in Anbar governorate (Sakai 2003, 144).

Saddam Hussein and his family—including half-brothers, sons, and sons-in-law—monopolized the most privileged economic opportunities, and this tendency intensified over the course of the international embargo. Davis (2005, 233) argues that the "continued consolidation of power within Saddam's immediate family intensified cleavages within the regime." This created particular tensions for tribes and regional groups that had been previously loyal to the regime but were economically marginalized under the embargo. For example, during the 1991 uprisings, the troops who successfully put down the rebellion were "drawn mainly from tribes that inhabited the Sunni provinces of Anbar and Salah al-Din" (Dawisha 2009, 236). According to the account of one tribal sheikh, in the wake of the uprisings Saddam Hussein said that it was the people of Anbar who held the country together (Haddad 2011, 101).

A major downsizing of the military particularly hurt western Sunnis, who were prominently represented in these units. Simultaneously, the regime began to create more elite military units that were intended to provide loyal support. According to Davis (2005, 232), these new military units "enjoyed high salaries and extensive privileges" that were not offered to others within the regime. Blaydes (2018) identifies patterns in recruitment for various Iraqi paramilitary groups, including the Fedayeen Saddam and the Jerusalem Army. These new military units drew heavily from tribes with strongholds located near Tikrit. Members of the Juburi tribe were heavily represented in these elite military units; the Juburis are particularly well represented in the districts directly north of Tikrit (Blaydes 2018).

What were the political implications of the narrowing of the regime's political base as a result of the economic embargo? One important impact of sanctions relates to an increasing number of attempts by regime elites to target Saddam Hussein himself. The mid-1990s witnessed a series of attempted coups reported in the international media. Many of these attempts were made by members of the military affiliated with tribal groups based in western Iraq.

Among the most prominent challenges to the regime emerged because of conflict with members of the Dulaim tribe, a group that is prominently represented in western Iraq. In fact, the governorate of Anbar was previously named Dulaim governorate because of the heavy concentration of Dulaimi tribesmen in that area. In 1995, General Mohammed Mazlum al-Dulaimi was arrested and accused of plotting against the Baathist regime. He was executed and his body was returned to his family with signs of torture, after which rioting broke out (Davis 2005, 234). A number of other western tribes, including the Jumailat, Anis, Rawis, and Kubaysis, were reported to sympathize with the Dulaimi.

Press reports from that time suggest that the rebellion was linked to a shrinking of Saddam Hussein's power base as a result of purges of various Sunni tribes.[49] It was reported that as many as 1,000 soldiers and officers from a Republican Guard unit were involved in the uprising.[50] A battalion led by General Turki al-Dulaimi reportedly attacked a radio transmitter and helicopter base at Abu Ghraib, on the outskirts of Baghdad.[51]

In addition to high-profile, documented coup attempts, rumors in the Baath Party archival collection make reference to anticipated or attempted coups (Blaydes 2018). Rumors of attempted coups were particularly common between 1996 and 1999. In July 1996, high-ranking army officers were thought to be conspiring to kill Saddam Hussein, but apparently the plot was discovered by the security apparatus and the conspirators arrested.[52] Later that month, a high-ranking military commander and cousin of Wafiq al-Samarrai reportedly attempted a coup.[53]

A rumor in January 1997 suggested the formation of a committee based in Anbar with the goal of assassinating government and party officials.[54] A rumor that circulated in July 1997 reported an aborted coup plot organized by military officers.[55] In June 1998, a failed conspiracy involving senior army officers was reported as well that was rumored to have been associated with attacks on party bases.[56] Failed coups were also reported in March, May, and July of 1999.[57] In the case of the reported July coup attempt, 73 military officers of a variety of ranks were reported to have been involved.[58]

Conclusion

For the Iraqi regime, there was considerable uncertainty about what sanctions sought to accomplish and how long they would last. There is little question, however, that sanctions affected Iraqi society in fundamental ways (Sassoon 2012, 242–43). While sanctions had a highly negative impact on the health and well-being of Iraqis, particularly Iraq's children, the embargo failed to unseat Saddam Hussein.

Scholars have long debated how the Baathist regime reconsolidated power and why the sanctions failed to instigate regime change. According to Mazaheri (2010, 264), the ill-defined nature of the demands made on Saddam Hussein may have hindered destabilization of the Baathist regime and may have strengthened, rather than weakened, Hussein's hold on power. Similarly, Sassoon (2012, 244) contends that Hussein capitalized on sanctions in ways that helped his political prospects. During this time, Hussein consolidated political power and sought to demonstrate the centrality of the regime to the population's survival (Khoury 2013, 148–49). At the same time, ordinary Iraqis became increasingly dependent on regime-distributed food rations to meet their daily caloric needs, while Iraqi elites depended on ties to the Baathist leadership for access to rent-seeking opportunities. An analysis of the case of Iraq, then, provides insights into how governments survive lengthy international sanctions or trade embargoes.

The impoverishment of Iraq's middle class made the "growth of a wealthy elite comprised of black marketeers, contractors, and Baath Party officials all the more egregious" (Davis 2005, 228). During this time, Saddam Hussein and his sons created numerous enemies, including some among influential tribes (Davis 2005, 238). The evidence I have presented suggests that Sunnis from areas peripheral to Tikrit, particularly those from western governorates like Anbar, saw significant declines in quality of life and, despite the instrumental role they had played in putting down the uprisings, did not enjoy the same levels of access, employment, and privilege as Sunnis from in and around Tikrit. The net result was that tribes that had been previously loyal to the regime—many of which were majority Sunni—"reacted against the economy's continued deterioration" (Davis 2005, 234). One political implication of a reduced support base for the regime was an increasing number of coup and assassination attempts that sought to unseat Saddam Hussein. In other words, the narrowing of the regime's support among co-"ethnic" elites increased the probability of overthrow by individuals from those increasingly dispossessed groups.

For ordinary citizens struggling to survive the embargo, the menu of possible resistance activities was highly constrained by Iraq's repressive environment. As a result, resistance activities tended to be covert rather than public acts. Rumor mongering during this period was common, and many of the rumors that circulated related directly to conditions of economic hardship.

NOTES

Many thanks to Will Bannick, Kayla Bostrom, and Tareq Samman for outstanding research assistance.

1. I make use of two main collections in this chapter. The first includes Baath Party records held at the Library and Archives of Stanford's Hoover Institution. Most of the documents came from the Baath Regional Command Collection (BRCC). The second collection is composed of the transcripts of tape-recorded meetings between Saddam Hussein and his advisers that were previously held at the Conflict Records Research Center (CRRC) at the National Defense University. See Blaydes (2018) for a more complete discussion of these archival collections.

2. Shih (this vol.) defines an economic shock as a contraction of available resources for a regime due to factors that are at least partly outside of the domestic economic environment. Harris (this vol.) discusses sanctions as a type of economic shock.

3. The ration system operated out of government-controlled warehouses, silos, and distribution points (Mazaheri 2012, 257).

4. According to one source, daily available calories in Iraq averaged 3,375 kilocalories per capita in 1987–88 (Pellett 2002, 188).

5. See the Food and Agriculture Organization of the United Nations for data on calorie consumption. Blaydes and Kayser (2011) provide a discussion on empirical applications of FAO data.

6. CRRC Doc. No. SH-BATH-D-000-492.

7. Ibid.

8. I adopt an operationalization of the infant and child mortality rate of an area as the probability of dying between birth and exactly five years of age expressed per 1,000 live births. To calculate the death rate I divide the number of those who died in each sample by the number of total births and multiply the resulting ratio by 1,000. To produce this statistic for 1990, I subset the data to individuals born on or after January 1, 1986, and only include deaths for those who died on or before December 31, 1990. To calculate the 1991 mortality rate, because the survey ended

on September 5, 1991, I look at all individuals who were born on or after September 1, 1986, and died on or before August 31, 1991.

9. To generate child mortality rates from these data, I use data from Iraqi mothers who were surveyed as part of the census and, in particular, use information about the number of children each woman had given birth to as well as how many of those children had died. While I am able to distinguish between mothers in the survey, I am not able to distinguish among individual children. For instance, if a mother gave birth to five children and lost three, it would be impossible to know which of those children had died, particularly if the children who died were under five or over five years of age. As a result, I subset the data to only include mothers whose children were all under five. The statistics presented here, therefore, should be interpreted as the child mortality rate for relatively young families, or those who had not yet had their first child reach the age of five.

10. Walter (2018) analyzes Iraqi petitions to the government, of which many dealt with people and families in crises. According to Walter (2018), citizens were concerned with receiving urgent medical treatment, food aid, and assistance with handling a son who deserted from mandatory military service or the need to report an abuse of power. In many cases, petitions could result in tangible benefits for individuals who sought assistance.

11. CRRC Doc. No. SH-PDWN-D-000-720, January 1996.

12. CRRC Doc. No. SH-BATH-D-000-492.

13. Ibid.

14. CRRC Doc. No. SH-SHTP-A-001-465, August 17, 1992.

15. CRRC Doc. No. SH-SHTP-A-001-478, c. 1994.

16. CRRC Doc. No. SH-PDWN-D-000-720, January 1996.

17. See Dimitrov and Sassoon (2014) for more on how rumors were an important source of information to the regime about people's feelings on various issues.

18. BRCC Doc. No. 005-3-3-0491, February 7, 1993.

19. BRCC Doc. No. 005-3-3-0480, February 14, 1993.

20. BRCC Doc. No. 005-3-3-0135, April 16, 1993.

21. BRCC Doc. No. 005-3-3-0081, April 19, 1993.

22. BRCC Doc. No. 01-3197-0001-0690, April 26, 1993; BRCC Doc No. 01-3197-0001-0601, May 2, 1993.

23. BRCC Doc. No. 01-3197-0001-0505, April 28 1993; BRCC Doc. No. 01-3197-0001-0646, April 29, 1993.

24. BRCC Doc. No. 01-3197-0001-0008, July 3, 1993.

25. BRCC Doc. No. 01-3197-0001-0463, May 10 1993; BRCC Doc. No. 01-3197-0001-0474, May 10, 1993.

26. BRCC Doc. No. 01-3197-0001-0400, April 29, 1993.

27. BRCC Doc. No. 01-3197-0001-0400, April 29, 1993.

28. BRCC Doc. No. 01-3197-0001-0463, May 10, 1993.

29. BRCC Doc. No. 01-3197-0001-0327, April 23, 1993.

30. BRCC Doc. No. 01-3197-0001-0263, May 29, 1993.

31. There was also a great deal of paranoia in Iraq about the role played by external actors. It was believed that Iraq's oil fields would be given to the United States in order to pay Iraq's debts (BRCC Doc. No. 005-3-3-0301, February 22, 1993); that the Kuwaitis were giving Kurdish traitors 500 million Iraqi dinars to buy dollars

from the Iraqi markets to harm the economy and make the Iraqis complain (BRCC Doc. No. 005-3-3-0081, April 19, 1993; and that some Iraqis going to Saudi Arabia were kidnapping women to sell in Saudi Arabia for 1 million dinars each. (BRCC Doc. No. 01-3197-0001-0681, April 26, 1993).

32. BRCC Doc. No. 01-3197-0001-0221, June 12, 1993.
33. BRCC Doc. No. 01-3197-0001-0070, June 26, 1993.
34. BRCC Doc. No. 01-3197-0001-0166, June 20, 1993.
35. BRCC Doc. No. 148-4-5-0958, August 3, 1996.
36. BRCC Doc. No. 148-4-5-0949, August 4, 1996.
37. BRCC Doc. No. 005-3-3-0141, April 10, 1993.
38. BRCC Doc. No. 148-4-5-0943, August 5, 1996.
39. BRCC Doc. No. 148-4-5-0949, August 4, 1996.
40. BRCC Doc. No. 148-4-5-0835, August 26, 1996. Davis (2005, 232) reports that Saddam Hussein built 26 new palaces during the 1990s, importing marble and expensive materials for this purpose.
41. BRCC Doc. No. 01-3197-0001-0639, May 2, 1993.
42. BRCC Doc. No. 01-3197-0001-0628, May 3, 1993.
43. A variety of rumors dealt specifically with the issue of public discontent over missing chickens. One rumor suggested that Libyan leader Mu'ammar Gaddhafi wanted to send 25 million chickens to the Iraqi people for Ramadan but that the Iraqi government sold those chickens to merchants instead of giving them to the Iraqi people (BRCC Doc. No. 148-4-5-0267, February 13, 1997). Only a few days later, it was rumored that Gaddhafi was angered because of the missing chickens (BRCC Doc. No. 148-4-5-0273, February 16, 1997). A third rumor suggested that Gaddafi's gift of 18 million chickens were intended for Iraqis, but instead they were given to the Sudanese people (BRCC Doc. No. 148-4-5-0012, February 18, 1997). Another rumor suggested that chicken sellers were not selling their poultry in Iraq but instead were sending their products to other countries (BRCC Doc. No. 040-4-2-0509, December 12, 2002).
44. BRCC Doc. No. 148-4-5-0723, September 6, 1996.
45. BRCC Doc. No. 148-4-5-0128, March 15, 1997.
46. BRCC Doc. No. 01-2912-0004-0136, August 12, 2001.
47. BRCC Doc. No. 148-4-5-0406, January 29, 1997.
48. BRCC Doc. No. 148-4-5-0301, February 6, 1997; BRCC Doc. No. 148-4-5-0095, February 26, 1997.
49. Ed Blanche, "Iraqi Rebels Claim Sunni Clans Gathering against Saddam," Associated Press, June 18, 1995.
50. Youssef Ibrahim, "Iraq Reportedly Cracks Down on Clan That Tried a Coup," New York Times, June 20, 1995.
51. Blanche, "Iraqi Rebels Claim Sunni Clans Gathering."
52. BRCC Doc. No. 148-4-5-0994, July 20, 1996.
53. BRCC Doc. No. 148-4-5-1006, July 22, 1996.
54. BRCC Doc. No. 148-4-5-0396, January 29, 1997.
55. BRCC Doc. No. 162-2-2-0291, July 24, 1997.
56. BRCC Doc. No. 01-3713-0000-0107, June 27, 1998; BRCC Doc. No. 01-3713-0000-0059, July 15, 1998.
57. BRCC Doc. No. 087-5-3-0470, March 16, 1999; BRCC Doc. No. 087-5-

3-0421, March 17, 1999; BRCC Doc. Nos. 087-5-3-0163 to 0165, May 20, 1999; BRCC Doc. Nos. 133-5-7-0742 to 0743, July 21, 1999.
58. BRCC Doc. Nos. 133-5-7-0742 to 0743, July 21, 1999.

REFERENCES

Ascherio, Alberto, Robert Chase, Tim Cot, and Godelieave Dehaes. 1992. Iraq Survey Data. *New England Journal of Medicine* 327 (13): 931–36.

Baram, Amatzia. 2000. "The Effect of Iraqi Sanctions: Statistical Pitfalls and Responsibility." *Middle East Journal* 54 (2): 194–223.

Bengio, Ofra. 2000. "How Does Saddam Hold On?" *Foreign Affairs* 79 (4): 90–103.

Blaydes, Lisa. 2018. *State of Repression: Iraq under Saddam Hussein*. Princeton: Princeton University Press.

Blaydes, Lisa, and Mark Kayser. 2011. "Counting Calories: Democracy and Distribution in the Developing World." *International Studies Quarterly* 55 (4): 887–908.

Davis, Eric. 2005. *Memories of State: Politics, History and Collective Identity in Modern Iraq*. Berkeley: University of California Press.

Dawisha, Adeed. 2009. *Iraq: A Political History from Independence to Occupation*. Princeton: Princeton University Press.

DiFonzo, Nicholas, and Prashant Bordia. 2007. *Rumor Psychology: Social and Organizational Approaches*. Washington, DC: American Psychological Association.

Dimitrov, Martin, and Joseph Sassoon. 2014. "State Security, Information and Repression: A Comparison of Communist Bulgaria and Ba'thist Iraq." *Journal of Cold War Studies* 16 (2): 3–31.

Gordon, Joy. 2010. *Invisible War: The United States and the Iraq Sanctions*. Cambridge, MA: Harvard University Press.

Graham-Brown, Sarah. 1995. "Intervention, Sovereignty and Responsibility." *Middle East Report* 193 (March–April).

Graham-Brown, Sarah. 1999. *Sanctioning Saddam: The Intervention Politics in Iraq*. London: I.B. Taurus.

Haddad, Fanar. 2011. *Sectarianism in Iraq: Antagonistic Visions of Unity*. London: Hurst and Company.

Jawaheri, Yasmin Husein Al-. 2008. *Women in Iraq: The Gender Impact of International Sanctions*. Boulder: Lynne Rienner.

Khoury, Dina Rizk. 2013. *Iraq in Wartime: Soldiering, Martyrdom, and Remembrance*. New York: Cambridge University Press.

Mackey, Sandra. 2002. *The Reckoning: Iraq and the Legacy of Saddam Hussein*. New York: W. W. Norton.

Marr, Phebe. 2004. *The Modern History of Iraq*, 2nd ed. Boulder: Westview Press.

Mazaheri, Nimah. 2010. "Iraq and the Domestic Political Effects of Economic Sanctions." *Middle East Journal* 64 (2): 254–68.

Pellett, Peter. 2002. "Sanctions, Food, Nutrition and Health in Iraq." In *Iraq under Siege: The Deadly Impact of Sanctions and War*, ed. Anthony Arnove. Cambridge, MA: South End Press.

Rohde, Achim. 2010. *State-Society Relations in Ba'thist Iraq: Facing Dictatorship*. New York: Routledge.

Sakai, Keiko. 2003. "Tribalization as a Tool of State Control in Iraq: Observations on the Army, the Cabinets and the National Assembly." In *Tribes and Power: Nationalism and Ethnicity in the Middle East*, ed. Faleh Abdul-Jabar and Hosham Dawod. London: Saqi Press.

Sassoon, Joseph. 2012. *Saddam Hussein's Ba'th Party: Inside an Authoritarian Regime*. New York: Cambridge University Press.

Scott, James. 1985. *Weapons of the Weak: Everyday Forms of Peasant Resistance*. New Haven: Yale University Press.

Walter, Alissa. 2018. "Petitioning Saddam: Voices from the Iraqi Archives." In *Truth, Silence, and Violence in Emerging States: Histories of the Unspoken*, ed. Aidan Russell. London: Routledge.

Wedeen, Lisa. 1999. *Ambiguities of Domination: Politics Rhetoric and Symbols in Contemporary Syria*. Chicago: University of Chicago Press.

Woods, Kevin, David Palkki, and Mark Stout. 2011. *The Saddam Tapes: The Inner Workings of a Tyrant's Regime, 1978–2001*. New York: Cambridge University Press.

TWO

Economic Shocks and Communist Survival and Collapse

Martin K. Dimitrov

Autocracies sometimes survive the impact of external shocks, but at other times these shocks contribute to their collapse. What determines the vulnerability of nondemocratic regimes to economic crises? The causal mechanisms may vary depending on regime type (single party; dominant party; no party), the type of crisis (collapse of trade with the main trading partner; externally imposed debt crisis; externally conditioned currency or stock-market collapse), and the time period under analysis (the preglobalized world of the Cold War or the current integrated economic world order). To maximize the likelihood of identifying causal mechanisms that explain the ability of authoritarian regimes to survive crises, this chapter offers case studies of four single-party communist regimes that experienced a rapid deterioration of trade with the Soviet Union, which was their main trade partner at the time. This research design holds constant regime type, the type of crisis, and the dominant economic world order under which the crisis emerged. Nevertheless, it identifies important variation with regard to the outcome of the crisis on regime stability: China and Cuba survived the end of trade relations with the Soviet Union in the 1960s and 1990s, whereas regime collapse in the German Democratic Republic and Bulgaria was due at least in part to substantial reductions in the supply of Soviet oil at subsidized Council for Mutual Economic Assistance (COMECON) prices (in addition, both countries suffered an externally imposed debt crisis). Thus, the paired comparison of China/Cuba and the GDR/Bulgaria allows us to explore within-regime variation in susceptibility to external economic shocks.

This chapter argues that the ability of single-party communist regimes to withstand a deterioration of relations with their main trading partner depends on whether they have established a welfare dictatorship (*Fürsorgediktatur*),[1] which features costly social spending commitments and economically debilitating subsidies aimed at maintaining consumer price stability; preferential trade with the Soviet Union was essential for making the system viable. Although the introduction of a welfare dictatorship may stabilize communist governance in the short run, eventually the costs of maintaining the system are so great that they can bring regimes to the brink of bankruptcy. The chapter argues that China survived the split with the Soviet Union in the late 1950s because the absence of a welfare dictatorship meant that there was no popular discontent as a result of frustrated expectations about social spending. In contrast, such expectations existed in Bulgaria and the GDR, where mass compliance was based entirely on performance legitimacy, thus leading to widespread discontent when welfare provision deteriorated as a result of the double whammy of declining Soviet subsidies and curtailed access to Western loans. These two countries illustrate the importance of relative expectations: in Bulgaria, the impact of the crisis was more severe than in the GDR, but the Bulgarian protests were smaller than the German because of more modest relative expectations. Finally, the case of Cuba (which also experienced a foreign debt crisis and deteriorating trade relations with the Soviet Union) demonstrates that welfare dictatorships with a strong ideological foundation may survive a prolonged economic crisis, especially when they open the exit option by permitting emigration. Collectively, these four cases allow us to understand what variables condition the impact of external economic shocks on the survival of communist regimes with centrally planned economies.

The argument advanced in this chapter gives rise to two questions. The first is why some communist regimes implement a welfare dictatorship and others do not. The answer is that because it is costly, the creation of this type of welfare regime will only be adopted as a legitimacy-generating strategy in response to a system-destabilizing domestic crisis (like the mass anti-regime protests in the GDR and Bulgaria in the 1950s) or a severe external shock (US sanctions against Cuba in the 1960s) (Dimitrov 2018a). China did not experience an event of this type until the 1989 Tiananmen protests, which explains why its welfare regime under central planning was quite modest by comparison with those established in Eastern Europe and Cuba. The second question concerns the mechanism through which communist regimes take stock of popular expectations with regard to the scope of the welfare dictatorship. The chapter argues that citizen complaints function as the main channel for communicating consumption preferences. As citizen complaints can be used to fine-tune social policy, communist regimes that have established welfare dictatorships actively solicit and carefully analyze them.

Because of its focus on how the presence of a welfare dictatorship conditions the impact of an externally imposed crisis in centrally planned economies, this chapter departs from the standard theories of rule in non-electoral autocracies, which focus on catering to the needs of the selectorate. Mass constraints loom large in the logic of a welfare dictatorship. Therefore, although the chapter acknowledges that the incumbent needs to secure the support of the selectorate, it argues that communist regimes also took very seriously the importance of building surplus coalitions by assessing and satisfying mass consumption preferences. Moreover, these preferences also informed the decision-making calculus of soft-liners within the selectorate during the process of regime breakdown and collapse. Because they index levels of popular trust in the system (Dimitrov 2014a, 2015), regime insiders can use aggregate complaints data to assess the popularity of the regime. In particular, the chapter argues that strategic members of the selectorate interpret a decline in citizen complaints as an indicator that they should prepare an exit strategy and turn against the incumbent.

The chapter is based on regime-generated primary sources from China, Bulgaria, and the GDR, which are supplemented by Soviet archival documents and by 62 interviews conducted in Bulgaria, China, Germany, and Cuba. For China, I collected materials at provincial archives (primarily the Shanghai Municipal Archive) and a range of internal-circulation (*neibu*) and classified (*mimi*, *jimi*, and *juemi*) serials and government documents. For Bulgaria, I relied on the State Security Archive (AMVR) and the Communist Party archive (TsDA). For the GDR, I used the Stasi archive and the Socialist Party archive (SAPMO). As access to archival documents remains impossible in Cuba, I supplemented official publications with a data set of citizen complaints that I compiled on the basis of library research conducted in Havana. The Chinese, German, and Bulgarian primary sources that form the empirical backbone of the chapter were produced for regime insiders and thus hold significant potential to reveal the internal logic of establishing and operating a welfare dictatorship.

The chapter is organized as follows. Section 1 provides further theoretical reflections on the conditions under which communist states successfully establish and sustain welfare dictatorships. Sections 2 and 3 respectively trace the evolution and collapse of the welfare dictatorships in East Germany and Bulgaria. Section 4 focuses on the effects of the Sino-Soviet split in China. Section 5 examines how the Cuban welfare dictatorship adapted to the end of Soviet subsidies. Section 6 provides broader reflections on scope conditions and concludes.

1. The Rise and Demise of Welfare Dictatorships

A standard interpretation is that communist regimes, which are understood as "shortage economies" (Kornai 1980), do not aim to satisfy the consumption preferences of the population (Friedrich and Brzezinski 1965), ruling instead by repressing the masses and rewarding members of the selectorate (Arendt 1951; Bueno de Mesquita et al. 2003). This received wisdom has been challenged by early scholarship that emphasized the decline in repression in post-Stalinist regimes (Dallin and Breslauer 1970), as well as by subsequent studies of the social contract, which argued that citizens would remain quiescent for as long as the regime provided them with stable access to jobs, housing, welfare benefits, and, importantly, consumer goods (Pravda 1980; Millar 1985; Hauslohner 1987; Cook 1993). The collapse of communist regimes led to an archival revolution that allowed scholars to assess the validity of arguments about centrally planned economies that were developed without access to primary regime-generated sources. Recent archival studies have confirmed the insights of the earlier literature concerning the importance that communist regimes attached to satisfying the consumption preferences of the population (Landsman 2005; Siegelbaum 2008; Betts 2010; Bren and Neuburger 2012; Koenker 2013). Research on welfare dictatorships has thus validated Václav Havel's astute observation that late socialism involved "the coming together of a dictatorship and a consumer society" (Havel 1979, 71).

This chapter extends the findings of the recent archival literature on socialist consumption (which has been developed exclusively by historians) by focusing on several interrelated questions that allow us to shed light on the political logic of welfare dictatorships. Namely, it addresses the following puzzles: When do communist regimes start paying attention to the consumer preferences of the population? How do they find out what these preferences are? How do they aim to satisfy these preferences? And how might they avoid systemic collapse following their eventual inability to respond to these preferences after an economic shock? By identifying a non-electoral mechanism for popular input into authoritarian governance, the chapter contributes to three literatures: the literature on welfare in autocracies (Cook 2007; Haggard and Kaufman 2008; Inglot 2008; Cook and Dimitrov 2017; Dimitrov 2018a), the literature on economic shocks and democratization (Haggard and Kaufman 1995), and more broadly, the rapidly expanding literature on durable authoritarianism (Magaloni 2006; Brownlee 2007; Levitsky and Way 2010; Bunce and Wolchik 2011; Blaydes 2011; Svolik 2012; Dimitrov 2013).

The Political Logic of Welfare Dictatorships

This chapter argues that, although welfare dictatorships may arise in response to external threats (as in Cuba, where social spending was strategically deployed to win popular support following the Bay of Pigs invasion in 1961 and the imposition of trade sanctions by the United States in 1962), the typical pattern involves a response to domestic threats to regime stability. In the GDR, Bulgaria, and the Soviet Union welfare dictatorships were established in response to unanticipated system-destabilizing mass protests about price and work norm increases. These protests made apparent to the leadership that consumption and discontent were intimately linked in communist regimes. The response necessitated a two-pronged strategy: the expansion of social spending and the collection of information that would allow communist regimes to anticipate future eruptions of discontent.

Regime-generated documents reveal that communist elites distinguished between two types of discontent: overt and latent (Dimitrov 2014b). Overt discontent involved public acts of opposition, such as the distribution of antiregime pamphlets, the creation of unauthorized civil society groups, and participation in unsanctioned protests and demonstrations, whereas hidden discontent (latent discontent) was limited to privately held dissatisfaction that typically stemmed from the regime's inability to meet its redistributive commitments to the population. Leaders were aware that latent discontent could also result from frustrated expectations for political concessions but believed that those expectations could be kept at bay through a relaxation of repression and increased spending on consumer goods, welfare, and services. Leaders thought that the two types of discontent were related and that the emergence of overt discontent represented a visible failure to identify and neutralize brewing latent discontent through redistributive concessions. Thus, the institutions of a welfare dictatorship emerge as a solution to the problem of tracking and responding to latent discontent prior to its transformation into system-destabilizing overt discontent.

Authoritarian leaders who want to assess popular discontent face a fundamental obstacle: the exceeding difficulty of collecting reliable information. First identified in the classic literature on totalitarianism (Friedrich and Brzezinski 1965), this problem poses a major challenge to governance in dictatorships. Friedrich and Brzezinski argue that in the absence of information, citizens are prevented from revolting solely through the systematic use of pervasive terror (Friedrich and Brzezinski 1965). Repression intensifies the information problem, because citizens in autocracies are unwilling to reveal their true level of support for the regime due to fear that criticism will be met with reprisals (Kuran 1995). Instead of showing their opposition to the system, therefore, citizens engage in preference falsification, which manifests itself as reluctant participation in ritualistic acts of public dissimulation ("as if" compliance), such as compulsory mass rallies, manifestations, and elections (Wedeen 1999). Preference falsification makes dictators fundamentally insecure, since they cannot know their true level of support and thus face an incalculable risk of being deposed through revolution or a coup (Kuran 1991; Lohmann 1994). Because dictators who repress are more insecure than those who do not (Wintrobe 1998), logically repression not only does not resolve the information problem but actually shortens the life span of dictatorships. And yet some dictatorships are especially durable (with communist regimes being the longest-lasting type of nondemocratic regime to emerge since World War I),[2] which suggests that they have found ways of mitigating the information problem.

Arguments about the effects of preference falsification on governance are built on the assumption that authoritarian leaders are unable to create channels that ameliorate the information problem (Kuran 1991, 47). In contrast, this essay argues that a range of bureaucracies in autocracies can be mobilized to compile the necessary information on the public mood. Because they control these bureaucracies, authoritarian leaders have access to data that allows them to assess the magnitude of this problem and to try to mitigate it. For this reason, the leaders of authoritarian regimes actively promote channels that would allow them to obtain information on the popular mood.

What might these channels be? One literature that addresses this question is the new research on electoral autocracies, which has highlighted how competitive elections can provide information to the regime about its level of mass support (Magaloni 2006; Gandhi and Lust-Okar 2009). Ongoing research has identified protests as a second channel for transmitting information about levels of discontent to the leadership in autocracies, with a recent study arguing that the Chinese government encourages protests because of its inability to gather information on discontent through other channels (Lorentzen 2013). A third line of inquiry has focused on news content published in commercialized media in post-Tiananmen China and on the monitoring of social media as valuable sources of information about public discontent (Stockmann 2013; King, Pan, and Roberts 2013, 2017; Pan and Chen 2018).

This essay argues that although they transmit information about popular discontent, elections, protests, and commercialized media do not function as the main avenues for collecting information in communist autocracies. This does not mean that the regimes studied here did not extract information about governance problems from these channels (Zaslavsky and Brym 1978). However, they did not actively promote them as solutions to the information problem because all of these channels had the potential to usher in systemic crisis rather than to help manage discontent. With regard to elections, the experience of Poland in 1989 demonstrates how competitive elections can precipitate regime collapse. Eastern Europe also illustrates how unconstrained mass protests can usher in regime instability and, eventually, regime collapse (Bunce 2003). Commercialized media and the internet also present a danger, because to the extent that the information about discontent is disseminated, it undermines stability by creating a coordination mechanism for discontented citizens (this confirms Kuran's prescient insight) (Kuran 1991, 47). For example, the liberalization of Soviet media during perestroika hastened regime collapse by revealing to citizens the pervasiveness of discontent with the Communist Party.

Another limitation of the channels emphasized in recent studies is that they do not provide indicators of latent discontent. Joining a protest is a highly visible public act of discontent, whereas spoiling a ballot or casting a negative vote sends a clear signal of opposition. Similarly, newspaper stories about popular grievances or social media posts about mass incidents help identify overt discontent. As valuable as such knowledge is, communist regimes prize more highly information on the spread of latent discontent. The reason is that they understand the emergence of overt discontent as a failure to detect and dissipate latent discontent. Furthermore, overt discontent, especially when it is widespread, requires either significant concessions or massive repression, both of which are very costly governance tools. From the perspective of a communist regime, information on latent discontent allows for a more nimble governance strategy, involving selective repression and targeted redistributive concessions.

Collecting Information on Consumption Preferences in Communist Regimes

Information is essential for the effective operation of a welfare dictatorship, as it allows for social spending to be consistent with popular preferences (it also facilitates the effective targeting of selective repression). Information on citizen preferences is either involuntarily extracted or voluntarily provided. Successful information gathering requires both a decline in repression (in order to reduce fear among the population and facilitate the collection of information) and an expansion of personnel to collect and process the information (both the East German Stasi and the Bulgarian Committee for State Security expanded their personnel as levels of repression declined).[3] One innovation in tracking latent discontent was to register rumors by dispatching informants to stand in queues (which were long and moved very slowly, providing a suitable venue for people to vent off their frustrations); this method is still used today in Cuba, where the survival of the food distribution system means that Cubans spend many hours each week in queues, thus allowing informants to engage in the registration of "spontaneous public opinion" (*opinión espontánea*) (*Revista Temas* 2013). In Bulgaria, rumors highlighted the major anxieties of the population, which concerned the prices of staples and of household necessities (TsDA, f. 1B op. 55 a. e. 1207 [1972]); the increase in the retirement age (TsDA, f. 1B op. 55 a. e. 1207 [1972]); and the curtailing of ethnolinguistic rights for minority populations (TsDA f. 1B op. 55 a. e. 1203 [1971]; TsDA f. 1B op. 101 a. e. 1140 [1984]). Another innovation was the use of opinion polling, which was conducted from the 1960s onward by sociologists working at newspapers, radio stations, academic research institutes, youth research institutes, and even at opinion research institutes located within the Central Committee (Niemann 1993). Prior to perestroika, the utility of polls in revealing latent discontent was limited due to preference falsification (Aslanov interview 2009). As preference falsification became less widespread during perestroika, opinion polls demonstrated almost instantly that citizens were dissatisfied with their standards of living, the scarcity of consumer goods, and the spread of corruption (TsDA f. 1B op. 55 a. e. 722 [1988]).

From the perspective of communist regimes, the problem with involuntarily extracted information was twofold. On the one hand, citizens were typically aware that information was being collected from them against their will. Because this collection occurred in an authoritarian setting, there was a non-negligible probability that individuals were falsifying their preferences in order to please those collecting the information and to avoid recrimination. A more serious concern was that the involuntary extraction of information did not bind citizens to the regime, because they could not expect to receive individualized benefits in exchange for providing accurate information, as they would when lodging complaints. These shortcomings of involuntarily extracted information raised the importance of incentivizing citizens to provide information voluntarily.

Citizen complaints served as the main channel for the voluntary provision of information in communist autocracies. In the assessment of the Communist Party itself, complaints functioned as a "barometer of public opinion" (TsDA f. 1B op. 55 a. e. 943 [1985], 9), which could reveal popular perceptions of governance problems under late socialism and thus help alleviate the shortage of information on how ordinary citizens viewed the performance of the regime. Because they are spontaneously produced matter-of-fact requests for services or benefits rather than hollow ritualistic displays of loyalty to the party, complaints provide information that is unlikely to suffer from preference falsification.

The discussion of complaints allows us to make a general theoretical point about the voluntary provision of information on latent discontent in communist regimes. Complaining in a communist regime (voice) represents trust that the government will take citizen concerns seriously; this is consistent with Hirschman's argument that "loyalty holds exit at bay and activates voice" (Hirschman 1970, 78). Loyalty in communist autocracies, however, is instrumental and contingent on responsiveness to complaints. In turn, because ongoing responsiveness is easier to implement under central planning (when more resources are controlled by the state), the voluntary transfer of information is most likely to emerge under a centralized system of resource allocation. This is one reason why China, which started to transition away from central planning in the late 1970s, never consolidated an East European–style comprehensive nationwide system for the systematic collection and analysis of information on citizen preferences contained in complaints.

In sum, the chapter argues that communist regimes establish welfare dictatorships following unexpected system-destabilizing internal or external shocks. They use social spending to prevent the transformation of latent discontent into overt discontent. Although this system may stabilize communist governance for some time, its long-term viability depends on access to substantial resources that are needed to underwrite social spending in order to continuously satisfy the ever-rising consumer expectations. When communist regimes lose the support of their main trading partner, the stability of the welfare dictatorship (and of the regime itself) is threatened, as demonstrated by the cases of the GDR and Bulgaria; the situation becomes even more precarious when an external debt crisis is added to the deterioration of trade relations with the main trading partner. Regimes that either have not established a welfare state (like China in the 1950s) or which have extensive stocks of legitimacy (like Cuba, where anti-American nationalism bolstered the Castro brothers in the 1990s) can survive the severing of trade relations with the main trading partner. The next four sections provide empirical details to address how the GDR, Bulgaria, China, and Cuba dealt with the ending of trade relations with the Soviet Union.

2. Internal and External Shocks and the East German Welfare Dictatorship

The German Democratic Republic was the first communist regime in post–World War II Europe to implement a welfare dictatorship. The rolling out of extensive commitments to social spending came as a direct consequence of the June 1953 worker uprising. As newly declassified documents from the GDR State Security Archive (Stasi Archive) make clear, the uprising itself reflected mounting discontent throughout 1952 as a result of forced collectivization, shortages of staples (butter, margarine, meat, vegetables, and sugar), and the difficulty of securing coal for winter heating (Engelmann 2013). The spark was the political opening created by the death of Stalin in March 1953, as well as the raising of prices for sugar products, and especially, the increase in work norms coupled with a decrease in salaries (Engelmann 2013). About a million people participated in protests and strikes that engulfed as many as 500 cities and villages throughout 14 of the 15 regional districts (*Bezirke*) of the GDR (Schroeder 2013, 146). Though Soviet tanks successfully quelled the uprising, the 1953 events demonstrated that the GDR regime was deeply unpopular and that it could not base its long-term survival on repression alone. The leadership aimed to ensure the quiescence of the population through a package of benefits and price subsidies. Instead of totalistic terror, social spending and selective repression formed the wellspring of regime stability.

The optimal operation of the welfare dictatorship required channels through which citizens could express their preferences with regard to social policies. The institution of citizen complaints (*Eingaben*) was actively promoted precisely because it allowed citizens to communicate with the regime about the allocation of benefits and simultaneously enabled the leadership to utilize resources more effectively by better targeting these benefits (Merkel 1998; Staadt 1996; Mühlberg 2004; SAPMO DY30/913 [1981]; SAPMO DC 20/16563 [1981]; SAPMO DC 20/16634 [1989]; and SAPMO DC 20/16635 [1989]). The party took *Eingaben* so seriously that districts were encouraged to compete for handling the highest volume of complaints (Betts 2010, 175). In parallel with the institutions for analyzing citizen complaints, the Central Evaluation and Information Group (Zentrale Auswertungs- und Informationsgruppe, or ZAIG) of the Stasi also collected information on discontent. The ZAIG was established in the aftermath of the 1953 uprising and tasked with producing timely assessments of the public mood that could be used to prevent the rise of another unanticipated expression of popular discontent through the deployment of targeted redistribution and selective repression (Dimitrov 2018b, 27). A third channel for evaluating citizen preferences with regard to social spending and the provision of consumption goods was provided by the reports of the Central Committee Opinion Research Institute (Meinungsforschungsinstitut beim ZK der SED), by the party departments in charge of municipal service provision, and by the Worker-Peasant Inspection (SAPMO DY 30/J IV 2/3 1272 [1967]). These multiple channels of information meant that the leadership was well apprised of the needs of the population.

In the aftermath of the June 1953 uprising and especially after the building of the Berlin Wall in 1961, the East German population came to expect a growing set of entitlements and an expanding range of consumer goods. The seriousness with which the leadership took these expectations is highlighted by the fact that the Stasi spent most of 1977, which was an otherwise "normal" year (Allinson 2009), trying to solve the "coffee shortage crisis" that had befallen the GDR (Bispinck 2012). The Stasi was also involved in securing the goods that were sold both in the Intershop/Genex chains (which operated with hard currency) and the Delikat/Exquisit shops, where one could use GDR marks to buy hard-to-find domestic and imported goods (Judt 2013). By the 1980s, however, economic difficulties made it increasingly challenging for the regime to respond to citizen preferences regarding social spending and consumer goods provision. The housing crisis, which had been a source of constant concern throughout the existence of the GDR, worsened. Although the GDR imported automobiles from other socialist countries and produced its own Trabant and Wartburg, there remained vast unmet demand for cars. And despite efforts to keep supermarkets and department stores well stocked, shortages became more palpable in the 1980s.

The inability of the regime to satisfy the consumption preferences of the public was closely connected to the decline in Soviet subsidies. The GDR had come to rely on access to cheap raw materials (primarily oil and gas) that were traded at submarket COMECON prices. Until 1980, two-thirds of East German trade was conducted with the Soviet Union and other COMECON countries. By 1989, the Soviet Union accounted for only 22 percent of GDR imports and 23.8 percent of its exports (Statistisches Amt der DDR 1990); during the 1980s, the EU emerged as the main trading partner for the GDR (Leibniz-Institut für Länderkunde 2005, 82–83). This reorientation of trade reflected a gradual reduction of Soviet oil shipments, which began in 1981 (Schürer 2014, 458–77). The decline was so bad that shipments in 1989 were equivalent to those of 1978, despite the fact that increasing oil consumption was essential if the East German regime wanted to satisfy the ever-increasing consumption expectations of the population. As Soviet oil had been used to meet both domestic needs and to earn hard currency through re-export, the GDR leadership had to borrow from the West in order to finance the expensive welfare state that it had created. Although the cumulative debt burden was relatively low (at 40 billion deutsche marks it was equivalent to only about 16 percent of East German GNP), but as a top-secret report prepared by Gerhard Schürer for the Politburo documented, the inability of the GDR to export to the West meant that by 1989 it could not secure any further foreign loans and was unable to make payments on its existing foreign debt (Schürer 2014). In short, spending on welfare had brought East Germany to the brink of bankruptcy (Schroeder 2013, 691). This information was made available to regime insiders in September 1989 and was a consideration when they removed Honecker on October 18, 1989 (Hertle and Stephan 2012, 103–33).

The other factor that led to Honecker's ouster was the massive protests that engulfed East Germany in 1989. From the public's perspective, the regime had reneged on its commitments under the socialist social contract by failing to deliver the anticipated volume of benefits and consumer goods. The tenor of complaints became angrier and citizens began to withdraw from the petitioning system. Despite the worsening economic crisis, the only category of petitions that saw a sizable increase in the second half of the 1980s was requests for permanent exit from the GDR and requests to visit West Germany (SAPMO DY30 6265 [1988], 26; SAPMO DY30 6266 [1989], 3). This showed that, having witnessed the failure of the regime to deliver on the socialist social contract, previously loyal citizens simply exited the system of citizen complaints and instead joined various opposition groups whose rapid growth in 1987–89 helped pave the way for the eventual dissolution of the system; latent discontent had been transformed into overt discontent. Far from being an isolated case, the GDR is paradigmatic of the conditions under which the welfare dictatorship emerged, operated, and eventually failed in the Eastern bloc.

Following the removal of Honecker, the new communist ruling coalition made a desperate attempt to secure Soviet economic assistance. Egon Krenz, the new general secretary, went on an emergency trip to Moscow on November 1, 1989. Although Gorbachev promised to fulfill the existing Soviet oil shipment obligations (Galkin and Cherniaev 2006, 232–45), these had been drastically reduced when compared to their levels in the 1970s. Krenz left Moscow knowing that he could not rely on much-needed additional Soviet assistance and that Gorbachev was opposed to his plans to seek emergency aid from the International Monetary Fund (Krenz 2014, 276). Facing an economic collapse, the entire East German Politburo resigned on December 1, 1989. The end of the welfare dictatorship was also the end of the East German regime.

3. The Bulgarian Welfare Dictatorship

In most other Eastern bloc states, the establishment of a welfare dictatorship followed a sequencing of events similar to those that unfolded in the GDR in 1953. The specific timing varied from country to country, but the logic was identical throughout the bloc. In Bulgaria, for example, the reorientation toward increased social spending resulted from a combination of domestic antiregime protests and the reactions of the leadership to events elsewhere in Eastern Europe. The most important instances of organized domestic discontent occurred in the spring of 1953, when textile workers in Khaskovo and tobacco-processing workers in Plovdiv went on strike due to poor work conditions, inadequate compensation, and massive layoffs (AMVR f. 1 op. 1 a. e. 2922 l. 5 [May 6, 1953]; AMVR f. 1 op. 1 a. e. 2811 [January 7, 1954]). Those strikes raised concerns that were amplified by the events in Eastern Europe, which in the understanding of the Bulgarian leadership resulted from the frustrated consumption preferences of the population (TsDA f. 1 op. 24 a. e. 125 [1953]; TsDA f. 1 op. 24 a. e. 188 [1954–1955]; TsDA f. 1B op. 64 a. e. 185 [November 21, 1953]). In response to these internal and external shocks (TsDA f. 317B op. 1 a. e. 133, l. 1–16 [October 31, 1956]), the Politburo decided to reduce the retail prices of staples, to increase the production of consumer goods, and to introduce various benefits and entitlements that constituted the Bulgarian socialist welfare dictatorship.

As in the GDR, the citizen complaints system was used to incentivize individuals to communicate their concerns about the fulfillment of social spending commitments and to thus bind them to the regime (Dimitrov 2014a). In 1970, the Bulgarian Politburo created a top-secret research institute that supplied the Central Committee of the Bulgarian Communist Party with classified information on trends in citizen complaints (TsDA f. 1 op. 35 a. e. 1235 [1970]), which were understood as a "barometer of public opinion" that could reveal popular perceptions of governance problems under late socialism in Bulgaria and thus help alleviate the dearth of information on how ordinary citizens viewed the performance of the regime (TsDA f. 1B op. 55 a. e. 943 [1985], 9). These complaints often focused on shortages that ranged from essential items like bread and car gasoline (TsDA f. 1B op. 55 a. e. 489 [1977]; TsDA f. 1B op. 55 a. e. 506 [1980]) to medicines, sanitary materials, and household medical devices (TsDA f. 1B op. 55 a. e. 508 [June 24, 1981]). The Information-Sociological Center saw such shortages as having potential economic, social, and political consequences. For example, the shortage of mass-consumption goods like spades, axes, hoes, adzes, pitchforks, wheelbarrows, metal buckets, electric pumps, stoves, door and window hinges, nails, forks, and spoons was considered a source of unfavorable economic, social, and political consequences: "The economic consequences include a slowdown of GDP growth; the social consequences include the creation of unnecessary obstacles for the consistent and full implementation of the [1972] December Program of the Party for Raising the Living Standards of the Population; politically, it gives rise to discontent and prompts public criticism" (TsDA f. 1B op. 55 a. e. 501 [December 29, 1979], 10).

Party leaders also received information about numerous complaints about the poor quality of various services provided to the population, such as telephone services (TsDA f. 1B op. 55 a. e. 485 [January 1977]), residential elevator service (TsDA f. 1B op. 55 a. e. 485 [January 1977]), taxicab services (TsDA f. 1B op. 55 a. e. 486 [March 1977]), general transportation services (TsDA f. 1B op. 55 a. e. 507 [December 30, 1980]), dental care (TsDA f. 1B op. 55 a. e. 529 [March 1986]), and health care (TsDA f. 1B op. 55 a. e. 497 [April 10, 1979]). Reports also alerted the leadership to the quality of food served in student and worker canteens (TsDA f. 1B op. 55 a. e. 487 [April 1977]; TsDA f. 1B op. 55 a. e. 496 [November 1978]), as well as the quality of organized vacation packages offered to workers (TsDA f. 1B op. 55 a. e. 512 [March 5, 1982]). No matter how small a problem might appear, all reports noted that it was already a source of popular discontent, and, if left unaddressed, it might have larger political consequences, such as creating doubt in the population with regard to the governing capacity of the Communist Party (Dimitrov 2012). For example, a report on housing repair services maintains that "the weaknesses and shortcomings in the maintenance and repair of the housing stock" have "political consequences," namely, "discontent among citizens"; the report warns that "if no decisive measures for improving this situation are taken, the question of the maintenance and repair of the housing stock will turn from a purely mundane problem into a political question" (TsDA, f. 1B op. 55 a. e. 502 [April 8, 1980], 16). Finally, a report about the poor quality of customer service provided in government offices highlighted the "political consequences" of this problem: "People form a negative opinion about the capabilities not only of government offices but of the governing capacity of the state as a whole" (TsDA f. 1B op. 55 a. e. 515 [November 25, 1982], 17).

Like the East German Stasi, State Security in Bulgaria also collected information on citizen perceptions about the fulfillment of social spending commitments. In the early 1980s, for example, State Security transmitted to the Politburo reports that indicated widespread understandings among ordinary citizens that "the Polish people supported Solidarity because they had nothing to eat" (AMVR f. 1 op. 12 a. e. 421 [1982], 61) and that "in light of the events in Poland, our government is aiming to maintain a wide assortment of food in the stores" (AMVR f. 1 op. 12 a. e. 421 [1982], 40). Such explicit linking of social stability with the availability of staples was not a surprise for the leadership, since it had been a part of State Security reports on the public mood for decades. Considering that most instances of antiregime protests prior to 1989 can be traced to either shortages of staples (typically meat) or to an increase in the price of staples (Dimitrov 2019a), Bulgaria is quite similar to other states in the Eastern bloc. Much like the Stasi, Bulgarian State Security also attempted to alleviate consumer discontent, usually by relying on industrial espionage to either steal trade secrets that would enable state-owned enterprises to manufacture higher-quality household cleaning agents or to acquire the design specifications of Western household appliances that could then be reverse-engineered and mass-produced (Dossier Commission 2013).

As elsewhere in the Eastern bloc, the rolling out of expansive packages of social benefits in Bulgaria was consistent with citizen preferences as expressed in complaint letters. In the late 1960s, the government provided a generous expansion of maternity leaves, engaged in the rapid construction of new housing, and legally sanctioned the private construction and ownership of countryside homes. The response to complaints also featured a further increase of salaries; support for families (child supplements and subsidies for mothers); attempts to augment the variety of domestic and imported goods offered in the stores; an increase in the volume and variety of services; and enhancements in health care and education. As the regime itself had promised, "The resolute improvement in the quality of all activities, production, and services is to become the main task in our future socioeconomic and cultural development" (BCP 1983, 13). The reasoning was powerful: "The fulfillment of this task has enormous political, ideological, economic, and social importance for every work unit, for every working man" (BCP 1983, 13). Attempts were also made to provide enough cars, and to thus satisfy the third leg of the socialist consumer dream: an apartment, a villa, and a car (Siegelbaum 2008; Bren and Neuburger 2012). Other concessions that resulted from persistent complaints included the increase in pensions and the attempt to alleviate consumer goods shortages by encouraging private activity.

In the 1980s, however, economic difficulties made the Bulgarian regime unable to respond to citizen complaints with redistributive concessions. The Information-Sociological Center reported that by 1988 as few as 14.5 percent of all complaints received a favorable resolution, a threefold decline from the early 1980s (TsDA f. 1B op. 55 a. e. 953 [1989], 19–20). The result of this erosion of effectiveness is not surprising: citizens started to withdraw from the system. From the public's perspective, the regime was failing to maintain adequate social spending and citizens were signaling their perception that the regime had reneged on its commitments to support welfare. There was a 50 percent drop in complaints between 1984 and 1988, followed by a further substantial reduction in the volume of complaints in 1989, at the height of the precollapse economic crisis. This showed that, having witnessed the failure of the regime to deliver on its social spending commitments, previously loyal citizens simply exited the system of citizen complaints and instead joined various opposition groups whose rapid growth in 1987–89 helped pave the way for the eventual dissolution of the system. Although the economic decline in Bulgaria was more serious than in the GDR, protest activity was more moderate, reflecting differences in relative expectations of economic well-being between the two regimes.

As in the GDR, the collapse of the welfare dictatorship had been prompted by a decline in Soviet subsidies. Bulgaria was even more dependent on Soviet aid than the GDR, as it conducted 80 percent of its trade with COMECON. Like the GDR, Bulgaria used Soviet oil to meet domestic demand and to secure foreign currency through re-export. The decline of Soviet oil shipments in the 1980s (these shipments were valued at $2 billion in world prices) led to a rapid accumulation of foreign debt. At $10 billion, the absolute value of the debt was low (about 20 percent of GNP, comparable to 16 percent of GNP in the GDR), yet according to a top-secret letter from the central bank that was circulated to Politburo members in July 1989, Bulgaria had no further export capacity and could no longer secure any additional foreign loans or make payments on its existing obligations to the West (TsDA f. 132P op. 15 a. e. 2 l.1–4 [July 18, 1989]). An additional letter from the central bank to the Politburo in October 1989 reiterated the gravity of the situation (TsDA f. 132P op. 15 a. e. 10 l. 3–4 [October 19, 1989]). Thus, when regime soft-liners decided to remove Zhivkov on November 10, 1989, they did so with the knowledge that the country was facing bankruptcy. As in the GDR, the demise of the welfare dictatorship was linked to regime collapse. A new communist ruling coalition was installed in November 1989, but it could not prevent regime change, which occurred in June 1990.

4. The Impact of the Sino-Soviet Split on China

China presents an important case of a communist regime that survived the deterioration of trade relations with the Soviet Union. The 1950s were a decade of extensive Soviet economic influence in China (Kong 2010; Kaple 1994; Shen 2013). Although Chinese adoption of the Soviet model was made possible by the presence of tens of thousands of Soviet advisers (Shen 2014), trade proved essential for economic integration (CASS 1991). Following the establishment of the People's Republic of China, the Soviet Union quickly assumed the status of main trade partner: in 1950 it accounted for 29.8 percent of Chinese trade; by 1952, for 54.8 percent; and by 1954, for as much as 56.9 percent (Lu 2008). The US embargo further elevated the importance of the relationship with the Soviet Union (Shu 2001; Shu 2014, 21–96). Thus, the Sino-Soviet split, which occurred in the midst of the famine during the Great Leap Forward, had a considerable economic impact on China (Lüthi 2008, 174–80). Soviet trade quickly collapsed: from 39.8 percent of trade volume in 1958, to 29.8 percent in 1961, and eventually to 1 percent of all trade in 1970 (Lu 2008; Hu 2015, 88). The question is how China survived this rapid deterioration of trade with its main trade partner.

In contrast to Eastern Europe, the absence of comprehensive nationwide social spending commitments meant that the regime was shielded from popular discontent in the wake of the Sino-Soviet split. Under Mao the social contract covered only a portion of urban residents working for government offices and state-owned enterprises: for example, in Shanghai, which was the city with the most extensive coverage in China, only 51 percent of the workforce (21 percent of the population) received welfare coverage in 1960 (Dillon 2015, 264). Coverage was even lower in other urban areas of China and did not extend to rural residents, who did not enjoy the package of labor insurance and cradle-to-grave welfare benefits that were accorded to privileged urban workers.

Maoist China provides an illustration of what information-gathering institutions look like when no welfare dictatorship exists. Analysis of a large corpus of archival materials (119 published reports from other provincial archives found in Zhou 2012, supplemented with over 1,000 party, government, and journalistic reports collected by the author at the Shanghai Municipal Archives), internal-circulation public security publications (*Renmin gong'an* and *Renmin gong'an zengkan*), and internal circulation news bulletins (especially *Neibu cankao*) reveals that information gathering during the Mao period (1949–76) was fragmentary and focused on the monitoring of overt discontent. Facts reported were rarely contextualized with regard to how representative they were of general trends. Although such lack of analysis might be understandable for reports produced at and below the provincial level (where the quality of the bureaucracy was lower), this was the norm at the national level as well. Let us take the example of the secret (*jimi*) bulletin aimed at Central Committee members entitled *Neibu cankao* (Internal Reference). The reports contained in this bulletin strengthen the impression that leaders were rarely presented with comprehensive information about national conditions. Reports from the 1950s and early 1960s are geographically specific, discussing events in a single large city (Beijing, Shanghai, Tianjin, Chongqing, Chengdu, Wuhan, Nanjing, Guangzhou, or Nanning), part of a province (Southern Jiangsu), a single province, or at the highest level of aggregation, a macro-region consisting of several provinces (the Southwestern Region; North China; or Northeast China). It is impossible to get a sense of national variation from these reports; in the GDR, by contrast, the Stasi aimed to provide leaders with mood assessments for each of the 15 provinces (*Bezirke*) in the immediate aftermath of the June 1953 worker uprising (BStU MfS SdM 249 Bl. 102–107 [1953]). Perhaps most distressing is that even party reporting was fragmentary: the most comprehensive report about hunger during the Great Leap Forward that has become available thus far covers only 16 provinces (Zhou 2012, 10–16), about three-fifths of China's 28 provinces, provincial-level municipalities, and ethnic autonomous regions at the time.

This might explain why, when confronted with evidence of hunger in some provinces, Chairman Mao reportedly interjected that the situation was better in other provinces (Dikötter 2010, 89, 335). Given the fragmented nature of information-gathering institutions in China, it is doubtful that even Mao had complete information on the spread of overt discontent.

After the death of Mao, information gathering slowly changed. Party and journalistic reporting was gradually being reoriented toward the monitoring of latent discontent. One early example is provided by a November 1976 investigation report commissioned by the Shanghai Municipal Party Committee on citizen reactions to a proposed change in the system for pork rationing (pork prices are so vital to the Chinese economy that they are still monitored by the government even today and used as a bellwether of food price inflation) (SMA B248-2-924 [1976]). A second area that experienced significant change was the content of the secret bulletins prepared for the Chinese leadership. Although coverage remained region-specific (rather than presenting comprehensive nationwide information), by 1980 both *Qingkuang huibian* and *Neibu cankao* had started to print longer, more in-depth reports that aimed to focus on important issues of broad significance. In contrast to earlier styles of reporting in such bulletins, in the post-Mao period, efforts were made to contextualize the specific incident that was described and to showcase how it might be representative of general trends; coverage of official corruption (*Neibu cankao*, No. 73/1981, 10–14; *Qingkuang huibian*, No. 549/1980) and of retaliation against petitioners (*Qingkuang huibian*, No. 365/1980) is exemplary of this new tendency. Finally, the creation of the Ministry of State Security in 1983 and the introduction of opinion polling in the mid-1980s further extended the ability of the state to eventually make a successful transition toward the involuntary extraction of information on latent discontent (Manion 1993).

The one area where progress was a lot more uncertain was the voluntary provision of information through citizen complaints. Vice Premier Xi Zhongxun opined in 1961: "Is it better to have more letters and visits or fewer? Of course it is better to have more. This means that the masses support us, love us, and trust us" (Diao 1996, 158). Yet building that trust was not a simple task. One problem was the relatively low use of the system: in 1979, the peak year for complaints during the entire 1949–89 period, the central complaints offices in China received 769 complaints per million people, which was 5.8 times lower than central-level complaints in East Germany (4,464 complaints per million people) and in Bulgaria (4,494 complaints per million people) (Diao 1996, 260; Mühlberg 2004, 177; TsDA f. 1B op. 55 a. e. 940 [1983], 5). But the key obstacle was the high levels of fear that persisted right up to Tiananmen and prevented the effective operation of the nascent institutions for collecting information on latent discontent. Some might question this claim. It is of course true that China was a lot less repressive in the 1980s than, for instance, in 1950: according to statistics published in a *neibu* compendium, no fewer than 1.8 million bandits (*tufei*) were exterminated (*jiaomie*) during the first 11 months of that year (MPS 2003, 19). However, China was still practicing capital punishment against those accused of counterrevolutionary crimes in the 1980s, and rates of execution had been increasing since the death of Mao (Scobell 1990, 513); contrast this with the GDR, which carried out its last execution in 1981 (curiously, of Werner Teske, a Stasi officer who attempted to defect) and where a grand total of 166 judicial executions were carried out in the four decades of communist rule (1949–89) (Marxen and Werle 2000). In China, the shelter and investigation, reeducation through labor (*laojiao*), and the gulag-like reform-through-labor (*laogai*) systems were all operating at a high volume throughout the 1980s. Though repression had declined by comparison with the 1950s or 1960s, this decline had not been sustained for a long enough period to translate into a diminution of fear among the population comparable to that in East European countries like the GDR.

In sum, China survived the Sino-Soviet split because it had not made commitments to universal welfare provision and could not be held accountable by the masses for a failure to sustain high levels of social spending. Neither the redistributive nor the information-gathering institutions that are essential for the effective operation of a welfare dictatorship existed in China in the 1950s. Moreover, these institutions were not established on a nationwide scale at any point prior to Tiananmen. Thus, it was only after the system-destabilizing antiregime protests of 1989 broke out that the regime was sensitized to the importance of monitoring latent discontent.

5. Surviving the End of Soviet Subsidies in Cuba

Cuba began to build a welfare dictatorship in the 1960s, when it guaranteed universal access to foodstuffs through the *libreta de abastecimientos* system; the trigger was an external shock in the form of the Bay of Pigs invasion and the imposition of sanctions by the United States (*Revista Temas* 2008). Welfare provision was understood as a mechanism for building popular support. It was expanded in the 1970s, following Cuba's entry into COMECON in 1972. By 1983, the Soviet Union accounted for 68.3 percent of Cuba's imports and 70 percent of its exports (Goskomstat SSSR 1985). Cuba financed its welfare dictatorship by exporting sugar at a price that was above market and importing Soviet oil at a price that was significantly below market. This model came to an abrupt end when Cuba suspended payments on its $10.9 billion debt to the Paris Club in 1986 and the Soviet Union announced that it would use market prices in trading with Cuba in 1990. The collapse of trade with the Soviet Union (and subsequently, with Russia) ushered in the *período especial*, which saw a plummeting of industrial production and living standards for Cubans, but not regime collapse. The system did not implode because the regime had ideological legitimacy due to the ongoing US embargo; because it allowed for an exit option by tolerating emigration; and because, even if food rations were reduced, other benefits like guaranteed employment, housing, and pensions were preserved. Enough of the welfare state survived to meet the relatively modest expectations of the Cuban population.

Cuba still maintains some semblance of a welfare dictatorship, despite rhetoric about reforming away from the planned economy. In the 1990s and 2000s, there have been some limited changes, such as the rise of small-scale private restaurants (*paladares*), the legalization of renting rooms in private homes (*casas particulares*), the emergence of cooperative markets (*mercados agropecuarios*) in the cities, and the multiplication of hard currency stores (*diplo-tiendas*). The market was allowed to penetrate some pockets of the economy, like the export-oriented sector, the tourism sector, and the small family-owned business sector (Corrales 2004). Important as they were, these changes were not incompatible with the planned economy and had, in fact, all existed in various national manifestations throughout the Eastern bloc in the 1970s and 1980s. Thus, on the eve of the Sixth Party Congress in April 2011, Cuba found itself with an unreformed planned economy. Yet reforms were urgently needed (Mesa-Lago 2012). At the Congress, Raúl Castro laid out an ambitious plan for economic reform, featuring price liberalization, the end of rationing, economic decentralization (although large enterprises would continue to be owned by the state), a massive expansion of market activities with the concomitant limiting of the role of the planned economy, and the layoffs of 1.3 million people (20 percent of the Cuban labor force) (Castro 2011). These reform plans called for nothing short of the dismantling of the welfare dictatorship.

Eight years after the Sixth Party Congress, the welfare dictatorship had survived largely intact.[4] The layoff targets had not been achieved (although the number of those employed in the private sector increased from 12 percent of the labor force in 2007 to 25 percent 2016) (ONEI

2017), price liberalization had not occurred, and rationing persisted in the form of the ubiquitous *libreta de abastecimientos* (supplies booklet), which entitles every Cuban citizen to purchase from one of the specialized groceries (*bodegas*) rations of sugar, rice, beans, bread, eggs, poultry, minced meat, pasta, salt, matches, soap, toothpaste, and coffee. These items are sold significantly below cost, with monthly rations costing no more than $2.50–$3.00, which is about an eighth of the average monthly salary. In addition, phone, electricity, and gas for cooking are available for another $2 a month per household. Public transportation, basic medicines, newspapers, books, and theater tickets are also very heavily subsidized. Finally, few Cubans pay rent, since most of them own their housing. Overall, the party-state has proven reluctant to abrogate its social spending commitments. The Seventh Party Congress in April 2016 reaffirmed the opposition of the ruling coalition to rapid implementation of economic reform. In April 2018, Miguel Díaz-Canel succeeded Raúl Castro to the post of president of Cuba; however, Díaz-Canel has not provided any indication that he will pursue rapid reforms.

The question that emerges is why these expensive subsidies have been preserved. The answer that one repeatedly hears in Havana is that they are the key to maintaining social stability. Many Cubans feel that the rations have already been reduced from their pre-1989 levels, when they included rum, cigarettes, milk, and even clothing; what they now get is the bare minimum, but they still receive something from the state. Ever since the special period came to an end in 1994, the Castro brothers have been relaxing repression. This relaxation elevated the need to reach out to Cubans through the mechanisms that made the welfare dictatorship functional in Eastern Europe. Cuba solicits public opinion through various channels: spontaneous registration of public opinion (based on publicly expressed opinion overheard by party cadres); opinion polling; and analysis of citizen complaints (*Revista Temas* 2013). In addition, since March 14, 2008, *Granma* has been publishing a regular section entitled *Cartas a la Dirección*, which prints letters to the editor containing complaints, criticisms, and suggestions that typically focus on concerns like the poor quality of municipal services and various types of shortages. The section rapidly grew in popularity. During the first year of its existence, about 10,000 citizens sent in letters by email or by post. In 2012, *Granma* received as many as 100,000 emails, letters, postcards, and phone calls. To accommodate the explosion in reader interest, *Granma* increased the size of the section from one to two printed pages. By *Granma*'s own assessment, this section is the most closely read portion of the Friday paper (*Granma*, January 4, 2013). Over time, responsiveness to citizen complaints has increased nearly fivefold, from 13.5 percent in 2008 (responses to 36 of the 266 letters published) to 65.1 percent in 2014 (responses to 164 of the 252 letters published) (Dimitrov 2019b). The other major newspapers (*Juventud rebelde*; *Trabajadores*; *Tribuna de la Habana*) and the monthly *Bohemia* also maintain sections in which they print citizen letters and responses to some of these letters from the authorities. The publication of such letters represents a visible gesture of government responsiveness to citizen concerns about the fulfillment of the social contract.

In sum, this section has maintained that though it is costly, a welfare dictatorship is established and maintained in communist regimes with a planned economy because, to the extent that citizen buy-in occurs, it allows for the maintenance of social stability without totalistic repression.

6. Conclusion

This chapter has argued that the institutions of a welfare dictatorship emerge in communist regimes as a solution to the problem of tracking and responding to latent discontent prior to its transformation into system-destabilizing overt discontent. By creating welfare dictatorships, communist regimes enter a devil's bargain: they maintain stability, but the price of doing so continuously increases, as their populations come to expect constant increases in the provision of welfare and consumer goods. Soviet subsidies were essential for maintaining these systems. For this reason, a rapid deterioration of trade relations with the Soviet Union (in conjunction with the nonavailability of Western loans) triggered instability in communist regimes that, unlike Cuba, could not resort to nationalism to shore up the system. In the GDR and Bulgaria, driven by the perception that the regime had reneged on its commitments to satisfy their consumption preferences, the masses engaged in system-destabilizing street protests. The actions of soft-liners in these regimes were at least in part guided by these mass expressions of overt discontent. Reformist members of the selectorate developed a strategy of unseating the incumbent with full knowledge of the widespread overt discontent stemming from the failure of the welfare dictatorship.

The argument presented in this chapter is not teleological. There is no assumption that all communist regimes would develop welfare dictatorships. The chapter maintains that communist regimes would not develop the information-gathering and redistributive institutions that comprise the welfare dictatorship until they experience system-destabilizing external or internal shocks. In the GDR, the shock was the 1953 worker uprising; in China, it was the 1989 protests. However, the chapter makes no claim that all communist regimes will experience such shocks.

The chapter has argued that the successful operation of a welfare dictatorship is facilitated by a system of central planning. Both the information-gathering and the redistributive institutions described in this chapter are most likely to emerge when the state exercises near-total control over resources. A market economy diminishes such control, thus limiting the ability of the state to supply uniform benefits and access to consumer goods. One reason why China never developed a welfare dictatorship as comprehensive as those found in Eastern Europe was that it did not experience a system-destabilizing shock until 1989; by then it had started to dismantle the planned economy, thus finding itself unable to follow the East European model and respond to the unanticipated eruption of overt discontent with the unrolling of a comprehensive welfare dictatorship.

At the broadest level of generality, this chapter argues that the effects of external shocks on communist regimes are conditioned by the presence of a welfare dictatorship. A country like China, which had no welfare dictatorship in the 1950s, could survive the severing of trade relations with the Soviet Union without worrying about popular discontent as a result of its failure to satisfy the consumptions needs of the population. This presents a sharp contrast to Eastern Europe, where regime collapse following the deterioration of trade with the Soviet Union was at least in part a result of frustrated popular social spending expectations that had been generated by the institutions of the welfare dictatorship. When economic conditions worsen, dictators have the choice of shrinking the support coalition, thus reducing costs; however, the expectations of a welfare dictatorship constrains the degree to which dictators can do so.

Cumulatively, these case studies illustrate the range of effects that the deterioration of trade relations with the Soviet Union had on communist regimes with centrally planned economies during the Cold War (maintenance of the status quo in 1950s China; a change in the ruling coalition in both the GDR and Bulgaria in 1989 that did not prevent regime change months later; and a very cautious implementation of limited reform by the precrisis ruling coalition in Cuba) and allow us to shed light on within-regime variation regarding the ability of single-party communist autocracies to survive external economic shocks.

NOTES

1. I extend a concept advanced by Jarausch 1998.
2. Communist regimes are the most durable type of nondemocratic regime, outlasting both noncommunist single-party regimes and nondemocratic monarchies. As of 2000, the average life span of noncommunist single-party regimes was 28.5 years and that of nondemocratic monarchies was 34.8 years. In contrast, communist single-party regimes had an average life span of 46.2 years as of 2000. My data set includes 39 noncommunist single-party regimes (based partially on Smith 2005), 20 nondemocratic monarchies, and 15 communist regimes. As of 2019, the five remaining communist regimes have an average life span of 62 years.
3. The staff of the East German Stasi, for example, increased from 12,976 officers in 1953 to 91,015 in 1989, even though the number of individuals prosecuted for political crimes declined from 12,520 in 1953 to 2,617 in 1989 (Gieseke 2006, 202–46, 317). In Bulgaria, the number of those sentenced for political crimes declined from 2,144 in 1952 to 206 in 1989 (Stoianova and Iliev 1991, 101). On the staff of the Bulgarian State Security, see AMVR f. 10 op. 6 a. e. 6 (1969).
4. Paragraph based on research conducted in Havana, May–June 2013 and May–June 2015.

REFERENCES

Allinson, Mark. 2009. "1977: The GDR's Most Normal Year?" In *Power and Society in the GDR, 1961–1979: The "Normalization of Rule"?*, ed. Mary Fulbrook. New York: Berghahn Books, 253–77.

Arendt, Hannah. 1951. *The Origins of Totalitarianism*. New York: Harcourt, Brace.

Aslanov, Yuri. 2009. Personal interview. Sofia, June 29.

Betts, Paul. 2010. *Within Walls: Private Life in the German Democratic Republic*. New York: Oxford University Press.

Bispinck, Henrik. 2012. *Die DDR im Blick der Stasi: Die geheimen Berichte an die SED-Führung 1977*. Göttingen: Vandenhoeck & Ruprecht.

Blaydes, Lisa. 2011. *Elections and Distributive Politics in Mubarak's Egypt*. New York: Cambridge University Press.

Bren, Paulina, and Mary Neuburger, eds. 2012. *Communism Unwrapped: Consumption in Cold War Eastern Europe*. New York: Oxford University Press.

Brownlee, Jason. 2007. *Authoritarianism in an Age of Democratization*. New York: Cambridge University Press.

Bueno de Mesquita, Bruce, Alastair Smith, Randolph M. Siverson, and James D. Morrow. 2003. *The Logic of Political Survival*. Cambridge, MA: MIT Press.

Bulgarian Communist Party (BCP). 1983. Reshenie na TsK BKP, MS, US na BZNS, TsS BPS, NS OF, and TsK DKMS "Za po-natatushno izpulnenie na Dekemvriiskata programa za povishavane na zhiznenoto ravnishte na naroda v suotvetstvie s resheniiata na XII kongres na BKP." Sofia: Partizdat.

Bunce, Valerie J. 2003. "Rethinking Recent Democratization: Lessons from the Postcommunist Experience." *World Politics* 55 (2): 167–92.

Bunce, Valerie J., and Sharon Wolchik. 2011. *Defeating Authoritarian Leaders in Postcommunist Countries*. New York: Cambridge University Press.

Castro, Raúl. 2011. "Informe Central presentado por el compañero Raúl." http://www.granma.cubaweb.cu/secciones/6to-congreso-pcc/artic-04.html

Chinese Academy of Social Sciences (CASS). 1991. *Zhongsu Maoyishi Ziliao*. Beijing: Zhongguo Duiwai Jingji Maoyi Chubanshe.

Cook, Linda J. 1993. *The Soviet Social Contract and Why It Failed: Welfare Policy and Workers' Politics from Brezhnev to Yeltsin*. Cambridge, MA: Harvard University Press.

Cook, Linda J. 2007. *Postcommunist Welfare States: Reform Politics in Russia and Eastern Europe*. Ithaca: Cornell University Press.

Cook, Linda J., and Martin K. Dimitrov. 2017. "The Social Contract Revisited: Evidence from Communist and State Capitalist Economies." *Europe-Asia Studies* 69 (1): 8–26.

Corrales, Javier. 2004. "The Gatekeeper State: Limited Economic Reforms and Regime Survival in Cuba, 1982–2002." *Latin American Research Review* 39 (2): 35–65.

Dallin, Alexander, and George W. Breslauer. 1970. *Political Terror in Communist Systems*. Stanford: Stanford University Press.

Diao Jiecheng. 1996. *Renmin Xinfang Shilüe 1949–1995*. Beijing: Jingji Xueyuan Chubanshe.

Dikötter, Frank. 2010. *Mao's Great Famine: The History of China's Most Devastating Catastrophe, 1958–1962*. New York: Walker.

Dillon, Nara. 2015. *Radical Inequalities: China's Revolutionary Welfare State in Comparative Perspective*. Cambridge, MA: Harvard Asia Center, Harvard University Press.

Dimitrov, Martin K. 2012. "Zhalbite na grazhdanite v komunisticheska Bulgariia." In *Da Poznaem Komunizma: Izsledvaniia*, ed. Ivailo Znepolski. Sofia: Ciela, 167–226.

Dimitrov, Martin K., ed. 2013. *Why Communism Did Not Collapse: Understanding Authoritarian Regime Resilience in Asia and Europe*. New York: Cambridge University Press.

Dimitrov, Martin K. 2014a. "What the Party Wanted to Know: Citizen Complaints as a 'Barometer of Public Opinion' in Communist Bulgaria." *East European Politics and Societies and Cultures* 28 (2): 271–95.

Dimitrov, Martin K. 2014b. "Tracking Public Opinion under Authoritarianism: The Case of the Soviet Union under Brezhnev." *Russian History* 41 (3): 329–53.

Dimitrov, Martin K. 2015. "Internal Government Assessments of the Quality of Governance in China." *Studies in Comparative International Development* 50 (1): 50–72.

Dimitrov, Martin K. 2018a. *Politicheskata logika na sotsialisticheskoto potreblenie*. Sofia: Institute for Studies of the Recent Past and Ciela Publishers.

Dimitrov, Martin K. 2018b. "Anticipating Crises in Autocracies." In *Crisis in Autocratic Regimes*, ed. Johannes Gerschewski and Christoph H. Stefes. Boulder, CO: Westview Press, 21–41.

Dimitrov, Martin K. 2019a. "Crises and the Creation of Institutions for Assessing Popular Consumption Preferences in Communist Bulgaria 1953–1970." In *Perceptions of Society in Communist Europe: Regime Archives and Popular Opinion*, ed. Muriel Blaive. London: Bloomsbury Academic, 123–39.

Dimitrov, Martin K. 2019b. "The Functions of Letters to the Editor in Reform-Era Cuba." *Latin American Research Review* 54 (1): 1–15.

Dossier Commission. 2013. *Durzhavna sigurnost i nauchno-tekhnicheskoto razuznavane: Dokumentalen sbornik.* Sofia: Voenno izdatelstvo.

Engelmann, Roger, ed. 2013. *Die DDR im Blick der Stasi: Die geheimen Berichte an die SED-Führung 1953.* Göttingen: Vandenhoeck & Ruprecht.

Friedrich, Carl J., and Zbigniew K. Brzezinski. 1965. *Totalitarian Dictatorship and Autocracy.* Cambridge, MA: Harvard University Press.

Galkin, Aleksandr, and Anatolii Cherniaev. 2006. *Mikhail Gorbachev i germanskii vopros: Sbornik dokumentov, 1986–1991.* Moscow: Ves Mir.

Gandhi, Jennifer, and Ellen Lust-Okar. 2009. "Elections under Authoritarianism." *Annual Review of Political Science* 12: 403–22.

Gieseke, Jens. 2006. *Der Mielke-Konzern: Die Geschichte der Stasi, 1945–1990.* Munich: Deutsche Verlags-Anstalt.

Goskomstat SSSR. 1985 *Narodnoe Khoziaistvo SSSR v 1984 g.* Moscow: Finansy i Statistika.

Haggard, Stephan, and Robert R. Kaufman. 1995. *The Political Economy of Democratic Transitions.* Princeton: Princeton University Press.

Haggard, Stephan, and Robert R. Kaufman. 2008. *Development, Democracy, and Welfare States: Latin America, East Asia, and Eastern Europe.* Princeton: Princeton University Press.

Hauslohner, Peter. 1987. "Gorbachev's Social Contract." *Soviet Economy* 3 (1): 54–89.

Havel, Václav. 1979. *Moc bezmocných.* London: Londýnské listy.

Hertle, Hans-Hermann, and Gerd-Rüdiger Stephan, eds. 2012. *Das Ende der SED: Die letzten Tage des Zentralkomitees.* Berlin: Ch. Links.

Hirschman, Albert O. 1970. *Exit, Loyalty, and Voice: Responses to Decline in Firms, Organizations, and States.* Cambridge, MA: Harvard University Press.

Hu Xiaoli. 2015. *Zhongsu Guanxi De Meiguo Yinsu 1949–1989.* Beijing: Zhongguo Shehui Kexue Chubanshe.

Inglot, Tomasz. 2008. *Welfare States in East Central Europe, 1919–2004.* New York: Cambridge University Press.

Jarausch, Konrad. 1998. "Realer Sozialismus als Fürsorgediktatur: Zur begrifflichen Einordnung der DDR." *Aus Politik und Zeitgeschichte* 20: 33–46.

Judt, Matthias. 2013. *Der Bereich Kommerzielle Koordinierung: Das DDR-Wirtschaftsimperium des Alexander Schalck-Golodkowski. Mythos und Realität.* Berlin: Ch. Links Verlag.

Kaple, Deborah A. 1994. *Dream of a Red Factory: The Legacy of High Stalinism in China.* New York: Oxford University Press.

King, Gary, Jennifer Pan, and Margaret Roberts. 2013. "How Censorship in China Allows Government Criticism but Silences Collective Expression." *American Political Science Review* 107 (2): 326–43.

King, Gary, Jennifer Pan, and Margaret Roberts. 2017. "How the Chinese Government Fabricates Social Media Posts for Strategic Distraction, Not Engaged Argument." *American Political Science Review* 111 (3): 484–501.

Koenker, Diane. 2013. *Club Red: Vacation Travel and the Soviet Dream.* Ithaca: Cornell University Press.

Kong Hanbing. 2010. "The Transplantation and Entrenchment of the Soviet Economic Model in China." In *China Learns from the Soviet Union, 1949–Present*, ed. Thomas Bernstein and Hua-yu Li. Lanham, MD: Lexington Books, 153–66.

Kornai, János. 1980. *Economics of Shortage*. Amsterdam: Elsevier.

Krenz, Egon. 2014. *Herbst '89*. Berlin: Edition Ost.

Kuran, Timur. 1991. "Now out of Never: The Element of Surprise in the East European Revolution of 1989." *World Politics* 44 (1): 7–48.

Kuran, Timur. 1995. *Private Truths, Public Lies: The Social Consequences of Preference Falsification*. Cambridge, MA: Harvard University Press.

Landsman, Mark. 2005. *Dictatorship and Demand: The Politics of Consumerism in East Germany*. Cambridge, MA: Harvard University Press.

Leibniz-Institut für Länderkunde. 2005. *Nationalatlas Bundesrepublik Deutschland— Deutschland in der Welt*. Heidelberg: Spektrum.

Levitsky, Steven, and Lucan A. Way. 2010. *Competitive Authoritarianism: The Origins and Evolution of Hybrid Regimes in the Post–Cold War Era*. New York: Cambridge University Press.

Lohmann, Susanne. 1994. "The Dynamics of Informational Cascades: The Monday Demonstrations in Leipzig, East Germany, 1989–91." *World Politics* 47 (1): 42–101.

Lorentzen, Peter. 2013. "Regularizing Rioting: Permitting Public Protest in an Authoritarian Regime." *Quarterly Journal of Political Science* 8 (2): 127–58.

Lu Nanquan. 2008. "Zhongsu Jingmao Guanxi Jianxi." *Eluosi Zhongya Dong'ou Shichang*, no. 6. http://www.cssn.cn/gj/gj_gjwtyj/gj_elsdozy/201311/t20131101_821308.shtml

Lüthi, Lorenz M. 2008. *The Sino-Soviet Split: Cold War in the Communist World*. Princeton: Princeton University Press.

Magaloni, Beatriz. 2006. *Voting for Autocracy: Hegemonic Party Survival and Its Demise in Mexico*. New York: Cambridge University Press.

Manion, Melanie. 1993. *Retirement of Revolutionaries in China: Public Policies, Social Norms, Private Interests*. Princeton: Princeton University Press.

Marxen, Klaus, and Gerhard Werle. 2000. *Strafjustiz und DDR-Unrecht*. Vol. 5, pt. 2. Berlin: De Gruyter.

Merkel, Ina, ed. 1998. *"Wir sind doch nicht die Mecker-Ecke der Nation": Briefe an das DDR-Fernsehen*. Cologne: Böhlau Verlag.

Mesa-Lago, Carmelo. 2012. *Cuba en la era de Raúl Castro: Reformas económico-sociales y sus efectos*. Madrid: Colibrí.

Millar, James R. 1985. "The Little Deal: Brezhnev's Contribution to Acquisitive Socialism." *Slavic Review* 44 (4): 694–706.

Ministry of Public Security (MPS). 2003. *Jianguo Yilai Gong'an Gongzuo Dashi Yaolan 1949–2000*. Beijing: Qunzhong Chubanshe.

Mühlberg, Felix. 2004. *Bürger, Bitten und Behörde: Geschichte der Eingabe in der DDR*. Berlin: Karl Dietz Verlag.

Niemann, Heinz. 1993. *Meinungsforschung in der DDR*. Cologne: Bund-Verlag.

Oficina Nacional de Estadística e Información (ONEI). 2017. *Anuario Estadístico de Cuba*. Havana: ONEI.

Pan, Jennifer, and Kaiping Chen. 2018. "Concealing Corruption: How Chinese Officials Distort Upward Reporting of Online Grievances." *American Political Science Review* 112 (3): 602–20.

Pravda, Alex. 1980. "East-West Interdependence and the Social Compact in Eastern Europe." In *East-West Relations and the Future of Eastern Europe: Politics and Economics*, ed. Morris Bornstein, Zvi Gitelman, and William Zimmerman. London: George Allen and Unwin, 162–87.
Revista Temas. 2008. *Último jueves: Los debates de Temas*. Vol. 2. Havana: ICAIC, 13–40.
Revista Temas. 2013. *Último jueves* debate on "Opinión pública y toma de decisiones." Havana, May 30.
Schroeder, Klaus. 2013. *Der SED-Staat: Geschichte und Strukturen der DDR, 1949–1990*. Cologne: Böhlau.
Schürer, Gerhard. 2014. *Gewagt und verloren: Eine deutsche Biografie*. Berlin: Edition Ost.
Scobell, Andrew. 1990. "The Death Penalty in Post-Mao China." *China Quarterly* 123: 503–20.
Shen Zhihua. 2013. *Lengzhan De Zai Zhuanxing*. Beijing: Jiuzhou Chubanshe.
Shen Zhihua. 2014. *Sulian Zhuanjia Zai Zhongguo 1948–1960*. Beijing: Shehui Kexue Wenxian Chubanshe.
Shu, Guang Zhang. 2001. *Economic Cold War: America's Embargo against China and the Sino-Soviet Alliance, 1949–1963*. Washington, DC: Woodrow Wilson Center Press.
Shu, Guang Zhang. 2014. *Beijing's Economic Statecraft during the Cold War, 1949–1991*. Washington, DC: Woodrow Wilson Center Press.
Siegelbaum, Lewis. 2008. *Cars for Comrades: The Life of the Soviet Automobile*. Ithaca: Cornell University Press.
Smith, Benjamin. 2005. "Life of the Party: The Origins of Regime Breakdown and Persistence under Single-Party Rule." *World Politics* 57 (3): 421–51.
Staadt, Jochen. 1996. *Eingaben: Die institutionalisierte Meckerkultur in der DDR. Goldbrokat, Kaffee-Mix, Büttenreden, Ausreiseanträge und andere Schwierigkeiten mit den Untertanen*. Berlin: Arbeitspapiere des Forschungsverbundes SED-Staat, No. 24.
Statistisches Amt der DDR. 1990. *Statistisches Jahrbuch der Deutschen Demokratischen Republik '90*. Berlin: Rudolf Haufe Verlag.
Stockmann, Daniela. 2013. *Media Commercialization and Authoritarian Rule in China*. New York: Cambridge University Press.
Stoianova, Penka, and Emil Iliev. 1991. *Politicheski opasni litsa*. Sofia: Sv. Kliment Okhridski Press.
Svolik, Milan W. 2012. *The Politics of Authoritarian Rule*. New York: Cambridge University Press.
Wedeen, Lisa. 1999. *Ambiguities of Domination: Politics, Rhetoric, and Symbols in Contemporary Syria*. Chicago: University of Chicago Press.
Wintrobe, Ronald. 1998. *The Political Economy of Dictatorship*. New York: Cambridge University Press.
Zaslavsky, Victor, and Robert J. Brym. 1978. "The Functions of Elections in the USSR." *Soviet Studies* 30 (3): 362–71.
Zhou, Xun, ed. 2012. *The Great Famine in China, 1958–1962: A Documentary History*. New Haven: Yale University Press.

ARCHIVAL MATERIALS

Bulgarian Central State Archive (TsDA)

TsDA. 1953. F. 1 op. 24 a. e. 125.
TsDA. 1954–55. F. 1 op. 24 a. e. 188.
TsDA. 1970. F. 1 op. 35 a. e. 1235.
TsDA. 1977. F. 1B op. 55 a. e. 485.
TsDA. 1977. F. 1B op. 55 a. e. 486.
TsDA. 1977. F. 1B op. 55 a. e. 487.
TsDA. 1977. F. 1B op. 55 a. e. 489.
TsDA. 1978. F. 1B op. 55 a. e. 496.
TsDA. 1979. F. 1B op. 55 a. e. 497.
TsDA. 1979. F. 1B op. 55 a. e. 501.
TsDA. 1980. F. 1B op. 55 a. e. 502.
TsDA. 1989. F. 1B op. 55 a. e. 506.
TsDA. 1980. F. 1B op. 55 a. e. 507.
TsDA. 1981. F. 1B op. 55 a. e. 508.
TsDA. 1982. F. 1B op. 55 a. e. 512.
TsDA. 1982. F. 1B op. 55 a. e. 515.
TsDA. 1986. F. 1B op. 55 a. e. 529.
TsDA. 1988. F. 1B op. 55 a. e. 722.
TsDA. 1983. F. 1B op. 55 a. e. 940.
TsDA. 1985. F. 1B op. 55 a. e. 943.
TsDA. 1989. F. 1B op. 55 a. e. 953.
TsDA. 1971. F. 1B op. 55 a. e. 1203.
TsDA. 1972. F. 1B op. 55 a. e. 1207.
TsDA. 1953. F. 1B op. 64 a. e. 185.
TsDA. 1984. F. 1B op. 101 a. e. 1140.
TsDA. 1989. F. 132P op. 15 a. e. 2.
TsDA. 1989. F. 132P op. 15 a. e. 10.
TsDA. 1956. F. 317B op. 1 a. e. 133.

Bulgarian State Security Archive (AMVR)

AMVR. 1953. F. 1 op. 1 a. e. 2922.
AMVR. 1954. F. 1 op. 1 a. e. 2811.
AMVR. 1982. F. 1 op. 12 a. e. 421.
AMVR. 1969. F. 10 op. 6 a. e. 6.

Shanghai Municipal Archive (SMA)

SMA. 1976. B248-2-924.

Chinese Internal (Neibu) Materials

Neibu cankao. 1981. No. 73.
Qingkuang huibian. 1980. No. 365.
Qingkuang huibian. 1980. No. 549.

East German Party Archives (SAPMO)

SAPMO. 1981. DC 20/16563.
SAPMO. 1989. DC 20/16634.
SAPMO. 1989. DC 20/16635.
SAPMO. 1967. DY 30/J IV 2/3 1272.
SAPMO. 1981. DY30/913.
SAPMO. 1988. DY30 6265.
SAPMO. 1989. DY30 6266.

East German State Security Archive (BStU)

BStU. 1953. MfS SdM 249 Bl. 102–107 (Meldung Nr. 7/53).

THREE

Of Eggs and Stones

Foreign Sanctions and Domestic Political Economy in the Islamic Republic of Iran

Kevan Harris

In January 2016, the Islamic Republic of Iran and the five permanent members of the United Nations Security Council plus Germany inaugurated the Joint Comprehensive Plan of Action (JCPOA), an agreement for a rollback of Iran's nuclear enrichment program in exchange for a reduction in foreign-imposed sanctions on the country's economy. Since the signing and ratification of this agreement in July 2015, the discrete impact of sanctions on Iran's decision-making process leading up to the JCPOA has remained under debate, even by those involved in the negotiations. "Sanctions was always a conundrum," Germany's ambassador to the United States stated during an interview. "Do the sanctions work, do they not work? We could never really tell" (Parsi 2017, 129–30).

Assessing the impact of sanctions in bringing the Iranian government "to the negotiating table" is hard to tell partly due to the lack of any smoking gun evidence that provides direct proof of a causal link between shifts in external economic conditions brought on by sanctions and shifts in internal decisions by Iranian policymakers. State actors involved in diplomatic negotiations, of course, tend not to reveal their entire hand. Iranian politicians contend that external sanctions on the country's oil purchases, international financial transactions, and insurance on the export trade did not cinch their decision to agree to reductions and monitoring of the enrichment of nuclear material. As Iran's foreign minister, Javad Zarif, asserted in 2014, "Sanctions didn't bring us to the table, we never left the table" (Tabatabai 2017, 226).

So how can we understand the effect of an external sanctions shock on Iran's internal political economy? Instead of a smoking gun that proves a direct link between externally imposed sanctions and a change in the domestic political order, or a Kremlinology of Iran's political elite that psychologically imputes such a link, I address this question on two levels. First, I discuss the institutions and networks of the postrevolutionary Iranian ruling elite. Due to the lack of a single ruling political party, the porousness of elite factional boundaries, and the role of perceived threats in fostering elite cohesion, the Iranian political system looks quite different from the game-theoretical predictions of a minimum winning coalition of dictator-selected allies that may withdraw regime support in response to an external economic shock. Yet this is the political system that was faced with an external shock in 2011–13, and thus should be analyzed as it actually existed.

Second, state control over the financial system in Iran helped to absorb the costs of lower government revenues and foreign exchange crises that resulted from externally imposed sanctions. Partly due to an uptick in non-oil exports, Iran maintained a positive balance of payments during the entire period of 2011–15. Though enacted before the brunt of sanctions, the Iranian government's concurrent policies of implementing universal cash transfers and injecting liquidity into the financial system also cushioned the effects of state revenue decline on much of the population. While these policies were not necessarily advantageous for long-term macroeconomic stability, Iran's long postrevolutionary experience of currency controls and channeling finance broadly across economic sectors—including the private sector—provided an improvised tool kit that managed to cushion the economic shock. As this chapter shows, foreign exchange distribution and export revenues in Iran were largely under the purview of the state. This helped to prevent the sort of rapid hyperinflation or massive capital flight which has been associated with abrupt political shifts in other cases.

This chapter concludes with a call to separate out the differences between the effect and the effectiveness of an economic shock. Not all authoritarian regimes are born of the same cloth, I argue, and the perceived type of shock as well as the structure of elite institutions can intertwine to produce a situation where sanctions can have a tremendous effect without being effective.

The Most Expensive Nuclear Program in the World

What are sanctions designed to accomplish as a tool of foreign policy? The debate over the impact of external sanctions on actions of internal political elites is difficult to resolve not simply because of the opacity of authoritarian state actors, but also because of a problem of concept operationalization. All in all, given the costs borne as a result of sanctions in 2011–15, Iran arguably possessed the most expensive nuclear enrichment program in the world. But how did the period of economic shock filter into Iran's political economy, both at the level of elite coalition and among broader networks of state and society? This is a *different* question than whether sanctions had their intended effect.

To start, the JCPOA negotiations should be put in a longer context of diplomatic endeavors over Iran's nuclear program. By the early 2000s, Iran's national security establishment—members of the executive branch as well as various unelected offices inside the Islamic Republic, including those appointed by the country's leader and supreme jurist—had been trying to find ways to leverage its nuclear program to make a deal that would reduce external pressures on Iran dating from the postrevolutionary period up to the late 1990s.[1] Iranian representatives regularly attended negotiations over the nuclear program with one or another group of other countries, from EU members and the United States to Brazil and Turkey, from 2002 onward. And after years of harsh sanctions and 20 months of continued negotiations, most strictures on Iran's nuclear program agreed upon in the 2015 JCPOA were *less stringent* than the 2004 Paris agreement between Iran and members of the European Union. In the latter, Iran agreed to voluntarily suspend all enrichment and reprocessing of nuclear material temporarily. The United States, under the Bush administration, torpedoed the 2004 agreement by demanding zero enrichment of any material permanently.

A year later, in 2005, Mahmoud Ahmadinejad was elected president of Iran, and then proceeded to jettison Iran's seasoned diplomats and ramp up nuclear enrichment activities. Given perceptions, by many members of Iran's national security establishment, of unfair treatment by the EU and the United States, Ahmadinejad's provocations were not, at the outset, widely opposed on the domestic front. In 2007, Iran issued a new currency note for the 50,000-rial bill, with an atomic symbol as a watermark, next to a phrase attributed to the prophet Muḥammad: "Men from the land of Persia will attain knowledge even if it is as far as the Pleiades." Nuclear enrichment was being associated, in nationalistic form, with the hard-won self-sufficiency and domestically financed technological gains of the country since the 1979 revolution. The increase of sanctions directed at Iran after 2010 should be viewed in the context of the previous breakdown of multilateral negotiations and the uptick in domestic nuclear enrichment.

As detailed below, the panoply of sanctions, especially from 2011 to 2015, certainly had an effect on Iran's economy. Average daily exports of oil shrank from 2.4 million barrels in 2011 to 1.0 million in 2013, rising to 1.4 million barrels in 2014 with temporary sanctions relief, and returning to 2.2 million barrels by fall 2017. The International Monetary Fund estimated that US$185 billion in oil revenue alone was lost during these years (IMF 2017, 6). In the wake of announcement by EU countries that oil purchases from Iran would be curtailed, but before the policy went into actual effect, a run on the Iranian currency in January 2012 led to a 25 percent depreciation in the parallel market. In September later that year, a new burst of speculation led to an additional 30 percent depreciation, prompting the Central Bank of Iran (CBI) to set up a foreign exchange center to coordinate the distribution of hard currency at tiered exchange rates. As Richard Nephew, the principal deputy coordinator for sanctions policy at the US State Department at the time and the subsequent author of *The Art of Sanctions*, later recalled, "For a moment, I thought that October 2012 was the beginning of our Tunisia [in the 2011 Arab uprisings] . . . when we saw that the currency lost about two-thirds of its value in a day. But then they regained control. In less than a day and a half . . . I was disappointed. Because I thought it was [going to] really lead to some real internal problems for Iran and force them to negotiate a way out of the sanctions" (Parsi 2017, 140).

Why did the expected relationship between economic shock and political shift not materialize as Nephew had anticipated? As Robert Jervis reflected shortly after the nuclear accord signed by Iran, changes in the external environment might be important, but any such change "works its effects through domestic configurations" (Jervis 2015, 609). The need to open up the black box of internal responses to external shocks is also what Stephan Haggard and Robert Kaufman noted over two decades ago when analyzing variations in state responses to economic crises: "The effort to explain policy preferences by reference to economic conditions . . . yields some insights, but . . . [such] explanations must often rely in the last instance on the way ideology shapes elite cognitions and values" (Haggard and Kaufman 1992, 22). Wesley Widmaier, Mark Blyth, and Leonard Seabrooke note that that wars and economic crises are not exogenous shocks that independently act upon a state in the absence of endogenous interpretation by both elites and popular masses: "The fact that the domestic price level of the U.S. fell off a cliff in 1929, or that 'the Germans took back the Rhineland' in 1936, does not telegraph to agents on the ground in 1929 or 1936 what such events mean and what (obviously) has to be done about it" (Widmaier, Blyth, and Seabrooke 2007, 748). In other words, relating external economic shocks to observed political outcomes requires attention to intermediate processes that are more directly linked to—that is, hold greater explanatory power for—the causal driver of internal changes.

Such methodological insights have a well-known predecessor in Mao Zedong's aphorism about the egg and the stone: "External causes are the condition of change and internal causes are the basis of change, and . . . external causes become operative through internal causes. In a suitable temperature an egg changes into a chicken, but no temperature can change a stone into a chicken, because each has a different basis" (Mao 1965, 314). Written from a guerrilla base in Yunnan, Mao's rustic metaphor for assessing external change and internal processes is useful for unpacking the Iranian case.

Indeed, during the period of heightened sanctions on Iran from 2010 onward, few practitioners believed in the power of sanctions to change state behavior. Iran had just gone through a dramatic election cycle in summer 2009, where claims of fraud against the incumbent president, Mahmoud Ahmadinejad, galvanized a cycle of social protest and mobilization from summer to fall, known as the Green Movement (Harris 2017). Though the movement eventually fizzled, the conservative allies of Ahmadinejad seemed even less amenable to any public form of negotiations with the United States.

Iran therefore presents us with a puzzle. In the wake of conservative political ascendance in Iran, a Washington-based analyst wrote in 2012, "The 2009 election and its aftermath may have made the Islamic Republic less receptive to sanctions and even positive inducements, and more likely to pursue a nuclear weapons program regardless of the costs" (Nader 2012, 213). Yet the opposite occurred, and in 2013 the Iranian government again agreed to sustained negotiations over a nuclear accord, finally completed in 2015. *How did a sustained economic shock from 2011 to 2013, in the form of reduced state revenues and other US-led financial sanctions, affect the Iranian state?* What was inside the Iranian egg?

Iran's Political Order: Diffuse and Undisciplined

Assessing Iran's political order in the wake of increased sanctions requires a look at how Middle Eastern states are conceptualized more generally. The Middle East used to be known as the last region in the world still catching up with history. The third wave of democratization from the 1970s to the 1990s, in Southern Europe, Latin America, East Asia, sub-Saharan Africa, and Eastern Europe positioned the Middle East as an embarrassing global outlier. Due to such unmet expectations, a cottage industry flourished on the subject of Middle Eastern authoritarian persistence (see Hinnebusch 2006). As case studies multiplied and theories converged, arguments became increasingly sophisticated. Authoritarian states were not historical hangovers hulking after the third wave. These polities contained a flexible set of institutions that utilized coercive and co-optive measures alike. Authoritarianism did not simply "persist" in the Middle East; it "upgraded" and thus remained "adaptable" and "resilient" (Heydemann and Leenders 2013).

The 2011 Arab uprisings across the Middle East forced social scientists to rethink two decades of theory-building on authoritarian rule. Without the dissolving of a formal imperial sovereign, such as occurred in the USSR, for instance, the protest wave and subsequent counterthrusts of 2011 looked more like Europe in 1848 than Eurasia in 1989 (Arjomand 2015).[2] As a result, the wide variation in regional outcomes, from pacted transition in Tunisia and authoritarian consolidation in Egypt to civil war in Syria, renewed attempts to explain the reproduction of authoritarian institutions, albeit no longer with the inevitable endpoint of democracy as a foundational consensus (Brownlee, Masoud, and Reynolds 2015; also see Yom 2015).

The Islamic Republic of Iran is a strange entity in the middle of it all. With a constitution part republican (rule by popular sovereignty) and part hierocratic (rule by clerics), Iran's 1979 revolution produced a hybrid type of "semi-democratic" or "competitive authoritarian" regime well before these terms became common parlance among social scientists (Keshavarzian 2005). For some comparativists who study Middle Eastern polities, state control over oil extraction remains the key to understanding regimes in the region, no matter their historical origins or institutional makeup. Yet as Michael Herb has shown, even in the most extreme cases of the rentier states of Kuwait and the United Arab Emirates, the political economy of state-society relations varies on nearly all matters that purportedly explain common political outcomes (Herb 2014). More notably, for the case of Iran itself, if oil rents were the key to understanding the politics of the Islamic Republic, we would not need to peer into the black box of Iran's postrevolutionary order. In fact, among some security analysts with little background in studying Iranian politics, the JCPOA between the Islamic

Republic and Western powers in 2015 is lauded as proof that economic strictures on states can directly change their behavior. Those who previously assumed that Iran's anti-Western ideological creed irrevocably prevented any major policy shift later accepted that the brute cudgel of economic sanctions did the intended job (Terhalle 2015). Yet other than macro-level correlations between oil prices, state revenues, and the timing of the JCPOA, little else has been demonstrated.

Rather than a modal form of hybrid regime or rentier state, the *origins* of the Islamic Republic turn out to matter more for the way in which economic shocks, when perceived as direct geopolitical attacks by hostile powers, affect the ruling political elite. As comparative scholars have more recently argued, authoritarian states are not all alike, partly because they are not born alike. Political coalitions and ruling parties that emerged during an initial period of regime formation condition the subsequent effects of economic shocks. Scholars have developed useful typologies for teasing out the differences, and we can combine them to better make sense of the Iranian case.

The first key difference is whether the regime was born in a social revolution, usually involving a violent struggle and mass participation, versus a top-down transformation, such as a coup or a relatively nonviolent transfer of power from colonial rule to independence. Nonrevolutionary parties emerging from top-down transformations tend to utilize patronage distribution and public spending to maintain an elite coalition—what Dan Slater (2010) calls "provision pacts." During ordinary periods of rule, patronage is often sufficient as a means to foster elite cohesion. During economic shocks or crises, however, the ruling party's capacity to maintain patronage is lessened or made uncertain. Shocks can disrupt patronage networks or provision of public goods, leading to elite splits in nonrevolutionary regimes—Indonesia under Suharto after the 1997 economic crisis is an example.

In revolutionary states, however, ruling parties or coalitions that emerged out of violent struggle tend to developing cohesive institutions that link political elites and security apparatuses in near existential fashion (Levitsky and Way 2015). Revolutionary regimes endure economic shocks far more often than nonrevolutionary ones, especially while the first post-revolutionary generation of elites is still in power. These regimes tend to create ruling coalitions that can often utilize legitimate threats from external or internal origin to bind together elites in "protection pacts," and are less reliant on patronage to maintain elite cohesion (Slater 2010). Economic shocks are less likely to disrupt such regimes—Cuba under Castro after the collapse of Soviet Union in 1989 is an example.

The second key difference is whether a state is governed by a centralized ruling party or a diffuse mix of ruling institutions. One-party states can more easily discipline wayward elites, coordinate the reproduction of power through electoral institutions, and make shifts in state policy even with elite dissension, such as in response to an economic shock—Mexico under the PRI (Partido Revolucionario Institucional) after the 1982 debt crisis is an example.

In most authoritarian states with electoral institutions, the capacity of rulers to dominate and control formal institutional arenas is crucial for the purposes of ensuring that the ruling party stays in power. Discipline inside a single-party organization is key, both for mobilizing constituencies and for maintaining the ability to punish outsiders or fence-sitters. Party splits can be dangerous for the reproduction of elite cohesion.

Iran is not such a polity. Instead, as Daniel Brumberg and Farideh Farhi have argued, the Islamic Republic exhibits a diffused set of competitive-authoritarian institutions. Power and authority are "unevenly spread and concentrated through a myriad of both formal and informal mechanisms and arenas" (2016, 8). The constitutional order does not provide an "agreed upon template of principles for the exercise of political or constitutional rights." These mutable institutional and legal mechanisms create a "feckless" pluralism, as Thomas Carothers called it, one that "seems to be incoherent, disorganized and constantly improvised, but which in fact uses such suppleness to channel, contain or diffuse challenges to regime hegemony and elite unity" (Brumberg and Farhi 2016, 8). For major shifts in foreign policy, therefore, such as a signing of the JCPOA, ruling elites in Iran operate through consensus. If an elite coalition in favor of a policy shift is too narrow, there is the likelihood of a veto by a holdout faction or power center.

Put simply, states with diffuse institutional rule tend to require a wider elite consensus to engage in major policy shifts, with more elite buy-in required across the political establishment. And here is where Iran lies. Picture a 2 × 2 matrix, with revolutionary versus nonrevolutionary states on one axis, and single party versus diffuse ruling institutions on the other axis: the Islamic Republic of Iran would be in the quadrant of postrevolutionary states with diffuse ruling institutions.

This institutional context allows us to better understand Iran's lurching coalitional shifts in the lead-up to the economic shock of sanctions after 2010. There have been four major political realignments in the Islamic Republic's short history, partly conditioned by the lack of a revolutionary party that could discipline and smooth out splits among the political elite.

The first realignment was the coalescing of a pro-Khomeini front by revolutionary participants in the initial years after the 1979 ouster of the shah, driving out other contenders for state power. The second realignment came after the 1989 death of Khomeini and the end of the Iran-Iraq War, when President Hashemi-Rafsanjani and his economically liberal supporters allied with conservative political elites to neuter the radical wing of the Islamic Republic's battle-forged leadership. Many of these radicals went into the political wilderness and emerged a few years later, speaking a new vocabulary and self-identifying as reformists.

The third realignment occurred during the late 1990s and early 2000s under the presidency of Mohammad Khatami (1997–2005). His circle of reformists increasingly sought common cause with Rafsanjani's technocratic-minded posse under a vague rubric of modernization. Conservative members of the political elite, mostly housed in unelected state institutions or the security apparatus, petulantly rebelled. Legislation and reform were blocked by fiat from above, while fresh recruits were mobilized from below. Mahmoud Ahmadinejad, an engineer who administrated the western provinces during the Iran-Iraq war and sidled his way into an appointment as Tehran's mayor, rose to the commanding heights of the state in this environment of self-perceived conservative crisis. Vertical patronage networks and clever machine politics lifted him up alongside a new generation of right-wing political entrepreneurs. Partly rehashing the radical rhetoric of the early 1980s and partly stealing the modernizing bromides of his opponents, President Ahmadinejad (2005–13) solidified support from conservatives while pushing the reformist-technocratic coalition almost completely out of the political order (Harris 2015).

The fourth realignment began in 2009 with a wave of postelection popular unrest labeled by participants as the Green Movement. The realignment hastened from 2011 to 2013 under increased sanctions and the onset of economic downturn. Conservative solidarity fractured, and the reformist-technocratic coalition mobilized in the fissures. Another wave of electoral mobilization and a dose of luck in 2013 propelled Hassan Rouhani to the presidency. Rouhani was a Rafsanjani confidant whose career up to that point had largely occurred through backstage politicking. The key to Rouhani's subsequent success, whether in negotiations with Western powers or domestic policy battles, was keeping conservatives divided while inviting old-guard segments into his own coalition.

As a result, what was unmentionable in Iranian conservative political discourse a decade prior—direct negotiations with the United States and the acceptance of strictures over a symbolically important but militarily insignificant nuclear enrichment program—was authorized and justified by

Iran's top mandarins, including the leader and supreme jurist of the Islamic Republic, Ali Khamenei. Once Khamenei publicly backed the negotiations, high-ranking members of the security apparatus also came on board, widening the elite coalition which could potentially back a policy shift. As Foreign Minister Javad Zarif mentioned at the height of the negotiations in 2013, the entire security establishment in Iran as well as Khamenei had given him the authorization to negotiate with the United States, though they all insisted that no capitulation was allowable. Of course, this was a negotiating tactic in itself, since Zarif could use the existence of a diffuse and undisciplined set of elites back in Tehran as a bargaining chip to frame Iran's offer as the best he could do.

In a diffuse institutional order such as Iran's, segments of the political elite can shift positions without necessarily appearing as outright defectors from the ruling coalition. Intraelite bargaining does not always map onto preexisting and formalized institutional cleavages. As discussed below, this realigning field of elite competition was already in progress *before* the intensification of sanctions. This ongoing realignment prefigured and conditioned the response to the economic shock after 2010. Though there was no single party in existence to endorse the negotiations with Western powers, there were "veto" points across the diffuse and undisciplined political order that could have blocked the process.

Postrevolutionary States and Protection Pacts

In considering the effect of economic shocks on a state such as Iran's, we should consider not only the diffused institutional structure of the political order, but also *how different types of shocks might lead to different elite responses*. A generalized economic crisis affecting states across a region, such as the 1980s Latin American debt crisis or the 1997 Asian economic crisis, is arguably perceived differently by governing elites than a shock targeted by outside powerful states, telegraphed in advance to rulers, and implicated with the goal of regime collapse or overthrow. This latter form of shock, when directed at postrevolutionary states with ruling elites that identify the status quo international order as hostile, can foster elite cohesion by incentivizing survival rather than conciliation.

As Dan Slater points out, legitimately perceived external threats against states that have historical memory of Western intervention or domination tend to generate high status anxiety among governing elites, even among those in the loyal opposition who could act as agents of democratization in other contexts (Slater 2011). These actors are less afraid of international ostracism and isolation than of status deflation and domestic vulnerability. In situations of high and increasing external threat, hard-line elites tend to thrive, while moderate elites are forced to back down. This is because believable external threats allow authoritarian rulers to extract compliance and resources from different groups with demonstrable power resources, whether the military, industry, the middle class, or communal/ethnic leaders, depending on the country (Slater 2010).

In such moments of legitimate threat perception, regimes can construct far more durable ruling pacts than in times of normal intraelite conflict. During the latter, state rulers must expend material and symbolic resources to maintain a semblance of cohesion, while in the former, elites will willingly sacrifice narrow interests and hand over resources to the state because their own power and status feels wholly threatened. Imminent threats by recognizably hostile actors tend to force elites together more than unreliable promises of shared material gain. This is why, Slater provocatively argues, patronage systems with clientelist networks of distribution are not sufficient to reproduce authoritarian power indefinitely (Slater 2011).

In the dramatic months of Green Movement protests in 2009, this form of "protection pact" was on display as the Ahmadinejad administration engaged in a new set of talks with the United States. The outgoing head of the International Atomic Energy Agency, Mohammad el-Baradei, arranged for a renewal of negotiations on Iran's nuclear program in fall 2009 in Geneva. The United States pushed for a drastic reduction in enriched nuclear material through a swap with Russia or an acceptable third party under the guidance of the IAEA. It was clear that a failure to reach any agreement would result in a new round of UN Security Council sanctions. It was a "take or leave it" proposal from Washington, as Secretary of State Hillary Clinton told the press.

Yet in Tehran, few politicians spoke out in support of the deal. Instead, nearly all political factions, across the domestic ideological spectrum, intimated that it was a capitulation, *including the opposition leader* of the Green Movement, former prime minister Mir-Hossein Mousavi. "If [the swap is] put in place, all the efforts of thousands of scientists will go to the wind," Mousavi wrote in a released statement. "If [it is] not put in place, the foundations will be laid for wide-ranging sanctions against Iran, and this is the result of a confrontational stance in foreign policy and the neglect of national interests and principles" (Parsi 2017, 97). Underneath Mousavi's objections was the fear that once a deal was inked with the United States, conservative elites would have a freer hand to purge their political competitors and crack down on social unrest. Without a coherent party apparatus to discipline political elite competition, President Ahmadinejad's attempt to renew negotiations was outflanked by politicians on multiple sides.

Even with a diffuse system of elite competition, however, could an intensification of sanctions lead to a cascade of shifting incentives among a majority of powerholders in the interest of regime survival? Countering such a possible cascade in Iran is the *differentia specifica* of postrevolutionary regimes that Steven Levitsky and Lucan Way (2015) identify. Unlike authoritarian states originating in top-down coups or putsches, postrevolutionary regimes such as China, Zimbabwe, or Iran are, as Sam Huntington long ago noted, a "product of struggle and violence" (1970, 13). Elite cohesion and partisan identities in Iran were born from a decade of revolutionary consolidation and a cross-border war with Baathist Iraq (1980–88). As Levitsky and Way argue, "Security forces created and staffed by veterans of the liberation struggle are less prone to coups and more likely to close ranks behind coercive measures in the face of opposition challenges" (2015, 103). External shocks to postrevolutionary regimes, when perceived as legitimate threats from ideological opponents, are more likely to produce a tightening of the bonds between the security apparatus and the ruling elite, rather than a widening schism.

In other words, the effect of external shocks is conditioned on the legacy of the origins of the authoritarian regime. As Levitsky and Way note, "Whereas economic downturns undermined authoritarian regimes in Albania, Benin, Indonesia, Ukraine, and Zambia during the post–Cold War era, autocracies in Cuba, Malaysia, North Korea, and Zimbabwe proved strikingly robust in the face of economic crises" (2015, 100). Their argument travels well into the Middle East, as it is historically rare for security apparatuses in postrevolutionary states such as Iran's to engage in coups against ruling elite coalitions. In states born from top-down constructions of political order, such as in Turkey or Egypt, however, coups and military putsches are commonplace. US policymakers in charge of sanctions policy did not take this *differentia specifica* of postrevolutionary states into consideration. At an off-the-record discussion of US policy toward Iran in 2013, "one of the architects of the sanctions" argued that a point would be reached, he predicted, "in which a senior Iranian Revolutionary Guard Corps official would have no choice but to confront Khamenei and implore him to succumb to Western demands lest Iran's economy collapse" (Parsi 2017, 188).

The path of JCPOA negotiations, however, traveled along the opposite route. As noted above, Iran's security establishment had already encouraged Ahmadinejad to pursue negotiations toward a nuclear deal in 2009–10. Due to the domestic chaos of the 2009 elections, and the refusal of the Obama administration at the time to accept any enrichment, the negotiating efforts were shifted to the sidelines. By 2011, Ahmadinejad himself had alienated other members of the conservative political elite, and a coalitional shift was taking place. One incident that illustrated such a shift was when Ahmadinejad attempted to dismiss the minister of intelligence in May 2011. Ali Khamenei then reinstated the minister, to the petulant outcry of the president, who refused to attend any cabinet meetings for nearly two weeks. Not only was he chastened by the leader and supreme jurist, but control over the nuclear negotiations was subsequently shifted completely out of the president's office. While he could still cast an informal veto, Ahmadinejad largely sat out the next two years of foreign policy decisions. But any shift on the nuclear program had to happen in such a way that it could be framed as bolstering the legitimacy of the Islamic Republic. In Iran's case, the shift was predicated on a US concession to relax their previous demand for zero nuclear enrichment.

Only after the United States telegraphed a possible acceptance of some level of nuclear enrichment in 2012 could members of Iran's governing elite work to build a coalition around the acceptance of negotiations, including convincing key members of the security apparatus. The potential for a US shift allowed a consensus to slowly form in Iran as various segments of the diffuse institutional order joined in. It was only once the leader and supreme jurist, Ali Khamenei, put the stamp of approval on the process that members of the IRGC publicly backed the negotiations. As Foreign Minister Zarif claimed in 2015, echoing Levitsky and Way's argument, "[Outside pressure] provided a means for ensuring domestic national consensus [in favor of the enrichment program]. So interestingly enough, you had this dichotomy where internationally, the nuclear issue provided consensus [against Iran within the P5 + 1] and domestically it provided consensus [against the United States]. . . . This was the single most effective way of uniting the Iranian people" (Parsi 2017, 185).

In sum, two key arguments can be made for the Iranian case in determining the effect of exogenous shocks on authoritarian rule. First, the diffuse character of ruling institutions made rapid shifts in government policy more difficult, as major changes required consensus across ruling elites to block the possibility of a veto being exercised even under exogenous duress. Second, the origins of the Iranian state in postrevolutionary struggle shaped the manner in which exogenous shocks were perceived. When shocks are seen as ideological challenges to the existing order targeted by external opponents, elite cohesion is produced rather than elite dissension.

As a result, any concept of a sufficient threshold of state capacity over which a state can bear the burden of an abstract exogenous shock needs to be contextualized. In the Iranian case, the state is strong (in the sense of reducing chances for regime collapse) because it is diffuse, while credible external threats strengthen, rather than weaken, the cohesion of ruling elites. Despite the diffusely institutionalized makeup of elite contention and competition incentivized by the lack of single-party rule, the nature of the economic shock matters. Since the shock faced by Iran stemmed not from a global/regional financial crisis or generalized commodity bust, but rather from direct geopolitical threats of war and encirclement, the effect was elite cohesion. Rather than a ratcheting up of sanctions, the loosening of US demands on limits to Iran's nuclear enrichment provided the impetus for a cascade effect across Iran's elite spectrum toward a settled deal.

Political Economy Foundations for the Cushioning of External Sanctions

Economic shocks on Iran during 2011–15 came in more than one form, and on top of existing sanctions periodically enforced from the 1990s onward. In March 2005, when Mohammad Khatami was president, Hassan Rouhani was secretary of the Supreme National Security Council (SNSC), and Javad Zarif was the ambassador to the United Nations, the Islamic Republic of Iran floated an offer to EU representatives to limit its nuclear enrichment program to 3,000 centrifuges with agreement to additional inspection beyond the requirements of the Non-Proliferation Treaty, of which Iran is a signatory. Zarif later claimed that the number of 3,000 centrifuges was itself arbitrary, chosen by the Iranians as an opening position, while even 1,000 centrifuges would have been possible for a final agreement (Parsi 2018, 20). As previously noted, however, the position of the United States under the George W. Bush administration at the time was that any enrichment in Iran was unacceptable.

Circa 2003, Iran possessed around 150 centrifuges for enriching nuclear material. When Barack Obama assumed the US presidency in 2008, Iran had amassed 8,000 centrifuges. The expansion seemed to be part of the gambit of the Ahmadinejad administration, which had assumed the presidency in 2005, to extract a more favorable settlement in future negotiations, not a mad rush to a nuclear bomb. Yet the provocative bluster of Ahmadinejad during this period proved counterproductive. While Rouhani and Zarif had spent political capital in 2002–4 attempting to keep the EU and the United States split over the issue of Iran's nuclear program, and thus lessen the chances of a UN Security Council vote on a new round of sanctions, Ahmadinejad provided a superb target for the United States to paper over previous differences with the EU. Once the Obama administration took over, it was far easier to corral other states into a plan to buy into new oil sanctions and collectively cut off Iran from the international financial system. The Ahmadinejad government underestimated how the change in US administrations facilitated an international coalition for increased sanctions.

The economic shock was delivered across multiple arenas over a short time line. In November 2011, the United States labeled Iran's entire financial system, including the CBI, as a jurisdictional arena of money laundering that threatened other governments. As a result, countries or firms that did business with Iranian banks could be subject to US penalties, as was imposed on the French bank BNP Paribas in June 2014 for the sum of US$8.9 billion. In December 2011, the US Congress adopted legislation to sanction foreign banks that transacted with Iran's central bank unless that bank's parent country reduced oil purchases from Iran, with each country's case reviewed every six months by the US president. In January 2012, the EU froze new contracts with Iranian oil firms and announced it would wind down existing contracts by July. The EU also banned insurance for shipping oil or petrochemicals from Iran and froze the assets of the CBI. In March 2012, the Society of Worldwide Interbank Financial Telecommunications (SWIFT) cut off Iranian banks from its network, significantly raising the transaction costs of financial transfers to and from Iran. In October 2012, the EU banned short-term export credits and insurance to Iran. In November 2012, the US Treasury Department announced that financial transactions with the state-owned National Iranian Oil Company would be sanctioned, and that banks that facilitated hard currency or gold transfers to Iran would be penalized. This forced Iran to trade oil for imported goods through escrow accounts with countries such as China and Korea, rather than through foreign exchange, using banks disconnected from SWIFT (IMF 2014, 9).

Over this period, oil production fell to a 20-year low, oil export revenues declined by more than half (about 15 percent of GDP), and Iran's currency lost 80 percent of its value in the parallel market. Two separate runs on Iran's currency in 2012 (January and September) put pressure on the rial, forcing the CBI to conduct forex transactions via three tiers of exchange rates over the most volatile period. To an extent, the 2012 currency devaluation was a product of speculative rushes on a currency that had long been perceived as overvalued by domestic traders, as overvaluation is common to most oil exporters. It was widespread knowledge that the currency was being propped up through CBI intervention, but it still took a collective rush of currency traders to spike market rates into short-term volatility.

However, Iran was no stranger to currency crises. During the 1980s Iran-Iraq War, the country implemented currency controls and a tiered set of exchange rates along with a regulated system of channeling cheaper foreign exchange to licensed importers. In 2002, after a decade of attempting to wean the system away from tiered rates, Iran converted the de jure exchange rate arrangement to a managed float against a basket of international currencies. During the 2012 currency run, the CBI returned to using exchange tiers in order to channel forex into particular sectors with high demand, creating lists of prioritized imports to be valued at the official exchange rate, and limiting individual sales of domestic currency in exchange for dollars and euros. In a sense, then, the CBI returned to the stabilizing exchange arrangement that had prevailed for most of the post-revolutionary period. But the speed of the devaluations contributed to an inflationary shock over the next several years.

Moreover, even with available domestic credit, key industrial sectors such as automobile production suffered knockoff disruptions in supply chains. While 1.42 million cars were produced in 2012, for instance, the number shrank to 624,000 in 2014. Overall, real GDP contracted by 6.6 percent in 2012 and 1.9 percent in 2013, returning to a positive rate of 4 percent growth in 2014 (IMF 2017).

For someone who traveled to Iran annually during this period and witnessed the run on the currency, it was remarkable how little these effects were visible at the everyday level other than a generalized worry about the price level (Harris 2013). The pain was eventually felt over time through stagflation, with inflation hitting 40 percent in 2014 amid a flat rate of economic growth. Yet a set of buffers existed in Iran, less understood at the time, that bear examining.

Some of these buffers can be seen at work in national accounts data. To the surprise of many, Iran's current account stayed positive during the entire period of economic shock (2011–14). As shown in table 3.1, Iran's current account balance as a share of GDP was actually lower in 2008–9, due to the effects of the 2008 global financial crisis on oil prices, than it was under sanctions in 2012–14. There are three main reasons for the positive balance remaining even under economic shock. First, oil prices stayed high during the latter period (partly due to global skittishness over the Iran crisis itself), so even with reduced volumes in oil exports, Iran still garnered a significant share of revenue from oil sales. Second, the currency devaluation contributed to an increase in non-oil exports, in goods such as petrochemicals, steel, cement, iron ore, agricultural products, and textiles.[3] Third, and uncommon to oil-exporting countries when oil prices move higher, a fall in imports helped to offset the decline in oil exports, driven by the high transaction costs of doing business abroad and the depreciation in the Iranian currency.

In addition, Iranian markets were sufficiently connected to the world economy for some form of substitution to take place among export destinations and import sources. The sanctions regime did not manage to create a fully encompassing cordon sanitaire. One study by a Lebanese economist, using Iranian firm-level data, is a case in point. Between 2006 and 2011, two-thirds of the value of Iranian non-oil exports believed to be destroyed by export sanctions were estimated to have been deflected to destinations that had not imposed sanctions. Large export firms were the most successful at shifting exports toward countries more politically amicable with Iran (Haider 2017). A thick web of cross-country trade networks across Central and East Asia allowed Iranian firms to compensate, albeit with higher transaction costs.

State Control over Domestic Financial Flows

Another set of buffers can be seen in budget and capital account data, shown in table 3.2. Unlike many Middle Eastern countries such as Leba-

TABLE 3.1. Iran Current Accounts Data 2007–8 to 2015–16 (in Billions USD)

	2007/08	2008/09	2009/10	2010/11	2011/12	2012/13	2013/14	2014/15	2015/16
Current account balance	32.6	22.9	10.9	24.4	59.4	26.3	26.5	15.9	9
(in % of GDP at market prices)	10.5%	6.5%	3.0%	6.0%	11.0%	6.6%	7.8%	3.8%	2.4%
Trade balance	39.4	31.1	20.9	37.5	67.1	31.0	33.1	21.4	12.2
Exports	97.7	101.3	87.5	107.5	144.9	98.0	93.1	86.5	64.6
Oil and gas	81.6	82.4	66.2	81.1	118.2	62.9	64.9	55.4	33.6
Non-oil and gas	16.1	18.9	21.3	26.3	26.6	35.1	28.2	31.1	31.0
Imports	−58.2	−70.2	−66.6	−70.0	−77.8	−67.1	−60.0	−65.1	−52.4
External debt (in % of GDP)	9.3%	6.1%	5.9%	5.4%	3.2%	1.9%	1.6%	1.2%	2.7%

Source: International Monetary Fund Article IV Staff Reports 2011, 2014, 2015, 2017.
Note: The Persian calendar runs from March to March.

non, Egypt, or Turkey, Iran's banking system was not reliant on foreign financing or domestic sources of private capital.

Iran's banking system consists of public commercial banks; state-owned specialized banks in sectors such as housing, agriculture, and industry; a number of semipublic banks that had recently become privatized; and thousands of small credit institutions. Iran's banking sector had also gone through a wave of privatization and deregulation in the late 2000s. As a result, the number of financial institutions in Iran increased, as well as asset holdings. Yet even in recently privatized banks, the government usually remained a main shareholder and retained control over management.

The cutting off from SWIFT did, of course, hamper Iran's connections with foreign banking sources. The number of international correspondent banks, institutions that acted as third parties for Iranian financial transactions abroad, went from 306 in 2012, to 27 in 2013, to 4 in 2014 (IMF 2017, 6). Yet these linkages were never key funding sources of finance for Iran. State-owned, commercial, specialized, and partially privatized banks largely relied on CBI funding to implement internal as well as governmental credit directives. These banks raised funds largely from deposits or special-purpose vehicles issued in domestic debt markets. In addition, nonfinancial public enterprises (NFPEs), such as large firms in industry, gas, and mining sectors, also utilized the public banking system for most credit needs.

As table 3.2 shows, Iran experienced a fiscal contraction in 2012–14, as revenue and spending declined as a share of GDP. Iran did not, however, experience a monetary contraction—far from it. Instead, the CBI continued to expand credit to the banking system, including to semiprivate banks and NFPEs. Throughout the economic shocks, then, monetary policy acted as a quasi-fiscal liquidity pump to keep banks and NFPEs solvent, albeit at the cost of increasing nonperforming loans, lowered profitability, and close-to-negative real interest rates. It was only in 2014, with the new Rouhani administration in place and the prospects for the JCPOA in view, that the central bank reined in monetary growth. The outcome was a dysfunctional banking sector wrought with stories of corruption, leading to state bailouts of numerous credit institutions and an implicit guarantee of deposits for lenders. Overall, then, the expansion of liquidity into the financial system did prevent a credit crunch, albeit at a high cost that kicked the challenges of inflation, underinvestment, underperforming banking assets, and high unemployment down the road.

In addition to a monetary cushion to the shock of sanctions, two more policies in Iran should be highlighted that complicate the claim that sanctions directly caused all of Iran's economic woes during this period. First, as seen in table 3.2, as of 2011 the government was spending 1.6 percent of GDP on a new cash transfer program entitled "Targeted Subsidy Reform." As long advocated by economic reformers inside Iran as well as the IMF itself, in late 2010 the Ahmadinejad government finally passed a bill to raise prices on heavily subsidized fuel, petrol, and electricity in exchange for a near-universal system of cash transfers to be delivered to individuals directly via their bank accounts. The switch to cash transfer policy was not a response to the 2011–13 increase in sanctions, since the policy had been under debate in years and took a full year to pass in the legislature during 2009–10 (Harris 2010). These per-person cash transfers were equivalent to US$45 per month when first introduced in 2011 and turned out to be an important buffer for low-income households over the following years. Indeed, partly because all households received the same monthly transfer, estimated overall inequality in the country went down. The Gini index of income inequality for Iran's household expenditure remained remarkably steady, at around .45, for most of the 1990s and 2000s. Inequality started to decrease in 2006, but there was a noticeable

TABLE 3.2. Budget and Monetary Sector in Iran, 2007/8–2015/16

	2007/08	2008/09	2009/10	2010/11	2011/12	2012/13	2013/14	2014/15	2015/16
Budgetary operations (% of GDP)									
Revenue	28.9%	25.1%	23.5%	23.4%	19.7%	15%	14.1%	14.6%	16.2%
Taxes	6.7%	7.1%	8.4%	6.5%	5.9%	5.8%	5.2%	6.4%	7.1%
Oil revenue	18.3%	13.8%	10.5%	14.5%	10.85	6.6%	6.5%	6.8%	7.4%
Expenditure	21.5%	24.5%	22.5%	21.7%	19.5%	15.3%	15%	15.7%	17.9%
Balance of targeted subsidy organization					−1.6%	−1.6%	−1.3%	0	0
Monetary sector (annual % change)									
Credit to the private sector	33.3%	11.4%	12.2%	31.9%	20.1%	17.7%	30.7%	16.7%	16.7%
Narrow money (M1)	29.7%	−2.1%	14.2%	24.9%	15.8%	29.1%	8.1%	0.9%	13.2%
Broad money (M3)	28.6%	15.2%	23.5%	26.7%	19.6%	30.6%	39.5%	22.3%	30%
Gross official reserves (in millions USD)	82.9	79.6	78.0	78.9	92.2	104.4	117.6	126.2	128.4
(in months of the following year's imports)	11.2	11.2	10.1	9.5	13.8	17.2	18	22.5	19.4

Source: International Monetary Fund Article IV Staff Reports 2011, 2014, 2015, 2017.
Note: The Persian calendar runs from March to March.

decline during the period of 2011–13, and the coefficient bottomed out at around .37. This was partly due to the cash transfer system as a mode of redistribution from middle and upper strata (who tend to consume more energy) to lower-income households (Salehi-Isfahani 2016). The Rouhani administration refused to adjust the cash transfers upward to adjust for inflation, but nevertheless the program carried over into the new government, as it was quite popular.

An additional program that funneled liquidity into the economy during the same period was a huge semipublic housing expansion known as the *Mehr* program. Beginning in 2007, the government provided land to private developers free of charge, and new homeowners received a 99-year lease to these properties developed on publicly owned land. The state-owned Housing Bank extended subsidized mortgage loans to new homeowners to finance their home purchases. The financing of the *Mehr* housing program through the Housing Bank was also placed on the Central Bank of Iran's rolls. In fact, CBI financing to the Housing Bank tripled in 2010, before the implementation of monthly cash transfers, and then doubled again after the transfer policy had begun. By the end of 2011, CBI financing to the Housing Bank *made up 40 percent* of base monetary flows into the economy. This was a huge injection of liquidity into an economy about to also experience a price shock from energy price reform and a currency shock from sanctions pressure (IMF 2017, 13).

The CBI eventually removed the financing of housing from its balance sheets, and the Rouhani administration curtailed the program in 2015 in order to shift housing policy expenditures back into the fiscal budget. But these two large social policies complicate our ability to claim that sanctions alone caused the economic troubles of Iran from 2011 to 2014. In reality, *three shocks, not one*, came to bear on the country at the same time. Nor did the government curtail these programs afterward, even as the country faced uncertainty on the negotiations front with United States.

In sum, partly due to its postrevolutionary origins amid a hostile geopolitical order, the Islamic Republic of Iran contained a set of economic institutions which buffered the economic shock of sanctions. The economy was diversified enough across sectors and interlinked enough across the world economy to support a fall in oil revenues with nonoil exports, as well as deflect some of the sanctions pressure. Domestic financial institutions, while not fully nationalized, were still reliant largely on state control over monetary policy and access to state-provided finance. Lastly, the social policies of the Ahmadinejad government, which spent on procyclical programs such as cash transfers and housing, did buffer the social effects of the sanctions, albeit in haphazard fashion.

Conclusion: Effect versus Effectiveness of Economic Shocks

As the case of Iran in 2011–15 shows, when operationalizing interstate sanctions as a particular form of economic shock, the concept of the "effect" of sanctions should arguably be defined differently than the concept of "effectiveness." It is easy to document the first concept, but it often conflated with the second concept. US officials who strove to build up a sanctions regime against Iran and garner international support from skeptical states such as Russia and China might have been subject to bureaucratic blinders or a silo mentality akin to the obsession with "body count" tactics during the US-Vietnam war. Detailed accounts of the period suggest that US efforts at increasing sanctions on Iran may have been more a process of holding off more hawkish opponents calling for outright war and corralling together a patchy international coalition, rather than crafting an assessable strategic lever on the calculations of the Iranian political elite. While painful for Iran, sanctions were also performative for the Obama administration—a signaling and coordination device with other states. Even members of the US negotiating team, including Secretary of State John Kerry, were not fully convinced that there was a relationship between the degree of sanctions and the willingness of Iran to agree to particular conditions. "Sanctioning Iran until it capitulates makes for a powerful talking point and a pretty good political speech," Kerry stated at a press conference in July 2015, "but it's not achievable outside a world of fantasy" (Parsi 2017, 316).

Taking a step back, one could even argue the sanctions were counterproductive, given the stated policy of the United States back in 2005 for permanent zero enrichment in the Islamic Republic. The Iranian nuclear program actually grew quite rapidly over the very years in which sanctions were increasingly applied, and the JCPOA accepted enrichment levels far above Iran's previous negotiating position. The expansion of nuclear enrichment and reprocessing might have partly been brinksmanship by the Iranian side, as later admitted, in order to pressure the United States to accept some enrichment capabilities. President Hassan Rouhani's chief of staff, Mohammad Nahavandian, quietly noted as such in 2015: "We escalated our nuclear activities to show what pressure would produce. Perhaps we really didn't need some of the nuclear facilities and activities we engaged in, but we deemed it necessary for breaking the mentality of the other side" (Parsi 2017, 118). Once the enrichment of any nuclear material was accepted by the United States, first communicated in secret talks coordinated through the sultan of Oman in summer 2012, the seed of an agreement slowly began to take shape.

Reconstructing the time line of Iranian politics over these years suggests that, even if we grant the assumption that pressure from sanctions was a necessary condition, it was by no means sufficient and could have led to alternative outcomes. Two other conditions were also necessary. First was the breakup of the conservative political coalition attached to Mahmoud Ahmadinejad, which *preceded* the imposition of increased sanctions in 2011. This coalitional shift eventually led to the election of Hassan Rouhani, the reinstatement of key diplomats from the 2002–5 period, and the endorsement of Iran's skeptical leader and supreme jurist, Ali Khamenei, of an approach of "heroic flexibility" toward the United States. Second was the perception inside the Obama administration by 2012 that the marginal payoff of sanctions was declining, not rising, and the United States faced the unraveling of its own coalition of support for maintaining international sanctions. In sum, coalitions on both sides had to align in a conducive way for JCPOA negotiations to take place and then succeed. Given the realignment on both sides, it is doubtful whether sanctions were a necessary, much less the key, ingredient.

In fact, by 2012 it was becoming clearer to the Obama administration that sanctions were having an effect on Iran's economy, but not being effective at changing the elite consensus in Tehran. At the same time, given economic losses for key allies such as Germany and France, which had foregone billions in exports to Iran, and the wilting of solidarity with states such as China and Russia, it was becoming clearer that the time line for keeping an international coalition together on sanctions was also running short. With hawkish pressure for a military strike coming from US allies, and Iran's nuclear enrichment gambit shrinking the breakout time for enough material to theoretically construct a bomb, the Obama administration perceived itself in a race between an act of war, a nuclearized Iran, and a diplomatic "roll of the dice" (Parsi 2017). This was the context for the concession on zero enrichment by the United States, and the beginning of the process of the JCPOA.

The cost to Iran was enormous in quantitative effect, but not qualitatively effective. As a postrevolutionary state with political elites who still could recall the many attempts by the extant geopolitical order to attack and overthrow the Iranian state, the sanctions imposed in 2011–14 were not likely to have produced a capitulation even if continued for several more years. The idiosyncratically diffuse political institutions of the Islamic Republic, however, meant that a wide swath of the political elite had to be convinced that accepting restrictions on a nationalistic nuclear policy could be framed as prorevolutionary resistance, not a capitulation to long-mistrusted enemies. The heat of the external environment rose in temperature, but it was the changes in the Iranian egg that mattered.

NOTES

1. Iran's Supreme National Security Council, created in 1989 through an amendment to Iran's 1979 constitution, consists of the positions of president, the speaker of parliament, the chief justice of the judiciary, representatives of the leader's office, the head of the army, the head of the Islamic Revolutionary Guards, the foreign minister, the interior minister, the intelligence minister, and the head of the Planning Organization. These offices span the elected (executive branch) and unelected (leader and judiciary) institutions of postrevolutionary Iran.

2. As much as the year 1989 symbolizes a wave of democratization today, we should remember the wide divergence among regime outcomes once socialist states in the Caucasus and Central Asia are included (Derluguian 2005).

3. Iran is the largest cement exporter to Iraq and Afghanistan. So, ironically, reconstruction efforts in these two countries partly sponsored by American aid and military spending helped to buffer Iran's balance of payments during the sanctions period.

REFERENCES

Arjomand, Saïd Amir. 2015. *The Arab Revolution of 2011: A Comparative Perspective.* Albany: SUNY Press.

Brownlee, Jason, Tarek Masoud, and Andrew Reynolds. 2015. *The Arab Spring: Pathways of Repression and Reform.* Oxford: Oxford University Press.

Brumberg, Daniel, and Farideh Farhi. 2016. "Introduction: Politics of Contention and Conciliation in Iran's Semiautocracy." In *Power and Change in Iran: Politics of Contention and Conciliation,* ed. Daniel Brumberg and Farideh Farhi. Bloomington: Indiana University Press, 1–33.

Derluguian, Georgi M. 2005. *Bourdieu's Secret Admirer in the Caucasus: A World-System Biography.* Chicago: University of Chicago Press.

Haggard, Stephan, and Robert Kaufman. 1992. "Institutions and Economic Adjustment." In *The Politics of Economic Adjustment: International Constraints, Distributive Conflicts, and the State,* ed. Stephan Haggard and Robert Kaufman. Princeton: Princeton University Press, 3–40.

Haider, Jamal. 2017. "Sanctions and Exports Deflection: Evidence from Iran." *Economic Policy* 32 (90): 319–55.

Harris, Kevan. 2010. "The Politics of Subsidy Reform in Iran." *MERIP Reports* 254: 36–39.

Harris, Kevan. 2013. "A Fistful of Tomans: Iran's Currency Wars." *London Review of Books* 35 (2): 28–29.

Harris, Kevan. 2015. "The Breakaway Boss: Semiperipheral Innovations and the Rise of Mahmoud Ahmadinezhad." *Journal of World-Systems Research* 21 (2): 417–47.

Harris, Kevan. 2017. *A Social Revolution: Politics and the Welfare State in Iran.* Oakland: University of California Press.

Herb, Michael. 2014. *The Wages of Oil: Parliaments and Economic Development in Kuwait and the UAE*. Ithaca: Cornell University Press.

Heydemann, Steven, and Reinoud Leenders. 2013. *Middle East Authoritarianisms: Governance, Contestation, and Regime Resilience in Syria and Iran*. Stanford: Stanford University Press.

Hinnebusch, Raymond. 2006. "Authoritarian Persistence, Democratization Theory and the Middle East: An Overview and Critique." *Democratization* 13 (3): 373–95.

Huntington, Samuel. 1970. "Social and Institutional Dynamics of One-Party Systems." In *Authoritarian Politics in Modern Society: The Dynamics of Established One-Party Systems*, ed. Samuel Huntington and Clement H. Moore. New York: Basic Books, 3–47.

Keshavarzian, Arang. 2005. "Contestation without Democracy: Elite Fragmentation in Iran." In *Authoritarianism in the Middle East: Regimes and Resistance*, ed. Marsha Pripstein Posusney and Michele Penner. Boulder: Lynne Rienner, 63–88.

International Monetary Fund (IMF). 2011. *Staff Report for the 2011 Article IV Consultation*. Washington, DC: International Monetary Fund.

International Monetary Fund (IMF). 2014. *Staff Report for the 2014 Article IV Consultation*. Washington, DC: International Monetary Fund.

International Monetary Fund (IMF). 2015. *Staff Report for the 2015 Article IV Consultation*. Washington, DC: International Monetary Fund.

International Monetary Fund (IMF). 2017. *Staff Report for the 2016 Article IV Consultation*. Washington, DC: International Monetary Fund.

Jervis, Robert. 2015. "Socialization, Revolutionary States and Domestic Politics." *International Politics* 52 (5): 609–16.

Levitsky, Steven, and Lucan Way. 2015. "Not Just What, but When (and How): Comparative-Historical Approaches to Authoritarian Durability." In *Advances in Comparative-Historical Analysis*, ed. James Mahoney and Kathleen Thelen. Cambridge: Cambridge University Press, 97–120.

Mao Tse-tung. 1965. *Selected Works of Mao Tse-tung*. Vol. 1. New York: Pergamon Press.

Nader, Alireza. 2012. "Influencing Iran's Nuclear Decisions." In *Sanctions, Statecraft, and Nuclear Proliferation*, ed. Etel Solingen. Cambridge: Cambridge University Press, 211–31.

Parsi, Trita. 2017. *Losing an Enemy: Obama, Iran, and the Triumph of Diplomacy*. New Haven: Yale University Press.

Parsi, Trita. 2018. "Roundtable on Losing an Enemy: Author's Response." *H-Diplo ISSF Roundtable* 10 (7): 17–22.

Salehi-Isfahani, Djavad. 2016. "Long-Term Trends in Poverty and Inequality in Iran." *Tyranny of Numbers* blog, March 29. https://djavadsalehi.com/2016/03/29/long-term-trends-in-poverty-and-inequality-in-iran

Slater, Dan. 2010. *Ordering Power: Contentious Politics and Authoritarian Leviathans in Southeast Asia*. Cambridge: Cambridge University Press.

Slater, Dan. 2011. Review of *Competitive Authoritarianism: Hybrid Regimes after the Cold War*. *Perspectives on Politics* 9 (2): 385–88.

Tabatabai, Ariane. 2017. "Negotiating the 'Iran Talks' in Tehran: The Iranian Drivers That Shaped the Joint Comprehensive Plan of Action." *Nonproliferation Review* 24 (3–4): 225–42.

Terhalle, Maximilian. 2015. "Why Revolutionary States Yield: International Sanctions, Regime Survival and the Security Dilemma. The Case of the Islamic Republic of Iran." *International Politics* 52 (5): 594–608.

Widmaier, Wesley W., Mark Blyth, and Leonard Seabrooke. 2007. "Exogenous Shocks or Endogenous Constructions? The Meanings of Wars and Crises." *International Studies Quarterly* 51 (4): 747–59.

Yom, Sean L. 2015. "The Arab Spring: One Region, Several Puzzles, and Many Explanations." *Government and Opposition* 50 (4): 682–704.

FOUR

Economic Shocks and Authoritarian Responses

Putin's Strategy after the Global Financial Crisis of 2008–9

Natalia Lamberova and Daniel Treisman

1. Introduction

Authoritarian leaders should fear economic downturns. Such downturns can threaten their position by several pathways. For one thing, poor economic performance casts doubt on the incumbent's competence, undermining confidence in his abilities both among members of the elite and within the population at large. Attempts to overthrow the incumbent may follow, whether by mass protest or insider conspiracy (Haggard and Kaufman 1995; Brancati 2014).

Besides motivating citizens to challenge their ruler, economic crises may make it easier to do so. A sudden economic shock can serve as a focal point, enabling discontented individuals or factions to coordinate on the timing of an uprising (Acemoglu and Robinson 2005). Meanwhile, unemployment and wage stagnation lower the opportunity cost for citizens to rebel (e.g., Acemoglu and Robinson 2001; Dagaev et al. 2015).

Even as they increase the odds of challenges, economic crises weaken the ruler's capacity to fight back. Poor economic performance shrinks government revenues, reducing funds for both co-opting critics and financing the police, army, and other agents of repression (Bueno de Mesquita et al. 2003). Dwindling domestic resources may create dependence on foreign patrons and donors, who rarely value a dictator's survival as much as he does. Together, these various effects of economic crisis have a significant impact. Empirical studies confirm that leaders of authoritarian states are more likely to be replaced in bad economic times (Londregan and Poole 1996; Bueno de Mesquita and Smith 2010; Treisman 2015).

Of course, not *all* economic crises produce a change of leader or regime. Dangerous as economic shocks are, some dictators survive them. Cuba's GDP per capita fell by more than one-third between 1990 and 1993, yet Fidel Castro's rule persisted. Mu'ammar Gaddhafi, Saddam Hussein, and Kim Jong-il all experienced years of severe depression without losing office. To some extent, such variation is explained by the different initial conditions that prevail when economic crisis strikes. Leaders who have saved or inherited large reserves can use them to compensate for shrinking revenues. So can those with access to foreign aid—although then the donors' objectives become important. If the ruler is initially popular, with a reputation for competence, an economic crisis may do less short-run damage than if it strikes a leader who is already widely reviled. The intensity of opposition may depend on both the existence of a credible alternative leader and the type of the authoritarian regime (Bermeo 2000; Magaloni 2008). Those with better outside options—a military junta, for instance, can often return safely to the barracks—may be more likely to step down. On the other hand, those with more effective tools of repression may be better able to weather economic shocks. In practice, the first effect seems to dominate for military regimes, which appear more vulnerable than other types to economic pressures (Geddes 1999). Finally, various contextual details affect how easily rulers can deflect the blame for economic problems onto others.

Besides initial conditions, the strategy with which a ruler responds to an economic shock is bound to matter. Of course, the strategy chosen will, itself, depend on the initial conditions, so disentangling the effects is difficult. For this reason, case studies offer a valuable opportunity to explore the mechanisms of authoritarian survival during economic hard times. In this chapter we examine the consequences for Russia of the global financial crisis that began in late 2008 and the successive responses attempted by the regime of Vladimir Putin.

This crisis, which began in the United States with a panic in the market for mortgage-backed securities and quickly spread around the world, hit Russia particularly hard. Its GDP plunged by almost 8 percent, the largest decrease of any G20 country (Guriev and Tsyvinski 2010). Although growth turned positive again in 2010, the rate soon dwindled, falling to 1.3 percent in 2013. In 2011, Russia's GDP per capita in real terms reattained the level of 2008. However, a second wave of crisis broke out in late 2014, as oil prices crashed from $109 a barrel in 2013 to $52 in 2015 and Western sanctions, imposed after the Russian annexation of Crimea, tightened access to credit.[1] The ruble lost almost half its value against the dollar between mid-2014 and early 2015, and GDP fell by 3.7 percent in 2015 and then by 1.2 percent (year on year) in the first quarter of 2016.

The abrupt end to the eight-year boom that had lasted until 2008 posed urgent challenges to the regime of President Putin, whose popularity had been based in large part on the steadily rising living standards of these years. From a peak of 88 percent in September 2008, Putin's approval rating drifted down to 61 percent in late 2013. The annexation of Crimea sent it soaring again above 80 percent, where it stayed until 2018. But, amid stagnant economic performance, it had fallen again by mid-2019 to the low 60s.

The next section discusses possible strategic choices of authoritarian leaders facing economic downturns in light of theoretical analyses of dictatorships. Section 3 characterizes the economic and political situation in Russia on the eve of the global financial crisis. Section 4 reviews the details of the economic shock Russia suffered after 2008 and examines the regime's economic and political responses. Finally, the concluding section explores to what extent the Kremlin's strategy fits the expectations of different theories.

2. Authoritarian Responses to Economic Crisis: Theoretical Expectations

How do economic crises affect the survival strategies of authoritarian rulers? Scholars have approached this problem in a number of ways. Guriev and Treisman (2015) see modern dictators as focused on maintaining a reputation for competence that can reconcile the population to their rule. Of course, democratic leaders also prefer to be thought competent, but authoritarian ones achieve this by distorting information flows to an extent incompatible with democracy. In an economically interdependent, globalized, and media-rich world, manipulating information to boost the leader's popularity is a less costly way of holding onto power than intimidating the population with violent repression. Dictators choose between, on the one hand, buying the silence of those who observe their incompetence (cooptation) and, on the other hand, blocking media messages that expose their inadequacies (censorship).

In Guriev and Treisman's model, dictators can often ride out small economic shocks—and may even see their reputations enhanced if they survive. But large economic downturns pose a greater threat, so they may force a change of strategy. Dictators switch from co-opting the informed elite to censoring critical media. If they are already censoring such media, they increase the resources devoted to such censorship relative to other expenditures. They also respond to large economic shocks by boosting relative spending on propaganda. Thus, this theory predicts that severe economic shocks should prompt an increase in relative effort on censorship and propaganda. Since the amount of available funds shrinks, one expects to see a decrease in spending to co-opt the elite.

Rozenas (2015), also modeling the dictator's information control problem, reaches close to the opposite conclusion. If economic crisis leads citizens to suspect the dictator's popularity is falling, he must correct this impression in order to forestall challenges. To do so, he needs credible communication channels. But to be credible, such channels must be relatively independent, since manipulated information sources are discounted. Rozenas develops this logic in the context of fraudulent elections, but it could apply more broadly to manipulation of the media. A dictator who is thought to be losing popularity because of economic crisis should commit *less* electoral fraud so that, when he receives a higher vote than some expect, citizens believe that he is genuinely popular. By the same token, such dictators should permit more media freedom so that the independent media can credibly report his stronger-than-perceived public approval.

By contrast, a dictator whose popularity has not been thrown into question—by economic deterioration or other events—does not need a credible channel to send persuasive messages. He can afford to manipulate elections and censor the media as much as he likes. The key difference from Guriev and Treisman's approach is that Rozenas assumes that the amount of manipulation can be observed, whereas Guriev and Treisman assume that at least some manipulation can be concealed. Based on Rozenas's argument, one might expect a dictator struck by economic crisis to reduce both censorship of the media and the broadcasting of propaganda.

Another common expectation, consistent with Guriev and Treisman (2015), is that, as its resources dwindle, an authoritarian regime should shift from trying to co-opt the elite and population with material benefits to providing (at least relatively inexpensive) symbolic goods. The dictator should substitute circuses for bread. This can involve stirring up nationalism by invoking external threats, and even provoking—preferably easily winnable—military conflicts. Scholars have suggested that economic deterioration may prompt diversionary wars. General Galtieri's invasion of the Falkland Islands is sometimes seen in this light (Levy and Vakili 1993; Hastings and Jenkins 1983). The same logic might lead to a search for internal enemies, who could be pitted against the circus gladiators.

The effect of economic downturns on the extent of corruption is unclear. On the one hand, the incumbent might cut back on lavish expenses to compensate for falling revenues and avoid having to change political strategy. In this case, one might observe a decline in corrupt self-enrichment by insiders. On the other hand, if the crisis shortens the incumbents' time horizon, it could prompt a rapid grab for movable wealth during what time remains (Olson 1993). It might also motivate the autocrat to lavish greater largesse on members of his selectorate in order to offset their losses caused by economic deterioration and keep them loyal (Bueno de Mesquita and Smith 2011).

All these predictions hold ceteris paribus. As noted in the previous section, monetary reserves, aid (plus any associated conditionality), the initial popularity of the leader, his ability to suppress dissent, the type of authoritarian regime, and other contextual factors will all affect the impact of economic shocks on leader and regime survival. These factors will also influence what strategy the incumbent chooses. Thus, no simple model is likely to accurately capture in all settings what approach the incumbent will choose. Rather, the different logics specified by the various arguments can inform a closer examination of individual cases.

3. Russia on the Eve of the Global Crisis

The global financial crisis that struck in 2008 caught Russia at the peak of a remarkable economic rebound. After the painful contraction of the 1990s, GDP per capita had been growing by 7 percent a year on average since 2000.[2] For eight years, the state budget had been in surplus. The country had paid off most of its foreign public debt, reducing the total from $139 billion in 1999 to $37 billion in 2008.[3] The authorities achieved this while simultaneously simplifying the tax system, slashing rates, and introducing a flat 13 percent personal income tax. The central bank's currency reserves had grown from $12 billion in 1998 to almost $550 billion in June 2008, an amount exceeded only by China and Japan.[4] Rather than spending windfall profits, the government had saved excess oil revenues in a stabilization fund that by early 2008 contained $157 billion.[5]

Living standards had grown even faster than output. The average wage rose by 14.7 percent a year during 2000–2007, adjusted for inflation, while the average pension increased by 11 percent a year. This surge in spending power had fueled a consumer revolution. Between 2000 and 2008, retail trade per person grew from $570 to $3,952 a year (at market exchange rates); computer ownership soared from 6 to 47 per 100 households; and the number of cars per 100 people increased from 13 to 21. Even among the relatively poor, both incomes and life satisfaction had risen substantially (Guriev and Zhuravskaya 2009). Between 2000 and 2007, the unemployment rate fell from 11 percent to 6 percent and the share of citizens in poverty from 29 to 13 percent.

Yet the economic picture was not all rosy. The impressive growth rates of 2000–2007 had four main causes: (1) a recovery after the previous collapse, (2) increased competitiveness because of the devaluation of 1998, (3) market reforms introduced in the 1990s and early 2000s, and (4) rising prices of oil and gas.[6] While the first three factors dominated in the early 2000s—the oil price increased only moderately in those years, rising from about $10 a barrel at the end of 1998 to $30 a barrel at the end of 2003—their effects had been exhausted by 2005. From that year, growth owed much more to the soaring price of hydrocarbons and the stimulus effect of a huge foreign borrowing binge by mostly state-controlled companies. Between 2004 and 2008, the foreign debt of Russian banks and corporations ballooned from $80 billion to $425 billion.[7]

The effects of higher oil prices and inflows of liquidity more than offset the effects of a simultaneous negative trend—the gradual decrease in the security of property rights. In 2003–4, the authorities dismantled the leading oil company, Yukos, supposedly to pay tax debt, and its main assets were sold cheaply to the state oil company Rosneft. Yukos's CEO, Mikhail Khodorkovsy, was imprisoned after a trial based on dubious evidence and procedural irregularities. However, the stock market continued to soar, rising 50 percent in the two years after Khodorkovsky's arrest.[8] In subsequent years, the term *reyding* entered the Russian language to refer to corrupt takeovers of companies with the help of judicial fraud and police threats or force. Meanwhile, certain old friends or associates of President Putin became extremely wealthy, acquiring control of major banks and other companies (Treisman 2007, 2011a).

The clearest example was Bank Rossia, which, led by an old Putin associate, Yuri Kovalchuk, rose from a little-known provincial bank to one of the country's leading financial institutions. Throughout the period, most of the largest banks were majority state-owned, and the two giants—Sberbank and VTB—were both headed by old Putin loyalists—German Gref, who initially worked with Putin in Saint Petersburg, and Andrei Kostin, a former Soviet diplomat posted in London (Aris 2015). This permitted the Kremlin to count on assistance from these banks when, for instance, it needed a reliable buyer for a failing private bank. In 2011, VTB purchased the Moscow city government's stake in Bank Moskva, which was later revealed to have accumulated $9 billion of problem loans. In turn, such Kremlin-connected banks could count on bailouts when needed; to cover Bank Moskva's losses, VTB later received a $14 billion state package.[9] Such close Kremlin ties also left Russia's leading banks in the firing line when the US imposed post-Crimea sanctions: both Sberbank and VTB were cut off from much international borrowing.

The dramatic improvement in living standards during this period made any political strategy almost superfluous. Putin's approval ratings spiked in late 1999, most likely reflecting a rally behind his leadership in the initial phase of the second Chechen war. But as support for his policy on Chechnya waned, the president's ratings were sustained by the country's buoyant economic performance (Treisman 2011b). Between January 2000 and December 2008, Putin's approval never fell below 60 percent, and it rose as high as 87 percent.

Putin's political strategists exploited their boss's overwhelming popularity to concentrate power within the Kremlin. This reflected not so much need—with such approval ratings, Putin could reliably get his way under the existing system—as opportunism. The Duma was rendered subservient. A number of legal changes and informal measures reasserted Kremlin authority over the country's regional governors. From 2005, these became presidential appointees rather than elected officials (Yakovlev and Zhuravskaya 2004). The "oligarchs" of the 1990s were ordered to withdraw from politics. A few who resisted—Boris Berezovsky, Vladimir Gusinsky, Mikhail Khodorkovsky—were forced to part with assets and sent to exile or jail. The Kremlin imposed control over the national television networks and began closely managing news coverage. The main previously independent television station, NTV, was acquired by the state-controlled oil company Gazprom, and editorial policy became much more supportive of the president (Becker 2004). The apparatus for organizing elections was turned in large part into a machine for manipulating and distorting the results.[10]

None of this dented Putin's popularity with the general public; in fact, the claim that he was rebuilding the state, restoring law and order, and fighting corruption among governors and oligarchs added to his appeal. With ratings in the 70s and 80s, Putin's approval was high among almost all identifiable social groups. What opposition existed consisted of a very small liberal fringe and, at the other extreme, antimarket and anti-Western communists and nationalists. Yet, although Putin's ratings were lower in these groups than among others, he still often enjoyed majority support among their members. Even among those who said in December 2007 that they would like to vote for the Communist leader, Gennady Zyuganov, in the next presidential election, 52 percent said that they approved of Putin's actions.[11]

Despite his moves against the most political oligarchs, and the growing pressures on other businessmen from the new Kremlin-connected corporate raiders, those magnates who survived remained decisively in Putin's camp. It was under Putin that the number of Russian billionaires rose from zero in 2000 to 83 in 2008.[12] Although a few of these were friends of the president, the vast majority were second-rank oligarchs of the Yeltsin era. For those that kept loyal, and were lucky enough to escape direct expropriation, the payoffs were enormous (Treisman 2016).

4. The Global Crisis and the Regime's Response

With little exposure to the "toxic assets" that had spread panic through US markets, Russian business and political leaders at first thought their country would avoid the storm. Speaking at Davos in January 2008, finance minister Aleksey Kudrin described Russia as an "island of stability."[13] But as international investors fled emerging markets, Russia's corporations found it harder to roll over their debt. After the US investment bank Lehman Brothers filed for bankruptcy in September, Russian financial markets froze, and the authorities had to close the stock exchanges for two days to curtail hysterical selling (World Bank 2008). Between mid-May and late October 2008, the RTS share index fell almost 80 percent, erasing $1 trillion worth of value (World Bank 2008). The country's currency reserves dropped by $220 billion in late 2008 and early 2009 as the central bank tried to slow the ruble's decline.

By early 2009, the crisis had spread from finance to the real economy. GDP dropped by almost 8 percent that year. Meanwhile, consolidated budget revenues fell from about 40 percent of GDP in 2007 to 35 percent in 2009 and 2010. Industrial enterprises were soon running into trouble. In the small town of Pikalyovo, southeast of Saint Petersburg, workers stormed the town hall and blocked highways to protest unpaid wages after all three of the town's enterprises were forced to close. Unrest spread rapidly. According to data compiled by Tomila Lankina, the number of protests nationwide peaked in 2009 at 1,093, falling to 810 in 2010, 701 in 2011, and 549 in 2012.[14] Data collected by the Moscow-based Institute of Collective Action and analyzed by Graeme Robertson (2013) show similar trends.

One can divide the Kremlin's economic policy responses to the crisis into several phases. The first phase was one of emergency management. The immediate priority was to prevent banks from collapsing and major corporations from losing assets to foreign creditors. The government issued about $40 billion in credits to banks and $50 billion to companies.[15] It bailed out the automobile producer AvtoVAZ with an $806 million credit and lent the oligarch Oleg Deripaska's aluminum concern, RusAl, $4.5 billion.[16] Russia also cut export tariffs on oil to compensate for falling world prices and raised tariffs on imported cars to protect domestic factories. Less successfully, the authorities wasted $5.3 billion trying vainly to prop up share prices, but quickly abandoned the effort.[17] These short-run measures of the government and central bank cost about 12 percent of GDP in 2009, according to Putin, constituting a much larger stimulus in relative terms than the United States' 5.5 percent of GDP.[18] Government budget spending rose from 34 percent of GDP in 2008 to 41 percent in 2009. In part, this reflected falling GDP, but the level of spending, in real terms, also increased by 5.4 percent.

These actions prevented mass bank failures and industrial bankruptcies. The government offered bailouts to a list of 78 companies in various sectors, but the terms were sufficiently onerous that many companies chose not to take them. It resisted calls to immediately nationalize troubled private companies. In these regards, finance minister Aleksey Kudrin and associated macroeconomic conservatives won in the short run. Analysts tended to see these early measures as effective (Guriev and Tsyvinski 2010).

The contraction of 2009 threatened to slash living standards and undermine the political model that had worked so well for the previous eight years. In 2009, the Kremlin tried to soften the blow. However, its leverage over the wage level in the economy at large was limited. This influence consisted mostly of the government's control over the minimum wage—which served as an anchor for various other wages—and its wage-setting for public sector jobs. From January 1, 2009, the minimum wage was raised by a massive 88 percent in nominal terms. State sector wages were also increased more than inflation. Yet the plunge in private sector wages meant that the average real wage in the economy fell by 3.5 percent in 2009. The government increased pensions by 11 percent in real terms in 2009 and another 24 percent in 2010. Overall, social and cultural spending rose from 51 to 58 percent of the consolidated budget between 2008 and 2010.

And, after the disorienting first months, the Kremlin settled on a political strategy. The focus was on using the media to show that Putin was *personally* in command and—as prime minister—was energetically fighting the fires as they arose, in a style that became known as "manual control." When the workers rioted in Pikalyovo, Putin flew out, accompanied by television cameras, to knock heads together and broker a deal. He was also shown in supermarkets berating their managers for raising prices.[19] To divert discontent, the Kremlin blamed the West for triggering the crisis.

By 2010, the economy had begun a fitful rebound. The growth rate bounced back to 4.5 percent in 2010 and 4.3 percent the next year. After their decline in 2009, real wages rose by 5 percent in 2010 and 3 percent in 2011. The stock market also recovered somewhat from its 2009 plunge. After the emergency response of 2009, the authorities now sought to rein in the surging consolidated budget deficit, reducing it from 6.3 percent of GDP in 2009 to 3.4 percent in 2010, and returning the budget to surplus the following year. The growth of social spending slowed.

The oligarchs, who had seen much of their wealth evaporate in 2009, were almost all saved by the rebound and, in some cases, government bailouts. The 10 businessmen who had topped Russia's *Forbes* list of billionaires in 2008 had watched as their total net worth crashed from $197 billion in 2008 to $54 billion in 2009. By 2011, it was back up to $155 billion. Yet a set of Putin-connected businessmen did even better. Gennady Timchenko, an old associate of Putin's who had created a business trading oil, raked in billions precisely during these crisis years. His wealth, according to *Forbes*, grew from $2.5 billion in 2008 to $9.1 billion in 2011 and $15.3 billion in 2014. Four Russian businessmen are often reported in the press to be old friends of Putin—Timchenko, Yury Kovalchuk, and the brothers Arkady and Boris Rotenberg. The combined net worth of these four according to *Forbes* increased from $4.4–$6.4 billion in 2008 to $22.4 billion in 2014.[20] Putin's friends at the head of state corporations lobbied hard to use the crisis to nationalize troubled private firms—into their holdings (Treisman 2011a).

Yet, while the superwealthy might have been relieved, the recognition that the previous boom would not be returning demoralized those who had risen into the middle class during the previous decade. Consumer confidence never regained its precrisis levels.[21] The strategy of blaming the West was clearly losing effectiveness. In December 2008, 39 percent of respondents had held the United States and other Western countries responsible for Russia's economic distress, compared to 22 percent that pointed the finger at the country's own leaders. By March 2010, 35 percent blamed Russia's leaders and only 30 percent the West. The proportion blaming large Western banks and corporations had also fallen from 22 percent to 18 percent.[22] Putin was becoming a target for economic discontent. In late 2010, even among those who thought the economy was in bad shape 51 percent still approved of the president's performance. By late 2011, only 28 percent did (Treisman 2014).

The second phase in the political strategy began in early 2012. To the Kremlin's surprise, Putin's decision to return as president in 2012, "castling" with his protégé Dmitri Medvedev, who took Putin's role as prime minister, prompted grumbling from the capital's elites. Insiders were also caught off guard when, after numerous observers documented fraud in the parliamentary vote of December 2011, tens of thousands took to the streets in Moscow demanding clean elections. These demonstrations actually mobilized fewer people in total and were more localized than those of 2009–10. But, unlike the economic protests in Pikalyovo and other cities, the Moscow events were explicitly political, brought out up to a 100,000 people in the country's capital, and attracted the most modern and globalized segment of the population, which had previously been mostly supportive of Putin or politically inert.

At first, the Kremlin wavered. Medvedev, in late December 2011, announced several political compromises, including a return to elections for regional governors—a reform later weakened by the addition of a screening mechanism—and easier registration procedures for political parties. But after Putin's inauguration in May, his team introduced a tougher line, seeking to intimidate and marginalize the Moscow protesters with a mix of hostile propaganda and relatively mild but effective political repression. This coincided with—and facilitated—a shift in power within the Kremlin, with security officials coming to dominate the technocratic managers.

To scare potential protesters off the streets, the Kremlin tightened relevant laws and undertook a number of very public prosecutions of opposition figures. The maximum fine for participating in an unauthorized demonstration rose from 300 to 300,000 rubles—about $9,000. In line with the view that the protests had been instigated from outside, a new law ordered nongovernmental organizations (NGOs) that were receiving foreign funding and engaged in "political activity" to register as "foreign agents." The definition of treason was broadened to cover cooperating with foreign organizations "against Russia's security." To signal the new environment, the performance artists of Pussy Riot, several left-wing activists, and the opposition leader Alexei Navalny were all tried and sentenced to jail for different offenses, although Navalny was immediately released to house arrest. Perhaps even more significantly, 27 previously unknown Muscovites who had marched in a May 6 rally on Bolotnaya Square were prosecuted on dubious evidence for allegedly attacking policemen. This sent a clear message to all potential protesters that they, too, could end up in a labor camp.

No authoritative accounting of politically motivated arrests exists. Still, a meticulous examination by the NGO Union for Solidarity with Political Prisoners (USPP) suggests the scale increased after 2011. In 2011–14, according to USPP, 139 political prosecutions were initiated, more than in the entire preceding 12-year period (Durnovo 2015). The human rights organization Memorial also tracks those it considers to be political prisoners. As of October 2013, its list contained 70 names. Several dozen of these—including the Pussy Riot performers and 30 Greenpeace activists arrested trying to scale a gas-drilling platform in the Pechora Sea—were freed in an amnesty that December. Putin also pardoned the jailed oligarch Mikhail Khodorkovsky, in what was viewed in the West as an attempt to improve Russia's image on the eve of the Sochi Winter Olympics.[23] By February 2014, Memorial's total had fallen to 40, but it began to rise again, reaching 50 by June 2015.

Already by early 2008, almost all the television channels broadcasting news had been brought under state control. But efforts to cow critical journalists from what remained of the independent print media continued. On his return to the presidency, Putin recriminalized defamation and slander, which Medvedev had decriminalized in his last months in office. In a notorious incident, the head of the Investigative Committee, Aleksandr Bastrykin, had *Novaya Gazeta* deputy editor Sergei Sokolov driven to a forest outside Moscow and allegedly threatened to kill him if Sokolov did not apologize for a critical article about Bastrykin.[24]

Before the protests of 2011–12, Putin had paid little attention to the internet, which he once described as containing "50 percent pornography."[25] That changed after Facebook and Twitter were credited with helping to coordinate both the Arab Spring and the Moscow demonstrations.[26] A new law in 2012 introduced a "blacklist" of websites, supposedly to filter out child pornography and other information harmful to children. But in December 2013, the law's scope was broadened to cover sites that promoted "extremist" information or publicized unsanctioned protests. The sites blocked included the blogs of opposition leaders Alexei Navalny and

Garry Kasparov. Between January 2012 and February 2013, Freedom House reported an approximately 60 percent increase in the number of websites blocked on the grounds of "extremism."

As in China, many of these measures seem aimed at preventing the use of the internet to coordinate protests (King, Pan, and Roberts 2013). But in other ways the Kremlin appeared committed to a more active agenda aimed at shaping opinion. A vigorous propaganda campaign sought to portray the West as morally decadent, while asserting conservative Russian values, rooted in Orthodox Christianity. The prosecution of Pussy Riot, various initiatives against "pro-homosexual" publications, and a law passed in late 2012 that banned adoptions of Russian children by Westerners all sent this message in different ways. Another new law, passed after the Pussy Riot affair, criminalized "public acts expressing manifest disrespect for society and carried out with the goal of insulting the feelings of religious believers."

State television became a venue for increasingly blatant attacks on the domestic opposition, casting them as agents of the West. In a series of conspiratorial documentaries produced by the journalist Arkady Mamontov, anti-Putin activists were portrayed as violent revolutionaries or social deviants. To counter such forces, the Kremlin set about mobilizing its own supporters. During President Putin's election campaign, the Kremlin had organized a mass rally of 130,000 loyalists in the Luzhniki Stadium; some came voluntarily, others were paid to participate. Educating youth in patriotic values also became a more urgent priority: the agency responsible for such work, Rosmolodezh, saw its budget rise from $12 million in 2012 to $31 million in 2013 and $36 million in 2015.

Whether because of the effectiveness of the Kremlin's propaganda and repression or just because of the natural wavelike dynamic of protest movements, the opposition demonstrations in Moscow dwindled over the course of 2012. At the same time, the Kremlin was shoring up its support among public sector workers, especially those required to implement the tougher approach. Between 2011 and 2013, wages rose nationwide by a total of 12 percent in real terms. But the increases were larger for many state employees—23 percent in health care and social services, 31 percent in education, 34 percent in justice and the courts, 58 percent in public order and security, and 61 percent in management of jails.

Although Putin's ratings remained at a level that most leaders would envy, they had nevertheless been sliding for several years. From a peak of 87 percent approval in December 2007, his rating had reached a low of 61 percent in November 2013. Other polls suggested a hollowing out of this support. The proportion that said they fully shared Putin's views and positions had dropped from 27 percent in May 2007 to 16 percent in August 2013. The share that said they used to like Putin but had recently grown disappointed in him had risen from 9 percent to 20 percent. Six weeks after his election in 2012, fewer than 40 percent of respondents thought Putin would still have won the presidency if Russia had "a free press and television, which could freely talk and write about abuses of the authorities" (Treisman 2014, 16). At the same time, the trend in the economy was, by 2013, unmistakably bad. The growth rebound, which had ended in 2011, was followed by five consecutive quarters of falling rates.

It was against this backdrop that Putin's political strategy changed again in early 2014. To what extent Russia's intervention into Ukraine reflected external political objectives or domestic concerns is not easy to say. But the domestic situation certainly worried political advisers. In February 2014, after the regime of President Viktor Yanukovych collapsed in Kiev, Putin ordered covert special forces troops to invade the Crimean Peninsula. After a hurriedly organized referendum conducted in the shadow of the Russian troops, the region was annexed to Russia. In a triumphant speech to the Federal Assembly, Putin declared that the West had placed Russia "in a position it could not retreat from," and demanded that others "take into account and respect" Russia's national interests. "In people's hearts and minds, Crimea has always been an inseparable part of Russia," he asserted.[27]

As the West responded with harsh criticism and economic sanctions, Putin's approval rating shot up to 86 percent that June.[28] Eighty-eight percent supported the annexation of Crimea.[29] Putin then rolled the dice again, providing covert support to anti-Kiev rebels in the predominantly Russian-speaking regions of Donetsk and Lugansk, at first in the form of nationalist volunteers with military experience who were allowed to infiltrate across the border, and later in the form of heavy weapons and interventions by Russian troops.

These actions made Russia's economic problems considerably worse. Western sanctions cut off major Russian companies and banks from Western financing, just as they needed to roll over the large foreign debt they had continued to accumulate through the crisis period. Sanctions exacerbated the effect of plunging oil prices. In late 2014, the ruble crashed, losing almost 50 percent of its value between June 2014 and January 2015. Real wages fell by 11 percent in the year after Crimea's annexation, and the average pension fell by about 4 percent. But approval of Putin remained strong, never dropping below 83 percent. The Kremlin succeeded in diverting the blame for deteriorating economic conditions onto

Western sanctions. Levada Center polls showed that 46 percent of respondents thought that foreign sanctions were aimed not at the elite but at the general population and 66 percent believed their aim was to "weaken and humiliate Russia."[30] Even Putin's self-punishing "antisanctions," which banned the import of European food into Russia, won the support of 70 percent of respondents.[31]

The renewed economic crisis of 2014—and Western sanctions—hit Russia's billionaires hard, but especially those closest to Putin. The combined total wealth of Russia's 10 richest men fell from $161 billion in 2014 to $137 billion in 2015. But that of the four "old Putin friends" on the *Forbes* list dropped from $22.4 billion in 2014 to $12.1–$14.1 billion in 2015, a much larger proportional decrease. This was despite remarkable efforts by the Kremlin to offset Western sanctions on these individuals by providing them with state-financed material benefits.[32] Analysis of the top recipients of Russian government contracts in 2010–15 shows that members of Putin's inner circle received about 142 times more money in such contracts than unconnected recipients (Lamberova and Sonin 2018). Indeed, the wealth of members of Putin's inner circle and their immediate contacts turns out to be particularly volatile and tied to hydrocarbon prices. Such Putin connections did far better than other major business people in years of high oil prices, but *worse* than others in years when prices were low (Lamberova and Sonin 2018).

Meanwhile, the Kremlin ratcheted up the censorship, propaganda, and pressure on potential protesters. On the propaganda front, a key change came in late 2013, when the relatively professional and politically restrained state news agency RIA Novosti was reorganized under the new name Russia Today and the leadership of the virulently anti-Western news anchor Dmitri Kiselyov. With the Ukraine events, the theme of state propaganda shifted from the attack on Europe's moral decadence to the military competition and even conflict with the West. As Kiselyov pointed out to viewers, Russia remained the only world power with capacity to reduce the United States to "radioactive ash." At the same time, propaganda operations on the internet were decentralized to hundreds of "trolls," who were hired to disrupt discussion of certain issues with their comments and promote the government view on other issues.[33]

New amendments in 2014 toughened penalties for violating public order and increased the police's authority to use violence. And a range of measures intensified pressure on what remained of the independent press. In October 2014, the Duma banned foreign ownership of more than 20 percent in any Russian mass media organization, prompting Axel Springer and other major foreign players to begin selling their holdings.[34] Reportedly under pressure from the Kremlin, cable providers cut off service to the small, liberal, Russian-owned Dozhd television station in January 2014, depriving it of 90 percent of its audience. A year later, the station was hit again by a new ban on advertising on paid television channels.

Simultaneously, control over the internet tightened. Pavel Durov, the founder of the largest social network, VKontakte, had since 2011 been resisting pressure to hand over users' data to the security services. In 2014, he was compelled to sell his stake in the company to pro-Kremlin investors, and he left the country shortly afterward (Thornhill 2015). A new 2014 law required foreign internet companies to store all Russian citizens' personal data within Russia, where they could be monitored by the security services. As of November 2015, it was not clear whether Facebook, Twitter, and other platforms would comply (Soldatov and Borogan 2015).

After Navalny published details of the vast real estate holdings of top officials, the law on privacy was amended to make it a crime to reveal information about the living conditions of individuals. Bloggers whose posts attracted more than 3,000 views were, from 2014, ordered to register as media, rendering them subject to various regulations. Resending "extremist" material was also criminalized, raising the possibility that a wrong retweet could lead to imprisonment. And anonymity was eliminated by a law that requires Russians to sign in with their phone number whenever they use Wi-Fi in public spaces. Preparing for possible new waves of protest, the authorities even tried simulating a complete cutoff of Russia from the global internet to be used in a crisis (Soldatov and Borogan 2015).

5. Conclusion

So how did the Putin regime adjust its political strategy—in particular, its use of repression, co-optation, censorship, and propaganda—in response to the global economic crisis? As we saw, this response passed through several phases.

The first, which lasted from 2009 to 2011, focused on emergency management. With extensive currency and fiscal reserves, the Kremlin could afford to delay any decisions about a more fundamental change. At the same time, Putin's remarkable approval rating at the start of the crisis—which hit 88 percent after Russia's brief war in Georgia—allowed him breathing room. In this period, the Kremlin concentrated on co-optation, boosting public spending to offset the pain felt by the population as the economy contracted. At the same time, the government allocated resources—albeit relatively sparingly—to bail out business interests. Yet, although this strategy deflected any major threat to the regime, it did not prevent the disillusionment of those in the upwardly mobile middle class who had been counting on the continuation of the previous boom. Increasing discontent among more modern and globalized circles in Moscow and other big cities contributed to the outburst of protest in 2011–12.

What brought this first phase to an end was both the shock of mobilized opposition to Putin in the streets of Moscow and the realization that, given the tepid pace of economic recovery, the Kremlin would need to conserve and target its reserves. The key objective of the second phase was to discredit and marginalize the urban opposition. Propaganda was stepped up, focused on the theme of Russian traditional values. Co-optation now targeted mostly core supporters—in particular, public sector workers—while repression and censorship (of both media and internet) were intensified in an attempt to block collective action and break the momentum of protests.

The theme of the third phase, which began with the covert invasion of Crimea, was war, first in Ukraine and later in Syria. From late 2013, Putin appeared to give up on a revival of rapid growth. With the international economy slowing down from Europe to China, depressing demand for oil, he largely abandoned co-optation and concentrated on blaming the West for the population's economic hardship, which he did less and less to alleviate. Indeed, Russia's open military confrontation with the West made economic conditions worse. Propaganda was raised to an unprecedented pitch, focused now on military conflict more than traditional values. Controls over media and internet were tightened still more, less at this point to disrupt the protest movement, which had in any case died away, than to dominate public discourse.

As economic conditions worsened and resources shrank, this did not lead—as might have been expected—to any observable reduction in favoritism toward Putin's close associates. Rather, the Kremlin sought to compensate these businessmen for losses suffered at the hands of Western governments, which sanctioned their travel and froze their foreign assets. At first sight, this might look like an attempt by the autocrat to shore up support within his selectorate (Bueno de Mesquita and Smith 2011). Yet the favored individuals—who include two old judo partners of Putin's and a former physicist turned banker—have no political resources that could threaten Putin's position. The special treatment might also reflect the Kremlin team's shortened time horizon, except that we know of no evidence that Putin sees his time in office as limited.

In sum, the case fits Guriev and Treisman's expectation that economic shocks can prompt the substitution of censorship and propaganda for co-optation of the opposition elite. It also fits the notion that leaders, facing a shortage of bread, may switch to circuses, or, in the Russian idiom, may seek to distract citizens from their emptying refrigerators with exciting drama on the television. Although the motives for Russia's interventions in Ukraine and Syria are more complicated, the initiation of military adventures after an economic shock is certainly consistent with the diversionary war view. That said, the change in strategy did not follow the economic crisis immediately, but materialized only after several years. Initial reserves of money and popularity allowed the regime to coast along for a while, waiting to see how economic conditions might develop.

We observe no effort by the authorities, in light of falling popularity, to strengthen their credibility by increasing media freedom and the honesty of elections. Rather, the fall in the reputation of the pro-Putin United Russia party during 2011 was followed by a parliamentary election that was plausibly portrayed as one of the most fraudulent in postcommunist history. Pressures on both the media and internet intensified. By contrast, it was in the era of post-Crimea soaring ratings that the Kremlin did seem concerned to reduce the appearance of fraud in the legislative elections of 2016. The long-serving head of the Central Electoral Commission, Vladimir Churov, nicknamed "the Magician" for his seeming ability to conjure up the Kremlin-favored electoral result, was replaced in March 2016 by a former human rights ombudswoman, Ella Pamfilova.[35] Nor do we observe any attempt to conserve resources by suspending corrupt favoritism in public contracts. While this could possibly reflect greater perceived insecurity of tenure among ruling circles, there is little supporting evidence for this view.

Whereas in some other countries well-organized ruling parties have been important tools by which authoritarian leaders maintained control at times of economic crisis, Putin's United Russia (UR) party is commonly viewed as a rickety construction, staffed by opportunists who would desert without hesitation if the party lost its dominance and funding. UR's reputation as the "party of crooks and thieves," as the opposition activist Alexei Navalny dubbed it, became such a liability that Putin himself sought to find some distance in 2011–12, setting up a loosely defined "National Front" as a parallel vehicle for mobilizing supporters. Instead, Putin's model depends on more direct mobilizational appeals that exploit his personal popularity and television image, as well as the "vertical of power" within the state. Governors and mayors are responsible for maintaining social order and ensuring electoral victories in their jurisdictions, and are managed in this regard by the political operatives of the presidential administration in the Kremlin.

NOTES

1. Spot price for Brent, average for year, BP, *Statistical Review of World Energy*, 2016, http://www.bp.com/en/global/corporate/energy-economics/statistical-review-of-world-energy.html

2. Except where indicated otherwise, all economic data cited are from the Russian state statistical agency Rosstat (previously Goskomstat). Its website is www.gks.ru

3. Data from the Central Bank of Russia at www.cbr.ru

4. Central Bank of Russia, *Byulleten Bankovskoy Statistiki* 12 (67) (1998), and 6 (181) (2008).

5. Ministry of Finance of the Russian Federation, www1.minfin.ru/ru/stabfund/statistics/volume/

6. See, for example, Guriev and Tsyvinski (2010).

7. Information from the Central Bank of Russia, at www.cbr.ru

8. MICEX stock index from October 24, 2003, to October 25, 2005, at www.moex.ru

9. Catherine Belton, "VTB in Bank of Moscow Victory," *Financial Times*, February 26, 2011; Catherine Belton, "Bank of Moscow Rescued with $14 billion State Bail-out," *Financial Times*, July 1, 2011.

10. Electoral manipulations and fraud had also existed in the 1990s, but the scale clearly increased in the 2000s (see, e.g., Fish 2005).

11. Authors' calculations from Levada Center *kurer* survey December 2007, available at sophist.hse.ru

12. This is the number as of March 2008, when *Forbes* published its global list. By the summer, when the Russian edition of *Forbes* published its list, the number had grown to 100.

13. Russia Today, "Russia Is an 'Island of Stability': Finance Minister," January 24, 2008. http://www.russiatoday.ru/Business/2008-01-24/Russia_is_an_island_of_stability_Finance_Minister.html

14. These data are based on reports posted on the namarsh.ru website, which compiles information from a network of regional correspondents as well as press and online sources. Web links to press coverage are provided to check accuracy of each event report.

15. Sergei Balashov, "Every Banker for Himself: While Businesses Must Now Swim on Their Own, the Government Is Reluctant to Economize on Social Spending," *Russia Profile*, May 27, 2009.

16. RIA Novosti, "Putin Instructs Government to Extend $806 Million Loan to AvtoVAZ," June 4, 2009; RIA Novosti, "Aluminum Giant RusAl Confirms $4.5 Bln Loan from VEB," November 5, 2008.

17. Ira Iosebashvili, "Medvedev Slams State Stock Purchase," *Moscow Times*, May 6, 2009.

18. RIA Novosti, "Russia's Anti-crisis Package to Hit 12% of GDP in 2009—Putin," Novokuznetsk, March 12, 2009; Reuters, "Factbox: How US Stimulus Plan Ranks against Other Programs," February 13, 2009.

19. Adrian Blomfield, "Vladimir Putin Humiliates Russian Supermarket Chiefs over Expensive Sausages," *Daily Telegraph*, June 25, 2009.

20. We can give only a range of estimates for 2008 since the Rotenberg brothers were below the $1 billion minimum threshold for *Forbes* in that year.

21. Levada Center, "*Dekabrsky indeks potrebitekskikh nastroenii*," December 30, 2015. http://www.levada.ru/old/30-12-2014/dekabrskii-indeks-potrebitelskikh-nastroenii

22. Authors' calculations from Levada Center *Kurer* surveys December 2008 and March 2010, available at sophist.hse.ru

23. David M. Herszenhorn, "Released Punk Rockers Keep Up Criticism of Putin," *New York Times*, December 23, 2013. http://www.nytimes.com/2013/12/24/world/europe/member-of-russian-punk-band-freed-under-amnestylaw.html

24. David M. Herszenhorn, "Russian Official Apologizes for Threatening Journalist," *New York Times*, June 14, 2012. http://www.nytimes.com/2012/06/15/world/europe/russian-official-apologizes-for-threatening-journalist.html

25. "Russia: Putin Goes from the Repressive to the Absurd," *The Guardian*, July 28, 2012. http://www.theguardian.com/commentisfree/2012/jul/29/observer-editorial-russia-putin-pussy-riot

26. Reporters Without Borders, "Vkontakte Social Network Targeted by Security Services," December 9, 2011. http://en.rsf.org/russie-vkontakte-social-network-targeted-06-12-2011,41519.html

27. Address by President of the Russian Federation, March 18, 2014. http://en.kremlin.ru/events/president/news/20603

28. Levada Center polls, "Odobrenie organov vlasti," http://www.levada.ru/indikatory/odobrenie-organov-vlasti/, last updated in Ocrober 2015.

29. Levada Center, *Prisoedinenie Kryma i uchastie rossiiskikh dobrovoltsev v konflikte na vostoke Ukrainy*, November 10, 2014. http://www.levada.ru/2014/11/10/prisoedinenie-kryma-i-uchastie-rossijskihdobrovoltsev-v-konflikte-na-vostoke-ukrainy/

30. "Rossiyane uvereny vo vrazhdebnosti zapada," Levada Center poll results, published on February 11, 2015.

31. In contrast to the capital account, the trade account has not posed any problems to the Kremlin. High exports of oil, gas, and other commodities have made for a trade surplus—and a current account surplus—in all years since Putin took office. The current account surplus in 2015 was $65.8 billion (see http://www.reuters.com/article/russia-economy-capital-idUSL8N1522RH).

32. H. Meyer, I. Arkhipov, and A. Katz, "Putin's Friends Reap Billions in Deals as Economy Teeters," Bloomberg, December 10, 2014. http://www.bloomberg.com/news/articles/2014-12-10/putins-friends-reap-billions-in-deals-as-economy-teeters

33. A. Garmazhapova, "Gde zhivut trolli. I kto ikh kormit," *Novaya Gazeta*, September 7, 2013. http://www.novayagazeta.ru/politics/59889.html; A. Chen, "The Agency," *New York Times*, June 2, 2015. http://www.nytimes.com/2015/06/07/magazine/the-agency.html?_r=0

34. Katherine Hille, "Axel Springer Joins Long Media March from Russia,"

Financial Times, September 17, 2015. http://www.ft.com/intl/cms/s/0/235ef22a-5d4f-11e5-97e9-7f0bf5e7177b.html#axzz3r8w7GvtG

35. See http://www.themoscowtimes.com/news/article/chairman-churov-removed-from-russian-central-election-commission/561443.html

REFERENCES

Acemoglu, Daron, and James A. Robinson. 2001. "A Theory of Political Transitions." *American Economic Review* 91 (4): 938–63.

Acemoglu, Daron, and James A. Robinson. 2005. *Economic Origins of Dictatorship and Democracy*. New York: Cambridge University Press.

Aris, Ben. 2015. "Russia's State Banks Are Rotten." *Business New Europe*, June 29. http://www.intellinews.com/russia-s-state-banks-are-rotten-500446794/?source=russia&archive=bne

Becker, Jonathan. 2004. "Lessons from Russia: A Neo-authoritarian Media System." *European Journal of Communication* 19 (2): 139–63.

Bermeo, Nancy. 2000. "Rethinking Regime Change." *Comparative Politics* 22: 359–77.

Brancati, Dawn. 2014. "Pocketbook Protests: Explaining the Emergence of Pro-democracy Protests Worldwide." *Comparative Political Studies* 47 (11): 1503–30.

Brückner, Markus, and Antonio Ciccone. 2011. "Rain and the Democratic Window of Opportunity." *Econometrica* 79: 923–47.

Bueno de Mesquita, Bruce, and Alastair Smith. 2010. "Leader Survival, Revolutions, and the Nature of Government Finance." *American Journal of Political Science* 54 (4): 936–50.

Bueno de Mesquita, Bruce, and Alastair Smith. 2011. *The Dictator's Handbook: Why Bad Behavior Is Almost Always Good Politics*. New York: PublicAffairs.

Bueno de Mesquita, Bruce, Alastair Smith, Randolph M. Siverson, and James D. Morrow. 2003. *The Logic of Political Survival*. Cambridge, MA: MIT Press.

Dagaev, Dmitry, Natalia Lamberova, Anton Sobolev, and Konstantin Sonin. 2015. "Recurrent Revolutions." Los Angeles: UCLA.

Durnovo, Grigory. 2015. "Politicheskie repressii v Rossii v 2011–2014 godakh: ugolovnie presledovania." OVDINFO.org. http://reports.ovdinfo.org/2014/cr-report/

Fish, Steven. 2005. *Democracy Derailed*. New York: Cambridge University Press.

Geddes, Barbara. 1999. "What Do We Know about Democratization after Twenty Years?" *Annual Review of Political Science* 2: 115–44.

Guriev, Sergei, and Daniel Treisman. 2015. "How Modern Dictators Survive: An Informational Theory of the New Authoritarianism." NBER Working Paper No. 21136. Cambridge, MA: NBER.

Guriev, Sergei, and Alex Tsyvinski. 2010. "Challenges Facing the Russian Economy after the Crisis." In *Russia after the Global Economic Crisis*, ed. Anders Aslund, Sergei Guriev, and Andrew Kuchins. Washington, DC: Peterson Institute, 9–38.

Guriev, Sergei, and Ekaterina Zhuravskaya. 2009. "(Un)happiness in Transition." *Journal of Economic Perspectives* 23 (2): 143–68.

Haggard, Stephan, and Robert Kaufman. 1995. *The Political Economy of Democratic Transitions*. Princeton: Princeton University Press.

Hastings, Max, and Simon Jenkins. 1983. *The Battle for the Falklands.* New York: Norton.
King, Gary, Jennifer Pan, and Margaret E. Roberts. 2013. "How Censorship in China Allows Government Criticism but Silences Collective Expression." *American Political Science Review* 107 (2): 326–43.
Lamberova, Natalia, and Konstantin Sonin. 2018. "The Role of Business in Shaping Economic Policy in Putin's Russia." In *The New Autocracy: Information, Politics, and Policy in Putin's Russia*, ed. Daniel Treisman. Washington, DC: Brookings Institution Press, 137–58.
Levy, Jack S., and Lily I. Vakili. 1993. "Diversionary Action by Authoritarian Regimes: Argentina in the Falklands/Malvinas Case." In *The Internationalization of Communal Strife*, ed. Manus I. Midlarsky. New York: Routledge, 118–45.
Londregan, John B., and Keith T. Poole. 1996. "Does High Income Promote Democracy?" *World Politics* 49 (1): 1–30.
Magaloni, Beatriz. 2008. *Voting for Autocracy: Hegemonic Party Survival and Its Demise in Mexico.* New York: Cambridge University Press.
Olson, Mancur. 1993. "Dictatorship, Democracy, and Development." *American Political Science Review* 87 (3): 567–76.
Robertson, Graeme. 2013. "Protesting Putinism: The Election Protests of 2011–2012 in Broader Perspective." *Problems of Post-Communism* 60 (2): 11–23.
Rozenas, Arturas. 2015. "Office Insecurity and Electoral Manipulation." New York: New York University.
Soldatov, Andrei, and Irina Borogan. 2015. "Putin Trolls Facebook: Privacy and Moscow's New Data Laws." *Foreign Affairs.com*, November 3. https://www.foreignaffairs.com/articles/russianfederation/2015-11-03/putin-trolls-facebook
Thornhill, John. 2015. "Lunch with the FT: Pavel Durov." July 3. http://www.ft.com/intl/cms/s/0/21c5c7f2-20b1-11e5-ab0f-6bb9974f25d0.html
Treisman, Daniel. 2007. "Putin's Silovarchs." *Orbis*, Winter.
Treisman, Daniel. 2011a. *The Return: Russia's Journey from Gorbachev to Medvedev.* New York: Free Press.
Treisman, Daniel. 2011b. "Presidential Popularity in a Hybrid Regime: Russia under Yeltsin and Putin." *American Journal of Political Science* 55 (3): 590–609.
Treisman, Daniel. 2014. "Putin's Popularity since 2010: Why Did Support for the Kremlin Plunge, Then Stabilize?" *Post-Soviet Affairs* 30 (5): 370–88.
Treisman, Daniel. 2015. "Income, Democracy, and Leader Turnover." *American Journal of Political Science* 59 (4): 927–42.
Treisman, Daniel. 2016. "Russia's Billionaires." *American Economic Review* 106 (5): 236–41.
World Bank. 2008. *Russian Economic Report* 17 (November). Washington, DC: World Bank.
Yakovlev, Evgeny, and Ekaterina Zhuravskaya. 2004. "State Capture and Controlling Owners of Firms." Center for Economic and Financial Research (CEFIR) Working Paper No. w0044.

FIVE

Crises, Coalitions, and Change in Indonesia and Malaysia

Thomas Pepinsky

In this chapter I examine the politics of economic adjustment under authoritarian regimes, focusing on two countries and two economic shocks: the 1980s crises and the Asian Financial Crises in Indonesia and Malaysia. Pairing these two countries and these two crises provides some useful analytical leverage over important factors that explain how authoritarian regimes in emerging market economies manage economic crises. These include the institutional structure of the authoritarian regime, the depth of the economic crisis, the specific nature of the crisis, the role of the opposition, and most importantly for my account, coalitional politics within authoritarian regimes. I will argue, drawing on previous research (Pepinsky 2008, 2009), that these cases illustrate the importance of the specific distributional consequences of economic crises and how their burdens fall across regime supporters for explaining when and how economic shocks unseat authoritarian regimes.

I will also highlight the scope conditions of my account, and address the comparisons that can be drawn across different types of crises at different points in time. Perhaps the most theoretically important claim that I aim to make is that strategies of economic adjustment affect coalitional politics over the medium term. The effects of crises on coalitions in the context of one shock can set the stage for which coalitions are in place during a subsequent shock. This longer perspective on how coalitions—or alternatively, factions or cleavages or interest groups—evolve over the medium to long term reminds us that authoritarian regimes are not fixed or static entities, but rather evolving orders.

A summary of the material to be covered appears in table 5.1. The mid-1980s crises in Indonesia and Malaysia led to further liberalization and privatization in each economy, which had implications for the coalitional foundations of each country's authoritarian regime without upsetting the regime itself.

A second, much more acute, and much more politically divisive economic crisis in the late 1990s had much starker policy consequences. Whereas in the 1980s both Indonesia and Malaysia found relatively straightforward policy solutions, the same was not true in 1998, and the two diverged dramatically in terms of both crisis response and political consequences.

Why did two different crises yield two different outcomes? In what follows I will argue that the 1980s crises in Indonesia and Malaysia were "easy" crises. In neither case was the crisis particularly severe, and, moreover, in neither case did adjustment measures place any fundamental stress on the coalitional alignments that undergirded either regime. The Asian Financial Crisis of 1997–98, by contrast, created "hard" crises in Indonesia and Malaysia. What made them difficult was not just the magnitude of the shock—which itself is endogenous to each country's response to it (see also MacIntyre 2001)—but rather the political conflict that the crisis unleashed. That conflict tore apart the New Order regime in Indonesia, and tested Malaysia's Barisan Nasional regime by galvanizing a broad opposition coalition. Importantly, key coalition partners in both Indonesia and Malaysia had seen their fortunes rise in the 1990s as a result of the liberalization

TABLE 5.1. The Comparisons in Brief

	Mid-1980s Crisis	*Asian Financial Crisis*
Indonesia	Policy consequence: liberalization and privatization Coalition effects: new capitalists, military balanced Regime outcome: survival	Policy consequence: structural adjustment Coalition effects: conflict between fixed and mobile capital Regime outcome: breakdown
Malaysia	Policy consequence: liberalization and privatization Coalition effects: new capitalists, masses balanced Regime outcome: survival	Policy consequence: heterodox adjustment Coalition effects: none regime outcome: survival

and privatization policies that had followed the 1980s crises. In this way, it is possible to link crisis responses to subsequent political conflict.

The lessons from these cases mirror some of the insights from other chapters in this collection. For example, Sean Yom's chapter describes how the oil crisis of the 1980s led to a sharp economic contraction in Jordan that restricted the Jordanian regime's ability to channel funds to traditional tribal elites. What followed was a shift toward a new business elite amid economic restructuring, with the implication that the coalitional structure of the regime had changed as an indirect consequence of the crisis. Relatedly, Lisa Blaydes's chapter describes how international sanctions during the 1990s crippled the Iraqi regime, forcing it to moderate its strategy of directing resources toward Saddam Hussein's core Sunni base. The consequence was a decline in support for Saddam from among his coethnic support base, representing a noticeable shift in the logic of regime maintenance in the regime's final years. These and other examples from this volume illustrate how coalitions can become the dependent variable of analysis during a more protracted crisis, even as they continue to constrain regime strategies in the short to medium term.

In the next section I review the basic macroeconomic facts from the two sets of crises, to illustrate just how the two countries differed during the two periods. I then give a broad overview of authoritarian rule in the two countries, focusing on their basic institutional architectures and the groups that supported the regime going into the 1980s. I then outline the policy choices that were adopted as a result of the 1980s crisis and the political consequences of each, and then describe how the late 1990s crises revealed fundamental tensions within Indonesia's authoritarian regime that ultimately drove Soeharto from power. The final section concludes with some reflections on the broader theoretical lessons that can be drawn from this comparative exercise, and interprets the defeat of Malaysia's authoritarian government in 2018 election in terms of the logic of regime maintenance outlined below.

Two Sets of Crises

The crises of the 1980s in Indonesia and Malaysia were external crises that resulted from the global economic slowdown that followed the oil shocks of the early 1980s. In Indonesia, net oil exports fell from a peak of US$ 9.3 billion in 1981–82 to US$1.4 billion in 1986–87 (World Bank 1994, Table 3.1). In the Malaysian case, falling petroleum prices combined with

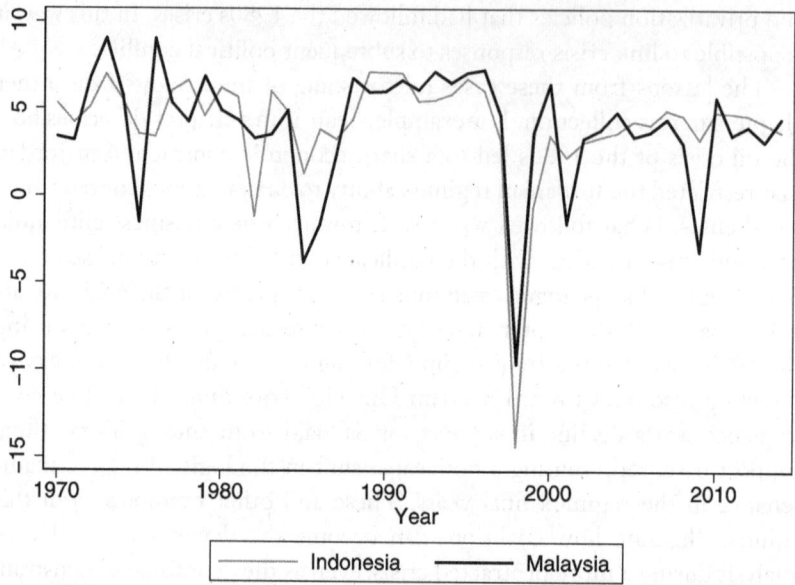

Fig. 5.1. Per Capita GDP Growth Rates, 1970–2014
Source: World Bank 2015b.

falling prices for other key commodity exports such as palm oil, rubber, and tin to produce a substantial fall in commodity export revenues (World Bank 1989, 15–16). Although these are sharp export contractions, when viewed in the contexts of the 1990s crises (described below), the economic setbacks of the 1980s were relatively mild. They did, however, persist for several years, resulting in anemic macroeconomic performance over half a decade rather than an abrupt reversal. Figure 5.1 charts the evolution of economic growth in the two countries from 1970 until 2014.

As the figure makes clear, Indonesia suffered one year of negative economic growth in 1982, but growth remained slow for the next several years. Malaysian growth remained positive until 1985, but the country then experience two years of economic contraction. At its worst, Indonesia's economy contracted at a rate of –1.2 percent per year, registered in 1982; in the case of Malaysia, the worst year of the 1980s saw its economy contract by –3.8 percent in 1985. On the whole, though, the entire decade of the 1980s saw only modest economic growth: an average of 3 percent per year in Malaysia and 4.1 percent in Indonesia.

When considering the potential political effects of these two crises, it is useful to examine effects on employment, government revenues, and government expenditures. Unfortunately, comparable time series data on employment and revenues are not available for either country in the 1980s. However, two OECD-sponsored analyses are useful sources of information. Demetry and Demetry (1992, 55–64) show that after years of strong employment in Malaysia, responding to strong growth in the construction sectors as well as active public investment in the 1980s, the mid-1980s witnessed a sharp rise in unemployment. At the same time, however, Malaysia saw rises in real wages, and precrisis levels of social development expenditures were maintained during the adjustment period. This suggests that the Malaysian government's adjustment measures mitigated the effects of the retrenchment on popular welfare. In the case of Indonesia, data on employment are scarce, but effects on wage rates are useful for capturing how the crisis was felt. Thorbecke (1992, 50–55) finds that only public sector employees experienced declining real wages; by contrast, manufacturing sector real wages continued to increase during the crisis, while other sectors saw wage rages stagnate. Poverty indicators, on the whole, continued to improve throughout this period. As in Malaysia, the conclusion is Indonesia's adjustment during the mid-1980s crisis shielded most of its citizens from bearing the brunt of the crisis.

Finally, we can examine the effects of the crisis on government expenditure. Figure 5.2 plots government final consumption expenditure, both in constant dollar terms and as a percentage of GDP, from 1970. The figures reveal that there was a slight dip in total government expenditures in both countries in the early 1980s. The dip also appears in expenditure to GDP ratios, but is hard to distinguish from the volatility characteristic of the preceding decade.

The more important finding from figure 5.2, though, is that *following* the crises of the 1980s, government expenditure as a percentage of GDP fell steadily, reflecting the privatization and liberalization policies that followed those crises.

The crises of the late 1990s differed starkly from the crises of the 1980s. Most immediately, the most striking difference was the severity of the contraction, with Malaysia registering a growth rate of –9.6 percent for 1998, and Indonesia a staggering contraction of –14.4 percent the same year. The second notable difference was in the abruptness of the shock. Relative to modest growth averages in the 1980s, between 1990 and 1996 Indonesia had grown on average by 6.2 percent and Malaysia by 6.7 percent. This represented a truly massive reversal in economic fortune for two countries that had enjoyed widespread acclaim as success stories among Asia's emerging markets.

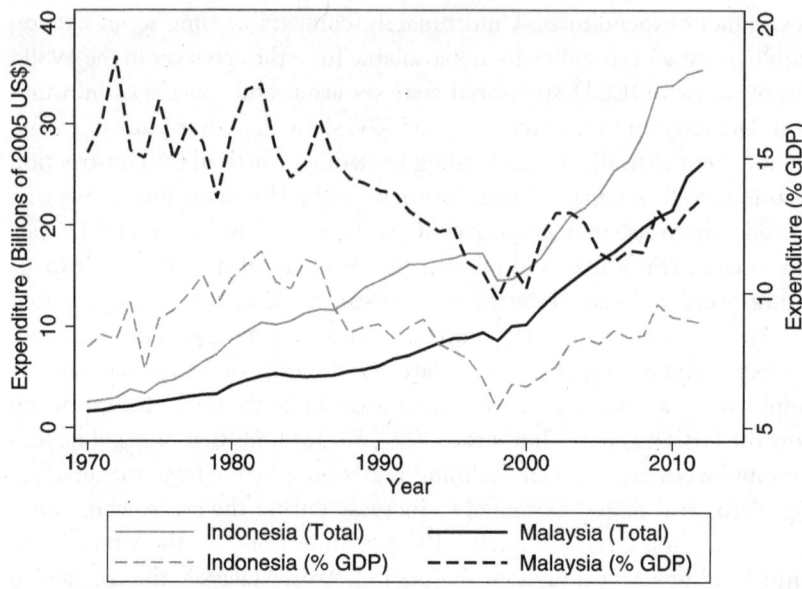

Fig. 5.2. Government Expenditure, 1970–2014
Source: World Bank 2015d.

What was the Asian Financial Crisis about? The literature on the causes of the crisis is enormous (for a diverse but incomplete set of views, see, e.g., Corsetti, Pesenti, and Roubini 1999; Montes 1998; Pempel 1999; Radelet and Sachs 1998; Woo, Sachs, and Schwab 2000). Rather than review it here, I highlight several important features of the two countries' economies. The first is *managed yet overvalued exchange rates*: both Indonesia and Malaysia had operated with quasi-pegged exchange rates that were significantly overvalued, which left them vulnerable to speculative attacks. The second is *imprudent financial management* of *financially open economies*, in which a lax regulatory environment allowed both banks and firms to borrow imprudently, and often without hedging against exchange rate risk. The third is *widespread directed credit*, often tied to individual cronies and corporate allies of ruling elites in both countries. This became particularly important during the freewheeling 1990s, during which market participants came to believe that the long-standing political regimes in these two high-performing economies would be able to protect the interests in the event of a negative downturn. The interaction of these three factors produced an accumulation of bad loans fed by buoyant expectations about future economic performance, but in a context of significant exposure to

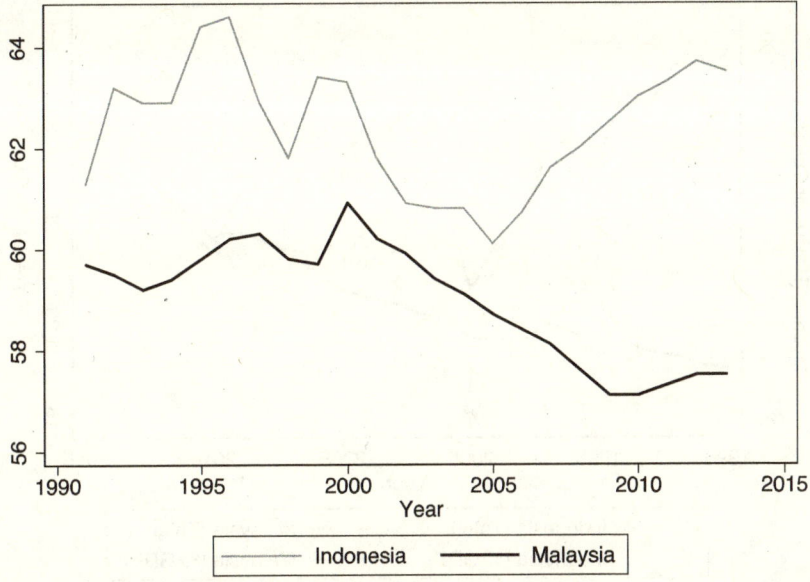

Fig. 5.3. Employment Rates, 1991–2014
Source: World Bank 2015c.

cross-border financial contagion. After the bursting of the Thai property bubble and the floating of the baht in summer 1997, speculators saw in Indonesia and Malaysia two countries with unsustainable currency pegs. The subsequent attacks against the ringgit and rupiah ultimately led to devaluations, after which the true depth of domestic financial mismanagement became even more apparent, thus beginning a vicious cycle leading to truly massive capital outflows, crises in the banking sector, wild swings in exchange markets, and fierce resistance by elites in both regimes to much-needed reforms.

I will outline the political battles unleashed by the Asian Financial Crisis in Indonesia and Malaysia below. For now, I turn to government revenues, expenditures, and unemployment. Unlike the 1980s, there are comparable data from the 1990s to gauge the consequences of the crisis for aggregate employment.

The dip in employment rates is clear in both countries, but the magnitudes are small relative to prior trends, with unemployment rates actually higher in the early 1990s in Malaysia than at the depth of its crisis. I will argue below that this reflects a deliberate strategy on the part of Malaysia's regime to adjust to the crisis in ways that would protect employment. In

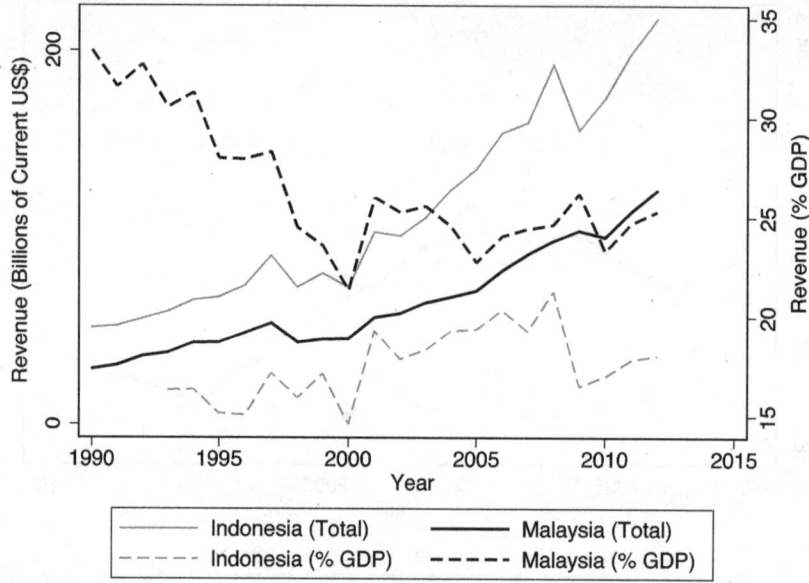

Fig. 5.4. Central Government Revenue, 1990–2012
Source: Author's calculations from International Monetary Fund 2013.

the case of Indonesia, the unemployment shock was larger. It is important to note, however, that these figures do not take into account the capacity of the rural sector to absorb those urban unemployed. It is likely, in other words, that Indonesia experienced much greater labor market churning during the crisis than those figures reflect. Figure 5.3 also illustrates that employment rates began to decline in the 2000s in both countries, well after the conclusion of the crisis itself, and in turn began to diverge in the late 2000s. I do not address the source of this postcrisis employment decline in this chapter, but my analysis would suggest that this is especially threatening for Malaysia's regime.

Comparable data also exist for revenue for the 1990s. In figure 5.4, I show trends in total central government revenue (solid lines) and revenue as a share of GDP. The revenue trends show clear dips below trends in both countries between 1998 and 2000. Because economic output shrank at the same time, though, we do not observe a similar dip in revenue as a share of GDP until 2000, when both economies had begun to grow once again.

Finally, in terms of government expenditures, we can return to figure 5.2. After a decade of steady declines in government expenditures as a fraction of GDP, the Asian Financial Crisis saw government expenditures reach their lowest points in each country's history. The total expenditure figures reveal as well that in 1998, total expenditures contracted in both countries. Malaysia, however, returned to trend in 1999, whereas Indonesia's expenditure figures remained lower than the precrisis peak for several more years.

Regime Structures and Support Coalitions

Having described the two sets of crises in the two countries, their origins, and their macroeconomic implications, I now step back to consider the political structures and support coalitions that undergirded each regime. First I consider each country's formal institutions and social structures, and then address what I consider to be the deeper politics of regime maintenance in both countries by describing the key coalitional alliances in each. My focus in this section is on describing institutions and social structures by the beginning of the 1980s, because my analysis below will turn to the ways in which these structures and coalitions evolved in the wake of the 1980s crisis.

Indonesia by 1980 was firmly under the control of the New Order regime. The name "New Order" (Orde Baru) reflected a decisive break from the government of Sukarno, which had struggled to balance competing nationalist, communist, and religious elements in the newly independent state. President Soeharto, by this time unchallenged as the peak figure in Indonesian politics, was a former general who had seized power from Sukarno following the abortive coup of September 30, 1965, and the subsequent extermination of the Indonesian Left. This meant that the Indonesian military played a central role in politics, with Soeharto's subordinates in the military occupying key positions in bureaucracy and administration, the fusion of military and police, the maintenance of the military's territorial command structure that placed military units throughout the country, and the promulgation of a military doctrine of dual function (*dwifungsi*) that considered the armed forces to have both a security and a "sociopolitical" function.

However, the New Order rested on far more than military control. It also adapted mass political institutions—themselves held over from Indonesia's brief period of liberal democracy in the early 1950s—for the purposes of mobilization, organization, and indoctrination. The key institution here was the corporatist body Golkar (*Golongan Karya*, or functional groups), which had emerged under Sukarno as an initial attempt to create an alternative to the fractious competition among different partisan groups (see Reeve 1985). Golkar was officially a "mass organization," not a political party, but it competed in controlled elections with two other political parties, the Indonesian Democratic Party and the United Development Party. Both were created in 1971, on Soeharto's directive, as controlled successors to various nationalist, liberal, socialist, Islamist, and other political parties that had previously competed in Indonesian elections. Representatives from each sat in the House of Representatives, and together with representatives from the armed forces, comprise the People's Consultative Assembly (MPR). While elections were never free or fair under the Soeharto regime, these legislative bodies did persist throughout the New Order, and did claim to provide a forum for interest representation. A final notable feature of the New Order was the central role of a core ideology, Pancasila, a set of five multireligious, developmentalist, and integrative principles held to represent the core values of the Indonesian nation. Pancasila too had its origins long before the New Order, but under the New Order became central to regime maintenance. By 1983, in fact, every organization in Indonesia was obliged to pledge that its sole foundation was Pancasila.

Malaysia, in 1980, had seen the consolidation of the Barisan Nasional regime. The Barisan Nasional—or "National Front"—is a coalition comprised of the United Malays National Organisation (UMNO), the Malaysian Chinese Association (MCA), and the Malaysian Indian Congress (MIC), alongside several smaller parties on the peninsula and an ever-changing roster of parties drawn from Sabah and Sarawak in East Malaysia. UMNO has always been the largest party in the coalition. In 1980, it held 69 out of the 154 seats in the Dewan Rakyat, Malaysia's lower house of parliament. By contrast, the MCA held 17 and the MIC only 3. In the 1982 elections UMNO would increase its seats to 70, with MCA increasing to 24 and MIC increasing to 4. The BN was formed in the wake of the suspension of parliamentary democracy from 1969 to 1971, which came on the heels of an unexpectedly poor electoral showing by the three main BN parties in 1969.[1] The suspension of parliamentary democracy from 1969 to 1971 was a critical juncture in Malaysian history, for it was the period that solidified UMNO control over Malaysian politics, and inaugurated critical policy and institutional changes in a decidedly more pro-Malay direction (Crouch 1996, 96–97; Goh 1971; Gomez and Jomo 1999, 21–23).

Unlike Indonesia, the Malaysian military has never played an active role in Malaysian politics. No prime minister of Malaysia has ever been drawn from the armed forces, for example. There has never been a coup, nor a serious threat of one. However, the nonpresence of the Malaysian armed forces as an active factor in national politics should not be confused with the military's irrelevance for Malaysian politics. As Enloe (1978) observed nearly four decades ago, Malaysia's military and police forces match patterns found in other countries where ethnicity and the military have been much more salient and contentious issues: the colonial government created the armed forces out of indigenous Malay majority, that pattern has persisted since independence, the independence period saw an armed conflict between the largely Malay security forces and a largely non-Malay communist resistance, there are few non-Malay military elites today, and non-Malays who are in the armed forces tend to occupy noncombat positions. Another revealing issue is that ministries such as Home Affairs, Defense, and Internal Security (the names and portfolios change periodically) have nearly always been held by either the prime minister or the deputy prime minister. The Malaysian security forces are "apolitical," then, precisely because they are so tightly fused to the country's civilian institutions.[2]

Institutionally, then, the key difference between Indonesia and Malaysia in 1980 was that Indonesia's New Order regime joined together both Golkar and the armed forces with explicit and formal roles in Indonesian politics, whereas Malaysia's BN regime was a civilian regime in which a dominant party stood at the apex of political power and ruled through a legislature. These institutional structures would remain in place throughout the 1980s and into the 1990s for Indonesia, and remain the case until today for Malaysia. The differences are readily apparent in three prominent authoritarian regime codings, as summarized in table 5.2.

The key difference between the countries is the presence of the military as integral to the New Order regime under Soeharto. Geddes, Wright, and Frantz (2014), importantly, code Indonesia as a "triple threat" in which elements of civilian, military, and personalist rule are all present. Soeharto is that personalist figure in Indonesia. In Malaysia, Mahathir

TABLE 5.2. Classifying Political Regimes

	Indonesia	Malaysia
Cheibub, Gandhi, and Vreeland 2010	Civilian dictatorship (1949–65) Military dictatorship (1966–98) Presidential democracy (1999–)	Civilian dictatorship (1958–)
Geddes, Wright, and Frantz 2014	Personalist (1950–66) Triple threat (1967–99)	Party based (1958–)
Wahman, Teorell, and Hadenius 2007, 2013	Military multiparty (1972–96) Limited multiparty (1997–2003) Democracy (2004–)	Democracy (1972–73) Limited multiparty (1974–)

Mohamad came to play a similar dominant role in the country's politics during the 1980s and 1990s, so much so that observers in the early 2000s began to describe Malaysian politics as having become "personalized" (Hwang 2003; Slater 2003).

If we turn away from the formal structure of government to the *informal* bases of authoritarian politics as rooted in each country's support base, another contrast between the two countries is apparent. That is between the ethnic *redistributivist* and fundamentally *mobilizational* BN regime in Malaysia, and the *developmentalist* yet ultimately *elite-focused* New Order regime. I have described this contrast and its historical origins at length elsewhere (Pepinsky 2009, 40–81), but the main contours are straightforward to describe. Indonesia's New Order did not depend on the support of the Indonesian masses, nor did it consistently appeal to them through programmatic policies. Instead, the New Order regime relied directly on the support of two fractions of capitalist interests, a set of indigenous (*pribumi*) entrepreneurs whose fortunes were nurtured by their access to state institutions such as the military and the bureaucracy, and a set of ethnic Chinese business cronies with substantial financial assets who profited from close access to Soeharto and other *pribumi* elites. In Malaysia, by contrast, the BN regime relied directly on the support of the country's Malay masses— UMNO is a party exclusively for *bumiputeras*, and campaigns openly and regularly on protecting the "special rights" reserved for Malays in the country's constitution. The New Economy Policy (NEP), promulgated in 1971 and continued under various new guises until today, targets *bumiputeras* in a range of redistributive economic and social policy schemes. In sum, UMNO ruled because it won elections, and it won elections because voters voted for the BN. UMNO paired electoral support with direct support from a class of *bumiputera* capitalists who provided funding and political support in exchange for the continuation of redistributive policies.

It is important not to confuse coalitional support for policy attention. Both New Order Indonesia and Malaysia under the BN were effective developmentalist regimes for the last third of the twentieth century. Under both, absolute poverty rates fell, human development indicators rose, and millions upon millions of Indonesians and Malaysians gained reliable access to basic human services. The difference between policy attention and coalitional support is that the latter implies an exchange of policy for quiescence, while the former does not, meaning that from the perspective of a regime, it must provide its supporters with desired policy or risk being overthrown. In the case of the New Order regime, the regime's indifference to representing mass interests meant that developmentalist policymaking was possible—and indeed, stabilizing—but not required for regime survival. In the case of the BN, regime survival without attention to Malay interests, both capital and the masses, was impossible.

As a consequence, the "veto players" under authoritarian rule in Indonesia and Malaysia differ in important ways, both in their number and in their interest profiles. Indonesia's veto players lay in the military and the burgeoning business sector; they were relatively few in number, had interests in political stability and economic order to facilitate capital accumulation, and were relatively indifferent to mass interests (but in no way opposed to widely shared growth and development). Malaysia's veto players lay both in the ruling party of UMNO, and indirectly, in its mass constituency of Malay voters. This means the veto players were more dispersed in number, and united in their preference for pro-*bumiputera* policies (but, too, in no way opposed to widely shared growth and development).

Finally, the role of each regime in managing finance is worthy of particular attention when discussing the politics of financial crises. Malaysia's financial sector features a large and relatively well-developed equity market, whereas prior to the 1990s Indonesia's financial sector was dominated by banks (and through the crisis of 1997 the Jakarta stock exchange remained relatively unimportant in a bank-based financial system). The origins of these differences can be traced to the colonial period (Pepinsky 2012), but in practice this means that Malaysia's stock market is more important for financial control than in Indonesia. UMNO's corporate allies benefited through the stock exchange from cheap tenders and government mobilization of popular savings, whereas Soeharto's allies tended to receive credit directly through loans. On one hand, this made UMNO particularly vulnerable to stock price fluctuations and to changes in investor sentiment. On the other hand, the Malaysian regime's ability to mobilize saving allowed non-Malay interests to profit from healthy stock performance, which allowed them to share in the fruits of development in ways that Indonesians frozen out of the New Order's coalition never could.

One consequence of this difference in capital market structures might have been differential amounts of cross-border diversification between Indonesians and Malaysians. However, data on cross-border asset holdings or portfolio flows in the two countries are scarce, especially dating back to the 1980s, and aggregate data would not allow for distinctions between supporters and opponents anyway. Qualitatively, it is clear that many ethnic Chinese cronies of the Soeharto regime also held assets overseas and invested overseas as well—recall that it was the ability to diversify overseas that was a precondition for their support for the Soeharto regime in the first place. But it is also true that many Malaysian Chinese firms have diversified overseas as well, with particular attention to Singapore, Hong Kong, and mainland China. This meant that both Indonesians and Malaysians had the ability to move assets overseas prior to the crisis of 1997–98. The more interesting question for most political economy approaches to Chinese business in Malaysia has in fact been explaining how Chinese capital that has remained in Malaysia has been able to accommodate pressures stemming from the NEP and the government's pro-Malay corporate and financial policies (Gomez 1999).

Crisis, Adjustment, Evolution, Crisis, (Sometimes) Change

In my previous work I have described just how the shock of unanticipated currency depreciation affected political conflict in Indonesia and Malaysia in 1997, arguing that it was battles over adjustment measures that lay at the center of Indonesia's authoritarian breakdown and that severely tested Malaysia's BN. In this section, I detail how responses to the crisis of the 1980s had set the stage for this conflict.

The crises of the mid-1980s were ultimately mild in nature. These were certainly viewed as crises by the governments of the countries experiencing them, but in the context of anticipated difficult external conditions over the medium term. The policy planning documents *Repelita IV* in Indonesia (Government of Indonesia 1984) and the *Fifth Malaysia Plan* in Malaysia (Government of Malaysia 1986) both describe a need for consolidating public expenditures and reducing dependence on external credit. But these were crises that would be overcome through economic reform. As outlined above, each country's economy shrank, but in neither country did economic contraction translate into mass economic dislocation or widespread business failures. There were several important corporate scandals during this period in each country, and widespread acknowledgment that in each country, regime insiders were profiting from government protection amid the crisis (see, generally, Liddle 1988; Mauzy 1987). Governments tightened their belts modestly.

But politically, the most important implication of the crisis in both countries was its effect on policy reform (on the politics of these reforms, see Jomo 1987; Robison 1987). Confronted with declining oil revenues and saddled with inefficient state sectors, each country embarked on a series of adjustment reforms directed toward deregulation and privatization, on the basis of a common belief that inefficient public enterprises would be

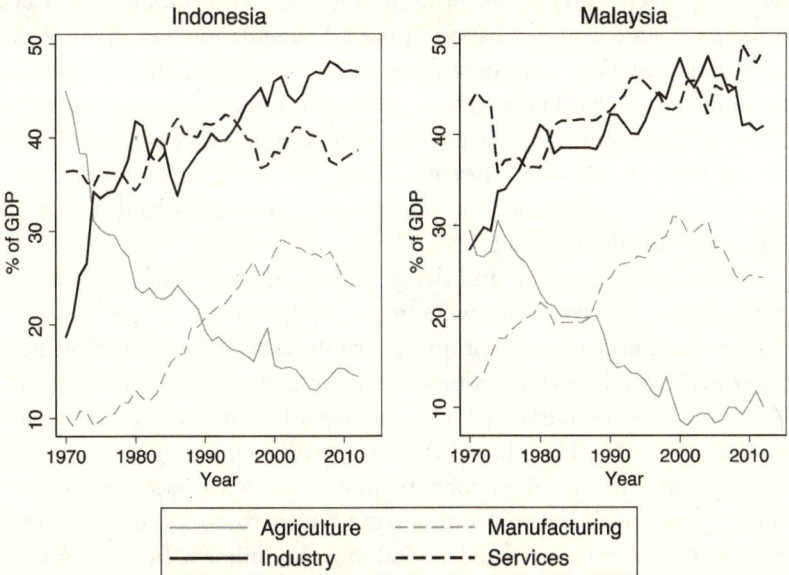

Fig. 5.5. Sectoral Value Added, Percentage of GDP
Source: World Bank (2015a).

replaced with more efficient ones once in private hands, and that the private sector would be better at allocating credit to worthwhile investments in sectors such as manufacturing, finance, and real estate. The implications for government expenditures of those deregulation and privatization measures can be observed in figure 5.2. Observers of Southeast Asian political economy frequently classify these policies as reflecting "Sadli's Law," that *bad times create good policies*.[3]

In point of fact, whether or not deregulation and privatization was on the whole "good" depends on how one evaluates the consequences, both immediate and long term. There is little doubt that privatization and deregulation invigorated domestic economies by allowing market mechanisms to operate more freely. In terms of deregulation as spurring market activity, adjustment measures were a success. The decade from 1986 until 1996 saw both countries' economies grow rapidly, with especially large gains in manufacturing and industry (see figure 5.5).

At the same time, however, deregulatory policies created few real losers. As detailed in various ways in multiple venues (Gomez and Jomo 1999, 75–116; Jomo 1995; MacIntyre 1994; Rasiah 1997; Robison 1997; Soesastro 1989), deregulation and privatization provided new opportunities for connected politicians, firms, businesses, and cronies to gain access to lucrative state assets at bargain prices. Deregulation and privatization worked because they were broadly consistent with the political coalitions that supported each regime. Thus, the mid-1980s crisis in no way forced either regime to reduce the size of its coalition or to restrict the perquisites flowing to those within it. Absent any fundamental conflict about adjustment, neither the crisis nor the adjustment measures adopted in its wake were politically destabilizing.

However, privatization and deregulation did change substantially the terms upon which coalitions were maintained, by empowering new capitalists and connected firms within the private sector who owed their newfound wealth to their connections with the regime (for a discussion of the Malaysian case, see Rasiah 1997; for a discussion of the Indonesian case, see Robison 1997). This shifted the relative balance of power within support coalitions in new directions. In Indonesia, newly ascendant cronies and members of Soeharto's own corrupt family rose to match the influence of older factions of fixed capital and the military. In Malaysia, the new Malay rich grew to increasing prominence in the country's political economy, enough that UMNO now was a party both of entrepreneurs and big business *and* of nurturing the still relatively poor Malay masses. It is not surprising that these changes—which had only accelerated developments in each country's political economy whose origins predated the crises of the 1980s—had political consequences. In Malaysia, UMNO experienced a fierce battle between a more traditionalist, establishment wing and newly ascendant Mahathirist faction; this ultimately led to an elite split and a near collapse of the party, only to see Mahathir's faction emerge victorious (Case 1993; Shamsul 1988; Singh 1991). In Indonesia, the rise of the cronies was accompanied by new factionalism within the military and conflict with the elites (Kammen and Chandra 1999), a new prominence among the country's long-repressed Islamic voices (Liddle 1996), which tended to align with the interests of *pribumi* capitalists, and other similar developments.

These political changes were not immediate consequences of the 1980s crisis itself. Rather, they were the indirect consequences of the crisis, which emerged endogenously from the adjustment measures that followed the crisis. It is of course true that these changes in each country's political coalition might have emerged without the 1980s crisis: Mahathir's aspirations would probably have conflicted with those of more traditional UMNO leaders even had Malaysia had a comfortable decade, and Soeharto had shown a particular blindness to his family's excesses for years. Counterfactually, we cannot know what would have happened had the mid-1980s not been lean times in Southeast Asia. But deregulation and privatization following the crisis, and the expansion of the relative political importance of the very same actors who benefited from those more market-oriented policies does suggest an evolution of each country's political order as an indirect consequence of that crisis.

Fast forward to mid-1997. The regimes in Indonesia and Malaysia now featured high-flying corporate sectors, buoyed by nearly a decade of strong economic growth and inflows of foreign capital under managed exchange rate regimes. When exchange markets turned against the rupiah and the ringgit, they exposed fragility within each country's financial sector, which led investors to update their beliefs about the sustainability of each country's economic model, further eroding exchange rates. Each country suddenly found itself suddenly experiencing a "twin crisis"—a simultaneous and causally interrelated banking and currency crisis (Kaminsky and Reinhart 1999; McKinnon and Pill 1998; Miller 1998). For the next two years, both countries struggled to find a way to restore confidence, expand the macroeconomy, protect domestic corporate allies, stabilize the exchange rate, and welcome back cross-border investment. The key to understanding why this mattered for authoritarian politics is to focus on how adjustment policies have differential impacts on different constituencies. Malaysia's BN found itself in the fortuitous situation that neither its corporate allies nor its mass base would oppose a heterodox adjustment strategy of repegging the ringgit, banning capital outflows, and implementing an aggressive macro stimulus. So after some delay, that is exactly what the regime implemented, with immediate salutary effects on economic recovery. Indonesia's New Order had no such luck: the bargain that united most of Soeharto's ethnic Chinese business allies with the newly ascendant *pribumi* entrepreneurs and the military was capital openness, which made a Malaysia-style heterodox adjustment plan politically impossible. The result was an incoherent, volatile reform strategy with reform pledges repeatedly broken and adjustment measures immediately undermined, with clear understanding that Soeharto himself understood that implementing serious reform would see him thrown out of office (see also Smith 2003).

That delay in Indonesia can be understood using a standard "delayed stabilization" framework, where the distributional costs of reform produce "blocking" (Alesina and Drazen 1991). But my larger argument is that it is this distributional conflict that produced authoritarian collapse in Indonesia (Pepinsky 2009, chs. 6 and 7). How exactly did this occur? It is helpful to begin with a review of some of the key developments of early 1998. The first was a prominent effort, spearheaded by one of Soeharto's daughters, to bolster the Indonesian exchange rate through a "Love the Rupiah movement" that encouraged Indonesians to donate gold and foreign exchange to the government, and to convert dollar holdings back into rupiah. This followed a meeting between several military figures and business elites (both ethnic Chinese and *pribumi*) to discuss how groups could work together to stabilize the economy. Also in January 1998, Golkar chairman Harmoko and retired general Syarwan Hamid spoke openly of "rats" who were betraying the nation by taking profits when others were showing loyalty by tightening their belts. At the same time, the Soeharto regime actually loosened what few restrictions existed on moving capital overseas, and stood by as bailout funds provided by Indonesian Bank Restructuring Agency to failed banks were converted into dollars and parked overseas instead of being used to stabilize balance sheets. After the March 1998 meeting of the MPR, which named Soeharto to his seventh five-year term as president and allowed him to install a number of close personal associates to important cabinet positions,[4] popular pressure began to mount for wholesale political change. University students played an important role, but so too did a broader range of civil society actors (see Aspinall 2005, ch. 8; Hefner 2000, chs. 6 and 7; Weiss 2005, ch. 7) who recognized that the erratic policymaking of the first half of 1998 reflected a regime fundamentally uninterested in protecting the interests of Indonesia's masses.

The microdetails about the actual fall of Soeharto in May 1998 are consistent with, if not themselves demonstrative of, a fracturing of the coalition between fixed capital (military, *pribumi* entrepreneurs) and mobile capital (ethnic Chinese cronies) that had undergirded the regime (in addition to the above sources, see Emmerson 1999; Forrester and May 1998; O'Rourke 2002). The key event preceding Soeharto's resignation on May 21 was mass riots in Jakarta that targeted, in particular, ethnic Chinese citizens. There is no consensus about the origins or ultimate responsibility for the riots; various interpretations hold that particular military officials, each with links to Soeharto but almost certainly not acting *on behalf of* or *on the orders of* Soeharto, fomented the disorder in order to force Soeharto's hand. One piece of evidence that the riots were somehow planned or encouraged is the ease with which they were stopped once the security forces chose to do so. In any case, these riots demonstrated to Soeharto's ethnic Chinese associates that the regime no longer had exclusive control over the security situation, and led to unprecedented—even for the time—capital flight.

It is unclear if the fracture of the coalition supporting Soeharto caused the riots, or if the riots brought that fracture to completion. We do know that over the next week, key figures—including Syarwan Hamid and

Harmoko—met privately with Soeharto and asked him to resign. Harmoko would later, in fact, become the first "inner circle" elite to announce publicly his demand for Soeharto's resignation. After a final two days spent in fruitless attempts to cobble together a new, Muslim-oriented coalition, Soeharto consulted with Wiranto, commander of the armed forces, to see if order could be restored under martial law. Assured that it could be but that there would be costs, Soeharto chose instead to resign. His successor, Vice President B. J. Habibie, would prove instrumental in overseeing Indonesia's transition to democracy in 1999 (for an account that emphasizes Habibie's importance, see Horowitz 2012).

Much of the intraelite politics of May 1998 remains unknown to us today, and may never be known. For example, we do not know if *pribumi* entrepreneurs were aware of impending moves within the military—I know of no evidence that they were. We also do not know the extent to which ethnic Chinese cronies spoke as a single voice. A group was called together by Soeharto in January 1998 and asked to contribute to economic recovery, but there is no evidence of deliberately coordinated behavior on the cronies' part.[5] However, one feature of this account that I did not emphasize in my previous work is that much rides on Soeharto's own personal decision to resign rather than to pursue those options that appear to have been available to him, cracking down decisively on protestors and employing the military's formidable special reserve forces to restore order. Whereas Liddle (1999) considers the last six months of Soeharto's rule to be an example of "failure of leadership," Soeharto's final act of resigning in favor of Habibie may be considered his last important accomplishment. Another noteworthy aspect of the final days of Soeharto's rule is the role played by protestors themselves. Their presence in the streets, and especially in front of the parliament building, is what led Wiranto to declare that restoring order would be costly. Had the costs of restoring order been lower, perhaps Soeharto would have been tempted to choose another, more militaristic course of action. That said, in my interpretation, protestors contributed to the fall of Soeharto by raising the costs of repression, not by directly forcing Soeharto from office. The key to the collapse of the regime in Indonesia was the fracture of the coalition of supporters within the regime, not pressure from without.

But why could elements of fixed and mobile capital not cooperate to bring the crisis to a close? After all, they had successfully coexisted—indeed, thrived—for three decades under Soeharto. The answer is because for the first time, the policies that would help fixed capital ran *directly contrary* to the interests of mobile capital. Even though these were only short-term distributional costs, and long-term cooperation plausibly would have left both factions better off, the severity of the adjustment costs would have almost certainly have pushed key firms out of business altogether. Theoretically, the problem is a standard intertemporal bargaining problem in which parties cannot credibly commit to respect their counterparts' interests in the future in exchange for sacrifice in the present (for formal treatments, see Acemoglu 2003; Acemoglu and Robinson 2006). The above discussions are evidence that key actors were aware of this problem, but under Soeharto's rule, no political institutions existed that would allow an intertemporal log roll in which one faction supporting Soeharto would bear the costs of crisis adjustment in exchange for disproportionate favoritism at some point in the future.

Concluding Thoughts and Speculations

I conclude this chapter by entertaining some theoretical considerations that emerge from related literatures on the politics of authoritarian rule, and that have particular implications for crisis politics. One particularly important question is whether "institutions mattered" in Indonesia and Malaysia. In my evaluation, it is hard to make a strong case that they did, at least based on a comparison of these four crises in these two countries. The best case for the success of authoritarian institutions would be Malaysia's UMNO and the 1990 elections. As noted above, these saw Mahathir reelected, and thus the defeat of the insurgent UMNO faction competing in alliances with each of the country's opposition parties. But I have argued elsewhere that the creation of "New UMNO" to sideline Mahathir's challengers is evidence not of the constraining or ordering effects of party institutions, but rather of the fundamental vulnerability of these institutions during periods of regime pressure (see Pepinsky 2014). That said, I do wish to emphasize that Mahathir's strategy worked because he and other members of his "Team A" could rely on state institutions that lay outside of the party itself: a registrar of societies who would transfer party assets to Mahathir's party, a judiciary that would rule in its favor, and so forth. This helps in illustrating just how states—not just parties—matter in shaping regimes' ability to endure over the long run (see Slater 2010, ch. 7).

Bringing in the Indonesian case for comparative reference, we also see that during the 1997–98 crisis, political institutions *did* do the work expected of them. The MPR session of 1998 returned Soeharto to office with strong support, for example. Golkar and the legislature remained united behind

Soeharto until the last week of his rule; indeed, Harmoko's turning against Soeharto was so powerful precisely because it was so unthinkable. These observations suggest to me that we must look elsewhere to understand regime collapse in Indonesia. The dangerous inference, one that we should avoid, is that we can conclude from the fact that Soeharto fell that Golkar and the legislature were somehow corroded or diminished as authoritarian political institutions.

Although the four crises provide ample evidence that the effects of institutions on regime survival are not as straightforward as they might appear to institutionalists, I do not think it is proper to pitch the argument I have made here, about how distributional conflict produces regime collapse, as an argument "against institutions." Complex outcomes such as regime survival and authoritarian breakdown have multiple antecedents, and we should understand any causal explanation as probabilistic. Had UMNO under Mahathir ruled Indonesia rather than Soeharto's New Order, perhaps a more orderly resolution of the Asian Financial Crisis would have been possible. Still, attention to the social bases of authoritarian rule and to the ways in which different groups of regime supporters produce different kinds of coalitions supporting authoritarian rule helps us to make sense of exactly when and why crises become threatening to incumbent regimes in the first place.

This point has implications for understanding the defeat of Malaysia's BN in 2018. The regime had been tested in unprecedented ways by the country's multiethnic opposition since 2008. The poor performance of Prime Minister Najib Razak both energized the opposition and ultimately led to a split within UMNO. However, Najib also fell victim to growing dissatisfaction with economic inequality and a series of high-level financial scandals. Does this comport with the logic of regime survival outlined in this chapter?

My presumption in answering this question is that the core logic of Malaysian politics had not changed between the 1980s and the mid-2010s, and that the coalition that confronted the Asian Financial Crisis—personnel changes aside—was essentially the same[6] right until Mahathir, Daim Zainuddin, and other UMNO elites defected to form a new Malay-based opposition party. This means that the regime continued to make policies that protected the economic position of the country's Malay masses and the regime's corporate allies, who were largely (if not exclusively) drawn from the *bumiputera* entrepreneurial elite. An economic shock that would bring down such a coalition would be one that could not be managed by redoubling redistributive policies toward the masses, or by paying off or bailing out corporate cronies—or even worse, set the two policies in opposition to one another, so that the regime cannot do both at the same time. In light of these considerations, the factional policies behind the "Malaysia Development Berhad" scandal were particularly important (Kassim 2015), as were recent trends of increased household indebtedness and growing federal budget deficits (Hazis 2015, 197–99). The former endangered the regime by highlighting the social costs of crony capitalism in a middle-income country. The latter endangered the regime by raising the fiscal costs of mass redistribution (note that the BN government introduced a highly unpopular goods and services tax in 2015). However, although these factors surely tested the BN, it was the ultimate defection of UMNO elites that explains the BN's defeat in the May 2018 general elections. This opened up the political space for two credible voices defending Malay interests, one of which was able to partner with the country's long-standing opposition movement to create an antiregime alliance. Although the path to regime change in Malaysia has not run through the mechanism of external economic crisis, the logic of authoritarian breakdown in Malaysia does reflect the logic of regime maintenance outlined above.

NOTES

1. Prior to 1969, the three main BN parties competed under the name the Alliance.

2. This point implies that if, counterfactually, events were to threaten seriously the BN regime, the military or police would intervene to stabilize the BN. I have heard suggestions from various Malaysians that this might be true; or more precisely, that it might have been true in the 1980s and 1990s.

3. The phrase is attributed to Mohamad Sadli, an Indonesian economist and New Order–era technocrat who is believed to have coined it, or at least popularized it, in the Indonesian context. See Hill and Wie 2008.

4. These include plywood tycoon Bob Hasan as minister of industry and trade, former tax authority director Fuad Bawazier as minister of finance, and Soeharto's daughter Tutut as minister of social affairs.

5. As I discuss in Pepinsky 2013, 93, distributional conflict does not require interest groups as conventionally understood.

6. For different articulations of continuity in Malaysian politics, see Case 2014 and Pepinsky 2015.

REFERENCES

Acemoglu, Daron. 2003. "Why Not a Political Coase Theorem? Social Conflict, Commitment, and Politics." *Journal of Comparative Economics* 31 (4): 620–52.

Acemoglu, Daron, and James A. Robinson. 2006. "Economic Backwardness in Political Perspective." *American Political Science Review* 100 (1): 115–31.

Alesina, Alberto, and Allan Drazen. 1991. "Why Are Stabilizations Delayed?" *American Economic Review* 81 (5): 1170–88.

Aspinall, Edward. 2005. *Opposing Suharto: Compromise, Resistance, and Regime Change in Indonesia*. Stanford: Stanford University Press.

Case, William. 1993. "Semi-democracy in Malaysia: Withstanding the Pressures for Regime Change." *Pacific Affairs* 66 (2): 183–205.

Case, William. 2014. "Malaysia in 2013: A Benighted Election Day (and Other Events)." *Asian Survey* 54 (1): 56–63.

Cheibub, José Antonio, Jennifer Gandhi, and James Raymond Vreeland. 2010. "Democracy and Dictatorship Revisited." *Public Choice* 143 (1–2): 67–101.

Corsetti, Giancarlo, Paolo Pesenti, and Nouriel Roubini. 1999. "Paper Tigers? A Model of the Asian Crisis." *European Economic Review* 43: 1211–36.

Crouch, Harold. 1996. *Government and Society in Malaysia*. Ithaca: Cornell University Press.

Demetry, David, and Lionel Demetry. 1992. *Adjustment and Equity in Malaysia*. Paris: Development Centre of the Organisation for Economic Co-operation and Development.

Emmerson, Donald K. 1999. "Exit and Aftermath: The Crisis of 1997–98." In *Indonesia beyond Suharto: Polity, Economy, Society, Transition*, ed. D. K. Emmerson. Armonk: M.E. Sharpe.

Enloe, Cynthia H. 1978. "The Issue-Saliency of the Military-Ethnic Connection: Some Thoughts on Malaysia." *Comparative Politics* 10 (2): 267–85.

Forrester, Geoff, and R. J. May, eds. 1998. *The Fall of Soeharto*. Bathurst, NSW: Crawford House.

Geddes, Barbara, Joseph Wright, and Erica Frantz. 2014. "Autocratic Breakdown and Regime Transitions: A New Data Set." *Perspectives on Politics* 12 (2): 313–31.

Goh, Cheng Teik. 1971. *The May Thirteenth Incident and Democracy in Malaysia*. Kuala Lumpur: Oxford University Press.

Gomez, Edmund Terence. 1999. *Chinese Business in Malaysia: Accumulation, Ascendance, Accommodation*. Richmon, Surrey: Curzon Press.

Gomez, Edmund Terence, and K. S. Jomo. 1999. *Malaysia's Political Economy: Politics, Patronage, and Profits*. New York: Cambridge University Press.

Government of Indonesia. 1984. *Rencana Pembangunan Lima Tahun Keempat, 1984/85–1988/89*. Jakarta: Bappenas.

Government of Malaysia. 1986. *Fifth Malaysia Plan, 1986–1990*. Kuala Lumpur: Economic Planning Unit.

Hadenius, Axel, and Jan Teorell. 2007. "Pathways from Authoritarianism." *Journal of Democracy* 18 (1): 143–56.

Hazis, Faisal S. 2015. "Malaysia in 2014: A Year of Political and Social Ferment." *Southeast Asian Affairs* 2015: 189–204.

Hefner, Robert W. 2000. *Civil Islam: Muslims and Democratization in Indonesia*. Princeton: Princeton University Press.

Hill, Hal, and Thee Kian Wie. 2008. "Moh. Sadli (1922–2008): Economist, Minister, and Public Intellectual." *Bulletin of Indonesian Economic Studies* 44 (1): 151–56.

Horowitz, Donald L. 2012. *Constitutional Change and Democracy in Indonesia*. New York: Cambridge University Press.

Hwang, In-won. 2003. *Personalized Politics: The Malaysian State under Mahathir*. Singapore: Institute of Southeast Asian Studies.
International Monetary Fund. 2013. "World Economic Outlook Database, October 2013." Retrieved from http://opendataforafrica.org/IMFWEO2013Oct/imf-world-economic-outlook-october-2013, November 16, 2015.
Jomo, K. S. 1987. "Economic Crisis and Policy Response in Malaysia." In *Southeast Asia in the 1980s: The Politics of Economic Crisis*, ed. Richard Robison, Kevin Hewison, and Richard A. Higgott. Sydney: Allen & Unwin.
Jomo, K. S., ed. 1995. *Privatizing Malaysia: Rents, Rhetoric, and Reality*. Boulder, CO: Westview Press.
Kaminsky, Graciela L., and Carmen M. Reinhart. 1999. "The Twin Crises: The Causes of Banking and Balance-of-Payments Problems." *American Economic Review* 89 (3): 473–500.
Kammen, Douglas, and Siddharth Chandra. 1999. *A Tour of Duty: Changing Patterns of Military Politics in Indonesia in the 1990s*. Ithaca: Southeast Asia Program, Cornell University.
Kassim, Yang Razali. 2015. "C015168 | 1MDB Crisis and Political Funding: Whither Malaysian Politics?" RSIS Commentary C015168 (August 12), available at https://www.rsis.edu.sg/wp-content/uploads/2015/08/CO15168.pdf
Liddle, R. William. 1988. "Indonesia in 1987: The New Order at the Height of Its Power." *Asian Survey* 28 (2): 180–91.
Liddle, R. William. 1996. "The Islamic Turn in Indonesia: A Political Explanation." *Journal of Asian Studies* 55 (3): 613–34.
Liddle, R. William. 1999. "Indonesia's Unexpected Failure of Leadership." In *Politics of Post-Suharto Indonesia*, ed. Adam Schwarz, and Jonathan Paris. New York: Council on Foreign Relations.
MacIntyre, Andrew. 1994. "Power, Prosperity and Patrimonialism: Business and Government in Indonesia." In *Business and Government in Industrializing Asia*, ed. A. MacIntyre. Ithaca: Cornell University Press.
MacIntyre, Andrew. 2001. "Institutions and Investors: The Politics of the Economic Crisis in Southeast Asia." *International Organization* 55 (1): 81–122.
Mauzy, Diane K. 1987. "Malaysia in 1986: The Ups and Downs of Stock Market Politics." *Asian Survey* 27 (2): 231–41.
McKinnon, Ronald I., and Huw Pill. 1998. "International Overborrowing: A Decomposition of Credit and Currency Risks." *World Development* 26 (7): 1267–82.
Miller, Victoria. 1998. "The Double Drain with a Cross-Border Twist: More on the Relationship between Banking and Currency Crises." *American Economic Review* 88 (2): 439–43.
Montes, Manuel F. 1998. *The Currency Crisis in Southeast Asia*. Updated ed. Singapore: Institute for Southeast Asian Studies.
O'Rourke, Kevin. 2002. *Reformasi: The Struggle for Power in Post-Soeharto Indonesia*. Sydney: Allen & Unwin.
Pempel, T. J., ed. 1999. *Politics of the Asian Economic Crisis*. Ithaca: Cornell University Press.
Pepinsky, Thomas B. 2008. "Capital Mobility and Coalitional Politics: Authoritar-

ian Regimes and Economic Adjustment in Southeast Asia." *World Politics* 60 (3): 438–74.
Pepinsky, Thomas B. 2009. *Economic Crises and the Breakdown of Authoritarian Regimes: Indonesia and Malaysia in Comparative Perspective*. New York: Cambridge University Press.
Pepinsky, Thomas B. 2012. "The Political Economy of Financial Development in Southeast Asia." In *East Asian Capitalism: Diversity, Continuity, and Change*, ed. Andrew Walter and Xiaoke Zhang. New York: Oxford University Press.
Pepinsky, Thomas B. 2013. "Pluralism and Political Conflict in Indonesia." *Indonesia* 96: 81–100.
Pepinsky, Thomas B. 2014. "The Institutional Turn in Comparative Authoritarianism." *British Journal of Political Science* 44 (3): 631–53.
Pepinsky, Thomas B. 2015. "Interpreting Ethnicity and Urbanization in Malaysia's 2013 General Election." *Journal of East Asian Studies* 15 (2): 199–226.
Radelet, Steven, and Jeffrey D. Sachs. 1998. "The East Asian Financial Crisis: Diagnosis, Remedies, Prospects." *Brookings Papers on Economic Activity* 1998 (1): 1–74.
Rasiah, Rajah. 1997. "Class, Ethnicity, and Economic Development in Malaysia." In *The Political Economy of South-East Asia: An Introduction*, ed. Gary Rodan, Kevin Hewison, and Richard Robison. Melbourne: Oxford University Press.
Reeve, David. 1985. *Golkar of Indonesia: An Alternative to the Party System*. Singapore: Oxford University Press.
Robison, Richard. 1987. "After the Gold Rush: The Politics of Economic Restructuring in Indonesia in the 1980s." In *Southeast Asia in the 1980s: The Politics of Economic Crisis*, ed. Richard Robison, Kevin Hewison, and Richard A. Higgott. Sydney: Allen & Unwin.
Robison, Richard. 1997. "Politics and Markets in Indonesia's Post-oil Era." In *The Political Economy of South-East Asia: An Introduction*, ed. Gary Rodan, Kevin Hewison, and Richard Robison. Melbourne: Oxford University Press.
Shamsul, A. B. 1988. "The 'Battle Royal': The UMNO Elections of 1987." *Southeast Asian Affairs* 1988: 170–88.
Singh, Hari. 1991. "Political Change in Malaysia: The Role of Semangat 46." *Asian Survey* 38 (1): 712–28.
Slater, Dan. 2003. "Iron Cage in an Iron Fist: Authoritarian Institutions and the Personalization of Power in Malaysia." *Comparative Politics* 36 (1): 81–101.
Slater, Dan. 2010. *Ordering Power: Contentious Politics and Authoritarian Leviathans in Southeast Asia*. New York: Cambridge University Press.
Smith, Benjamin B. 2003. "'If I Do These Things, They Will Throw Me Out': Economic Reform and the Collapse of Indonesia's New Order." *Journal of International Affairs* 57 (1): 113–28.
Soesastro, M. Hadi. 1989. "The Political Economy of Deregulation in Indonesia." *Asian Survey* 29 (9): 853–69.
Thorbecke, Erik. 1992. *Adjustment and Equity in Indonesia*. Paris: Development Centre of the Organisation for Economic Co-operation and Development.
Wahman, Michael, Jan Teorell, and Axel Hadenius. 2013. "Authoritarian Regime Types Revisited: Updated Data in Comparative Perspective." *Contemporary Politics* 19 (1): 19–34.

Weiss, Meredith L. 2005. *Protest and Possibilities: Civil Society and Coalitions for Political Change in Malaysia*. Stanford: Stanford University Press.

Woo, Wing Thye, Jeffrey D. Sachs, and Claus Schwab, eds. 2000. *The Asian Financial Crisis: Lessons for a Resilient Asia*. Cambridge, MA: MIT Press.

World Bank. 1989. *Malaysia: Matching Risks and Rewards in a Mixed Economy*. Washington, DC: World Bank.

World Bank. 1994. *Indonesia: Stability, Growth and Equity in Repelita VI*. Washington, DC: World Bank.

World Bank. 2015a. "Agriculture, value added (% of GDP)(NV.AGR.TOTL.ZS), Industry, value added (% of GDP)(NV.IND.TOTL.ZS), Manufacturing, value added (% of GDP)(NV.IND.MANF.ZS), Services, etc., value added (% of GDP)(NV.SRV.TETC.ZS)." Available at http://data.worldbank.org/data-catalog/world-development-indicators

World Bank. 2015b. "Constant GDP Per Capita for Malaysia [NYGDPPCAPKDMYS] and Constant GDP Per Capita for Indonesia [NYGDPPCAPKDIDN]." Retrieved from FRED, Federal Reserve Bank of St. Louis https://research.stlouisfed.org/fred2/series/NYGDPPCAPKDMYS/ and https://research.stlouisfed.org/fred2/series/NYGDPPCAPKDIDN/

World Bank. 2015c. "Employment to Population Ratio, 15+, Total (%) (Modeled ILO Estimate)(SL.EMP.TOTL.SP.ZS)." Available at http://data.worldbank.org/data-catalog/world-development-indicators

World Bank. 2015d. "General Government Final Consumption Expenditure (Constant 2005 US$)(NE.CON.GOVT.KD) and General Government Final Consumption Expenditure (% of GDP)(NE.CON.GOVT.ZS)." Available at http://data.worldbank.org/data-catalog/world-development-indicators

SIX

Pathways to Stability and Instability in the Midst of Prolonged Slowdown
The Case of China

Victor C. Shih

Of all the surviving authoritarian regimes, the Chinese Communist Party (CCP) seems the most prepared for long-term rule. Indeed, China's astonishing economic performance during the 2008–9 global financial crisis attested to the regime's staying power. While the rest of the world struggled with negative growth and financial meltdowns, the CCP mobilized a wide range of economic and financial institutions under its control and pumped trillions of dollars in investment into the economy, thus producing an astonishing 11.7 percent in real growth in 2009. Similar to the case of Taiwan in the Wong chapter, such impressive capacity to mobilize economic resources seemingly made it invulnerable to economic shocks. However, similar to the case of Malaysia after the Asian Financial Crisis described in Dan Slater's chapter in this volume, resource mobilization from 2008 to 2009 might have planted the seed for prolonged slowdown in the post-2012 period, which may pose a challenge to authoritarian stability in the medium term.

In the analysis below, I first describe the key selectorates in the CCP regimes, followed by a discussion on party and financial institutions. Unlike noncommunist regimes, the CCP did not need to negotiate with actors from outside of the party because, as wealthy as some of them were, they could not directly affect high-level political outcomes. Instead, the selectorates were embedded entirely within the CCP and were incentivized by party institutions to maintain the status quo. In addition, the CCP maintained control over all major financial institutions in China and ran a sizable positive balance of payments through much of the past 20 years. This endowed the regime with ample capacity to confront an economic shock. In the medium term, because institutions within the party were malleable, changes in these institutions might have shifted the elites' incentive to maintain the status quo of one-party rule.

I then discuss two cases of economic shocks, one generated entirely externally and another partly produced by policies from the first shock. In essence, the ruling elite mobilized its impressive machinery, which depleted much of the regime's financial resources in the 2008–10 period. Although China produced impressive economic performance in 2008–9, the binge credit expansion also gave rise to overcapacity and an unsustainable debt dynamic by 2012. The economy began to slow after that point. However, politically, the new secretary general, Xi Jinping, consolidated both formal and informal power to an extent unseen since Mao's death in 1976. This led to a swifter policy process, but its arbitrariness may have weakened elite incentives to maintain the status quo. Although China likely will maintain stability in the foreseeable future, the interaction between a financial crisis and weakened elite incentives to maintain the status quo may provide the backdrop to instability, defined as an unexpected leadership change or the introduction of a new, although not necessarily democratic, regime.

Selectorate

Of all of the surviving authoritarian regimes in the 2010s, China arguably had the strongest one-party system. The Chinese Communist Party governed over a strictly hierarchical one-party state with deep grassroots penetration. Most of the viable selectorates were actors within the CCP, which had multiple mechanisms to incentivize and to monitor party members. Purges launched by Secretary General Xi Jinping starting in 2013 further centralized power in his hands and strengthened an important mechanism for monitoring party cadres, the discipline and inspection committees. Even as China faced an economic slowdown, in 2018 it still had one of the highest growth rates in the entire world at over 6 percent. Finally, the regime still controlled vast resources via state-owned enterprises (SOEs) and the state banks, as well as a US$3 trillion foreign exchange reserve, which afforded the regime ample economic resources with which to deal with economic shocks, at least those with relatively short duration.

Unlike most other authoritarian regimes, communist regimes, when they took control over countries, typically sought to destroy all other autonomous social organizations, replacing them with Communist Party organs or social organizations tightly controlled by the party. As Walder (2015, 60) observes about the CCP's control over rural society, "The first step in the extension of state power was to destroy social groups that exercised authority, and to obliterate the economic foundation for their elite status." Similarly, Soviet Union decimated the kulaks soon after taking power (Montefiore 2003). In consolidating control over Chinese cities, the CCP imprisoned some 1.2 million potential "counterrevolutionaries," while 710,000 regime opponents were executed (Walder 2015, 65). In essence after 1958, there were only scattered and isolated pockets of autonomous social organizations, including commercial ones, and the surviving ones often had the protection of local cadres (Zhang, Liu, and Shih 2013).

Thus, at the dawn of economic reform in 1978, most of the selectorate of the Chinese Communist regime, defined as "the set of people whose endowments include the qualities or characteristics institutionally required to choose the government's leadership" (Bueno de Mesquita et al. 2003, 42), were embedded in the party. Even with the rise of private entrepreneurs with billions in assets, the party had little need to negotiate with or to reassure elites outside of the Chinese Communist Party because all the major decisions were made within the party by high-level party members alone.

The key selectorate body was the Central Committee, especially higher-level members sitting in the Politburo and the Politburo Standing Committee (Shirk 1993; Lieberthal 2004; Schurmann 1968). Members of the Central Committee occupied all of the important positions in the regime, including provincial party secretary positions, ministerial positions, senior offices in the People's Liberation Army and the People's Armed Police, as well as executive positions in important SOEs, state banks, and media organs. These organs provided the regime with what Slater (2003) calls "infrastructural power" of ruling over the country. Not only did these individuals control vital organs in the economy and in the polity, which provided potentially lucrative rent-seeking opportunities, they also participated in high-level decision-making, which gave them a stake in the system.

Besides members of the Central Committee, the military was often a crucial selectorate during times of political uncertainty, such as after Mao's death and in 1989 (Baum 1994). After 1989, an increasingly professionalized military was an important, but not necessarily pivotal, actor in the political system (Cheung 2001). Finally, although the internal security apparatus under the Central Law and Politics Committee became a powerful actor during the Hu Jintao years (Wang and Minzner 2015), the purge of Zhou Yongkang saw the entire apparatus downgraded to a Politburo-level organ, instead of a Standing Committee–level organ under Zhou Yongkang. Nonetheless, compliance by the security apparatus remained a crucial ingredient for stability in China. The millions of officers, foot soldiers, and informants in the public security and state security organs, as well as in the People's Armed Police, prevented and quelled over 100,000 "mass incidents" per year (Tanner 2014).[1]

A sharp reduction of benefits to the security agencies may decrease their effort, which can quickly introduce large-scale social instability. As Haggard and Kaufman point out, wealthy oligarchs with major monopolies often form alliances that threaten incumbents in dictatorships (Haggard and Kaufman 1995, 29). Indeed, the defection of wealthy Chinese investors from the ruling coalition might have precipitated or at least sped up the collapse of the Suharto regime (Pepinsky 2009). Since the reform in 1978, a sizable and wealthy class of entrepreneurs and corrupt officials has emerged in China. According to the *2015 Global Wealth Report* authored by the Boston Consulting Group, there were over 1,000 Chinese households with wealth over $100 million, second only to the United States (Boston Consulting Group 2015). There were also four million or so millionaire households in China. Together, the *financial* wealth of all of the millionaire households in China may have exceeded US$20 trillion by the end of 2014 (Boston Consulting Group 2015).

Despite their growing wealth, high-net-worth households remained largely at the mercy of the party. According to a growing body of research, private entrepreneurs were co-opted into business associations, the Political Consultative Conference, and the People's Congress at various levels so that the party could both listen to their concerns and monitor their activities (Dickson 2003; Kennedy 2005; Truex 2016). Some entrepreneurs exerted considerable influence on local policymaking, even to the point of subverting normal policy processes to enhance private gains (Tsai 2007; Caixin 2014).

If their patrons got into political trouble, however, even very wealthy and "connected" entrepreneurs found themselves in jail or even facing the gallows (Caixin 2014). For example, billionaire Huang Guangyu, the owner of the largest consumer electronic chain in China, fell afoul of the top leadership and was sentenced to a 14-year jail sentence for "insider trading," even though it was a common practice among the wealthy in China

(Yang, Mao, and Sang 2015). Under former security czar Zhou Yongkang's protection, millionaire Liu Han literally got away with murders, but the fall of Zhou resulted in Liu Han's speedy execution (Caixin 2014). In 2015, scores of fund managers and brokers, some of whom highly connected, were arrested for "maliciously shorting" the stock index and for insider trading (Wang 2015). Although the wealthy bought political connections, these connections were fleeting.

As a class, high-net-worth households in China had little capacity to challenge party rule, but they still exerted important influence. The enormous wealth of the rich in China had two potential implications for regime stability. First, even if they did not challenge the party directly but lost confidence in the regime, wealthy households in China could trigger capital flight that would have introduced a negative shock to macroeconomic stability and growth. If Chinese millionaires indeed had US$20 trillion in financial assets, even moving one-sixth of that wealth offshore would have wiped out China's US$3 trillion in foreign exchange reserve. China's loss of close to US$1 trillion in reserves between mid-2015 and mid-2016 illustrates the potential shock of capital flight. Second, it is conceivable that the wealthy in China could form an alliance with senior officials within the regime to challenge the incumbent if the regime faces sufficient stress.

Party and Financial Institutions

Political institutions in China have been some of the most robust among authoritarian regimes because of their ability to incentivize regime insiders to support the status quo and to facilitate an adaptive policymaking process. However, the party is not an immutable being, and specific institutions within the regime have been changed by high-level leaders, which may affect institutional stability in a later period.

As Svolik (2012, 167) points out, authoritarian parties serve three crucial functions: "hierarchical assignment of service and benefits, political control over appointments, and selective recruitment and repression." In essence, by institutionalizing a system of allocating spoils according to a set of relatively predictable criteria and following a set of predictable formal and informal procedures, actors in a party are incentivized to follow internal party rules in order to obtain more spoils, instead of overthrowing the existing system (Brownlee 2007). On top of that, Communist parties typically have multiple monitoring mechanisms for high-level party leaders to observe the behavior of their subordinates, or even colleagues. This helps enforce the coordination game between the elite in a one-party state. Indeed, empirical research has shown that one-party authoritarian states have been much more resilient than military dictatorships or monarchies (Geddes 1999; Magaloni and Kricheli 2010).

Indeed, as of the mid-2010s, the Chinese Communist Party was a hierarchical party in which higher-level officials typically were entitled to more power and more rent-seeking opportunities, which incentivized them to pursue their careers within the party hierarchy according to explicit and unspoken rules. According to official rules, higher-level officials were entitled to higher pay and state-allocated privileges, such as larger apartments and a car and driver. Ministerial-level officials, for example, were entitled to personal cars and drivers, several secretaries, and superior health care (Qian 2012).

Furthermore, under the one-level-down appointment system, a provincial party secretary, for example, had enormous discretion over the appointments of mayors within a province (Landry 2008). To the extent that subordinates had to share rent with higher-level officials in order to obtain promotions, the provincial party secretary or other high-level party figures of a wealthy province partook in the rent generated from all the cities in the province, netting them millions in income (Zhu 2008). Likewise, as recent corruption cases revealed, property developers and other businesses approached senior party leaders to give them equity stakes, cash, and other benefits in order to obtain land, lucrative state contracts, inside information, and government-sanctioned monopolies (Caixin 2014; Reporters, Staff 2015). These payouts amounted to hundreds of millions of dollars for Politburo-level officials (Forsythe 2015). Although Xi Jinping's anticorruption campaign likely reduced the degree of corruption, it was pursued selectively, and in the medium term, a high-level official in the CCP still expected sizable benefits from rent-seeking activities, providing that the economy maintained its growth trajectory.

The high benefits enjoyed by top officials, as well as retirement rules that so far have forced most senior officials to give way to younger officials at regular intervals, incentivized lower-level officials to obey the formal and informal rules within the party in order to maximize their power within the system, which also conferred significant rent-seeking opportunities. Although promotions in the CCP were driven by both formal and informal considerations (Shih, Adolph, and Mingxing 2012), as long as those in the system understood the rules clearly, party elites could maximize their chance of promotions in accordance with those rules. In other words, actors in the party had an incentive to adhere to the rules of the game, both formal and informal, because the game had a high potential payout for the winners.

In addition to the pyramidal structure of the party, the revolutionary legacy in the party also endowed it with an adaptive policymaking process. In essence, the party had long recognized that conditions varied depending on localities and that major shocks could change the optimal set of policies, which led to a continuous process of policy adjustments (Heilmann and Perry 2013). This has provided the CCP regime with additional resilience.

Instead of a coherent process of policy innovation coordinated by the top leader of the party, however, one can interpret policy experiments as local or ministerial actors advancing their power and careers via experiments in jurisdictional expansion. According to this interpretation, policy experiments by competing agencies or localities could lead to policy deadlock or enormous waste. Moreover, if actors suddenly lose the incentive to engage in policy experiment because the payoffs of innovation have fallen, the added resilience from adaptive policymaking also diminishes.

In terms of financial institutions, all but a small handful of banks were state-owned, and all financial institutions, with the possible exception of foreign institutions, had party committees that overlapped with the top management to a large extent (Shih 2008). Thus, financial institutions more or less followed instructions from the party. Moreover, China for the last two decades had had a great deal of control over the domestic financial system due to a persistent current account surplus, which infused the banking system with new high-powered money, as discussed below. Institutionally, China has been in a very strong position to deal with economic shocks during this period. Indeed, despite both a sharp global shock in 2009 and a prolonged growth slowdown after 2013, the Communist Party continued to rule over China without even major adjustments to the ruling coalition.

2008–9: A Noncrisis in China

In essence, the global financial crisis in 2008 had little impact on China either economically or politically because financial repression, fixed exchange rates, and years of current account surplus had endowed the financial system with many resources with which to counteract the economic slowdown. In combination with the party's ability to coordinate most of the economic actors in the country, rent-seeking opportunities to regime insiders likely rose dramatically during the global crisis, which increased regime insiders' incentive to protect the status quo. The rule of the party and its leaders likely strengthened during the 2008 global crisis.

By 2008, China had the third largest economy in the world behind only the United States and Japan, making it more resilient to external and internal economic shocks. Moreover, after China joined the WTO in the early 2000s, China's trade surplus expanded, leading to large inflows of foreign exchange (figure 6.1). Nonetheless, the global crisis did have an initially large impact on the economy. Exports plunged by 20 percent in the first quarter of 2009, while first-quarter growth in 2009 was the lowest since the early 1990s.

Still, the previous decade of healthy foreign exchange inflows provided the financial system with a powerful cushion with which to counteract the economic shock. When money flowed into China from its current account surplus, from foreign direct investment, or from hot-money inflows, the recipients of dollars sold them to banks in return for renminbi (RMB), China's official currency. When banks ran short on RMB, they had to sell their dollar holdings to the People's Bank of China (PBOC), which printed high-powered money to purchase banks' foreign exchange sale. Thus, indirectly, the creation of high powered money by the PBOC allowed foreign exchange earners to increase their RMB deposits while exchange rates remained at roughly the same level. At their height in early 2008, net inflows over a 12-month period increased deposits by 7 percent of bank assets.

The US$5 trillion in deposits allowed China to immediately accelerate the pace of investment growth to an astonishing 34 percent in 2009. In one year alone, financial institutions in China released over US$2 trillion in credit to finance a massive binge in infrastructure and industrial investment (People's Bank of China 2015b). The banking recapitalization in the late 1990s was too successful, in a sense. When the world financial crisis descended on China, Chinese banks were so well capitalized and had so much liquidity that they could boost lending by over 30 percent in one year. After 2009, Chinese banks' balance sheets continued to grow at a rapid clip, such that bank assets, when one takes into account assets in the shadow banking sector, approached 300 percent of GDP (Dobbs et al. 2015).

Institutionally, the party's control over all financial institutions, as well as many strategic firms and local governments, meant that the state could order banks to lend to local governments and SOEs and could also coordinate the allocation of trillions of dollars in bank loans from the banks (Shih 2010). Local governments formed thousands of local government financing platforms, which borrowed trillions of RMB from the banks on

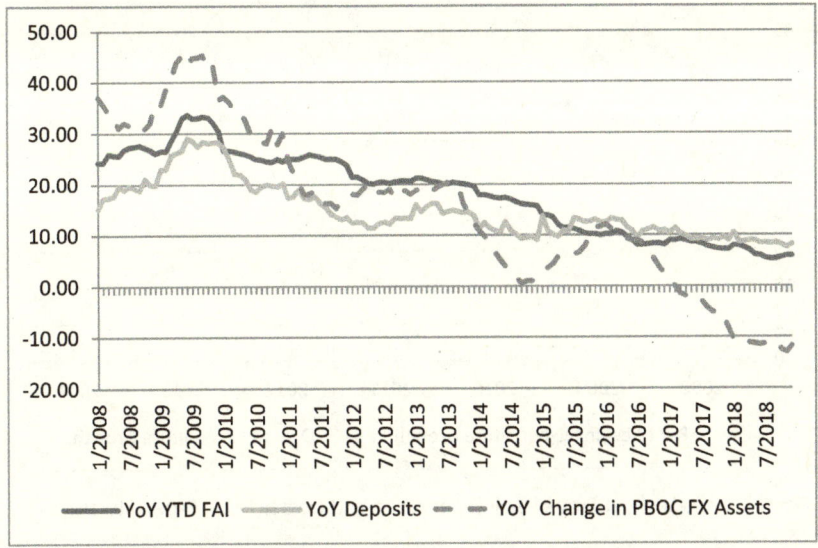

Fig. 6.1. Year-to-Date Fixed-Asset Investment, Deposits, Foreign Exchange Inflows (%)
Source: People's Bank of China 2018.
Note: Figures are year over year (YoY).

the basis of land collateral and government guarantees (Shih 2010). Within weeks of receiving the money, planning authorities across China directed these platforms to commence thousands of construction projects. As a result of this effort, GDP growth in China rebounded to above 10 percent by the fourth quarter of 2009.

Although the precise amount of rent seeking is unknown, one can derive indicators to measure changes in rent seeking over time. One approach is to compare the growth of fiscal expenditures that are prone to rent-seeking activities with the growth of overall fiscal expenditure. In essence, construction-related fiscal expenditures in the budget were prone to corruption. To be sure, state construction mainly relied on bank loans for financing instead of budgetary disbursement. Nonetheless, most state-related construction projects use 10–20 percent of the funds from the state budget, with the rest financed by bank loans (Shih 2010). Therefore, the year-on-year change in construction-related budgetary items should provide a sense of the over-time changes in rent-seeking opportunities.

The rent-seeking expenditure indicator in figure 6.2 records the annual percentage change in the sum of expenditure on urban and rural community affairs, agriculture, forestry and water conservancy, transportation, and

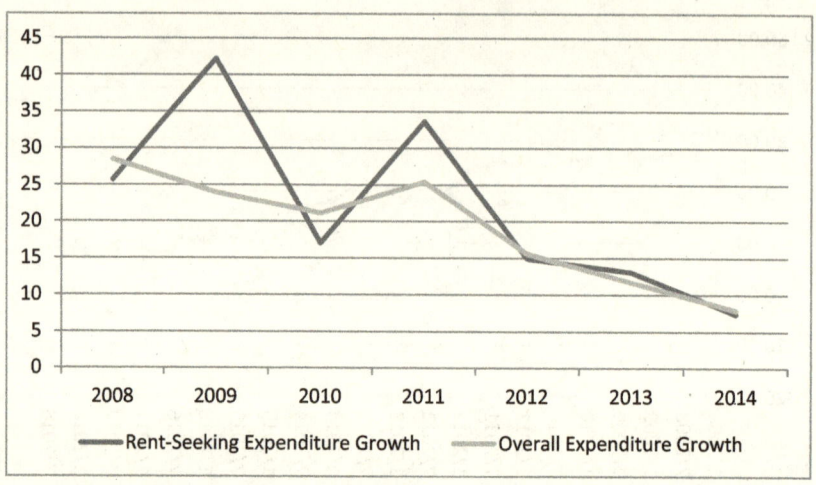

Fig. 6.2. Rent-Seeking-Prone Fiscal Expenditure and Overall Fiscal Expenditures (%)

housing security, all of which are dominated by construction. In addition, I also include general administrative expenses and expenditures on grain, oil, and material reserve management, an item often prone to corruption (Pei 2006, 118).

As one can see in figure 6.2, the growth of rent-seeking expenditures spiked in 2009 and again in 2011 as the regime engaged in countercyclical stimuli. To the extent that construction, administrative expenses, and management of state strategic reserves provided officials with rent-seeking opportunities, 2009 and, to a lesser extent, 2011 boosted the "gray income" of officials throughout the system to a considerable extent. In contrast, the growth of overall fiscal expenditure fell in almost a straight line starting 2008. Until the end of 2012, holding an important position in the Chinese Communist Party meant looking forward to substantial increases in rent-seeking opportunities year after year, which furnished strong motivations for protecting the status quo.

Politically, the 2008–9 economic shock did not in the slightest jeopardize the positions of Secretary General Hu Jintao or Premier Wen Jiabao. In fact, throughout the spring and summer of 2009, Premier Wen Jiabao was seen gallivanting around China to inspect progress in construction projects, and to approve trillions of RMB in new projects (Li 2009). Even before his retirement in 2013, scholars and even some government officials had begun to criticize Wen Jiabao for the stimulus in 2009 because it had led to an unsustainable accumulation of debt (Liu 2012). However, doling out trillions of RMB in investment projects likely made the top leaders of China extremely popular among mid-level officials, who profited handsomely during the stimulus years. The 2012 revelation of the Wen family's lucrative private equity and consulting deals did not have any noticeable impact on Wen's position as the premier of China (Barboza 2012). Even after his retirement, he and his family have been immune from the anticorruption drive, at least as of 2018.

The Party in Prolonged Austerity

The Chinese economy began to slow after 2013 partly because foreign exchange flows no longer infused the financial system with new liquidity every year. In addition, the high debt level in the economy meant that more and more liquidity was needed to service and roll over existing debt. These two dynamics led to a prolonged period of stagnant growth in China. In addition to a secular slowdown of growth, the CCP launched anticorruption and austerity campaigns to reduce the amount of rent-seeking activities. To be sure, anticorruption helped consolidate the power of Xi Jinping in the party. He further consolidated day-to-day control over policies with institutional changes in the policymaking process and with a constitutional revision that allowed him to serve as state president for life. The question, though, remains whether a *prolonged* period of austerity, coupled with reduced opportunities for advancement and rent seeking due to the contraction of the winning coalition and institutional changes, will encourage party insiders to defect from the ruling regime. Some cases in this volume, such as Iraq, suggest that prolonged austerity may not necessarily unseat the incumbent, although the risks of political instability rise.

Figure 6.1 shows that the growth of foreign exchange (FX) inflows slowed dramatically toward the end of 2012. This likely was caused by a combination of China's rising labor costs and its rapidly rising real effective exchange rate, which both slowed export and enhanced expectation of RMB devaluation vis-à-vis the dollar (People's Bank of China 2015a). By July 2012, net FX inflows only brought in deposits equivalent to 0.5 percent of bank assets over a 12-month period. Even as late as mid-2011, net FX inflows still increased deposits equivalent to 3.5 percent of bank assets over a 12-month period. Foreign exchange inflows rebounded in late 2013, but dropped again in the second half of 2014. In fact, China experienced consecutive months of FX *outflows* in 2015 and 2016, which exerted a contractionary impact on money supply.

The enormous size of China's banking system and the end of easy liquidity from foreign exchange inflows have important implications for China's monetary policy after 2013. First and foremost, without active PBOC interventions to increase money supply, the pace of lending would slow to a level that is detrimental to the targeted growth rates, which have been moderated after 2010. Indeed, since 2013, the PBOC has redeemed PBOC sterilization bills and lowered reserve requirement ratio to release high-powered money into the economy. These mechanisms succeeded in maintaining M2 growth in the low teens throughout 2014–15, but M2 growth fell below 10 percent by 2017 (fig. 6.1). In addition, the growth of fixed-asset investment has slowed substantially from previous years (fig. 6.1). Growth in 2015 was the slowest growth China has experienced since the early 1990s.

Moreover, the enormous debt built-up from the 2008–10 period, as well as subsequent leveraging, has created credit nearly three times the size of the economy. As figure 6.2 reveals, bank assets, which represented the vast majority of credit, were over 300 percent of GDP by 2017, which meant that even at an average interest rate of 7 percent, *interest servicing* on bank credit alone required funding equivalent to nearly 21 percent of nominal GDP. In 2017, nominal GDP grew only around 10 percent, which meant that borrowers in China in the aggregate could not have used new income to service all of the *interest* that had to be repaid that year. Either they used their savings to pay interest, or the central bank printed money to capitalize interest payments into principal, thus creating new credit that generated no new cash flows for the debtors. In a subsequent period, more credit will have to be generated to repay both interest and principal of the zombie credit.

Over time, this dynamic required the central bank to generate more and more new credit simply to service existing debt without improving the economy in any meaningful way. Also, this dynamic is not easily reversible. Even if the government had the courage to push thousands of inefficient SOEs into bankruptcy and to use fiscal resources to write down trillions of RMB in nonperforming loans arising from the bankruptcies, the government itself would need to issue trillions of RMB in fiscal debt, which also would require cash flows to service. The central bank would have to purchase government securities, or the government would need to raise new taxes from corporations and households, both of which represent heavy taxes and would slow growth for years to come. Without government write-downs, the central bank would need to lend money to banks on a larger and larger scale, which would ultimately tax households indirectly via both inflation and currency devaluation.

As things stood in 2018, without the PBOC's short-term facilities in the form of reverse repos and medium-term lending facilities, as well as reserve requirement ratio cuts, growth likely would have collapsed. This contrasted sharply with the 2003–8 period, when the PBOC only had to guard against inflation because banks all had plenty of liquidity with which to lend to firms. After 2012, the PBOC needed to be ever more vigilant against liquidity shortage in the interbank markets and intervened in a timely manner to prevent spikes in interbank rates, which would have precipitated a wave of defaults by debtors. In essence, without the central bank constantly injecting liquidity in various ways, interbank rates would have spiked, which in turn would have forced banks to charge debtors high interest. This would have forced thousands of firms into bankruptcy.

For firms in China, the era of easy credit from the banks is over. As bank deposit growth slowed sharply after 2011, the real cost of capital for firms also rose, despite rate cuts by the PBOC. The slowdown in liquidity affected firms' cost of capital in two ways. First, slowing investment led to weaker pricing power by firms, especially those in upstream industries such as coal mining and steel production. Second, the need to roll over an ever larger pile of debt has kept nominal rates relatively high despite a slowing economy. After 2011, real rates for firms approached 10 percent due to a prolonged period of worsening Producer Price Index for firms. Smaller firms had an even harder time borrowing from the banks, forcing them to borrow from trust companies and underground banks at much higher rates. Even larger real estate firms have had to borrow from trust companies at high yields (Reuters 2010). Although the forced closure of thousands of firms in the coal and steel industries in 2016 and 2017 brought the PPI up temporarily (People's Bank of China 2018), overcapacity and the PBOC's hawkish attitude soon increased the costs of financing and slowed the growth of credit.

As banks ran short of liquidity, their ability to finance construction projects and other rent-seeking activities also diminished. As figure 6.2 shows, rent-seeking expenditures slowed dramatically after 2012 and converged with overall fiscal expenditures, which also slowed to around 7 percent. The monthly data also reveal a persistent slowdown in rent-seeking resources. Figure 6.1 shows that the growth of fixed-asset investment has slid continuously in recent years to 5 percent in 2018, the lowest level seen since the early 1990s. Although the government has begun to front-load fiscal expenditures, the year-end growth of expenditures dropped to around 7 percent by 2018, down from 15 percent growth in 2013 (Ministry of Finance 2019). Such a spectacular reduction in overall expenditure necessarily reduced the growth in rent-seeking-related expenditures because the other expenditures were guaranteed line items related to civil service and teachers' salaries.

Politically, the party leadership likely anticipated an economic slowdown and implemented harsh austerity and anticorruption measures to reduce rent seeking. This in essence was a re-engineering of the ruling coalition such that the vast majority of officials were no longer entitled to large sums of "gray income" outside of normal salaries and bonuses. Soon after Xi Jinping took power in late 2012, he convened a Politburo meeting to implement the "Eight Regulations," which forbad cadres from a range of ostentatious activities, including holding large weddings or birthday banquets, convening unnecessary meetings at resorts, and using official cars for personal purposes (Chen 2015b). In the first nine months of 2015, the party's discipline and inspection commission investigated over 27,000 cases of violating the "Eight Regulations," resulting in nearly 24,000 cadres receiving administrative or party disciplinary punishment (Chen 2015b).

On top of the new austerity, Wang Qishan, an old friend of Xi Jinping, took control over the Central Discipline and Inspection Commission (CDIC), the party's anticorruption organ, and began to prosecute numerous high-level cadres, even retired Politburo member Xu Caihou and retired Politburo Standing Committee member Zhou Yongkang (Wu and Li 2013). Between the 18th Party Congress in late 2012 and November 2015, some 59 current provincial/ministerial officials, as well as scores of retired ministerial level officials, were charged with corruption (Chen 2015a). This constituted the largest cleansing of the senior party ranks since the removal of the Gang of Four in the late 1970s. Thus, much of the reduction in rent-seeking expenditures seen since 2012 might have been driven by the contraction in the demand of corruption caused by the anticorruption campaign. Still, the contraction of liquidity in the financial system meant that even if the anticorruption effort had come to an end, aggregate rent-seeking activities in China likely could not rise by too much.

The anticorruption campaign also had a noticeable impact on the relative power of Xi Jinping. In figure 6.3, I calculate the number of key officials, defined as heads and vice heads of central party organs, ministers of key economic ministries, as well as commanders of PLA departments and military regions, who had ties with various senior leaders in the party over time. Ties are identified using the Shih, Lee, and Meyer Central Committee (CC) data on the basis of overlapping work experience when the clients served within two administrative steps of the patron in the past, up until the patron's entry into the Politburo (Shih, Lee, and Meyer 2015). As figure 6.3 shows, after the 18th Party Congress, the number of Hu followers occupying key positions plummeted, while the number of Xi Jinping and Wang Qishan followers in key positions rose substantially.

To be sure, figure 6.3 shows that the largest change in power came from regular retirement and promotion, which took place at the 18th Party Congress. The congress saw 14 Hu Jintao followers retiring from the Central Committee due to age, thus dramatically lowering the number of his followers in key positions. The retirement process even affected the younger Xi Jinping, who also lost a couple of followers. Former president Jiang Zemin seemed able to maintain his influence by placing 10 followers in key positions after the 18th Party Congress, over a decade after his formal retirement. Another major beneficiary of the anticorruption campaign was Wang Qishan, the anticorruption czar, who saw the number of his followers occupying key positions rise from 10 in 2012 to 15 in 2017. By 2017, the factions of Xi Jinping and Wang Qishan combined occupied twice as many key positions as followers of former secretary general Hu Jintao, a major reshuffling in the space of five years. It is likely that Xi's followers continued to have latitude to engage in corruption, but surviving elites from other factions likely reduced their rent-seeking activities on the margin in the midst of the crackdown.

In addition to reshuffling the selectorate, Xi also enacted important institutional changes to top-level policymaking. Instead of discussing and deciding important issues at Politburo Standing Committee meetings, Xi formed a large number of leading groups that took over key decision-making power from the Politburo Standing Committee (PSC) (Huang 2014). After ascending to power in 2012, Xi formed new leading groups on economic reform, national security, internet security, and reform of the military, all of which were chaired by Xi himself (Keck 2014; Huang 2014). The only new leading group not chaired by Xi was the leading group on football reform, chaired by Vice Premier Liu Yandong. Many decisions that had been discussed and voted on in the PSC were decided by the leading groups, where Xi could personally drive the agenda (Huang 2014; Johnson and Kennedy 2015). Xi further strengthened the role of the leading groups in 2018 by transforming some of them into party commissions, which implying greater staff, resources, and decision-making power. Finally, in 2018 he provided himself with an option to rule China for life by removing the clause in the constitution limiting incumbency of the state president to two terms.

By rerouting policymaking through the leading groups instead of the PSC, Xi consolidated decision-making power in his own hands. He also

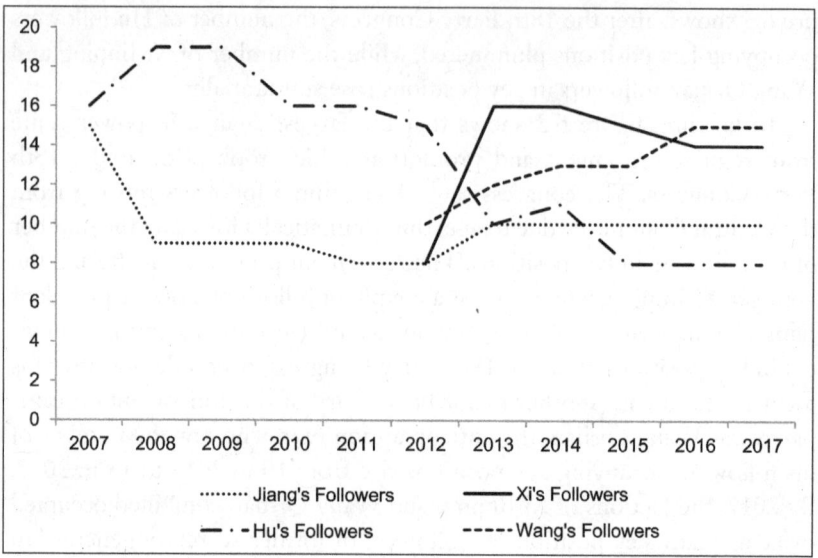

Fig. 6.3. The Number of Jiang Zemin, Hu Jintao, Xi Jinping, and Wang Qishan Faction Members in Key Positions, 2007–17

took away decision-making power from the hands of his colleagues in the PSC. For example, whereas economic policymaking was solely controlled by the premier through the State Council Standing Committee meetings in the Hu-Wen administration, the Leading Group on Reform now considered a large number of long-term economic policies, marginalizing the State Council for these decisions (Johnson and Kennedy 2015). The leading group on military reform also likely excluded other PSC members from military-related policy reform.

In sum, the post-2012 period was characterized by a prolonged period of austerity, caused both by a fundamental reduction in liquidity and by anticorruption and antiwaste campaigns. It further was characterized by the consolidation of power by Xi Jinping both through anticorruption purges and through changing the decision-making institutions at the top level. Thus, although the number of elites represented in high-level institutions, that is, the Politburo and the Central Committee, remained largely the same, their latitude to benefit personally from their positions and the extent of those benefits have reduced drastically since 2012. This power consolidation at first glance seems to provide a strong foundation for continual political stability in China under the current regime. The next section discusses whether this indeed may be the case.

Potential Paths of Stability and Instability in China

As the previous section discusses, China likely has entered a prolonged period of slow growth, perhaps punctuated by episodes of temporary stimulus and negative growth. The CCP regime, however, seems to be in a good position to weather even a prolonged episode of slow growth. First of all, all the relevant political actors are in the ruling Chinese Communist Party, or embedded in organizations tightly controlled by the CCP. This means that the selectorate in the regime is incentivized by promotion prospects in the party to support the regime. Although the benefits accruing to officials in the regime have been reduced by anticorruption efforts and by austerity measures, the CCP still maintains a comfortable living standard for most officials in China, at least relative to the outside options for these officials. The removal of scores of senior officials also opened up those positions for those lower in the hierarchy to advance.

The party also instituted greater monitoring of lower-level officials, which reduced their ability to accumulate resources with which to challenge the incumbent. The CCP also continues to use adaptive policymaking to derive new policy measures to deal with various manifestations of instability, including selective internet censorship targeted at potential collective action (King, Pan, and Roberts 2013). Finally, Xi Jinping eliminated his enemies and consolidated decision-making power in his own hands, which means that he can respond to emergency situations in a speedy manner. The centralized decision-making process also should help the leadership institute deep economic reform, if the leadership sees fit to implement it (Nelson 1993). Given these preconditions, regime stability is still the most likely outcome during Xi's tenure.

However, there are some potential pathways to instability, even in such a consolidated one-party regime with a high degree of power concentration. The first path is caused by a financial crisis alone. As previous discussions reveal, China had an unsustainable amount of debt that was still growing at a rate of over 10 percent as of 2018. While dollar interest rates remained at nearly zero, China could ease monetary policy without triggering large-scale capital flight. However, if the Federal Reserves hiked interest rates aggressively, nominal rates in China may well be lower than nominal US dollar rates, intensifying outflows from China. Expectation of higher rates in the United States likely contributed to the US$1 trillion reduction in China's foreign exchange reserve between early 2015 and the middle of 2016.

US rate hikes in 2018 pulled additional billions out of China's foreign exchange reserves late in the year, and further rate hikes may intensify this pressure. More important, when money leaves China, domestic money supply contracts as investors give RMB back to the central bank in exchange for dollars, thus extinguishing money supply. The central bank can allow rates to rise to arrest this process, but this would put an enormous burden on highly indebted firms and would cause a wave of bankruptcies. The other option is to devalue the currency substantially, but that may invite even more outflows and greater pressure for devaluation, as well as high inflation. Devaluation also would invite further protectionist measures from OECD countries.

In either case, an economic crisis will have emerged, which may cause two dangerous dynamics to emerge. First, political actors in the regime may interpret the crisis as a significant and long-lasting reduction of their payoffs from the status quo (Haggard and Kaufman 1995, 32). Second, economic hardship will increase the cost of maintaining stability as disaffected citizens engage in protests or even rioting. If protests emerged in several major cities simultaneously, elites who already have an exit option might not find it worthwhile to engage in costly repression. Alternatively, if lower-ranking "stability maintenance" staff expects a reduction or even a cessation of payments from the government, they may stop engaging in repression, thus allowing an escalation of protests (Kuran 1991). These dynamics would be very destabilizing for the regime.

Besides economic triggers, recent political changes also laid the groundwork for political triggers of instability. First, the dominance of Xi Jinping and his close followers meant the size of the selectorate has shrunk dramatically. With the destruction or weakening of all the other factions, officials in the losing factions in essence faced a dramatically lower chance of receiving promotions and fewer opportunities to engage in rent seeking (Shih and Lee 2018). Even followers in Xi's own faction faced much weaker incentives with the likely Xi tenure for life after the 2018 constitutional revision. His decision to serve for life signaled to rank-and-file officials that senior followers in the administration also will stay on beyond the normal retirement age, thus lowering mid-ranking officials' chance of moving to top-level positions in the medium term. By consolidating power and by scrapping the retirement age, Xi weakened the incentives of the vast majority of officials to help maintain the status quo.

To be sure, their outside options are also limited, as there are no viable political alternatives in the country. In addition, consolidation of power by Xi means that challenging Xi's power directly bears much greater risks today than when Xi first took power. Elites may have no choice but to help maintain the status quo given the uncertainties of the alternatives. However, if a smaller selectorate is faced with an economic crisis, which reduces the expected payoffs of all officials in the system and raises the costs of repression even more, they may become indifferent between the status quo and the uncertainties of regime change, especially if they can form an alliance with the wealthy elite with substantial offshore wealth (Haggard and Kaufman 1995).

Institutional changes at the top level may also interact with a crisis in a similar manner. Consolidating decision-making in the leading groups dominated by Xi in essence reduced the eventual payoffs of "winning" the inner-party promotion game because the power of an ordinary PSC member was reduced. To be sure, the secretary general position became much more powerful, but aspiring officials would not have given themselves a high chance of landing in the secretary general position before their own retirement, which was on a much stricter time table than Xi's own retirement.

A PSC seat no longer meant automatic control over a major policy area and plenty of rent-seeking opportunities in that area. An official who was promoted to the PSC after 2012 either had to accept a significantly smaller political payoff than his predecessors or to engage in highly risky political struggle to obtain the top position. Either way, the expected payoff of a Politburo Standing Committee seat was reduced. Coupled with an economic crisis, which further reduced payoffs, the institutional changes Xi enacted after he took power may well cause a wave of elite defection.

Neither the political nor the economic dynamic suggests imminent instability in China. In fact, the authorities can deploy a number of measures to forestall political and economic effects. On the financial front, the government can preemptively enact a one-shot devaluation to forestall capital flight. Alternatively, the government can tighten capital control, although capital control may not work well in the long run against market pressure. On the political front, the leadership can undo some of the institutional and factional changes in recent years and revert to a more decentralized mode of policymaking. That may restore the party elite's incentive to help maintain the status quo, although policy deadlocks may be the price.

NOTE

1. This number may be much higher than 100,000 because there are no data on how many protests are prevented.

REFERENCES

Barboza, David. 2012. "Billions in Hidden Riches for Family of Chinese Leader." *New York Times*, October 25.

Baum, Richard. 1994. *Burying Mao: Chinese Politics in the Age of Deng Xiaoping*. Princeton: Princeton University Press.

Boston Consulting Group. 2015. "Global Wealth 2015: Winning the Growth Game." In *Global Wealth Reports*. Boston: BCG.

Brownlee, Jason. 2007. *Authoritarianism in an Age of Democratization*. New York: Cambridge University Press.

Bueno de Mesquita, Bruce, Alastair Smith, Randolph M. Siverson, and James D. Morrow. 2003. *The Logic of Political Survival*. Cambridge, MA: MIT Press.

Caixin. 2014. "Zhou Yongkang Hong yu Hei" (The red and black of Zhou Yongkang). *Caixin*, July 29.

Chen, Lei. 2015a. "59shenbuji guanyuan luoma fanfu xinqushi: gengjiatuchu 'biaoben jianzhi'" (59 provincial and ministerial level officials fell; new trends in anti-corruption will emphasize "curing the symptoms and causes simultaneously"). *Legal Daily*, November 13.

Chen, Lei. 2015b. "Zhongjiwei jinnian yilai tongbao chachu27328 qi weifan baxiang guiding jingshen wenti" (The CDIC revealed and investigated 27,328 cases of violation of the spirit of "Eight Regulations"). *Legal Daily*, November 26.

Cheung, Tai Ming. 2001. "The Influence of the Gun: China's Central Military Commission and Its Relationship with the Military, Party, and State Decision-Making System." In *The Making of Chinese Foreign and Security Policy in the Era of Reform*, ed. David M. Lampton. Stanford: Stanford University Press.

Dickson, Bruce J. 2003. *Red Capitalists in China: The Party, Private Entrepreneurs, and Prospects for Political Change*. New York: Cambridge University Press.

Dobbs, Richard, Susan Lund, Jonathan Woetzel, and Mina Mutafchieva. 2015. *Debt and (Not Much) Deleveraging*. New York: McKinsey Global Institute.

Forsythe, Michael. 2015. "Wang Jianlin, a Billionaire at the Intersection of Business and Power in China." *New York Times*, April 28.

Geddes, Barbara. 1999. "What Do We Know about Democratization after Twenty Years?" *Annual Review of Political Science* 2: 115–44.

Haggard, Stephan, and Robert R. Kaufman. 1995. *The Political Economy of Democratic Transitions*. Princeton: Princeton University Press.

Heilmann, Sebastian, and Elizabeth J. Perry. 2013. "Embracing Uncertainty: Guerrilla Policy Style and Adaptive Governance in China." *China Analysis* 103, May. Trier, Germany: University of Trier.

Huang, Cary. 2014. "How Leading Small Groups Help Xi Jinping and Other Party Leaders Exert Power." *South China Morning Post*, January 20.

Johnson, Chris, and Scott Kennedy. 2015. "China's Un-separation of Power." *Foreign Affairs*, July 24.

Keck, Zachary. 2014. "China Creates New Military Reform Leading Group." *The Diplomat*, March 20.

Kennedy, Scott. 2005. *The Business of Lobbying in China*. Cambridge, MA: Harvard University Press.

King, Gary, Jennifer Pan, and Margaret Roberts. 2013. "How Censorship in China Allows Government Criticism but Silences Collective Expression." *American Political Science Review* 107: 1–18.

Kuran, Timur. 1991. "Now out of Never: The Element of Surprise in the Eastern European Revolution of 1989." *World Politics* 44 (1): 7–48.

Landry, Pierre F. 2008. *Decentralized Authoritarianism in China: The Communist Party's Control of Local Elites in the Post-Mao Era*. New York: Cambridge University Press.

Li, Bin. 2009. "Guanjian shiqi bunengsong- Wen Jiabao Zongli zai Shandong kaocha ceji" (One must not relax during an extraordinary period, a record of Premier Wen Jiabao's inspection of Shandong). *Xinhua*, June 29.

Lieberthal, Kenneth. 2004. *Governing China: From Revolution through Reform*. 2nd ed. New York: Norton.

Liu, Lillian. 2012. "Wen Jiabao Defends China's 2008 Stimulus." *Finance Asia*, September 12.

Magaloni, Beatriz, and Ruth Kricheli. 2010. "Political Order and One-Party Rule." *Annual Review of Political Science* 13: 123–43.

Ministry of Finance. 2019. "Guanyu 2018 nian zhongyang juesuan baogao" (Report concerning the final central budget of 2018). Beijing: Ministry of Finance.

Montefiore, Sebag. 2003. *Stalin: The Court of the Red Tsar*. London: Weidenfeld & Nicolson.

Nelson, Joan. 1993. "The Politics of Economic Transformation: Is Third World Experience Relevant to Eastern Europe?" *World Politics* 45: 433–63.

Pei, Minxin. 2006. *China's Trapped Transition: The Limits of Developmental Autocracy*. Cambridge, MA: Harvard University Press.

People's Bank of China. 2015a. "Report on Monetary Policy in the First Half of 2015." In *PBOC Monetary Policy Report*. Beijing: PBOC.

People's Bank of China. 2015b. *Sources and Uses of Credit Funds of Financial Institutions—Various Years*. Available from http://www.pbc.gov.cn/diaochatongji/tongjishuju/gofile.asp?file=2006S03.htm

People's Bank of China. 2018. "Report on the Implementation of Monetary Policy in 4th Quarter of 2017." In *PBOC Monetary Policy Report*. Beijing: PBOC.

Pepinsky, Thomas B. 2009. *Economic Crises and the Breakdown of Authoritarian Regimes: Indonesia and Malaysia in Comparative Perspective*. New York: Cambridge University Press.

Qian, Haoping. 2012. "Zhongguo zhengbuji gangbu daiyu qiemi" (Revealing the pay and benefits of full ministerial cadres in China). *Nanfang Zhoumo (Southern weekly)*, February 21.

Reporters, Staff. 2015. "Chinese Spy Chief Ma Jian Detained as Corruption Crackdown Widens." *South China Morning Post*, January 11.

Reuters. 2010. "China Curbs Off-Balance Sheet Trust Lending: Sources." Reuters, July 4.

Schurmann, Franz. 1968. *Ideology and Organization in Communist China*. 2nd ed. Berkeley: University of California Press.

Shih, Victor C. 2008. *Factions and Finance in China: Elite Conflicts and Inflation*. New York: Cambridge University Press.

Shih, Victor C. 2010. "Local Government Debt: Big Rock Candy Mountain." *China Economic Quarterly* 2010 (June): 26–32.

Shih, Victor C., Christopher Adolph, and Liu Mingxing. 2012. "Getting Ahead in the Communist Party: Explaining the Advancement of Central Committee Members in China." *American Political Science Review* 106 (1): 166–87.

Shih, Victor C., and Jonghyuk Lee. 2018. "Locking In Fair Weather Friends: Assessing the Fate of Chinese Communist Elite When Their Patrons Fall from Power." *Party Politics*. https://doi.org/10.1177/1354068818801143

Shih, Victor C., Jonghyuk Lee, and David Meyer. 2015. "An Updated Database of Central Committee Members of the CCP." San Diego: Institute of Global Conflict and Cooperation.

Shirk, Susan. 1993. *The Political Logic of Economic Reform in China*. Berkeley: University of California Press.

Slater, Dan. 2003. "Iron Cage in an Iron Fist: Authoritarian Institutions and the Personalization of Power in Malaysia." *Comparative Politics* 35 (1): 81–101.

Svolik, Milan. 2012. *The Politics of Authoritarian Rule*. New York: Cambridge University Press.

Tanner, Murray Scot. 2014. "China's Social Unrest Problem." Washington, DC: US-China Economic and Security Review Commission.

Truex, Rory. 2016. *Making Autocracy Work: Representation and Information in Modern China*. New York: Cambridge University Press.

Tsai, Kellee S. 2007. *Capitalism without Democracy: The Private Sector in Contemporary China*. Ithaca: Cornell University Press.

Walder, Andrew G. 2015. *China under Mao: A Revolution Derailed*. Cambridge, MA: Harvard University Press.

Wang, Duan. 2015. "Guotai Jun'an Guoji Yan Feng shilian, he Yao Gang guanxi buyiban" (Guotai Jun'an International Yan Feng has disappeared, had an unusual relationship with Yao Gang). *Caixin*, November 23.

Wang, Yuhua, and Carl Minzner. 2015. "Rise of the Security State." *China Quarterly* 222: 339–59.

Wu, Rujia, and Zijing Li. 2013. "Wang Qishan Nianpu: lujiyuxian zaijia zuofan zhaodai laoyou" (The Facebook of Wang Qishan: Self-disciplined and invites old friends to his home for dinner). *Phoenix Weekly* 34.

Yang, Yishen, Weihao Mao, and Dan Sang. 2015. "Huang Guangyu tiqian chuyu? zhengquan shichang xujia xinxi heyi mantianfei" (Will Huang Guangyu get out of jail early—false rumors fly in the stock market). *Xinhua*, May 17.

Zhang, Qi, Mingxing Liu, and Victor C. Shih. 2013. "Guerilla Capitalism: Revolutionary Legacy, Political Cleavage, and the Preservation of the Private Economy in Zhejiang." *Journal of East Asian Studies* 13: 379–407.

Zhu, Jiangnan. 2008. "Why Are Offices for Sale in China? A Case Study of the Office-Selling Chain in Heilongjiang Province." *Asian Survey* 48 (4): 558–79.

SEVEN

Maladjustment

Economic Shock and Authoritarian Dynamics in Malaysia

Dan Slater

1. Introduction

Economic shocks are expected to affect authoritarian regimes like kryptonite affects Superman. No matter how strong they are, dictatorships should be weakened in the face of sudden and severe economic downturns. Funds should immediately become less available for buying off key supporters. Elites should get conspiratorial; the masses should become restless. Whatever regime was in power when the crisis hit should receive the brunt of the blame for allowing it to occur. Opportunistic political entrepreneurs should seize the moment to proclaim the regime bankrupt, not just economically but politically. Their claims should find a ready audience among desperate countrymen seeking an alternative approach—almost any approach—to make the economic pain and uncertainty go away. Powerful external funders should see the shock as a golden opportunity to push for major economic and political reforms that the prostrate dictatorship will have diminished capacity to resist. Even if it does not kill Superman, the kryptonite of economic shock should leave him a shell and shadow of his former self.

Malaysia's experience during the epochal economic shock of the Asian Financial Crisis (1997–99) casts serious doubt on these seemingly straightforward expectations. The facts themselves are puzzling on their face, in at least four distinct respects. First, Malaysia's long-ruling authoritarian party (the United Malays National Organization, UMNO) and coalition (National Front or Barisan Nasional, BN) survived the crisis with relative ease, despite the fact that it was by any reckoning a truly massive financial shock. This puzzle of *regime stability* is the most obvious one to arise from the Malaysian case. Second, the economic shock's immediate political effect was not elite defections and mass protests, but 13 long months of continued regime cohesion and societal peace. The period from August 1997 through August 1998 thus presents us with an additional puzzle of *crisis quiescence*. Third, when elite splits and mass protests did finally erupt, it was not when the economy was cratering, but when it was already recovering thanks in part to a muscular government response. Herein lies the puzzle of *protest delay*. Fourth and finally, the primary source of these protests was the majority ethnic Malay population, who undeniably had long been at the heart of the ruling coalition, and whom the regime had targeted with increased economic support to preserve their loyalty. By contrast, the ethnic group that rallied most strongly behind the regime—first by overwhelmingly eschewing participation in mass protests, and then by strongly supporting the BN regime in the national election of October 1999—was the minority Chinese population, despite its much weaker position within the ruling coalition. We might call this the puzzle of *coalitional inconsistency*.

The essay to follow attends to all four of these puzzles. My overarching argument is that Malaysia's surprising political stability throughout the darkest economic days of the Asian Financial Crisis was primarily a product of the UMNO/BN regime's *inherited institutional and coalitional strengths*. Indeed, the regime entered the crisis in such a strong political and economic position that it scarcely needed to pursue economic adjustment policies at all to survive it. What is most striking about Malaysia's experience with adjustment policies during economic crisis is not *how* its authoritarian regime adjusted, but *how little* it needed to adjust to survive such a massive shock. Understanding authoritarian responses to economic shocks demands attention to institutional capacity, not just policy choice. Dictatorships with strong institutions have more policy choices at their effective disposal than dictatorships with weak ones.

Inherited regime strengths quite efficiently explain the first two puzzles: those of regime stability and crisis quiescence from August 1997 until September 1998. To put it in terms of the metaphor that opened this essay, Malaysia's Superman regime was strong enough to withstand a very heavy dose of kryptonite. Yet the Malaysian case also provides reason to believe that the kryptonite metaphor is misguided at a fundamental level. Economic shocks can ironically solidify an authoritarian regime's position by providing it with a rationale to increase popular spending programs in a countercyclical manner: that is, priming the pump. Especially for regimes that were born in crisis and generate their appeal in part by acting as if they are the only actors capable of preventing the country from plunging back into chaos, economic shocks are a perfect chance to prove their crisis-fighting mettle. From this perspective, an economic shock is less like sudden exposure to kryptonite than like a villainous kidnapping of Lois Lane. Like Superman, an authoritarian regime comes out looking even stronger after seemingly saving the day.

To make sense of the latter two puzzles—those of protest delay and coalitional inconsistency—it is essential to complement a historically oriented focus on inherited authoritarian strengths with careful attention to authoritarian dynamics arising from the crisis and response. Although Malaysia's dictatorship is often depicted as one that is strictly of, for, and by its ethnic majority Malay population, the fact of the matter is that UMNO (a Malay party) has always ruled the country through a multiethnic party coalition (the BN) that UMNO undeniably dominates. This durable coalition has never been a product of *economic provision* alone; rather, its extraordinary strength has always lain in its origins in *physical protection* for Malays and non-Malays alike (Slater 2010).

This helps explain why Malaysia's political crisis did not erupt until September 1998, fully 13 months after the economic crisis began, and in the specific way that it did. Prime Minister Mahathir Mohamad offended Malay middle-class sensibilities at the beginning of that pivotal month by sacking his popular deputy Anwar Ibrahim, and slandering him as a homosexual. Mass protests erupted in direct response to the sacking, beating, and imprisonment of Anwar, and not to the nearly simultaneous imposition of capital controls, which were seen as practically uncontroversial and unobjectionable within Malaysia (unlike their nearly hysterical denunciation *outside* Malaysia) at the time. In short, a growing number of Malays turned against Mahathir because they increasingly perceived him as *a producer of violence instead of a protector from violence*, despite his regime's stepped-up efforts to buy off Malay support.

By contrast, the ethnic Chinese minority solidly maintained its backing for the regime: first by largely eschewing participation in the mass *reformasi* protests that followed Anwar's ouster, and then by rallying behind the BN coalition in the 1999 elections that returned it to power with a reduced majority due to dropping Malay support for UMNO. In part this was surely because the Chinese community had not been expected to pay any significant costs for economic adjustment. But at a deeper level, it was because the "protection pact" between Malaysia's long-ruling authoritarian regime and the Chinese minority remained stronger than its pact with the Malay majority—especially in the shadow of ominous anti-Chinese riots taking place amid democratic transition in neighboring Indonesia.

This brings us, in the final analysis, to the longer-term dynamics of economic shock and authoritarian survival in Malaysia. The Asian Financial Crisis did not mark the end of Malaysia's authoritarian regime; but it did mark the beginning of the end of the protection pact that had historically sustained it. It also marked Malaysia's entry into an authoritarian "bittersweet spot" in which it maintained sufficient regime strength to concede deep reforms—even fully democratic reforms—without losing its electoral grip on power (Slater and Wong 2013). Yet this window of opportunity was badly squandered. After 1998, Malaysian authoritarianism began sustaining itself with the kind of deficit spending that proves unsustainable over the long haul. It also generally retained the kind of authoritarian repression that got the UMNO/BN regime into so much trouble with the country's rising urban population in the first place. By rejecting all kinds of economic and political reform during the Asian Financial Crisis, Malaysia's rulers chose to avoid rather than confront the costs of economic adjustment.

UMNO and the BN would ultimately pay a steep price for avoiding reform, however: at the ballot box. Fifteen years of pump-priming, deficit spending, megaproject-driven development, and repression of dissent after the Asian Financial Crisis hit, the regime inherited by Mahathir Mohamad's successors after his voluntary resignation in 2003 found itself in worse shape than it ever was when the economy was in a virtual free-fall.[1] This was most dramatically expressed in the elections of 2013, when the BN lost the popular vote and its two-thirds control over parliament for the first time. By the elections of 2018, the long-ruling coalition would lose power outright. The upshot of the shock was *not adjustment but maladjustment*, in which short-term survival trumps all concern for long-term sustainability. Economic shock did not quickly debilitate the UMNO/BN regime like kryptonite. More like a dose of radiation, its effects proved cancerous for the regime in both their slowness and severity.

2. Broad Coalition, Hegemonic Institutions: 1950s–1990s

Authoritarian ruling coalitions are not necessarily narrow and elitist. In contrast to median-voter theory (e.g., Acemoglu and Robinson 2006), and in close harmony with a wide range of new research critical of that paradigm (e.g., Albertus 2015), I argue that authoritarian regimes are quite commonly motivated to build broad coalitions and rule through the many rather than the few. Perhaps more controversially, I also challenge the assumption of selectorate theory that coalitions should be defined strictly in terms of who benefits from economic policies and disbursements. The defining trait of a coalition partner lies in offering a regime some form of active political support; whether that coalition member receives economic blandishments in exchange for that support should be an empirical question rather than a definitional entailment (Bueno de Mesquita et al. 2003).[2]

These correctives to predominant visions of authoritarian coalitions are vital for making sense of Malaysia's coalitional strength when crisis struck in August 1997. Malaysia's dominant UMNO party has housed a cross-class alliance of ethnic Malays ever since it was formed in 1946 to block British efforts to grant the colony's ethnic Chinese minority political status equal to that of Malay "sons of the soil" (*bumiputeras*). Contrary to median-voter theory's expectations, UMNO pursued relatively mild redistributive policies during Malaysia's democratic period from 1957 to 1969, but stepped up redistribution under the newly authoritarian regime's New Economic Policy from the early 1970s onward. These policy adjustments indicated a ruling coalition that was shifting in emphasis but not necessarily shrinking in size. Under the authoritarian auspices of the BN coalition as during the democratic period of the Alliance, UMNO ruled in tandem with its ethnic Chinese partners, particularly in the Malaysian Chinese Association (MCA).[3] Malaysia thus possessed a coalition that was resolutely both cross-class and cross-ethnic throughout its first 40 years of independence.

This enduring coalitional strength has manifested in a wide variety of institutional domains. For starters, UMNO constituted and commanded an electoral juggernaut. After the Alliance briefly saw its two-thirds majority threatened in the May 1969 elections, the formation of a broader BN party coalition helped its component parties romp to landslide after landslide throughout the 1970s, 1980s, and 1990s. Indeed, the 1995 national election was the BN's strongest result ever, as the coalition secured over 65 percent of all votes and nearly 85 percent of federal parliamentary seats. Hence when the Asian Financial Crisis struck Malaysia in 1997, it struck a regime that was truly at the apex of its authoritarian powers.

Malaysia's powerful and popular ruling parties were bolstered by their connection to an unusually strong postcolonial state. Forged in the violent social conflicts of the 1940s, 1950s, and 1960s, Malaysia's state was as effective at extracting taxes and other revenues from its population as the Alliance and BN were at attracting votes. This underscores the vital point that supporters of the BN did not merely support it out of appreciation or in exchange for economic services rendered. At both the elite and the mass level, the BN was widely perceived as a necessary physical protector against a recurrence of the deadly ethnic conflicts of the decolonization and early independence eras. This gave the regime leverage over its coalition partners, allowing it to generate ample political support without squandering its abundant economic resources in the process.

The economic might of Malaysia's authoritarian Leviathan was clearly expressed in its command over the country's financial sector (Jesudason 1989). Finance boomed throughout Malaysia's rapid-growth period; but it did not become autonomous from the BN regime in the process.[4] To the contrary, finance's economic rise in Malaysia was attained through total political dependence on UMNO/BN leadership. Foreign banks made few inroads except as minority shareholders in local financial institutions owned by highly connected Malaysian capitalists. As discussed further below, this regime dominance over financial capital was predicated on the state's long history of mobilizing revenue through the national tax system and forcing savings through the Employees Provident Fund (EPF), among other vehicles for aggrandizing sovereign wealth. In stark contrast to Indonesia and Thailand, its main Southeast Asian economic competitors, Malaysia's economic boom was largely funded by local institutions, and its boom-era debts were mostly denominated in local currency. This would have profound implications for the politics of economic adjustment and regime stability when the Asian Financial Crisis hit.

The Malaysian party-state's institutional might has always had a coercive as well as an economic side. Battling a decade-long emergency against communists in the 1940s–1950s had given rise to an unusually powerful coercive apparatus that was tightly wedded to the ruling party. Far from being a militarized state, Malaysia has always quite literally been a police state, in the sense that its coercive capacity rests in police rather than military institutions. Ironically, the efficiency of coercive institutions meant that Malaysian authoritarianism had to fall back on outright physical repression less often than most dictatorships. As Harold Crouch (1995) persuasively argued as of the mid-1990s, Malaysia's BN had long been a "repressive-responsive regime" in which any signs of mass protest would be countered, first, by punishing the movement's leaders, and then by responding effectively to whatever concern prompted the unrest, thereby nipping the problem in the bud.

Yet as Malaysia neared the Asian Financial Crisis, its ruling regime was narrowing and becoming more muscularly coercive in one important respect: the regime's growing personalization under the rule of Prime Minister Mahathir Mohamad, who had assumed power in 1981 (Slater 2003). Whereas his predecessors had generally ruled collectively and consensually, at least within the confines of UMNO and the BN's highest reaches, Mahathir brooked no opposition from either inside or outside his regime. This had prompted a nasty UMNO split in 1987 and Mahathir's use of draconian colonial-era security laws, particularly the Internal Security Act (ISA), to help him survive it. Having responded to political crisis in the late 1980s with a mixture of repression and dirty tricks, Mahathir had learned that a coercive response to regime crisis could prove extremely effective in the context of a highly capable authoritarian party-state. This would pale in comparison to the repressive response that Mahathir unleashed during the political crisis of the late 1990s, as I discuss in the following section.

In sum, Malaysia's UMNO/BN regime and its strong-armed prime minister were in the proverbial catbird's seat on the eve of the Asian Financial Crisis. Mahathir had become effectively the only veto player in a regime that could command the political, economic, and symbolic support of an extraordinarily wide set of actors at both the elite and the mass level. The economy had been booming and generating revenue surpluses for decades, leaving Malaysian businessmen much less dependent for their fortunes on short-term dollar-denominated liabilities than the corporate sector in much of East and Southeast Asia. The financial sector remained firmly in state control. This helps explain why even an economic shock as devastatingly powerful as the Asian Financial Crisis did not force Malaysia's authoritarian regime to shortchange its coalition partners or alter its approach to governance with any political or economic reforms. It would only be in the long run that the costs of such adjustment avoidance would take their toll.

3. Exogenous Shock: The Asian Financial Crisis, 1997–98

Emanating outward from Thailand after the forced devaluation of its baht currency, the Asian Financial Crisis had devastated the Malaysian economy by late 1997.[5] The Malaysian ringgit lost more than 50 percent of its value and the Kuala Lumpur Stock Exchange lost more than 60 percent of its capitalization, leaving the bourse "littered with penny stocks" (*Business Times* [Singapore], July 15, 1998). Even worse for Mahathir, his own missteps were widely blamed for the severity of the downturn. He initially responded to falling asset prices by unleashing a vitriolic tirade against foreign portfolio investors and currency traders. Such "blame-the-speculators pronouncements propelled the ringgit to new depths" (*Asiaweek*, February 20, 1998). As the economy plummeted, even UMNO members began to criticize Mahathir's mismanagement. "People are getting fed up with his constant attack on foreigners," said one UMNO official. "It's beginning to hurt us" (*Far Eastern Economic Review* [*FEER*], July 2, 1998). By March 1998, *Asiaweek* reported that "Mahathir finds his legacy in limbo, his country in jeopardy, and his backers in retreat" (*Asiaweek*, March 27, 1998).

Mahathir may have been playing his hand quite badly—but the bigger point is that he had inherited a strong hand. Thanks to the Malaysian state's fiscal power, public debt remained at manageable levels, and much of the private sector's gargantuan debt was owed to domestic rather than foreign institutions. Malaysia "managed to stave off an Indonesian-style crisis only because, unlike much of Asia, the bulk of its debt is in local currency" (*FEER*, April 30, 1998). Thanks to these stronger fundamentals, Malaysian authorities kept interest rates lower than in neighboring countries throughout the crisis—Indonesia's rates were more than three times higher than Malaysia's by late April 1998, more than four months *before* Malaysia imposed capital controls—and used domestic funds rather than International Monetary Fund monies to buy out the banking sector's enormous overhang of dud loans.

In short, the Asian financial crisis delivered a similarly powerful punch in Malaysia as in Indonesia, but the Malaysian private sector enjoyed access to a much stronger state to cushion the blow. Malaysia's authoritarian Leviathan entered the crisis with a cornucopia of funding sources that had gotten ever more bountiful over the preceding decades. The most important were the well-managed state oil company, Petronas, and the state provident fund, the EPF. Each had accumulated more reserves than Malaysia's central bank when the crisis hit—approximately US$25 billion for Petronas, and US$34 billion for the EPF. The EPF reserves alone amounted to a whopping 55 percent of Malaysia's annual GDP (*FEER*, April 30, 1998). As corporate debt skyrocketed, economic elites looked to these funds—and the BN officials pulling the purse strings—for their financial salvation. As a comedy troupe in Kuala Lumpur lampooned the lobbying of Malaysian corporate leaders: "We don't want the IMF [International Monetary Fund]. All we need is the EPF" (*FEER*, April 30, 1998).

Despite the severity of the financial shock, there was never any prospect that Mahathir's UMNO/BN regime would respond by cutting mass spending programs or letting powerful concessionaire businessmen go belly-up. To the contrary, after some initial rhetorical signaling of a willingness to cut public spending to appease panicky foreign lenders, spending grew through pump-priming rather than shrinking through austerity. Even during the first, worst year of the downturn, nobody of consequence in Malaysian politics was calling for spending cutbacks that might affect the pivotal ethnic Malay majority. Economic crisis provided an occasion to *increase* government spending to lessen the public pain, not a time to *decrease* spending to restore shattered investor confidence. Malaysia's Superman was rushing to rescue Lois Lane instead of wilting in the kryptonite of economic crisis.

While continued public subsidies and spending programs remained locally uncontroversial, corporate bailouts proved a touchier subject—not so much over *whether*, but over *how*, to rescue Malaysia's ailing, fledgling corporate giants. Most portentously, disagreements over the proper amount of public support for insolvent firms worsened the friction between Mahathir and his deputy, Anwar Ibrahim. While Anwar publicly expressed concern that bailouts should not compromise foreign investor confidence or squander the savings of EPF contributors, Mahathir remained committed to avoiding Schumpeterian creative destruction. Tensions worsened in March when Petronas, under Mahathir's control, announced that one of its subsidiaries was buying Konsortium Perkapalan Berhad (KPB), a heavily indebted shipping concern. The deal would use US$220 million in state funds to wipe out the personal debts of KPB's chief executive—Mirzan Mahathir, the prime minister's oldest son. When Anwar insisted upon an independent audit of KPB's value, he aggravated worries in Mahathir's inner circle that Anwar might not be a reliable champion of crony capital should he capture power.

Mahathir became increasingly defensive about his regime's financial support for well-connected firms. He recognized that the bailout issue threatened to catalyze middle-class opposition, since government largesse could only go so far. "If a person is a satay seller," Mahathir bristled, "surely we can't award him the Bakun dam project" (*The Star*, June 27, 1998). As UMNO's June general assembly approached, Anwar was forced to decide whether to make a bid for the UMNO presidency, or to defend his boss against growing criticism. If there was ever a time when Mahathir was vulnerable, this was it.

Yet expulsion from UMNO had always meant instant political marginalization, even for Malaysia's most popular politicians. Anwar thus tread cautiously. He encouraged his ally Ahmad Zahid Hamidi, the leader of UMNO's powerful youth wing, to "raise the issue of nepotism and cronyism in a way that indirectly challenged Mahathir's leadership" (Hwang

2003, 302). Mahathir and his allies responded forcefully, "releasing a list of names which showed that Anwar's relatives and close associates, including Zahid, had also benefited substantially from privatized state contracts and special share allocations" (Hwang 2003, 302). Zahid backpedaled: "We do not want anyone to doubt our loyalty to the party leadership or the country" (*The Star*, June 13, 1998). Anwar was equally conciliatory. Party unity was of "paramount importance," he insisted. "We have only one leader and skipper, our Prime Minister Dr. Mahathir" (*The Star*, June 22, 1998). With all the institutional weapons of the party-state in Mahathir's hands, Anwar calculated that his best option was to bide his time, hoping to remain the prime minister's chosen successor. The most serious public expression of regime fragmentation during the Asian Financial Crisis' first year—Zahid's elliptically critical speech at the June 1998 UMNO assembly—had ended with a whimper of cohesion instead of a bang of elite defection.

Despite Anwar's protestations of loyalty, "Mahathir's distrust of his protégé became irreversible" (Hwang 2003, 302). The trick for Mahathir was to dispose of his deputy without sending financial markets into a tailspin, since Anwar was viewed internationally as the only leading government figure committed to structural economic reforms. Mahathir found the solution in a one-two punch: on September 1, he imposed capital controls and fixed the value of the national currency, making it impossible for foreign investors to repatriate their capital or speculate against the ringgit. This was a viable strategy in Malaysia because the state had the institutional capacity to administer capital controls effectively, as well as the fiscal power to fund the immense cost of economic recovery from within. With capital controls in place, Mahathir had Anwar expelled, first from the cabinet, and then from UMNO—ostensibly on the grounds that he was a homosexual and had abused his power to stonewall a police inquiry into his private life.

4. Maladjustment amid *Reformasi:* 1998–99

The purging of Anwar and introduction of capital controls in early September 1998 moved Malaysia's crisis into an entirely new phase—but not because it meant a radical departure from the economic policies of the previous 13 months, which had already been more expansionary than austere. To be sure, capital controls had some short-term economic benefits. They allowed the regime to fix the value of the ringgit at a slightly stronger value; to force all ringgit being held overseas back into the country; and to nudge interest rates downward, alleviating the ongoing banking and corporate debt crises.

Here, the Malaysian party-state's command relationship with private finance was critical.[6] In what was effectively a grand political-economic quid pro quo, UMNO/BN leaders rushed to recapitalize Malaysia's reeling financial institutions with public funds in exchange for stepped-up, countercyclical private bank lending to keep the country's concessionaire capitalist class afloat. Alongside capital controls, Malaysia's central bank, Bank Negara, imposed a mandatory 8 percent loan-growth requirement on all private lenders, coercively counteracting private banks' prudential impulse to clean up their balance sheets in a time of spreading business bankruptcies. Mahathir appointed a political loyalist as Bank Negara governor to ensure banks would not forget that state-funded recapitalization was fully conditional on their active assistance in the UMNO/BN regime's campaign for increased lending. "We will monitor the progress of banking institutions in their lending activities on a weekly basis," the new governor warned. "Banking institutions which show no progress in their lending activities will be called for discussion with Bank Negara" (*The Star*, September 15, 1998). Regime leaders were paying the piper with funds for recapitalization, so it was calling the tune of rapid reflation.

Almost without question, capital controls helped Malaysia return to a growth trajectory from a recessionary one more quickly than would have been the case in the absence of such controls. Yet it was already abundantly clear many months before the capital controls that Malaysia would be able to navigate the Asian Financial Crisis without needing to seek the kind of massive external bailout that proved almost instantaneously necessary in Thailand, Indonesia, and South Korea. Since external capital had already fled Malaysian markets, forbidding further repatriation of the ringgit largely amounted to locking the barn door after the horse had already bolted. Thus in strictly economic terms, the short-term effects of capital controls and the fixed value of the ringgit—surely the most dramatic adjustment policies pursued throughout the entire economic crisis—could best be described as modest.

It is vitally important to appreciate that these heterodox economic policies did not salvage a regime at death's door. To the contrary: *the capital controls marked the onset rather than the termination of Malaysia's worst-ever political crisis*. The reason is that Mahathir did not implement capital controls to rescue the economy, but to assist him in killing off his main political rival: Anwar Ibrahim, the most popular politician in the country. Purging

Anwar provided both motive and opportunity for newly radicalized opposition to Mahathir's rule in particular, and to UMNO/BN hegemony more generally. Before the purge, the only real risk to Malaysian authoritarianism was that Anwar would take power and begin pursuing "democracy through strength," as reformist leaders had previously done in Taiwan, South Korea, and Indonesia (Slater and Wong 2013). This would have ended authoritarian rule, but not UMNO/BN rule. After the purge and subsequent crackdown on Anwar's supporters, however, Malaysia briefly flirted with a scenario of outright regime collapse through "democratic revolution."

There are many potential reasons why Mahathir and his repressive brand of authoritarian rule survived the *reformasi* movement. To mediate among these multiple explanations, it is prudent to consider the broader dynamics of crisis and response: especially the composition of the movement as well as the timing of its rise and decline. To return to the third and fourth puzzles that animated this paper from its outset: surely we can learn something deeper about the character and limitations of *reformasi* by considering the matters of *protest delay* and *coalitional inconsistency*. What does it tell us that protests did not break out until after capital controls were imposed and the economy was on the mend? And what does it tell us that majority ethnic Malays were by far the predominant participants in the protest movement, despite the fact that countercyclical spending policies were unambiguously targeted at Malays?

The overarching lesson I draw is that economic crises do not directly weaken authoritarian regimes because authoritarian regimes are not purely economic creatures. One must consider the noneconomic as much as the economic sources of regime cohesion and durability (Levitsky and Way 2012). *Protesters did not start biting the hands that fed them in Malaysia because those hands were underfeeding them in economic terms, but because those hands were increasingly strangling them in political terms.* In short, protests arose among Malaysians for whom Mahathir's authoritarian regime had devolved from a "protection pact" into more of a classic protection racket. Unfortunately for the fate of political and economic reform in Malaysia, the opposition coalition could not match the power of the ruling coalition throughout the duration of the Asian Financial Crisis.

The regime was held together more by shared fear than shared benefits.[7] In a society where mass mobilization has historically been associated with communal instability, authoritarian rulers have an easier time using scare tactics to dissuade average citizens from joining or supporting street protests. Mahathir's backers played on Malaysians' historical fears by persistently exaggerating both the communalism of the movement and the violence of the protests. In portraying *reformasi* as violent and communalist, Malaysian authorities had more than history on their side—they had the contemporary specter of communal violence in neighboring Indonesia to aggravate nervous souls. For reasons of shared language as much as shared political intentions, Malaysian oppositionists had adopted the same "reformasi" slogan used by the anti-Suharto movement in that same year. But Indonesia's democratic transition and aftermath had been marred by anti-Chinese violence, providing the BN with a golden opportunity to remind Chinese Malaysians of their insecure communal position. "Supporters of Mahathir depicted the anti-Chinese violence from Indonesia as a threat to the success of the Malaysian state in maintaining social and political order," write Ariel Heryanto and Sumit Mandal. "Images and reports were reproduced in the mass media that tended to intimidate the general public by hinting at the chaos the *Reformasi* movement would lead to in Malaysia if Malaysians followed the example of Indonesians by taking to the streets" (Heryanto and Mandal 2003, 10).

The BN's scare campaign was by no means limited to hints. When pressed to defend his decision to incarcerate Anwar, Mahathir replied: "It was clear he was working up emotions the way it was done in Indonesia, where the people rioted daily in order to overthrow the government" (*Asian Wall Street Journal*, September 23, 1998). Mahathir again played the race card in an interview with five Chinese-language dailies: "I worry that the power of UMNO will be weakened and the moderate political parties will be swept away." He insisted that the BN was uniquely capable of "taking overall control to maintain racial harmony," ignoring the *reformasi* movement's emphatically noncommunalist agenda (*Time International*, November 16, 1998). The attitude expressed by one Indian Muslim shopkeeper captured a common sentiment among opponents of *reformasi*, which I heard in various guises on dozens of occasions in the KL area in late 1998: "Look at Indonesia. As long as we can survive, we are grateful" (*Asian Wall Street Journal*, September 21, 1998).

The rhetoric and reality of riots intimidated Chinese Malaysians most of all. So long as "Chinese Malaysians were forced to contemplate the fearful implications for Malaysia of the racialized atrocities in neighboring Indonesia," it was unsurprising that "citizens of Chinese descent were not as politically active as those in Indonesia in challenging authoritarianism in the streets" (Heryanto and Mandal 2003, 8, 9). Anthony Loke, a Chinese student leader at the time of the protests and now an elected parliamentarian for the Democratic Action Party (DAP), agrees that the BN's manipulation of Indonesian unrest dampened Chinese support for *reformasi*: "You saw it every night on television: a few minutes of footage from Indonesia, showing burning cars and burning buildings." Such tactics help explain why as of 1998, pro-BN Chinese voters would "look at the Philippines and Indonesia, and think Malaysia is heaven."[8]

While Indonesian violence exacerbated Chinese Malaysians' fears of communal unrest, it by no means created it. For more than 30 years, Chinese Malaysians have been told, and often tell themselves: "Politics is not your cup of tea." Loke attributes this depoliticization to Malaysia's legacy of racial unrest. "Since 1969, for the Chinese, staying out of politics has become a norm." When asked whether his fellow Chinese students were deterred from participating in *reformasi* protests primarily by the threat from above (state repression) or by the threat from below (Malay communalism), Loke scarcely hesitates: "The big fear is from the bottom up." In light of the certainty and severity of government reprisals meted out to students who actively oppose the BN regime, this is powerful testimony to the lingering fear of ethnic unrest afflicting Malaysia's Chinese community as of the late 1990s.

Such fears helped keep Chinese voters wedded to the BN in the general elections of November 1999. Chinese support compensated for UMNO's loss of ground among Malay voters, who increasingly turned to the Malaysian Islamic Party (PAS) and Keadilan, the new multiracial party led on behalf of Anwar by his wife during what would prove to be Anwar's six-year prison term. While UMNO lost 20 of its 92 parliamentary seats, and relinquished the state of Trengganu to PAS in a rout, support for the MCA and Gerakan stayed firm. The BN retained its two-thirds majority with ease, in spite of the severity of the recent economic crisis and the plummeting popularity of Mahathir. The BN's weaker performance in the 1999 vote can be almost entirely ascribed to Malay anger at Mahathir over his handling of the Anwar affair, and not to any structural weakening of the BN. Internal UMNO polls before the elections suggested that up to 80 percent of Malay state officials disapproved of Mahathir's handling of the country's economic and political crises (Weiss 2006, 273 n. 37), as many of UMNO's bedrock supporters in the civil service "came to view Mahathir as repugnant" after his brutal dismissal of his popular former deputy (Case 2001, 50). Whatever political mileage Mahathir might have gained from introducing capital controls and priming the pump, it could not compare to the damage done to his reputation by his violent reaction to the challenges of Anwar and *reformasi*.

Malay voters felt freer than Chinese voters to reject the BN in 1999—especially in states with overwhelming Malay majorities—because historical Malay fears of Chinese political domination had all but evaporated. According to a leading oppositionist, Tian Chua, such fears had weakened among Malays only recently. As recently as the national elections of 1990, Chua argues, "The Malays still had not graduated from the fear that [DAP leader] Lim Kit Siang would become prime minister."[9] Yet Chua perceived little Malay anxiety about Chinese political intentions while playing a leading role in organizing the *reformasi* protests of the late 1990s.

The protection pact remained strong among Chinese voters, however. When asked why *reformasi* failed to gain as much support among Chinese as Malays, despite economic policies systematically favoring the latter over the former, Chua replied: "The Chinese fear that if they rock the boat, they will be punished." In terms of the argument presented here, Chinese support for the BN stems more from ethnic protection than from economic provision. "The BN gets maximum support from minimum concessions" among Chinese voters, says Chua. *"It's fear that holds it together."*

In sum, Malaysian oppositionists failed to generate the sort of sustained urban groundswell of cross-class protest that helped topple authoritarian regimes in the Philippines and Indonesia. In comparative perspective, Malaysian democratic mobilization was "limited, ephemeral, and unsuccessful" (Hedman 2001, 951). This was because the movement had virtually no backing whatsoever from elites, who remained firmly in the maw of Malaysia's cohesive and capable authoritarian Leviathan. Mahathir's claims to be acting as a protector of broad elite interests against the threat of renewed communal instability proved widely credible, especially among Malaysia's sizable ethnic Chinese population. Even a massive economic crisis could not shift Malaysian elites from a stance of authoritarian acquiescence to one of democratic action against a regime showing no hint of buckling from within.

5. Maladjustment after Crisis: 1999–Present

Skies only got brighter for the BN as the millennium turned. When Mahathir stepped down as prime minister and UMNO president in October 2003, a popular ruling party was freed from the grip of an autocratic and widely feared leader. The anti-Mahathir protest vote that shook UMNO in 1999 vanished in the elections of March 2004, delivering a landslide victory to BN parties across the board. This was something of a "honeymoon" election for new prime minister Abdullah Badawi, who came into power with a far less autocratic image and track record than his predecessor. The BN's vote share leaped from 56.5 percent to 64.4 percent, and its edge in parliamentary seats swelled from 147–42 to 198–20. UMNO was the biggest winner, boosting its total seats from 71 to 109. PAS lost 20 of its 27 seats, while Keadilan, the party of *reformasi*, was nearly annihilated as Anwar languished in prison, retaining only one of the seven seats it had won in 1999.

The scale of the BN's 2004 landslide cloaked the regime's structural problems that the Asian Financial Crisis had exposed and that the crackdown on *reformasi* had exacerbated. With its protection pact with the majority Malay population increasingly eroded, UMNO depended on increased public spending to win back urban Malay support, especially. The party also clearly benefited from Badawi's reformist image, even while ironically continuing to benefit from Anwar's ongoing imprisonment. Hence as of 2004, the UMNO/BN government had seemed to return to another apex of power, as in 1995. This made the regime ideally positioned to pursue "democracy through strength," yet unmotivated to do so, since Mahathir's combination of repression, pump-priming, and abdication from the prime ministership had seemingly sufficed to deliver UMNO/BN back to its authoritarian glory days.

With Chinese political power no longer a major pressing concern and the protection pact essentially in abeyance if not entirely expired in the Malay community, Malay voters were free to choose UMNO over PAS on the basis of more quotidian factors such as economic policy and the clean reputation of new prime minister Abdullah Badawi, rather than any lingering concerns with Malay needs for ethnic protection. Ironically, then, *UMNO secured its strongest electoral result just as its strongest justification for Malay support was evaporating*. Demographic shifts have swollen the Malay majority, and no Chinese political organization holds even remote hopes of capturing the political pinnacle. Yet ruling through patronage alone almost inevitably produces elite foes as well as friends, and saps the fiscal resources that an authoritarian Leviathan needs to maintain support in a "postprotective" era.

A worsening of factionalism within UMNO and other BN parties in the wake of its 2004 electoral landslide provides a partial explanation for the BN's shocking reversal of fortune in the March 2008 elections. For the first time since 1969, UMNO and its partners failed to capture a two-thirds majority of parliamentary seats. The BN's national vote plummeted from 64.4 percent to 51.2 percent, UMNO lost 30 of its 109 seats, and its major Chinese and Indian partners each surrendered more than half of their total seats to the opposition. PAS recouped most of its losses from 2004, bouncing back from seven seats to 23. But the spectacular opposition gains came from the DAP, which converted its 31–12 seat deficit vis-à-vis the MCA into a stunning 28–15 edge; and Keadilan, which came back from the political dead to capture 31 seats and become the largest party in opposition, just four years after it was a series of recounts away from having no seats in the national parliament. The states of Penang (DAP), Selangor (Keadilan), and Kedah (PAS) fell into opposition hands for the first time, while PAS easily recaptured Terengganu and maintained its grip on Kelantan.

While any single election result can only be adequately explained with reference to contingent as well as structural factors, the opposition's dramatic gains in 2008 are better explained by tectonic shifts in Malaysia's political context than in its economic context. In the final fiscal quarter before the 2008 election, Malaysia had the fastest economic growth (7.3 percent) and the lowest inflation (2.7 percent) in Southeast Asia, while unemployment remained minimal at 3.1 percent (*The Economist*, March 22, 2008, 101–2). The economy had been far worse in 1999, when the BN had fared far better. What had diminished between 2004 and 2008 was not Malaysians' level of well-being, but the levels of *coercion* the regime was using to repress opposition forces, and the levels of *confidence* elites felt that the BN was a surer protector of Malaysia's communal order than the multiethnic opposition alliance.

One cannot possibly explain Keadilan's political rebirth without appreciating the reduction in state repression the party faced after the 2004 vote. Most important, Anwar's release from prison after a federal court overturned his sodomy conviction in September 2004 permitted him to play the kind of active leadership role in 2008 that he could not in 1999 or 2004. The Mahathir government had also detained five other Keadilan leaders under the ISA from June 2001 until June 2003, and prevented several of these oppositionists from contesting in the 2004 election because their legal cases were still in process. Thus 2008 marked the first occasion when Malaysian voters could witness a largely unmolested electoral campaign by a truly ecumenical opposition party.

If Chinese voters had become much more inclined to perceive UMNO as a racketeer instead of a legitimate protector by 2008, UMNO had only itself to blame. As factionalism within the party intensified during the fat days following the 2004 landslide, ethnic outbidding increased. The most flagrant example came when UMNO Youth head Hishamuddin Hussein—the grandson of party founder Onn Jaafar and the son of former prime minister Hussein Onn—provocatively brandished a ceremonial *keris* dagger at the nationally televised UMNO General Assembly in June 2006.

Rather than backing down in the face of widespread criticism for the move, Hishamuddin went even further at the 2007 assembly, not merely waving a *keris* but receiving it from his underlings in an elaborate formal ceremony. In the interviews I conducted in Kuala Lumpur in late March 2008, Hishamuddin's menacing symbolism was portrayed as a watershed in Malaysian ethnic politics.

UMNO/BN's shocking 2008 electoral setback prompted the replacement of Abdullah Badawi with Najib Razak as UMNO president and Malaysian prime minister. Yet this was no solution to the regime's structural problems. Even more than Badawi, Najib tried to retain hegemony through unsustainable practices of elite patronage and public spending, without shoring up the regime's historical fiscal footing. The pre-1998 age of fiscal balances has given way to a post-1998 age of fiscal deficits. Moves to introduce a regressive national sales tax marked a decisive departure from Malaysia's history of extracting impressive amounts of revenue from economic elites through direct taxation. Najib also tried to restore the BN's strength with a more assertive rhetorical campaign to embrace the Chinese minority through a "1Malaysia" public-relations campaign, and through promising to discard Malaysia's atavistic authoritarian security laws such as the ISA.

These superficial steps were insufficient to arrest UMNO/BN's declining electoral fortunes in 2013. Especially due to collapsing support among the Chinese minority and urban voters more generally, the BN vote share declined from 50.3 percent to 46.5 percent, meaning Malaysia's opposition had secured a majority of the popular vote for the first time in the nation's history. Severe malapportionment kept the BN in power with 59.9 percent of all national seats (down from 63.1 percent in 2008). But the days when UMNO and the BN could count on electoral majorities by virtue of being seen as the only credible protector against a renewal of ethnic unrest appear to be gone entirely. It was only through increased repression (including the rejailing of Anwar Ibrahim and a reversal of promises to discard all draconian security laws), increasingly unsustainable borrowing and spending policies (as manifested in the shocking 1Malaysia Development Berhad [1MDB] scandal under Najib's leadership), and a devolution into increasingly rancid racist rhetoric against the minority Chinese population that UMNO/BN still managed to remain in power from 2013 to 2018.

None of these approaches could restore the regime's impressive historic majoritarian popularity. In a word, the regime's coalition and institutions had *shriveled*. The seeds of this decline can be located in the regime's failure to respond to the Asian Financial Crisis with either political or economic reforms of any kind. Having missed its golden opportunities to pursue "democracy through strength" in the mid-1990s and mid-2000s, UMNO could no longer concede democratic reforms with confidence that its BN coalition would win fully free and fair national elections. The regime's decisive defeat in the 2018 election, despite the usual battery of authoritarian controls, proved the most eloquent testimony to the regime's gradual postcrisis decline.

6. Conclusion: Economic Crisis as Authoritarian Opportunity

This chapter has attempted to leverage the case of contemporary Malaysia to rethink the role of economic shocks in undermining authoritarian regimes. As sudden as they are, economic shocks might only weaken dictatorships over the long run if they fail to respond to the economic and political signals that the crisis delivers: namely, that the salad days of rapid authoritarian-led development and widespread middle-class quiescence are over and done with.[10] Rather than assuming that economic shocks produce lean political times, we might consider how downturns prompt increased public spending in ways that can redound to a dictatorship's short-term benefit. Indeed, *economic crises are ideal times for dictators to borrow against the future in politically popular ways if they enjoy enough inherited fiscal strength to do so.*

Economic crises are never merely economic events. Hence economic variables like shifts in unemployment, inflation, interest rates, GDP growth, and exchange rates can only tell us so much about the political dynamics that follow. We need to take coalitions seriously, not merely as passive recipients of government largesse, but as the most important active contributors to authoritarian durability. We need to consider how physical repression of elite and mass opponents can play a key role in a dictatorship's survival of crisis, particularly if coercive institutions are both capable and cohesive. Whether the coercive arms of the state prove up to the repressive task will depend not merely on short-term economic considerations, but on long-term political dynamics of the ruling coalition and subtle shifts in its defining logics of rule.

At a deeper theoretical level, this essay suggests a need to transcend both median-voter theory and selectorate theory in our analyses of economic shocks and authoritarian rule. The breadth of an authoritarian coalition is always a historical and empirical question; it can never be apprehended by assumption. Careful case-based assessment of authoritarian dynamics is essential to determine what groups are in, what groups are out, and what the terms of coalitional inclusion—and exclusion—are (Yom 2015). Of particular importance is the direction in which economic, political, and even symbolic resources are flowing: mostly from the country's diverse elites into the hands of the authoritarian Leviathan, or from the authoritarian Leviathan toward those elites. Only then can we know if the regime is increasing or squandering its power resources in a dynamic sense. And only then can we know if an authoritarian regime's repressive maltreatment of actors who refuse to acquiesce in exchange for economic blandishments might be doing deep coalitional damage from which a dictatorship can never fully recover.

The Malaysian experience should also incite us to think of economic shocks as powerful political signals. In particular, they can signal that an authoritarian regime has passed its apex of power, and is entering the "bittersweet spot" where the regime is losing its capacity to maintain stability through purely authoritarian means, yet remains strong enough to thrive under democratic conditions. This was the case in Malaysia after both the economic shock of 1997–98 and the electoral shock of 2008. If Anwar Ibrahim and his allies had prevailed in his factional struggle with Mahathir Mohamad at the height of the Asian Financial Crisis, Malaysia would most likely have followed in the "democracy through strength" footsteps of ruling parties in Taiwan, South Korea, and Indonesia. If Abdullah Badawi had recognized that his 2004 landslide was a referendum in favor of his reformist image and not Mahathir's repressive and free-spending practices, another chance for UMNO/BN to concede democracy without conceding defeat could readily have been seized. And if Najib Razak had realized that he could only start winning back Malaysia's urban and Chinese voters, especially, with substantive and not merely superficial and rhetorical stabs at economic and political reform, yet a third opportunity for Malaysia to pursue "democracy through strength" was well within UMNO/BN's grasp. But instead of responding to its historical "bittersweet spot" by democratizing, the regime merely devolved into an increasingly embittered brand of authoritarianism. It would take Malaysia's multiethnic opposition three tries—2008, 2013, and finally 2018—to overcome UMNO/BN's inherited strengths and authoritarian controls to bring the country to the precipice of democratic transition.

NOTES

1. Economic data and analysis affirming Malaysia's increasingly debt-driven development trajectory since the Asian Financial Crisis can be found in Shahrir 2013.

2. This revisionist understanding of coalitions is more fully explored in Slater 2010.

3. Despite the formal coalition of 40-plus years between UMNO and MCA when the Asian Financial Crisis struck in 1997, Pepinsky (2009) argues that mobile Chinese capital was excluded from the BN coalition. This differing interpretation stems from our differing definitions of coalitions more than any disagreement on the character of BN rule. Our fundamental agreement that the BN protected its partners from the costs of adjustment is more important than any disagreement on the exact contours of Malaysia's coalition. Whether one considers mobile Chinese capital part of the coalition or not, the argument still holds that "the BN's supporters, elites and masses alike, stood behind the regime *because they faced no short-term sacrifice*" (Pepinsky 2009, 223). Yet this does not explain why favored Malays instead of disfavored Chinese made up the overwhelming bulk of protesters to the Mahathir regime, or why they did so only after capital controls were imposed for their putative benefit.

4. On the importance of financial-sector autonomy for the development of a unified political opposition in authoritarian contexts, see Arriola 2012.

5. This section draws heavily from Slater 2010, 211–13.

6. For biographical details on UMNO-linked Malay business leaders and their holdings in the financial sector (among others), see Pepinsky 2009, 71–74.

7. The remainder of this section draws from Slater 2010, 218–21.

8. Interview with the author, Kuala Lumpur, February 16, 2004.

9. Interview with the author, Kuala Lumpur, February 16, 2004.

10. In retrospect, the *Asian Wall Street Journal*'s editorial projection of September 4, 1998, just days after capital controls were announced, seems rather prescient: "The most optimistic scenario is only a short-term one in which pump priming and capital controls and the like will produce an illusion of economic well-being that lasts just long enough for Dr. Mahathir to declare victory, call an election, and eventually leave the inevitable mess for an unlucky successor." Quoted in Pepinsky 2009, 212.

REFERENCES

Acemoglu, Daron, and James A. Robinson. 2006. *Economic Origins of Dictatorship and Democracy*. New York: Cambridge University Press.

Albertus, Michael. 2015. *Autocracy and Redistribution: The Politics of Land Reform*. New York: Cambridge University Press.

Ariel, Heryanto, and Sumit K. Mandal. 2003. "Challenges to Authoritarianism in Indonesia and Malaysia." In *Challenging Authoritarianism in Southeast Asia: Comparing Indonesia and Malaysia*, ed. Heryanto and Mandal. New York: Routledge-Curzon.

Arriola, Leonardo. 2012. *Multiethnic Coalitions in Africa: Business Financing of Opposition Election Campaigns*. New York: Cambridge University Press.

Bueno de Mesquita, Bruce Alastair Smith, Randolph M. Siverson, and James D. Morrow. 2003. *The Logic of Political Survival*. Cambridge, MA: MIT Press.

Case, William. 2001. "Malaysia's Resilient Pseudodemocracy." *Journal of Democracy* 12 (1): 43–57.

Crouch, Harold. 1995. *Government and Society in Malaysia*. Ithaca: Cornell University Press.

Hedman, Eva-Lotta E. 2001. "Contesting State and Civil Society: Southeast Asian Trajectories," *Modern Asian Studies* 35 (4): 921–51.

Hwang, In-won. 2003. *Personalized Politics: The Malaysian State under Mahathir*. Singapore: Institute for Southeast Asian Studies.

Jesudason, James V. 1989. *Ethnicity and the Economy: The State, Chinese Business, and Multinationals in Malaysia*. Singapore: Oxford University Press.

Levitsky, Steven, and Lucan A. Way. 2012. "Beyond Patronage: Violent Struggle, Ruling Party Cohesion, and Authoritarian Durability," *Perspectives on Politics* 10 (4): 869–89.

Pepinsky, Thomas B. 2009. *Economic Crises and the Breakdown of Authoritarian Regimes: Indonesia and Malaysia in Comparative Perspective*. New York: Cambridge University Press.

Shahrir, Raja Ahmad. 2013. "15 Years of Pump-Priming, but Little to Show for It." *Malaysiakini*, October 22.

Slater, Dan. 2003. "Iron Cage in an Iron Fist: Authoritarian Institutions and the Personalization of Power in Malaysia," *Comparative Politics* 36 (1): 81–101.

Slater, Dan. 2010. *Ordering Power: Contentious Politics and Authoritarian Leviathans in Southeast Asia*. New York: Cambridge University Press.

Slater, Dan, and Joseph Wong. 2013. "The Strength to Concede: Ruling Parties and Democratization in Developing Asia," *Perspectives on Politics* 11 (3): 717–33.

Weiss, Meredith L. 2006. *Protest and Possibilities: Civil Society and Coalitions for Political Change in Malaysia*. Stanford: Stanford University Press.

Yom, Sean L. 2015. *From Resilience to Revolution: How Foreign Interventions Destabilize the Middle East*. New York: Columbia University Press.

EIGHT

Authoritarian Durability in East Asia's Developmental States

Surviving the 1973 Energy Crisis in Taiwan and South Korea

Joseph Wong

During the 1950s and 1960s, Taiwan's and South Korea's economies grew each year at nearly a 10 percent clip, hastening their transformations from backward economies into industrializing ones. Though authoritarian, the developmental states won the ruling regimes in Taiwan and Korea considerable political legitimacy by delivering sustained economic development. Into the 1970s, the Taiwan and Korean economies initiated another transformation, as they shifted gears to focus on export-oriented economic growth as well as the development of heavy industries and new higher-value economic sectors. But then the OPEC price spikes happened. In November, 1973, the price of imported oil suddenly quadrupled. As energy-dependent—and energy-poor—economies, Taiwan's and Korea's economic prospects looked bleak, if only temporarily. From a political point of view, the regimes' legitimacy formula based on sustained economic growth also looked shaky. In other words, the 1973 energy crisis could have derailed the authoritarian developmental states in both Taiwan and Korea.

As it turns out, the OPEC crisis neither derailed authoritarian rule nor an economic growth trajectory in Taiwan and Korea. Both developmental states weathered the price spikes and continued thereafter to grow and industrially upgrade their economies. In addition to righting their economies, the Kuomintang (KMT) party-state in Taiwan and the Park Chung-hee regime in Korea maintained, and even deepened, their political dominance well after the 1973 crisis.

What is noteworthy, however, is *how* the two regimes pursued very different strategies to economically and politically manage the crisis. The KMT, on the one hand, purposely slowed the Taiwan economy to a halt, reining in inflation to stabilize the economy. In doing so, the KMT's policies also contributed to a short-term trade deficit. Park Chung-hee's strategy, on the other hand, was to push Korea's export drive, ramping up foreign debt to cover a ballooning energy import bill. Korea did not experience a trade deficit, though inflation lingered much longer than it did in Taiwan. Whereas Taiwan's economic growth was deliberately slowed in the wake of the 1973 price spike, Park chose to essentially export Korea's way out of the crisis. Remarkably, Korea posted a nearly threefold jump in exports from 1972 to 1974 and a GNP growth rate of 8 percent in 1974, precisely at the time when most economies were reeling (Kwack 1990). In other words, the KMT chose a conservative though stabilizing route for handling the 1973 price spike, and Korea's developmental state decided upon a much more aggressive response to the crisis.

Both strategies were politically risky to the authoritarian regimes in Taiwan and Korea, to be sure. Had they failed to manage the economic crisis, the regimes may have been particularly vulnerable, their political dominance brought into question. But instead of politically threatening the regime, the KMT's and Park Chung-hee's economic responses contributed to each of the regime's political survival amid the crisis, and to the regimes' authoritarian durability over the longer term. What is more, the two regimes ensured their political durability for different reasons, reflective of the different political economic logics of their crisis management policy choices.

This chapter compares the Taiwanese and Korean developmental states and their distinctive responses to the energy price spikes of the early 1970s and explains how their respective responses contributed to regime survival. The first section of this chapter examines the political and economic significance of the 1973 oil price spike, and specifically the impact it *could have had* on regime survival and economic development in Taiwan and South Korea. The second section then provides an overview of how Taiwan's KMT and the Park regime in Korea responded to the energy crisis. I specifically examine the policies each developmental state put into place during the period 1973 to 1975, both as they initially reacted to the inflationary pressures of the price spike and their subsequent efforts to get each economy back on track. In this regard, Taiwan and Korea present a comparative study of contrasts, as the developmental state in the former chose a conservative strategy to stabilize the economy, while in the latter, the Park regime chose to pursue an aggressive, high-growth strategy. The particular economic circumstances at the time in Taiwan and Korea, I argue, were critical in shaping each government's policy response.

But economic conditions alone are insufficient to explain each regime's policy decisions; there was a political story as well. The third section of this chapter offers a political explanation of these distinctive policy choices. In Taiwan, the KMT regime swallowed a bitter pill of economic adjustment in order to diffuse the economic pain of the government's policy choices, preventing the emergence of political opposition to the authoritarian party-state. In the Korean case, however, the political conditions for the Park regime at the time of the crisis were considerably more contested than in Taiwan. Korea needed to continue a high-growth trajectory to maintain performance legitimacy for the Park regime, as the ruling party was just emerging from an intensely fought contest between Park and the opposition, led by Kim Dae-jung. Politically speaking, the high-growth strategy deepened the political economic alliance between the government and the big-business sector. Hence, whereas Taiwan's KMT strategy for authoritarian survival was to prevent an opposition coalition from forming against the regime, Park's strategy was to create a winning political coalition to support his regime. The last section concludes by highlighting two distinct models of authoritarian durability that emerged amid economic crisis in East Asia's developmental states. The concluding section also draws out important downstream implications of these political economic choices, and how they shaped democratization and the end of authoritarian dominance differently in both cases.

Crisis

During the initial postwar period, the authoritarian developmental states helped the ruling regimes consolidate their power in Taiwan and South Korea. In Korea, the nominally democratic regime under President Syngman Rhee proved dysfunctional and rife with corruption. The Rhee regime ended in 1960 when his administration confronted a groundswell of social movements and political opposition. The subsequent and short-lived democratic experiments in 1960 gave way to military strongman Park Chung-hee, who successfully launched a coup in 1961. President Park immediately reorganized the state apparatus and put into place many of the key technocratic institutions of the developmental state, notably the centralized and powerful Economic Planning Board. Park's regime oversaw Korea's rapid economic growth and industrial development, and is credited for Korea's postwar economic miracle. The KMT arrived on Taiwan in 1949 after it was defeated by the communists in the Chinese Civil War. Early on in Chiang Kai-shek's reign on Taiwan, the KMT's goal was to defeat the Communist Party and eventually retake the mainland to reestablish the Republic of China. Thus the party's stay on the island was intended to be temporary and short. In the meantime, however, the KMT had to govern Taiwan as a mainlander émigré regime without a popular political base. To consolidate its political authority, the KMT initiated a thorough party reorganization campaign starting in 1950. Remaking the KMT into a strong Leninist party meant tremendous effort was put into strengthening the party's internal discipline, to rid the party of corruption, and to institutionalize the KMT's capacity to penetrate Taiwanese society. To be sure, party membership doubled between 1950 and 1952 (Tien 1989, 85).

The developmental states in Taiwan and Korea sought above all else to grow their economies. This was in part to strengthen national security, as both were bulwarks against communist expansion in the region. But economic growth was also integral to the regimes' political legitimacy and survival. During the late 1940s and early 1950s, the Taiwan and Korean authoritarian regimes initiated thorough land reform in the countryside, redistributing plots to formerly landless tenants in the Japanese colonial land tenure system. The developmental states also put into place during the 1950s and early 1960s economic policies stimulating import substitution industrialization (ISI) to foster the growth of light manufacturing industries. Meanwhile, the state centrally managed the "commanding heights" of the economy, notably for key inputs such as energy and power through the state-owned enterprise sector, and in the case of Korea, the nationalized banking sector. Early economic development helped the authoritarian regimes consolidate their political power.

By the early 1970s, Taiwan and Korea confronted a potentially disruptive inflection point with the convergence of critical events in their political economic development. On the economic front, the ISI strategy had begun to run its course, prompting industrial policymakers to begin to shift the economies toward a more export-oriented program. The Taiwan and Korean economies were moving onto much shakier ground. At the same time, both ruling regimes faced severe political crises. The KMT, as the government of "Free China," lost its seat at the United Nations in 1971. Literally overnight the KMT regime, which had staked part of its legitimacy in Taiwan on its sovereignty claim over the whole of China, was internationally derecognized. Diplomatic gestures between the United States and the People's Republic of China soon thereafter cemented Taiwan's—and the KMT's—international isolation (Gold 1986; Haggard 1990). That Chiang Kai-shek's health was ailing at the time (he would pass away in 1975) portended a potential leadership success crisis within the KMT as well. Meanwhile in Korea, Park narrowly defeated opposition candidate Kim Dae-jung in the 1971 presidential election, prompting Park to declare martial law in 1972. That year he imposed the authoritarian Yushin constitution, which essentially stalled any progress toward liberalizing political reform.

Both the KMT and Park regimes were vulnerable in the early 1970s. It was against this backdrop that Taiwan and Korea experienced their first major economic crisis since the high-growth period began more than a decade earlier. In November 1973, the OPEC cartel unilaterally raised global oil prices, immediately quadrupling the price of oil in Taiwan and Korea. This affected not only the consumer price for energy, but also the price of inputs needed to power Taiwan's and Korea's industrializing economies. The effect on the economy was potentially devastating.

Following a decade of 10 percent growth and an average consumer price index inflation rate under 3 percent, Taiwan's economy was shocked into stagflation soon after the November 1973 oil price increase. Between 1973 and 1974, the consumer price index inflation rate jumped from 8 percent to almost 50 percent, and the wholesale price index increased from 23 percent to 41 percent over the same time period due to cost-push pressures from rising import prices on intermediate inputs. Taiwan's economy ground to a halt. Economic growth in 1974 was just 1.1 percent (Kuo 1999, 64–67) and Taiwan experienced a rare trade deficit (Wade 1990, 97). Stagflation was short-lived in Taiwan, however. With the swift implementation of several conservative stabilization measures, inflation was brought down to just 5 percent in consumer prices and negative rates for wholesale prices by 1975. Economic growth rates rebounded as well, growing to over 4 percent in 1975 and returning to 13 percent in 1976. The KMT pursued a "cold turkey" adjustment program (Kuo 1999, 69), deliberately slowing the economy down in order to stabilize it.

The effect of the 1973 OPEC price spikes was similar in Korea. Inflation skyrocketed after 1973, increasing from just 3.2 percent to about 25 percent in 1974 and 1975. The wholesale price index inflation rate jumped to over 40 percent in 1974 (Kwack 1990, 80). Though the inflationary effect of the energy crisis was similar in both Taiwan and Korea, the Korean response was different. Rather than slow the economy, President Park Chung-hee pushed Korea's export drive and the growth of its heavy and chemical industries. Borrowing from abroad to cover its energy import bill, Korea's exports actually increased from US$3.3 billion to US$4.5 billion between 1973 and 1974, growing again in 1975 to US$5 billion (Kwack 1990, 110). The share of heavy and chemical industry outputs in Korea's total exports also grew over the same time period. In contrast to the Taiwan case, where economic growth was traded off for economic stabilization, Korea's economy expanded at around 7 percent during and immediately after the OPEC price spikes. Whereas Taiwan's strategy to manage the 1973 energy crisis was to correct domestic prices, rein in money supply, and stabilize the economy to absorb the near-term blow of the crisis, the Korean strategy was to essentially export its way out of it. Tun-jen Cheng thus concludes that on "a macroeconomic level, South Korea expanded and inflated, while Taiwan contracted and stabilized" (1990, 163; see also Scitovsky 1990, 171).

Choices

What choices did the KMT government make in Taiwan, and how were those choices different from the ones pursued by the Park regime in South Korea? The KMT strategy consisted of two parts: an initial stabilization adjustment in early 1974, followed with a government investment plan for economic recovery. In Taiwan, the initial adjustment deliberately slowed the economy. After the November price spikes, expectations for rapid inflation (the "psychology of inflation") sparked a rapid decrease in bank deposits, fueling real inflation. In January 1974, the government imposed a battery of "stabilization measures," including a "one-shot" interest rate increase of 33 percent on deposits and 26 percent on loans. The effect of the one-shot increase was a "prompt and continuous increase" in deposits beginning in February 1974. Money was effectively reined in (Kuo 1999, 69). A second, complementary measure was implemented in January: a one-shot adjustment to domestic energy prices. Electricity prices grew by 79 percent in 1974. The average price of oil and oil products increased steeply, by 88 percent that year.

The longer-term inflationary effect of the one-shot energy price increase, however, was mitigated by the government's conservative monetary program and its ability to absorb the costs of the stabilization policies, which brought the month-to-month inflation rate down by as early as March 1974; it continued to decrease throughout the rest of that year. The "pain" of the energy price adjustment was mitigated in other ways. For instance, the 88 percent domestic price increase for oil was considerably lower than the actual market price Taiwan paid to import oil (which had quadrupled after 1973). State-owned enterprises (SOEs) such as the China Petroleum Corporation and Taiwan Power, which had been extremely profitable during the preceding decade of the 1960s, absorbed the difference in price (between the imported price and domestic price) by taking losses on their balance sheets in 1973 and 1974. In other words, the state, through its SOEs, distorted the price of oil to absorb the inflationary impact of the price spikes on Taiwan's consumers and manufacturers (Crane 1989–90, 14–15). In addition, the 88 percent price increase for oil and oil products was the *average* price for consumers and importers. The jump in diesel fuel prices, for example, was considerably less severe at only 50 percent. According to Robert Wade, differentiated energy prices were used to "soften the cost increases" on public sector services such as public transportation, as well as for the benefit of important political constituents such as farmers and fishermen who were more likely to use diesel fuel (Wade 1990, 252).

Indeed, the ruling party's main political objective was to maintain economic stability in postwar Taiwan, rather than pursue inflation-driven growth. Specifically, the ruling party was keen to prevent runaway inflation. From an institutional point of view, like the Chinese Communist Party in China (see Shih's contribution in this volume), the KMT enjoyed considerable control over Taiwan's financial institutions and was therefore able to pursue a radical but nonetheless short-term adjustment.

The roots of this economic position are also partly historical, a legacy of the nature of the KMT's authoritarian roots. The KMT upon first arriving in Taiwan immediately set out to gain control over the financial sector in order to "prevent inflationary outbreaks and prevent the private holders of money from exercising power over industry" (Wade 1990, 263). The formal banking system remained firmly under the regulatory power of the state. The central bank was insulated from industry pressure. For instance, investment credit was doled out conservatively in Taiwan by both government-controlled banks and highly regulated commercial entities, unlike in Korea, where state-managed credit fueled industrialization and where conglomerate firms were encouraged to establish their own banking houses. The secondary lending market was eventually permitted to flourish in Taiwan, though it too was monitored by the state and very closely managed so that speculation and inflation through the informal money markets could be quickly quashed. As an indication of just how severely the KMT managed the financial sector under martial law, any actions deemed by the state to be "disrupting the money market" was an offense punishable by death. According to economist Tibor Scitovsky (1990), a key element of the KMT's economic policy "philosophy" was to prevent inflation, which he contrasts with the Korean monetary policy model, in which a looser, more inflationary policy regime was used to facilitate industrial deepening.

After the initial adjustment measures reined in inflation in Taiwan, the KMT government set out to steer Taiwan's economic recovery. First, the government recalibrated its tax schemes, including a reduction in income taxes in order to jump-start consumer spending, a decrease in import tariffs on consumer goods and intermediate inputs for manufacturers, and a reduction in commodity taxes. The government took a significant fiscal hit by adjusting the tax schemes, with estimates that across-the-board tax reductions amounted to a reduction in fiscal revenues of over 11 billion NTD, or about 13 percent of the government's total tax revenues in 1974 (Kuo 1999, 72). Second, the SOE sector in Taiwan played an important role in maintaining industrial productivity and employment, particularly as the private sector's share of productivity and domestic capital formation decreased between 1971 and 1974. The SOEs' share of gross domestic capital formation, for example, grew from 27 percent to 43 percent between 1973 and 1975, and the government's share in industrial investment increased from around 8 percent to 14 percent during the same time period (Crane 1989–90, 14–17).

And third, the developmental state implemented the Ten Major Projects industrial upgrading program in 1973. Despite the oil price shocks, the KMT government pushed the program forward, which accounted for nearly 20 percent of government investment in 1975 and 1976. The Ten Major Projects focused on infrastructural improvements—cross-island highways, railways, ports, and a new international airport—that were intended to facilitate Taiwan's export-oriented industrialization. Government funds were also used to push investment toward the growth of new capital-intensive industries, including in petrochemicals and integrated steel production. The government's 1976 Six-Year Plan, in response to the OPEC crisis, began to shift investment resources to non-energy-intensive sectors, which laid the foundation for Taiwan's eventual turn to high-tech industries (Breznitz 2007; Gold 1986, 98–101; Wong 2011).

The KMT strategy for managing the 1973 OPEC price spikes and getting the Taiwan economy back on track contrasted with the Korean approach to handling the crisis. While the KMT hit the "reset" button in the wake of the crisis, the Korean strategy hinged on the expectation that "better export performance would somehow get Korea out of this hole" (Woo 1991, 128). In 1972, one year before the energy crisis, President Park imposed the authoritarian Yushin constitution and martial law and centralized political power in the presidency. The sudden oil price spikes posed a severe threat to Park's regime. Unlike in Taiwan, where the KMT deliberately put a brake on rapid growth in order to stabilize the economy, Park ordered the bureaucracy in Korea to implement the planned "big push" in the heavy and chemical industries (HCI) drive and also accelerate the state's plan to grow South Korea's export industries. To achieve this, Park further concentrated power within the presidential Blue House, such that he increasingly bypassed the bureaucracy altogether (Kim 1997, 146). As Jun-eng Woo puts it, "Seoul simply bulldozed ahead its course of expansion," despite the economic crisis (Woo 1991, 128). Korea's exports tripled, from US$3.3 billion to over US$10 billion between 1973 and 1977, and overall economic growth continued unabated through the energy crisis.

Whereas the Taiwan economy mitigated the effects of the energy price shock through monetary adjustments to reduce inflation quickly, the Korean developmental state ran an inflationary policy to keep the engine of its export economy running. Inflation rates stayed high through the rest of the 1970s, ranging from a low of 10 percent to nearly 30 percent per year (Kwack 1990, 80), unlike in Taiwan, where inflation rates were brought down soon after the crisis. The Korean economy absorbed higher prices for oil and oil-based industrial inputs, financing the growing import bill by quickly depleting the state's foreign exchange reserves and foreign borrowing. According to Korea's Economic Planning Board (EPB), the total amount of foreign loans nearly tripled between 1973 and 1975, from just over US$1 billion to US$2.85 billion. Short-term loans increased dramatically from just US$75 million to US$1.1 billion, presumably to cover Korea's skyrocketing energy import bill (Kwack 1990, 118). Over the same time period, foreign debt grew by 42 percent and the government's current account deficit quadrupled (Woo 1991, 128). Korea's debt service amount rose from only US$3.4 million in 1972 to approximately US$5 billion in 1981 (Kwack 1990, 119).

Park's commitment to the HCI campaign and to continuing to grow Korea's export economy meant, in a way, betting on the success of Korea's large conglomerate firms, the chaebol. According to Park, the chaebol, by virtue of their economies of scale and internal diversification, were in a good position to sustain and even upgrade their business operations into new and higher-value-added sectors. This was not a new strategic vision, but consistent with Park's economic plans prior to the 1973 energy crisis. In 1972, for instance, Park implemented the Emergency Decree for Economic Stability, which was intended to essentially bail out large Korean firms increasingly saddled with loans and debt in the curb market. The 1972 decree, prepared by Park's inner circle of advisers in the Blue House and not the economic ministries, froze the curb market and transferred all business loans to the centrally controlled banking system, giving indebted firms favorable conditions (interest rates and terms) to repay the loans. Banks also raised bonds to provide short-term relief funds for indebted businesses. The chaebol were favored. The "chaebol were the main beneficiaries of the Emergency Decree, while the small and medium-sized enterprises were not helped substantially" (Kim 1997, 149). To be sure, the 10 largest conglomerate firms in Korea grew five to nine times faster than the Korean economy during the 1970s, such that by the early 1980s the chaebol dominated in industrial output and productivity, exports and employment.

In macroeconomic terms, the different choices made by the KMT and Park regimes in Taiwan and Korea can be explained, in part, by the different economic circumstances in each place during the 1970s. Put another way, economic context mattered in determining the viable options that were available to each developmental state. In Taiwan, for example, the state enjoyed a significant foreign exchange asset base in the Central Bank of China, providing it the fiscal capacity to absorb the shock of induced stagflation immediately after the 1973 price spike. Foreign assets in the central bank grew from 885 million NTD to nearly 53 billion NTD from 1966 to 1972. Taiwan's current account increased dramatically as well in the decade prior to the 1973 energy crisis. Between 1966 and 1972, for example, exports grew 50 percent faster than imports, such that by 1969 Taiwan enjoyed a positive trade balance, shrinking the deficit and generating surpluses thereafter. In 1969, Taiwan's economy had posted a negative 1.9 billion NTD balance of payments, though by 1972, this had reversed to a 19.8 billion NTD surplus (Chang 1974). Taiwan's foreign debt load was comparatively small.

Whereas the KMT government in Taiwan had the fiscal capacity to absorb, at least for the short term, the inflationary pressures and economic slowdown brought by the 1973 energy price spikes, the Korean state confronted very different macroeconomic circumstances. According to the Bank of Korea (cited in Kwack 1990, 110), Korea experienced a negative trade balance throughout the 1960s and into the 1970s, and in fact, the pace of growth in imports was much faster than exports, resulting in a growing, rather than shrinking, negative balance of trade up to 1971. Accordingly, Korea's current account balance remained negative between 1966 and 1977. And unlike Taiwan, Korea was an aggressive borrower. From 1965 to 1973, Korea's total foreign debt grew from US$206 million to US$4.2 billion, a 20-fold increase in less than a decade. In 1973, total debt in Korea equaled 32 percent of GNP. This figure increased to 53 percent by 1984, amounting to US$43 billion. To put this into comparative perspective, Taiwan's total debt in 1984 was US$12 billion, or just 21 percent of GNP. In economic terms, then, there was no option to slow the economy in Korea in the wake of the 1973 energy crisis. Park had little choice but to pursue an aggressive growth policy with the hope that growth in economic productivity would allow Korea to export its way out of the crisis.

Surviving the Crisis

The developmental state regimes in Taiwan and Korea made big bets on how they would steer their economies through the abrupt economic crisis of 1973. To be sure, both economies were in relatively good shape on the eve of the crisis. Unlike some of the other political economies described in this volume, Taiwan's and Korea's economies were in a relatively strong position during the early 1970s. Rot and economic mismanagement were not pervasive.

That said, both regimes managed the crisis well. Park's "big push" in Korea eventually paid off. With the expansion and diversification of big business, the Korean economy barely dipped in performance immediately after the energy price spike, and rebounded thereafter as exports increased into the late 1970s. The KMT's economic bets paid off as well, but in a different way. Whereas the Park regime sought growth to mitigate the effects of the crisis, the KMT government pursued a conservative policy of stabilization by reining in inflation, slowing the economy down, and leveraging the SOE sector to absorb a good deal of the adjustment pain, especially in offsetting high energy prices.

The bets made by the KMT and the Park regime were also intended to sustain their authoritarian rule; these were not just economic adjustments but also *strategies for their political survival*. After all, the 1973 OPEC price spike came at a time when both authoritarian regimes were politically vulnerable. Park had narrowly defeated charismatic opposition leader

Kim Dae-jung in 1971 and subsequently imposed the authoritarian Yushin constitution. The KMT, meanwhile, had lost its seat at the United Nations and found itself internationally isolated, governing Taiwan as an émigré regime from the mainland. Simply put, the different adjustment strategies were politically motivated, adhering to distinct political logics.

The Park regime politically survived because it renewed its economic performance legitimacy pact, but more specifically by allying the state more closely with the chaebol sector. The Korean developmental state's adjustment policies after 1973 were intended to concentrate the benefits of growth in order to win the regime political support. The KMT's political survival strategy, on the other hand, adhered to a different political logic. Whereas the Park regime courted big business by concentrating and funneling resources to favored chaebol firms, the KMT in Taiwan pursued an adjustment strategy that deliberately minimized political opposition to the regime. The KMT's conservative response distributed the pain of economic adjustment across all sectors. As Shih stresses in this volume's introduction, the KMT did not instigate a major shift in its support coalition. To the extent any particular actor or sector was hit hard by the 1973 crisis, it was the KMT government's coffers, though as I have argued, it had the fiscal capacity and the control over financial institutions at the time to endure the near-term pain of the adjustment. But whereas business clearly won with Park's big push, few in Taiwan gained from the government's conservative policies; indeed, most everyone felt some pain. Yet no one experienced too much pain, and if they did, it was for a relatively short time. In other words, the Korean authoritarian regime survived the early 1970s by *concentrating the economic gains of adjustment to consolidate political support* from the powerful business sector, while the KMT regime in Taiwan survived the crisis because it *spread the pain of adjustment to prevent the emergence of any serious political opposition.*

The divergence between the adjustment strategies in Taiwan and Korea—minimizing opposition in the former and concentrating political support in the latter—can be partly explained by the key difference between their political systems during the early 1970s. The KMT ruled as a one-party state in Taiwan, while in Korea, the Park regime needed to win elections. Authoritarian Taiwan was not even nominally democratic during the 1970s. Prior to the lifting of martial law in 1987, opposition parties were banned in Taiwan. Though limited elections were held throughout the 1960s and 1970s, opposition candidates could only contest as independent candidates, with little chance of unseating KMT incumbency (Rigger 1999). The KMT's dominance, in this respect, was virtually unassailable

(Chao and Myers 1997). Accordingly, to weather the 1973 crisis, the KMT did not need to win support per se, but rather *it just needed to not lose*. This was not the case in Korea. Park Chung-hee's hold on power was considerably more precarious at the time. Prior to the imposition of the Yushin constitution in 1972, political parties, including opposition parties, contested elections to determine the composition of the National Assembly and the presidency in Korea. Though the electoral rules were skewed to favor the ruling party, opposition party candidates were competitive throughout the 1960s and early 1970s. In 1971, Kim Dae-jung increased the opposition's vote share to over 45 percent, a 4 percent increase over the 1967 election. Park's continued dominance, therefore, was not a foregone conclusion on the eve of the 1973 OPEC price spikes; he needed to win and consolidate support if his regime was to survive. Hence, whereas in Korea Park's political strategy was to *concentrate the gains* of reform to his political allies, the KMT's survival depended on *spreading the pain* of adjustment.

In Taiwan, spreading the pain to prevent opposition made good sense, given the nature of the KMT's authoritarian regime. According to Tun-jen Cheng, the KMT's authoritarianism endured into the 1970s because of the regime's reliance on a broad and "diffuse coalition" of support. By distributing the pain of adjustment during the early 1970s crisis, the KMT avoided breaking up this coalition. In this respect, the 1974 reforms were not intended to win the KMT political support, but rather to prevent the party from losing what legitimacy it had to authoritatively rule Taiwan. As a result, the medium-term political implications after the crisis were not that severe, in contrast to cases such as Malaysia, as described by Slater in this volume.

The postwar regime in Taiwan was a *distributive* developmental state (Slater and Wong 2018), one that strategically implemented social and economic policies that intentionally encompassed Taiwan's different classes, sectors and interests. The KMT nurtured a politically docile nation by putting into place, early on, broadly inclusive socioeconomic policies. As Cheng notes, the KMT "successfully preempted political opposition by sponsoring a broad yet low cost distributional coalition" (1990, 168). Land reform during the late 1940s, for instance, increased agricultural productivity, a key input into Taiwan's industrialization, but also redistributed land to tenant farmers. The countryside was thus never a political threat to the KMT regime. This was replicated in the cities. Despite repressive policies on labor mobilization, industrial wages were permitted to rise with labor market rates, meaning artificial wage compression through authoritarian measures were less conspicuous in Taiwan than in other authoritarian regimes, such as in Korea (Amsden 1989). As a result, Taiwan—and the KMT state—benefited from a very equitable distribution of income amid rapid growth throughout the 1960s and 1970s.

The same political logic—minimizing opposition as opposed to winning support—was also evident in how industry was organized in Taiwan. Unlike in Korea, where industrial activity during the 1970s was increasingly concentrated in state-favored conglomerate chaebol firms, the KMT instead fostered the growth and proliferation of small and medium-sized enterprises (SMEs). Rather than leverage the scale advantages of the Korean chaebol, Taiwanese firms instead thrived mainly due to their market agility and their ability to plug into globalized and segmented value chains. While in Korea, a significant share of industrial employment was accounted for by the largest firms during the 1970s and 1980s, in Taiwan, nearly 98 percent of all firms were SMEs and the primary source of industrial employment. Taiwan's industrial organization also encouraged greater levels of socioeconomic mobility among Taiwanese, mitigating potentially powerful political cleavages between the haves and have-nots and opposition to the KMT government.

The KMT government was keenly aware of how distributive politics and ethnic identity politics in Taiwan could potentially threaten the authoritarian regime. The infamous "228" tragedy of 1947, when the KMT security apparatus crushed Taiwanese protests, reinforced the fact the KMT was an émigré regime and incited the stirrings of ethnic conflict in Taiwan (Wachman 1994). This was obviously not good for the party's prospects of effectively governing Taiwan. Though the party managed to soften the repressive nature of the state through gradual political liberalization and the so-called Taiwanization of the party starting in the late 1960s (Tien 1989), the KMT was nonetheless perceived to be a mainlander, outsider, and even neocolonial regime. It was in the party's interest to facilitate inclusive economic development for Taiwanese.

The party implemented broadly inclusive socioeconomic policies such as land reform, a commitment to full employment in the city and countryside, the minimization of corruption and graft, and the growth of SMEs (Wong 2004). The KMT needed the Taiwanese to economically prosper, as this strengthened not only the economy but also the party's performance legitimacy and the KMT's hold on political power. Hence, while overall growth was critical for the party's political survival on Taiwan, the KMT understood that it needed to also prevent the concentration of wealth, especially among ethnic Taiwanese. The KMT's strategy to grow the SME sector was therefore motivated as much by economic considerations as political concerns to "prevent large-scale capital from acquiring enough autonomy to shape the regime." In line with the KMT's "anti-big capitalist bias," the party sought to keep business at arm's length and to keep firms relatively small (Wade 1990, 270, 272).

The KMT's political logic of economic development also impacted the degree to which the state was "embedded" in society (Evans 1995). The relationship between the state and the private sector was "distant" and "cool." Unlike in Korea, where the authoritarian state politically depended on big business for its political survival, business and the state in Taiwan "resist[ed] being seen in a collective huddle" (Wade 1990, 276). The nationalized commercial banking system in Korea, for instance, provided the state tremendous financial leverage with which to develop important political and economic patronage ties with big business (Woo 1991; Amsden 1989; Haggard 1990). Eun Mee Kim characterizes Park's economic policies favoring the chaebol as "a political gesture by the Park regime to solidify its ties to large business" (1997, 149). The private sector in Taiwan, on the other hand, did not rely on such state largesse for industrial investment or for protected markets. The KMT government eschewed the use of publicly managed funds for industrial credit. Instead the state relied on the strategic allocation of foreign direct investment and fiscal (i.e., tax-based) incentives to carry out its economic plans (Cheng 1990; Haggard 1990). Unlike the Park regime in Korea, where the president surrounded himself with a coterie of the country's top industrialists (Evans 1995; Kwack 1990), the KMT leadership kept its distance from business. To be sure, prior to the 1980s, there was not a single member in the cabinet, the Council for Economic Planning and Development, or its advisory council with a background in business. In the early 1980s, only one member of 27 on the KMT's standing committee was from the private sector (Wade 1990, 276).

Another way in which the KMT minimized potential political opposition during the economic tough times of the early 1970s was to distance the ruling party from the policy decision-making process. The policy process in Taiwan during the 1973 oil price spikes was by and large technocratic. As Robert Wade describes, the KMT always retained a veto on economic policies, though the government bureaucracy nonetheless wielded enormous authority in setting the economic policy agenda and implementing reform. Stephan Haggard's (1990) historical analysis of Taiwan's developmental state reaffirms this point, describing in great detail the central role played by technocrats in economic policymaking. As he and others point out, political leaders tended to not interfere with the day-to-day operation of the ministries and the bureaucracy. This pattern did not change when

Chiang Ching-kuo became premier in 1972 or when he was put in charge of the executive and the ministerial bureaucracies. Known to be politically moderate, Chiang did not intervene during the oil price crisis.

Taiwan's experience stands in direct contrast to Korea's. Whereas Chiang Ching-kuo tended to more hands-off when it came to economic policymaking, Korea's Park Chung-hee played a critical role in economic policy more generally, but also in how the Korean government managed the 1973 crisis specifically. During the 1960s and especially after the start of the 1970s, Park centralized the economic policymaking process first within the Economic Planning Board, over which he presided, and then later to the presidential Blue House. For Park, the "big push" agenda to accelerate the development of Korea's heavy and chemical industries (HCI) beginning in the 1970s was a "political obsession." As Jung-en Woo explains, the HCI drive reflected Park's political agenda to legitimate the authoritarian Yushin constitution. Woo elaborates: "The architects and executors of the heavy industrialization program were not the technocrats of the Economic Planning Board, as might be expected, but a coterie headed by a political appointee at the Presidential Palace." The energy crisis thus deepened, rather than abated, Park's "political resolve" to see the HCI program through (Woo 1991, 128–29, 131). For Park, the HCI drive was to generate selective political support from the business sector.

For the Park regime in Korea, the 1973 crisis provided an opportunity to further push the government's politically motivated plans to develop new capital-intensive industries and jump-start its export-oriented economy. Park's political strategy was to gain the authoritarian regime support through its management of 1973 energy crisis; for the Park regime, survival was about claiming political credit for orchestrating Korea's continued industrial transformation. In Taiwan, on the other hand, the technocratic response by the government had less to do with political credit-claiming and more to do with stabilizing the economy to prevent the mobilization of opposition to the regime. The KMT's strategy, to distance itself from the policy process by allowing the bureaucracy to pursue a technocratic and conservative response to the 1973 oil price spikes, was more about diffusing—and in turn politically defusing—blame.

Comparing Authoritarianisms

For Taiwan and Korea, the 1973 OPEC price spikes entailed a significant shock. Both economies, which until then had developed at a very rapid clip, were at a political economic crossroads. Politically, the authoritarian regimes were vulnerable. In 1971 the KMT government in Taiwan was derecognized and its claims to mainland China were undermined. In that same year, the Park Chung-hee regime suffered a devastating electoral hit, and though the ruling party retained power, its base of support was clearly dwindling. Yet both regimes steered their economies through the 1973 crisis, and both managed to politically survive. In retrospect, therefore, the energy crisis is a footnote in their political economic histories, an important *nonevent* in the end.

But this does not mean the 1973 crisis cannot shed important light on the developmental trajectories of Taiwan and South Korea. Taiwan and Korea are often characterized as successful developmental states, treated as most similar cases when in fact they were quite different. How each regime handled the 1973 crisis illuminates such differences. This chapter explains why, from both economic and political points of view, the two regimes pursued different strategies. Most accounts of the OPEC price spikes merely describe how the KMT and Park Chung-hee approached the crisis; understanding the political logic of why they made the choices they did, however, is barely covered in the literature. In this chapter, I have argued that the economic policy choices each of the regimes made during the 1973 crisis contributed to their political survival, though in very different ways and according to different political logics. In this respect, then, comparative analysis of the two cases allows conceptual work to be done about different means of political survival among authoritarian regimes during moments of crisis, and more generally, *different styles of authoritarian durability* over the long run.

Models of Authoritarian Durability

In Taiwan, the KMT pursued a conservative economic strategy to manage the oil price spikes. The government, through its tight grip on the central bank and its large state-owned enterprise sector, reined in money supply by increasing short-term interest rates and imposing a one-shot price increase for energy. The KMT enjoyed both strong party institutions and control over financial institutions. Economically speaking, the government's plan ground Taiwan's economy basically to a halt, though soon after, with some public sector funding, it recovered to pre-1973 productivity. The KMT favored stability and inflation control and, in so doing, spread the short-term pain of economic adjustment. There were no winners in this KMT strategy, but there were no extraordinary losers either. In Taiwan, economic adjustment did not result in defections from the ruling party's support coalition, unlike in many cases described in this volume. The economic strategy for diffusing the pain of adjustment allowed the regime to prevent or minimize opposition against the regime. This was, I argue, the KMT's modus operandi since long before the 1973 crisis. The KMT, since its arrival in 1949, was steadfast in fostering political and economic stability by implementing a distributive developmental state and preventing the concentration of wealth, especially among the ethnic Taiwanese. For the KMT, maintaining authoritarian rule always had less to do with winning support than it did with preventing a viable opposition. That the energy crisis was so short in duration also contributed to the party's ability to retain its support coalition, unlike the fate of other regimes examined in this volume.

The Korean approach to the 1973 crisis was dissimilar due to a different logic of political survival and authoritarian endurance. For Park, who suffered a severe blow in the 1971 elections, the key for his regime's survival was to win support. The KMT, on the other hand, operating in a one-party system in which the opposition was banned under martial law, never needed to worry about winning elections; its power was unassailable provided no opposition emerged to challenge the KMT regime. However, the stakes in nominally democratic Korea and for Park's regime were different. Despite the 1973 energy crisis, the Park regime forged ahead— "bulldozed"—even more aggressively its "big push" into heavy capital-intensive industries and export manufacturers. Thus whereas the Taiwan government chose to stabilize and pull back on growth in the face of the 1973 price spikes, the Park regime aggressively borrowed from abroad and drew down its foreign reserves to finance continued growth. As part of this big push, the Korean government leaned heavily on the big-business sector for economic productivity and political support in exchange for state-led investment credit. The Korean state made winners by concentrating investment into the chaebol, and thus concentrating the gains of economic adjustment.

Economically, in Taiwan, the government spread the pain, while in Korea, the Park regime concentrated the gains. Politically, the KMT sought to preemptively undermine any potential opposition to the regime, while the Park government looked to consolidate support in the business sector. What we have, therefore, are two models of authoritarianism and authoritarian durability. To be sure, the authoritarian regimes in Taiwan and Korea were similarly highly repressive; they similarly played politics on a deliberately uneven playing field; and for both, political survival was the ruling party's paramount interest. But though the regimes were similar in many of these regards, what explains their political survival in the wake of the 1973 crisis and their longer-term authoritarian durability was actually quite dissimilar. One model of authoritarianism, exemplified by the KMT in Taiwan, featured the regime's ability to *prevent and minimize opposition to the regime*. The other model of authoritarianism, reflected by the Park regime in Korea, depended on that regime's ability to *secure and maintain selective though powerful coalitions of political support for the regime*.

Democratic Consequences

The downstream consequences of how authoritarian durability was maintained in Taiwan and Korea were not trivial when it came to democratic transition in the two places. Though the two regimes survived the 1973 crises—and several others thereafter—both authoritarian regimes did eventually come to an end when Taiwan and Korea democratized during the late 1980s and into the early 1990s. But unlike other instances of regime transition, in which the severely weakened and delegitimated ancien régime is overthrown, democratic transformation in Taiwan and Korea was prompted by the authoritarian ruling parties themselves. Dan Slater and I describe this process as "democracy through strength," whereby authoritarian regimes concede democratic reform not from a position of extreme weakness but rather from a position of strength (Slater and Wong 2013).

In both Taiwan and Korea, the authoritarian regimes during the late 1980s remained relatively strong, especially vis-à-vis the emerging opposition. This "antecedent strength" endowed them with the confidence that by conceding democracy, they also enjoyed a high probability of continuing to rule. As we put it, conceding democracy is not tantamount to conceding defeat. The KMT, after it lifted martial law in 1987 and contested its first full election in 1992, remained Taiwan's dominant governing party. The KMT candidate also handily won the founding presidential election. Likewise in Korea, Roh Tae-woo of the incumbent authoritarian party won the first presidential election in 1987. His party also retained a plurality of seats in the National Assembly in 1988 and formed Korea's first democratically elected government since the 1950s.

Slater and I are also careful to point out that, despite having undergone similar processes of democracy through strength, not all authoritarian parties are created equal, and that the course of democracy through strength does not imply that all authoritarian parties are equally strong when they concede democracy. We contend that strong parties are arrayed along a *spectrum of strengths*. It thus follows that those parties that are stronger at the time they concede are also more likely to translate their authoritarian strengths into democratic ones; on the flip side, those that are less strong tend to fare less well subsequently in democratic contests. Authoritarian-turned-democratic parties, we argue, move from "relative strength to relative strength." Understanding the political basis of authoritarian durability over the longer term—and the variable models of authoritarian durability such as we see in Taiwan and South Korea—suggests that different *kinds of authoritarianisms* that precede transition impact the democratization process differently. The authoritarian regime in Korea was strong (strong enough to concede), but because it had relied upon a strategy of winning support to maintain its authoritarian rule, the party's antecedent strengths were precarious and certainly less broadly encompassing than the KMT in Taiwan. Put simply, the authoritarian ruling party in Korea was strong, but it strengths depended upon selective support. The KMT, meanwhile, conceded democracy during the late 1980s from a position of comparatively extraordinary strength, precisely because its authoritarian durability was not based on gaining selective political support, but instead on skillfully preventing broad-based opposition to the ruling party. The KMT was able to move from dominant strength to strength because it faced little opposition when it conceded democracy.

REFERENCES

Amsden, Alice. 1989. *Asia's Next Giant: South Korea and Late Industrialization*. New York: Oxford University Press.

Breznitz, Dan. 2007. *Innovation and the State: Political Choice and Strategies for Growth in Israel, Taiwan and Ireland*. New Haven: Yale University Press.

Chang, Chen Fu. 1974. "The Balance of Payments of Taiwan, 1966–72." *Asian Survey* 14 (6): 546–57.

Chao, Linda, and Ramon Myers. 1997. *The First Chinese Democracy: Political Life in the Republic of China on Taiwan*. Baltimore: Johns Hopkins University Press.

Cheng, Tun-jen. 1990. "Political Regimes and Development Strategies: South Korea and Taiwan." In *Manufacturing Miracles: Paths of Industrialization in Latin America and East Asia*, ed. Gary Gereffi and Donald Wyman. Princeton: Princeton University Press.

Crane, George. 1989–90. "State Owned Enterprises and the Oil Shocks in Taiwan: the Political Dynamics of Economic Adjustment." *Studies in Comparative International Development* 24 (4): 3–23.

Evans, Peter. 1995. *Embedded Autonomy: States and Industrial Transformation*. Princeton: Princeton University Press.

Gold, Thomas. 1986. *State and Society in the Taiwan Miracle*. Armonk, NY: M.E. Sharpe.

Haggard, Stephan. 1990. *Pathways from the Periphery: The Politics of Growth in the Newly Industrializing Countries*. Ithaca: Cornell University Press.

Kim, Eun Mee. 1997. *Big Business, Strong State: Collusion and Conflict in South Korean Development, 1960–1990*. Albany: SUNY Press.

Kuo, Shirley. 1999. "Government Policy in the Taiwanese Development Process: The Past 50 Years." In *Taiwan's Development Experience: Lessons on the Roles of Government and Market*, ed. Erik Thorbecke and Henry Wan. Boston: Kluwer.

Kwack, Sung Yeung. 1990. "The Economic Development of the Republic of Kora, 1965–1981." In *Models of Development: A Comparative Study of Economic Growth in South Korea and Taiwan*, ed. Lawrence Lau. San Francisco: International Center for Economic Growth.

Rigger, Shelley. 1999. *Politics in Taiwan: Voting for Democracy*. New York: Routledge.

Scitovsky, Tibor. 1990. "Economic Development in Taiwan and South Korea, 1965–1981." In *Models of Development: A Comparative Study of Economic Growth in South Korea and Taiwan*, ed. Lawrence Lau. San Francisco: International Center for Economic Growth.

Slater, Dan, and Joseph Wong. 2013. "The Strength to Concede: Ruling Parties and Democratization in Developmental Asia." *Perspectives on Politics* 11 (3): 717–33.

Slater, Dan, and Joseph Wong. 2018. "Game for Democracy: Authoritarian Successor Parties in Developmental Asia." In *Life After Dictatorship: Authoritarian Successor Parties Worldwide*, ed. James Loxton and Scott Mainwaring. New York: Cambridge University Press.

Tien, Hung-mao. 1989. *The Great Transition: Political and Social Change in the Republic of China*. Stanford, CA: Hoover Institution Press.

Wachman, Alan. 1994. *Taiwan: National Identity and Democratization*. Armonk, NY: M.E. Sharpe.

Wade, Robert. 1990. *Governing the Market: Economic Theory and the Role of Government in East Asian Industrialization*. Princeton: Princeton University Press.

Wong, Joseph. 2004. *Healthy Democracies: Welfare Politics in Taiwan and South Korea*. Ithaca: Cornell University Press.

Wong, Joseph. 2011. *Betting on Biotech: Innovation and the Limits of Asia's Developmental State*. Ithaca: Cornell University Press.

Woo, Jung-en. 1991. *Race to the Swift: State and Finance in Korean Industrialization*. New York: Columbia University Press.

NINE

Bread, Fear, and Coalitional Politics in Jordan

From Tribal Origins to Neoliberal Narrowing

Sean Yom

What happens when economic crisis drains a resource-poor autocracy's finances, instigates regime supporters to riot, and compels the leadership to make democratic concessions? Our accumulated knowledge of authoritarianism suggests that economic *trauma* brings political *drama*: wobbling dictators are exposed as their patronage pools dry up, while opposition forces—infused with both hard-line dissenters and newfound defectors from the ranks of former regime loyalists—revolt to cause serious political change.

However, the opposite happened in the Hashemite Kingdom of Jordan, whose ruling monarchy weathered financial meltdown in the late 1980s, but nonetheless retained its core ruling coalition of tribal support. That its traditional constituencies of tribal communities, one whose fealty long required the expensive provision of jobs, services, and other patronage, remained supportive despite suffering economic hardship represents the entrée to the puzzle. The larger part of the puzzle began after this shock, when that tribal-state compact continued to erode due to the official response to fiscal emergency: simultaneous market-oriented economic restructuring and political liberalization reforms, including allowances for parliamentary elections and civil society. By the 2000s, these new policies had enabled the regime to reconfigure its support coalition, slowly demoting many tribal communities in favor of a smaller stratum of new business elites. Today, the monarchy maintains this commitment to coalitional reconfiguration by continuing to politically favor its vanguard capitalist elite—investors, bankers, merchants, and industrialists enriched from market-oriented shifts through privatization and trade. Increasingly less favored is the regime's old tribal bedrock. Tribal forces simmer with frustration but seem resistant to creating revolutionary explosion, even during the 2011–12 Arab Spring, when other Middle East dictatorships were overthrown after their citizens suffered similar levels of deprivation.

Many analysts of Jordan have explained the persistence of the monarchy's tribal coalition during and since economic crisis with the answer of political liberalization. In the 1990s, the Jordanian regime embarked upon quasi-democratic reforms that relaxed repression, though stopping far short of constitutional monarchism (Lucas 2005; Ryan 2002). Thus, in a new era of neoliberal austerity, novel political goods such as parliamentary competition, electoral clientelism, and civic society became functional substitutes for the material patronage that the old statist economy could no longer provide. The proposition resonates with conventional wisdom regarding authoritarian survival strategies, particularly models of "liberalized autocracy" that predict rulers will allow for controlled political competition and other concessions during periods of economic difficulty as a way of alleviating the frustrations of their coalitional base (Brumberg 2002). While Jordan's political liberalization has rolled back since the 2000s, as the argument goes, the kingdom remains undeniably more open and pluralistic than before the watershed 1990s—and, consequently, its tribes are still supportive of the ruling monarchy.

Yet though political liberalization is useful for many dictatorships, it does not explain Jordan's outcome. It is not mild freedom that keeps tribal forces wedded to the Hashemite monarchy, but rather two less quotidian mechanisms—*bread* and *fear*. Regarding the former, tribal communities have been so historically tied to social and economic entitlements that not just their redistributive preferences but their political loyalties are sticky, or resistant to change even in the face of privation. These ties do not merely trend back a few decades; they began with the formation of Jordan itself a century ago, which catalyzed the social and political incorporation of tribes into the heart of the state apparatus. For as long as Jordan has existed, there has been a monarchy; and for as long as there has been a monarchy, the tribes have staffed its state and earned its protection. To be sure, these constituencies have always expressed diverse interests, including opposition and dissent during periods of financial austerity. However, the consistent absence of radical mobilization in pursuit of regime turnover reflects the enduring legacy of past coalitional investments, which gave generations of tribal Jordanians a powerful stake in protecting state institutions and political arrangements under the Hashemite crown.

The fear refers to an emotive factor, namely the regnant belief by tribal communities that even as neoliberal economics wear down their conventional status as the privileged nucleus of political order, monarchist rule still represents the most preferable outcome. Revolutionary change would mean the replacement of this autocratic status quo with a more democratic government that would be representative of Jordan's nontribal majority of Palestinians. By contrast to tribal communities, Jordanians of Palestinian origin have historically had little access to power and patronage; despite comprising much of the urban middle class, they have suffered political marginalization and discrimination as the result of the tribal-state compact. Given this communal cleavage, the ascent of a Palestinian-dominated regime could end the institutional favoritism and protections afforded to tribal communities. For many tribal actors, then, it is better to be diminished by the state they trust than by Palestinians whom they do not.

In addition to bread and fear are two facilitating variables that, at various junctures, have further reinforced the logic of the Jordanian autocracy's tribal coalition. The first is foreign aid from strategic donors, particularly the United States. The provision of economic and military rents has often alleviated fiscal shortages, and more recently has enabled the regime to ensure that the spigot of tribal patronage is only gradually constricted rather suddenly stopped. The second factor is the institutional nature of ruling monarchism itself. The Jordanian regime has survived crisis and realigned its coalition despite not possessing a *ruling party*—a feature long described in the literature as the desideratum of durable authoritarianism. The absence of such a mobilizing institution has not prevented the monarchy and its bureaucratic organs from reaching into the tribal populace, distributing patronage deftly, mediating conflicts, and shaping interests from above. Indeed, within autocratic monarchies like Jordan, the existence of a hegemonic party approaches contradiction: royal incumbents derive their legitimacy not from electoral domination and popular consent, but from dynastic claims upon state power enshrined in symbolic and constitutional routines that, by definition, lay beyond contestation of voters and protesters. However, the absence of ruling party institutions has not prevented Jordanian kings from maintaining power.

When contextualized against the other cases of this book, though, parts of Jordan's trajectory of persistence also ring familiar. That inherited social loyalties give this regime the capacity to absorb sudden financial blows resonates with Dan Slater's case study of the Malaysian UMNO and BN coalitions. That a cash-strapped autocracy responded to economic decline by doubling down, knowing this would probably fuel new forms of manageable dissent, also runs parallel to Lisa Blaydes's understanding of Iraq under international sanctions. And that an authoritarian leadership would engineer an armada of political initiatives masquerading as liberalism is common to many cases of postcrisis adjustment, such as Russian politics under Putin as described by Natalia Lamberova and Daniel Treisman.

What makes Jordan unique ultimately is the combination of state patronage, tribal fear, foreign aid, and ruling monarchism that has collectively generated political equilibrium on the east bank of the Jordan River. The kingdom is perennially characterized by Western analysts as "on the brink" of collapse given its structural weaknesses, among them scarce natural resources, indefensible borders, artificial origins, and conflict-ridden neighborhood. This is a near-absolutist but also near-insolvent dictatorship. Yet the Hashemite monarchy remains the only regime in the entire Levant area of the Middle East that has never fallen to internal coup or popular revolution, or drowned within internecine wars like those that befell Lebanon, Syria, and Iraq. This persistence is especially fascinating given the dramatically different coalitional strategy the Jordanian regime now pursues. The new business elites favored by the monarchy are distinctive. Unlike tribal communities with their high overhead costs of welfarist maintenance, these magnates eschew state interventionism in favor of technocratic proceduralism and economic openness. Unlike the Palestinian middle sector, they are agnostic in regards to the politics of popular representation, and have little desire for democracy. Indeed, their rise suggests that capitalism is supplementing communalism as the basis of coalitional politics, but with the tribal base still warily following.

This chapter traces the origins and pathway of coalitional politics in Jordan. It attends to the historical trajectory of state-building, because the coalitional dynamics of today stem from antecedent strategies made during early periods of state formation. First, it highlights bread—that is, patronage-fueled creation of a tribal foundation from the colonial 1920s through 1940s, as well as the renewal of patronage through the social conflict caused by the infusion of Palestinians through the 1960s. Second, it explores fear, namely the communal schism between tribal Jordanians and Palestinians left by the 1970 civil conflict, which hardened the tribal-state compact and turned the state into an ethnocratic one that further redistributed patronage among its tribal constituencies. Third, it shows how despite the economic meltdown of the late 1980s and tribal-state tensions, the tribal coalition remained largely attached to the crown through the 1990s—the product of social hostility and sticky loyalties. Fourth, it explores the neoliberal economic reforms that changed coalitional politics in the 2000s, relegating tribal privilege in favor of new capitalist elites. It concludes by extending the implications of this coalitional narrowing to new frontiers of opposition and political resistance.

Bread: Origins and Growth of the Tribal-State Compact

In Jordan, social conflict has been the crucible of coalitional mobilization since the colonial period, when the British-installed Hashemite monarchy traded bread for loyalty among local tribal residents. Historical sources map out well the kingdom's creation through the midwifery of British colonialism in 1921, implanting an imported monarchy under the Hashemite family into a nearly landlocked hinterland with neither oil nor water (Musa 1989). Residing in the British protectorate were about 225,000 mostly tribal residents, or *Transjordanians*. Though the British would retain major control over the fledgling regime's finances and policies for decades, the tribal-state compact linking tribal Transjordanian communities to the royal center began to form quickly. This constituted what we now recognize as a coalitional *pact*, one reflecting reciprocal expectations and bargained arrangements struck between two actors with overlapping preferences (Heydemann 1999).

From the start, the monarchical regime's nucleus consisted of the ruler, Emir Abdullah, and various bureaucratic and military factotums. The first coalitional layer of support secured from Transjordanian society were mercantilist families and trading notables, whose support was captured through economic concessions such as land regulations, import-intensive provisions, and mortgaged lending reform (Amawi 1994, 167–84). These early merchants accumulated significant capital through World War II, and enjoyed access to royal power. Beyond this, raw materials for social mobilization would come from tribal communities ranging from the nomadic Bedouin to settled farmers. There was no traditional class of landowners to co-opt, because unlike larger fertile Arab states such as Egypt, Syria, and Iraq, Jordan neither had abundant arable land nor suffered from widespread feudal land tenure. Still, loyalty to the imported monarchy was hardly automatic. Indeed, early hostilities from Bedouin confederations and their sheikhs (chieftains) required the fledgling regime to use British military muscle in the first years to pacify incipient rebellions (Alon 2007, 37–60).

What forged the tribal-state compact was conflict and vulnerability. First, the Hashemite regime felt geopolitical pressure from the south. The newly consolidated Saudi state not only rejected the dynasty's historic claim over Mecca and Medina, it also sparked militant raids deep into Jordanian territory. Second, tribal communities were endangered after the mid-1920s, as droughts followed by the Great Depression caused food shortages and starvation. Herein came the exigency of mutual survival, and thus the basis of the tribal-state pact—a struggling monarchy that required popular backing, and a tribal populace needing state support due to privation and loss. With British support, the Jordanian regime began distributing private and public goods to tribal communities whose survival was tied to land, such as title grants, tax relief, rural services, and public works (Tell 2013, 84–101). Economic safeguards against hardship also came with political integration into decision-making, as leading sheikhs plus the merchant notables gained symbolic representation into legislative councils and other organs of political voice (Abu Nowar 2006, 199–204). Another coalitional mechanism was militarized welfarism via through the army, known then as the Arab Legion. Led by British officers, the Arab Legion recruited heavily among Bedouin tribes, furnishing not only salaries but also education, food, housing, and medical services to tribal soldiers and their families.

When the emirate graduated from British tutelage to become the independent Kingdom of Jordan in 1946, the monarchy had managed to mobilize a coherent ruling coalition, with royal and merchant elites at its apex and tribal communities at the base. Transjordanians were now structurally tied to regime patronage: "Soldiering, subsidies, and relief work had replaced the claims on clan and *shaykh*, which guaranteed survival in the past" (Tell 2013, 112). Such pacting, however, also brought the institutional consequence of making this autocracy extremely dependent upon foreign aid. For instance, the Arab Legion was almost exclusively funded by British subsidies (Vatikiotis 1967, 79). The necessity of British support in various forms, from underwriting the royal budget to subsidizing the Legion, began a pattern of rentier redistribution in which the regime would aggressively seek international assistance in order to satisfy the domestic needs of its coalitional allies. For instance, Jordan's 1946 independence still tethered the regime to Britain through treaty relations: London would transfer economic grants and military aid equaling about £10 million per annum for 20 years, while retaining various territorial and strategic rights, such as maintaining control over the Legion. Reliance upon external rent in turn curtailed the development of domestic extractive capacity. For the Hashemite regime, the frequent use of tax abatements to win tribal support meant that revenues often fluctuated drastically, but the availability of foreign aid obviated any need for the costly act of direct taxation from Transjordanian communities.

Founded in mutual need, but expressed through generous patronage and little taxation, the tribal-state compact underwent stress in the 1950s and 1960s due to demographic change within society caused by the entry of Palestinians, which eventually culminated in civil conflict and the renewal of tribal support for Hashemite rule. After the 1948 Arab-Israeli War, 800,000 Palestinians, including 350,000 refugees, entered into a preexisting population of around 400,000 mostly tribal Transjordanians. Early on, some political incorporation occurred. Jordan was the only Arab country to grant Palestinians full citizenship, and the monarchy's newfound confederal control over the West Bank and Jerusalem gave it symbolic importance in the Arab world as a standard-bearer for the Palestinian cause. Domestically, though, the regime was reticent to broaden its coalitional base beyond what was, essentially, a tribalized "patriarchal oligarchy" (Aruri 1972, 73). More urbanized and mobile than the mostly tribal Transjordanians, the new Palestinian majority drastically transformed the political equation. For instance, the first confederal elections for the kingdom's 40-seat legislative assembly in 1950 featured 304,000 registered voters, whereas the prewar 1947 elections featured only 100,000 Transjordanian balloters (Wright 1951, 454). The assembly was long tolerated because of its generally conservative, promonarchical composition; now, it would become a vector of change.

By the early 1950s, Palestinian activists had helped introduce new opposition currents into public life. They founded local chapters of party-based opposition movements active elsewhere in the Middle East, such as the Arab Nationalist, Communist, and Baathist parties. These eventually coalesced to form a national opposition movement that demanded democratic reforms and the curtailment of Western influence (Anderson 2005, 117–46). Tensions came to bear in the mid-1950s, when a fierce period of contentious politics played out in parliament, the press, and the streets. After opposition parties captured a parliamentary majority, King Hussein was forced to appoint an opposition-led government, which moved to curtail royal authority. With constitutional monarchism or even overthrow a possibility, the regime flexed its muscle and enacted a vicious crackdown through its tribalized coercive apparatus that decimated the opposition

(Tal 2002, 44–53). Again reflecting the importance of exogenous support, this campaign of repression relied upon new American patronage, as the United States under the Eisenhower Doctrine moved to secure Jordan as its newest anti-Soviet client state. From April through June 1957, a period of fiscal emergency, the United States dispatched over $30 million in emergency cash grants and arms replenishments. This was an enormous gift in a year when the Jordanian state, saddled with political conflict and dysfunction, would collect $27.6 million in revenues but would spend nearly $37 million on policing and army salaries alone (Yom 2016, 174).

The destruction of the Jordanian opposition would echo for decades. Political parties would be permanently crippled, and there would be no more meaningful parliamentary life until the 1990s. Yet the crisis also reinforced the tribal-state compact. After the mid-1950s, development spending skewed heavily eastward; the Palestinian West Bank was reduced in status to agricultural workhorse and tourism draw, while land grants and subsidized housing on the east bank helped sedentarize many Transjordanian tribes. State-directed investments also seeded new industries that became communes for tribal employment, such as cement production and phosphates. The government itself became a work sponge for tribal labor: in 1961, the civil service alone recorded 24,000 Transjordanian employees, or a quarter of the nonagricultural workforce (Mazur 1979, 112). While a few Palestinian merchant families did become incorporated into the regime in the same way as Transjordanian mercantilists did a generation earlier, most state institutions, including the army, remained the preserve of Transjordanian loyalists. The army grew with a dual function of both protecting the regime and distributing rural welfarism; during the 1957–67 period, military manpower had more than doubled in size from 23,000 to 55,000. By the late 1960s, up to 70 percent of the tribal populace depended upon the salaries, housing, food, and medical care provided to military families (Tell 2013, 107). The royal court, a bureaucracy unto itself, became an important liaison to tribal communities, in which local sheikhs could interface with the monarchy through special representatives.

Much of this patronage required financial resources the nonextractive Jordanian state did not possess. Here, the importance of Western support cannot be overestimated, as rent-seeking foreign policy became central to Jordan's coalitional maintenance. After 1957, the United States became the monarchy's economic guarantor as well as sovereign safeguard against regional threats such as the Arab nationalist regimes of Egypt and Syria. The United States provided $500 million in assistance during 1958–67—cash grants, development spending, food aid, military arms, intelligence shar-

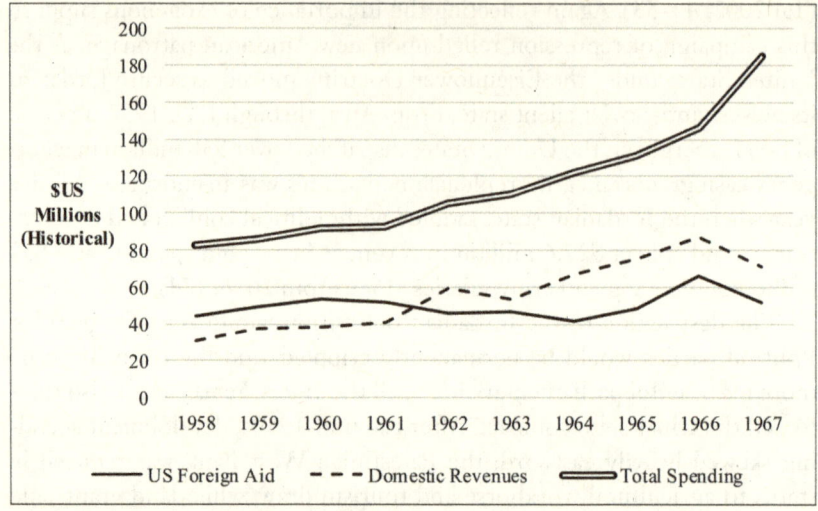

Fig. 9.1. US Aid, Domestic Revenues, and Total Spending in Jordan, 1958–67
Source: USAID 2018; Central Bank of Jordan (serial), *Annual Statistical Yearbook*.

ing, and so forth—that in turn underwrote the aforementioned networks of tribal provisions (Hammad 1987, 11–31). Jordan also received assistance from the United Nations Relief and Works Agency for its refugee population, alongside grants from other Western donors, but the United States remained paramount. During 1958–62, a period of regime consolidation through greater reliance upon tribal support, American foreign aid exceeded total domestic revenues (figure 9.1).

Fear: Ethnocracy and Coalitional Hardening, 1970–88

If political and economic bread accounts for the inception of the tribal-state compact underlying Jordanian autocracy from the colonial period onward, the 1970s and 1980s represented the apogee of this coalitional formula through communal conflict. The Transjordanian foundation underpinning Hashemite rule deepened after the Black September civil conflict of 1970, which ingrained within both tribes and monarchy the fear of being overrun by a Palestinian majority that saw little need for either. As a result, the Jordanian regime's coalitional strategy became increasingly ethnocratic through the 1980s, focused as much on *excluding* Palestinians from state institutions and political life as it was patronizing its tribal base through increasingly bloated, aid-fueled patronage networks.

While communal Transjordanian-Palestinian tensions first arose in the demographic flux following the 1948 Arab-Israeli conflict, the proximate trigger for the civil conflict was the 1967 Arab-Israeli War. The loss of the West Bank produced over 200,000 new Palestinian refugees, and led Palestinian guerilla forces operating regionally to relocate their liberation struggle to Amman. By summer 1970, friction between these groups and Jordanian security forces exploded in street battles. Palestinian armed commandos drew support from local Palestinian communities, some of whom began calling for the deposal of the Jordanian monarchy (El-Edroos 1980, 437–45). The resulting September 1970 war was short but bloody, as the Jordanian army liquidated the insurgency. Past investments into the tribal-state compact paid off; the army, described by one scholar as Bedouin "tribesmen in uniform," proved cohesive and effective in battle, with almost no defections (Axelrod 1978).

What followed for the next two decades was not just more royal patronage to tribal supporters, but the inverse gravitation of those supporters toward the monarchy out of fear. Such fear operated, as Dan Slater has described in other work, as an emotive mechanism designed to convince social forces that their primary enemy was not an authoritarian state capable of repression, but *other* societal groups whose ascendance would emasculate their privileges and property (Slater 2010, 20). After Black September, tribal sheikhs, military officers, cultural writers, and other voices of Transjordanian nationalism expressed this fear in lucid terms. In their eyes, a Jordanian state whose politics reflected its demographic reality would mean the end of the Hashemite throne, and with it the institutions that made rural tribal communities the guardians of political order.

Hence, despite that most Palestinians in Jordan had not only become citizens by 1970 but also refused to openly support the guerrilla insurgency, this demographic majority bore the brunt of this ethnocratic turn. Immediately, thousands of Palestinians were purged from state institutions, including the ministries and police, in acts of retribution designed to eliminate the small traces of Palestinian representation imprinted in previous decades (Susser 1994, 156–57). The national allegiance of Palestinians was frequently questioned; indeed, only a handful of Palestinian elites, by virtue of their wealth or service, ever managed to become ministers or royal advisers following the civil conflict. Alongside harsher repression through martial law levied especially at Palestinian-dominated urban areas and refugee camps, the monarchy also stoked a new cultural discourse—manifest in literature, textbooks, media, and other forums of national identity—that portrayed Palestinians as unwelcome guests while celebrating true Jordanians as *abna' al-'asha'ir*, or tribal sons (Abu Odeh 1999, 190–236).

As before, bankrolling this regime strategy was exogenous capital in the form of foreign assistance. Emergency US aid and arms during Black September rightly convinced the regime that Western interests were sufficiently staked to its survival as an anti-Soviet client state, enabling it to unleash unadulterated coercion during the conflict without fear of Western reproach. The United States also mobilized overseas military forces to discourage any foreign support of the Palestinian guerillas, including convincing the Israeli government to ward off a Syrian invasion (Joyce 2008, 49–66). Afterward, US economic and military aid per annum jumped from $4.1 million in 1970 to over $200 million in 1979; over this decade, Jordan would receive nearly $1.5 billion in American assistance, from cash grants and military arms to food (primarily wheat) and commodities. In addition, pan-Arab aid soon catapulted Jordan into unprecedented economic heights. In 1974, King Hussein secured $300 million in annual support from the Arab oil exporters, such as Saudi Arabia, in return for grudgingly recognizing the Palestinian Liberation Organization as the sole representative of the Palestinian people; the 1978 Arab League meetings went further, promising $1.25 billion in annual aid so long as Jordan rejected the Camp David peace process. In this way, Jordanian foreign policy became subservient to its "budget security"—that is, its capacity to find financial resources abroad that could then be redistributed at home to satisfy its domestic political commitments (Brand 1995).

One pernicious result of such aid-based rentier dependency was the continued weakness of domestic extractive capabilities. The Jordanian state never learned to live within its fiscal means because it seldom *had* to do so. By 1980, total internal revenues collected measured only half of external aid receipts (figure 9.2). Tax evasion was rampant and administrative capacity weak. In 1975, for instance, there were only 120,000 personal income taxpayers in a population of 2.3 million, with the vast majority of tax revenues collected through tariffs and other indirect means (Pillai 1982, 9). Thus, external aid financed a broad range of state functions, in particular public payrolls. By 1975, the public sector encompassed 157,000 Transjordanians, or almost half the entire national workforce (Mazur 1979, 113). Within the civil service, redundancy and corruption became commonplace, as underqualified Transjordanians regularly captured bureaucratic sinecures over better-educated Palestinian applicants who suffered systematic discrimination. While the old merchant elite were allowed to capitalize light sectors and amass fortunes in banking and retail, the state dominated labor-intensive industries like potash production and phosphate mining, which in turn gave rural tribal communities better access to employment

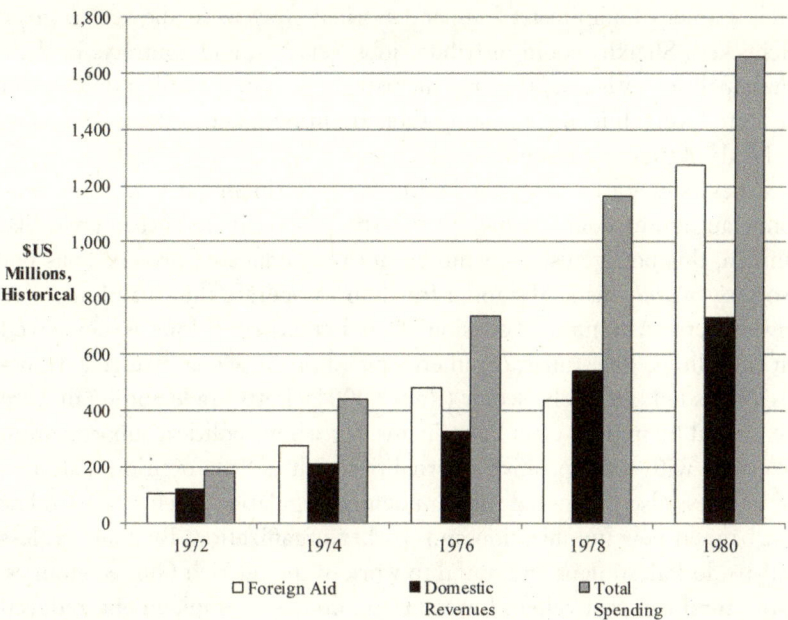

Fig. 9.2. Jordan's Foreign Aid and Domestic Revenues, 1970s
Source: Central Bank of Jordan (serial), *Annual Statistical Yearbook.*

and social services (Piro 1998, 37–58). Price subsidies, wage raises, and food cooperatives further protected Transjordanians reliant upon public salaries from inflationary pressures. Likewise, militarized welfarism under the army expanded through conscription, technological upgrading, and social services. The swelling defense budget gives indication of this: annual military spending more than quadrupled to an average of over $454 million during the 1970s, equaling over 43 percent of total government spending.

Institutionalizing the dependence of Jordan's tribal minority upon state patronage went hand in hand with political outreach that capitalized on its fear of Palestinian dominion. In official royal proclamations, King Hussein celebrated tribal values (and especially the Bedouin lifestyle) as the pillar of Jordanian identity, protecting them from social criticism: "Because of the close association between Jordan's tribes and the King, an attack on tribes could be construed as a veiled attack on the King" (Layne 1994, 104). The royal court arranged frequent consultations with sheikhs, and also experimented with various councils designed to give tribal notables more formal political venues for airing their opinions, such as the 1971 National Union and 1978 National Consultative Council (Al-Shraah 2012). At the local level, municipal administrations under tribal sway were allowed to grow unchecked. Sheikhs could distribute jobs, services, and contracts in their municipalities with ease, allowing the patronage system to filter down from the state level while also boosting their traditional authority as social figureheads of their communities.

If democracy was not forthcoming for Palestinians, at least some economic autonomy could be had. In Palestinian-dominated urban areas like Amman, this bourgeoisie—including not only educated professionals but also *petit-capital*—had substantial freedom to operate the small but active private sector. A communal division of labor emerged; so long as they stayed out of politics, Palestinian commerce could profit, while inversely Transjordanians led the public sector (Reiter 2004). Petty trade and retail were dominated by middle-class Palestinians, for whom political subordination also came with some positive externalities such as little taxation. Palestinian business also prospered through benign regulation, such as a 1976 law that banned new unionization and worker organization. By contrast, less well-to-do Palestinians emigrated to work in the oil-rich Gulf economies, a structural exit that relieved pressure on domestic employment, reduced the pool of political troublemakers, and infused the economy with remittance income. The state had all the means to encourage such emigration, since its security institutions controlled the distribution of exit visas.

Coalitional Loyalty in Hard Times: 1988–2000

By the 1980s, this coalitional recipe for monarchical rule in Jordan had succeeded in inverting its geography and demography. Palestinians constituted the numeric majority of society, resided in central urban areas, and propelled private sector commerce; yet they were relegated to the political margins. Inversely, tribal Transjordanians represented a populational minority living on the rural periphery, materially dependent upon patronage and statist development—but they represented the political heartland. In their own role as a supportive but small elite, the traditional merchant families flourished thanks to trade protections, sectoral capitalization, and monetary controls. Above all, fueling this formula was foreign aid, and access to regional markets and trade networks. The period after 1970 Black September conflict produced the financial peak of this ethnocratic political economy, with GDP leaping from $678 million to over $5.1 billion during 1971–85. By 1988, 75 percent of all working Transjordanians received a public salary in some form (Kanovsky 1989, 46–49).

At the decade's end, however, economic crisis threatened this framework of stability, as material scarcity and structural adjustments forced the Jordanian state to begin living within its means. Despite exposure to sudden hardship, however, tribal communities continued backing the monarchical regime due to the legacies of the redistributive loyalties and fear of Palestinian domination. The end of the boom began when global oil prices halved during 1981–85, which forced pan-Arab aid donors to renege on their aid payments. The economic contraction of the Gulf oil-exporters also meant a steep decline in remittances and export income. In 1988, the central bank recorded just $417 million in foreign aid, the lowest since 1977; to give some window as to how vital such capital flows were in a context of vapid taxation, in the previous year, public spending totaled $2.5 billion against domestic revenues of only $1.6 billion. The bubble burst in 1988, when capital flight precipitated a collapse of currency and total foreign debt hit $8 billion (twice the GDP). The resulting International Monetary Fund and World Bank loan interventions required structural adjustment policies, beginning with the retraction of fuel subsidies.

After years of material decline, sudden subsidy withdrawals sparked violence. In April 1989, the spiking price of fuel instigated tribal rioting in the worst outbreak of popular unrest since Black September, quelled only by the army. Yet notably, tribal protesters did not target the monarchy, nor did they call for radical political change; their actual demands were remarkably measured (as was the police response), consisting of calls for the appointed government to resign alongside the restoration of fuel subsidies (Yom 2016, 200–201). While ministers were dismissed to pacify tribal protesters, a return to the subsidy regimen was impossible given the regime's debt load and structural constraints. Indeed, economic conditions would only worsen after 1989. Nearly 300,000 Jordanians were deported from the Gulf kingdoms after the liberation of Kuwait, a punitive measure after the monarchy's surprising support for Iraq during the Gulf War; the influx of these returnees pushed the jobless rate to 30 percent and poverty rate to 33 percent by the early 1990s (Le Troquer and Al-Oudat 1999, 40–42). In August 1996, another round of IMF-imposed austerity doubled the price of bread and other basic commodities, creating more rural demonstrations in the tribal south.

The 1990s was a "lost" decade in terms of economic development and growth, for it marked the exhaustion of the statist economic policies that allowed the tribal coalition to flourish in decades past (Knowles 2005, 71–89). Tribal forces should have revolted—not just during the 1989 crisis, but also in this decade of welfarist withdrawal. Whereas the Palestinian middle class commanded more market resources, rural reliance upon public salaries and militarized welfarism made tribal communities extremely sensitive to state retreat. Even minor perturbations in social safety nets were felt in tribal households; for instance, the modest decline of subsidy spending from 3.3 percent of GDP in 1989 (or 7 percent of the budget) to just 1 percent in 1994 helped to more than double poverty rates in rural tribal communities (Zakharova 2004, 102). Compounding the problem, most government institutions were forced to freeze hiring. In 1995, the public sector and the military accounted for nearly 300,000 mostly Transjordanian employees, equivalent to about half the entire active labor force, while public sector wages and salaries represented over 52 percent of all current spending (Kanaan 1995, 24). The regime could not expand either given its fiscal shortages. Perhaps the only major concession made to tribal constituencies during this period, apart from the promise to not outright lay off workers and soldiers, was avoidance of direct taxation despite IMF and World Bank pressures to ratchet up domestic revenues. Instead, the state chose to raise badly needed funds through a general sales tax in 1994 while freezing public spending.

Why did tribal Jordanians not outright demand drastic political change? The traditional explanation is the "democracy for bread" argument: no longer able to give economic goods, the monarchy instead opted for political liberalization. Shortly after the 1989 tribal riots, the regime embarked upon a series of democratic reforms, including the release of political prisoners, new elections for parliament, abrogation of martial law, and legalization of political parties. Hence, the 1990s witnessed the return of civil society, parliamentary life, and critical media. Such venues gave Jordanians space to articulate opinions and mobilize openly, something missing for decades. And indeed, Transjordanians protested alongside Palestinians against several critical policies during the 1990s, from continued financial austerity to the normalization of relations with Israel. Moreover, the electoral system for parliament was especially engineered to privilege tribal supporters by maintaining Palestinian exclusion through extreme malapportionment of districts and the obscure single nontransferable voting system (Abu Jaber and Fathi 1990, 72–73). This allowed tribal leaders and notables to dominate the legislature, and reap the trickle-down clientelism that the parliamentary system proffered by facilitating access to state services and new resources.

However, political liberalization does not suffice as the reason for tribal loyalties to the crown. For one, tribal communities did not *need* democratic reforms to retain their privileged social and political status; their centrality depended upon not whether sheikhs could win parliamentary elections or create civic organizations, but instead whether they could communicate with royal decision-makers and obtain resources on a regular basis. For another, the very notion of democracy was anathema to the tribal-state compact. After the Black September conflict, the imperative among many Transjordanian nationalists was preventing any political opening that might translate Palestinian demography into political power. While the regime certainly took steps to contain this scenario, for instance by manipulating electoral laws to favor rural representation, it could not control all the implications of allowing for more pluralism. For instance, liberalization gave the Muslim Brotherhood an opportunity to mobilize and evolve as a political force, with its ranks infused by Palestinian cadres and its agenda increasingly oriented toward the Israeli-Palestinian conflict rather than grassroots issues of religiosity at home.

The more convincing explanation rests in the intersection between bread and fear. Tribal Jordanians remained tethered to a withering state unable to expand its patronage networks, but no other viable alternative existed in terms of welfarist provision and social protections. Moreover, while the ceiling of patronage could no longer be raised, it was not crashing down either. One major reason was the reticence of the IMF and World Bank in executing the full agenda of structural adjustment, such as downsizing the public sector and thus laying off Transjordanian labor, which would introduce even more political instability in a vital Western ally (Harrigan, Al-Said, and Wang 2006). Another was the well-timed arrival of more foreign aid. The 1994 peace treaty with Israel generated a wave of US-led economic support, food shipments, and multilateral debt relief; and while this did not close budgetary deficits during the decade, it at least guaranteed that civil service and military payrolls would not be subject to sharp contraction.

Beyond this lay the emotive factor of fear. Hostile anxieties against Palestinian identity remained visible within the public sphere during the 1990s, instigated by several geopolitical events (Lynch 1999, 100–112). One was Jordan's official disengagement from the West Bank in 1988, which ended the kingdom's financial and institutional responsibilities over the Palestinian territory since its 1967 occupation by Israel. Another was the recurrent idea birthed by Western voices that the Israeli-Palestinian conflict could be resolved by Jordan becoming the "alternative homeland" for Palestinians, an incendiary proposal that many Transjordanian advocates believed would submerge tribal communities in a sea of Palestinian interests and political domination. In sum, tribal communities were not pleased about their diminishing status, but they were more willing to accept retrenchment during economic crisis by a centralized, authoritarian monarchy they still trusted than take their chances under a democratic political order, one where their patronage and protection would most likely suffer more drastic devaluation. The redistributive preferences of Transjordanians were sticky—but so too were their loyalties.

Loyalties Tested: Coalitional Narrowing, 2000-Present

By the time young King Abdullah ascended to the throne in 1999, Jordan was only beginning to climb out of its long decade of economic stagnation. Politically, the strategy adopted during the incoming 2000s was coalitional *narrowing* through the instigation of neoliberal reforms to overhaul the entire economy in favor of privatization, free trade, and investment protocols. This shuffling would gradually transform the monarchy's ruling base; while Transjordanian tribalism still inhabited state institutions and the military, a new wave of business elites would emerge with a strikingly different relationship to the royal center. As manifest today, they desire not more government interventionism, but less; and they represent a market-based, globally oriented stratum that the regime prefers to push forward as Jordan's vanguard class. As before, bread and fear continue to keep tribal communities incubated within their monarchical compact, but signs of increased resistance and dissent are growing as welfarist promises continue to shrink.

Soon after his installation, King Abdullah placed hundreds of new technocratic reformers to revamp the institutional infrastructure of state power (Bank and Schlumberger 2004). These elites markedly differed from past regime insiders, such as the old merchant captains and tribal sheikhs. They were communally diverse, with many claiming Palestinian origins, and also hailed from Western-educated and usually private sector business backgrounds. They nurtured a marked distrust of state enterprise, associating it with endemic corruption and bureaucratic inefficiencies (Carroll 2003, 57–65). Among their early reform successes were Jordan's accession to the World Trade Organization in 2000; the US-Jordan Free Trade Agreement in 2001; and liberalized investment protocols that helped secure new foreign capital. Starting in 2003, the World Economic Forum held annual meetings on the Jordanian side of the Dead Sea, highlighting the regime's foreign policy orientation toward Western cultural and economic institutions.

Domestically, this neoliberal political economy clashed with tribal redistributive demands. A seminal example was privatization. As late as the mid-1990s, the Jordanian government commanded the majority of all shares among the 109 public firms listed on the financial exchange. By the early 2000s, however, the sell-off and divestment of many parastatal companies in sectors like mining, telecommunications, and transportation was proceeding apace, with job losses hitting rural areas especially hard. At the same time, the private sector industries anointed as engines of growth—skill-intensive fields like technology, pharmaceuticals, and financials—had little need for Transjordanian labor.

Hence, tribal communities faced creeping dislocation starting in the 2000s on multiple fronts. While the public sector outside of state-owned enterprises was in little danger of contraction in terms of absolute size, it could no longer expand to absorb Transjordanian labor. Neither the military nor the civil service could add more than marginal jobs to their distended payrolls despite tribal demands for more state employment. For instance, in 2014 the civil service counted nearly 250,000 employees, but over 200,000 more Jordanians had passed the Civil Service Exam and were waiting to obtain a bureaucratic position (Amer 2014). While the army remained a tribal institution, positions became extremely competitive; for instance, by 2012, 10,000 tribal applicants were vying for less than 1,000 military spots that opened annually (Yom 2015, 298). Military service, long a birthright of many tribal communities, became privileges reserved only for well-connected applicants. Further, subsidies underwent cyclical withdrawals during budgetary crunches, as planners began replacing blanket protections for bread, petrol, and other commodity prices with means-tested assistance and income-based programs. Finally, at the local level, in 2001 the national government reduced the number of municipal administrations from 328 to 94. This was a fiscally sound move, but it also obliterated the localized patronage that sheikhs could funnel to their constituencies.

This economic retooling went hand in hand with a renewed pro-Western foreign policy that, in line with its need for budget security, proffered a steady stream of outside monies. Rebuffing resistance from civil society, the monarchy burnished Jordan's peaceful relations with Israel, supported the US-led war on terror after 9/11, facilitated the Iraq War, and otherwise promoted American interests in the region. In return, it reaped massive aid through debt relief, development funding, military purchase credits, and direct payments, the latter of which were treated as fungible revenues to compensate for continually low domestic taxation. From 2000 to 2018, Jordan received nearly $18 billion in combined American economic and military aid, making it the third highest recipient of US foreign aid in the world (after Israel and Iraq). During the 2011–12 Arab Spring, Jordan also began receiving significant cash transfers from Saudi Arabia and several other Gulf kingdoms, as well as intermittent IMF and World Bank financing.

In place of a broad tribal base is the new elite business constituency, which the Jordanian autocracy sees as advantageous for three reasons. First, it is *cheaper*. Distinct from the old echelon of merchants present during the kingdom's formative decades, these new leaders of commerce were enriched greatly by post-1989 economic reforms, and are diversified across multiple capital-intensive sectors—pharmaceutical production, real estate development, energy trading, and investment banking, for instance. Unlike the regime's tribal constituencies, these voices make few demands for overt state interventionism, such as material patronage or communal protections. They want less government inference concomitant with open market protocols that will allow for greater integration with the global economy. This has paradoxically also allowed them to access state capital for industrial projects that express the globalizing, Western-oriented vision of the monarchy, such as real estate and trade complex megaprojects (Peters and Moore 2009, 277–78).

Second, it is *antidemocratic*. Unlike the views of many Palestinian activists, this new elite is at best agnostic to the question of democratization, which would entail not just dismantling the coercive apparatus, but also replacing royal absolutism with an empowered parliamentary government elected through a competitive voting system. Their preference is not the participation and accountability that such regime change would bring, but rather stability and order furnished by a reliable structure of predictable autocratic power. Rule of law is important insofar that it ensures property rights and contract enforcement, not horizontal accountability and mass enfranchisement. Indeed, their influence with decision-making circles is mediated not through formal institutions, but personalized access to ministers, officials, and the king—ties lubricated through money, favors, and service. Hence, much as it has rolled back tribal patronage since the 2000s, the Jordanian regime has also curtailed its prior push for political liberalization, installing a battery of newly restrictive laws and punishments since the late 2000s that have dampened the civic and oppositional momentum gained a decade earlier (Moss 2014).

Third, this support group transcends *communalism*. The new business elites do not identify themselves primarily along the lines of the

Transjordanian-Palestinian divide, the identity cleavage that fueled past periods of ethnocracy and social tension. The new coalitional constituency hails from both Palestinian and Transjordanian backgrounds; their families are tied to neither land nor community, and bound more by shared norms, education, and access to mobile capital. This comports with the regime's own political project to replace the worst parts of Transjordanian chauvinism within Jordan's national identity discourse with a newly contrived vision of Jordanian citizenship that emphasizes unity, patriotism, and love of Hashemite rule (Greenwood 2003). That Queen Rania is Palestinian herself weighs heavily in this reframing exercise. This markedly diverges from the prejudice latent in many tribal circles, where the decline of state largesse and rise of new business elites has wrought the belief that "Palestinians, long the base of the social pyramid, are perceived to be climbing to the top, while the Transjordanians feel the ground collapsing beneath their feet" (Ryan 2010).

As expected, the waning salience of the tribal-state compact has produced a rising tide of dissatisfaction. Starting late in the first decade of the new century, select Transjordanian luminaries—former ministers, tribal sheikhs, military veterans, and others—began periodically criticizing the monarchy for its technocratic inclinations through public petitions and street marches. Wildcat strikes in privatizing industries, especially phosphates and port logistics, became regular occurrences late in the decade (Adely 2012). The closest that tribal groups came to broaching red lines of dissent occurred during the Arab Spring. While this transformative regional event spurred more than a year of weekly protests from various social forces, from leftist movements and student groups to the Muslim Brotherhood and professional associations, rural communities contributed one of the most memorable popular mobilizations in the form of the *hirak*, or tribal activist movements (Yom 2014, 232–36). Often defying directives from their tribal elders and security forces alike, these young protesters authored thousands of contentious events from 2011 through mid-2013, some of which defaced the monarchy's symbols and demanded a return to the past.

As King Abdullah closes in upon two decades of power, however, such agitations must be contextualized against the wider trajectory of Jordanian regime persistence. The credible threat of repression, alongside other fatiguing factors that have drained collective energies for mobilization since the Arab Spring—the Syrian refugee crisis, the battle against the Islamic State, frictions with Israel—have reduced the propensity for large-scale protests. Rare exceptions, such as the urban uprising against another round of IMF-imposed austerity in June 2018, have followed past patterns in targeting the cabinet government but not the monarchy itself. Indeed, even the most radical outbursts of *hirak* mobilization during the Arab Spring did not call for the overthrow of the monarchy, but instead suggested the replacement of King Abdullah with another prince from the Hashemite family. The tendency even for ardent tribal activists to demure from impugning royal power, and instead fall back upon the familiar demands of sacking of ministers or reversing policy, underscores the legacy of past redistributive demands combined with anti-Palestinian fear. The regime still needs phalanxes of Transjordanian loyalists to staff the civil service and army, and both militarized welfarism and social entitlements—supported by aid rents garnered from foreign patrons—still diffuse outward to many tribal communities.

In this milieu, expectations for continued stability during future economic shocks is predicated upon not just the structural (if still declining) pull of these patronage and protection ties between tribe and state, but also the persistent belief among many tribal constituencies that the Hashemite monarchy remains the optimal purveyor of political order. The alternative scenario of political change driven by tribal insurrections depends upon a critical and unlikely shift—communal recognition among Transjordanians that the uncertainty of regime turnover, including the possibility of relegation under a Palestinian-majoritarian government, is more promising than continuing to suffer as losers of coalitional shuffling. Conventional wisdom suggests this is not likely; but as the Arab Spring illustrated that agents of revolution can emerge from unlikely quarters, it also should not reside outside the realm of possibility.

Conclusion: No Party, No Problem

Coalitions are not static. The pacts and bargains linking social forces to autocratic regimes change over time as both are subjected to economic busts and financial crises. The preceding analysis illuminated such an historical trajectory of coalitional evolution within monarchical Jordan, from the colonial creation of the tribal-state compact and ethnocratic reorganization of the political economy, to the economic shock of the late 1980s and the revealed unsustainability of this coalitional overhead. Reconfiguration through economic reforms has stressed the tribal-state compact, but a combination of inherited loyalties and communal fears of Palestinian domination—and not, pointedly, democratic political concessions—has proven sufficient to keep tribal support intact. Such stickiness has endured even as the monarchy promoted a new base of commercial elites, the beneficiaries of neoliberal economic adjustments made after the 1990s. As a result, the ruling coalition has become narrower, as popular rural support is replaced by a smaller stratum of urban business figures whose economic and political preferences diverge from traditional Transjordanian demands for patronage and protection.

Compared with most other chapters in this book, a vital element seems to be missing in this analytical narrative: there is no ruling party institution, one that either encases the authoritarian incumbent within organizational power or enshrines coalitional commitments within a mobilizational infrastructure that can flex its grassroots muscle through ideological or performance-based appeals. In fact, the Jordanian case underlines how neither incumbent survival during crises nor coalitional realignments afterward requires a hegemonic party. Four reasons account for this. First, within Jordan's ruling monarchy, executive power is inherited rather than contested, and decision-making organs such as the cabinet government and coercive apparatus are directly appointed by the king to carry out his wishes. Because the principals of these institutions are not drawn from the elected (though toothless) parliament, there is no systemic need for a dominant party apparatus aimed at winning elections or other venues of contestation. Second, the Jordanian regime has proven capable in terms of reaching into its social bases of support without the mediating functions of a party organization and rank-and-file cadres. The Hashemite royal court, a bureaucracy devoted solely to maintaining monarchical interests, serves as the central entity that allows the king to reach into society and directly engage supporters and rivals alike. Moreover, state institutions are able to distribute patronage to tribal labor through their everyday employment and welfarist functions; there is no ideological need to "recruit" tribes first.

Third, there is a peculiar historical factor. The monarchy's clashes with leftist and nationalist parties during the 1950s was so contentious, and the resulting decades of martial law so restrictive, that there is little support among either regime elites or Jordanian society for strong, cohesive party organizations. Pointedly, despite their legalization in the early 1990s, political parties remain extremely weak and small—not only because of restrictive laws, but also because most Jordanians (including oppositionists) simply do not see them as effective vehicles of interest articulation. Finally, monarchism itself offers a winning institutional design for authoritarian powerholders in Jordan. All of the political recalibrations needed to run this autocracy—implanting new elites into the state, dismissing unpopular governments, directing new policy imperatives, allocating repressive resources to trouble spots—have occurred through the efficient exercise of royal authority, either directly or indirectly through the king's will. Moreover, public officials, particularly the prime minister, usefully absorb public anger during episodes of popular discontent, and then are discarded for the next elite lieutenants down the line; this buffers the palace from both scrutiny and attacks. Though not immune to political change, given the uneven record of absolutist kingships elsewhere, it has worked well in sustaining the lineaments of authoritarianism in Jordan.

Lacking a ruling party, Jordan's pathway of crisis survival and coalitional reconfiguration deposits two further important lessons for theorizing about authoritarianism during hard times. First, it underscores that historical loyalties are not given but rather made—and once made, they can last for very long periods of time, particularly when infused with the emotive power of fear oriented against competing social forces. The redistributive demands of tribal groups made upon the Hashemite monarchy reflect a nearly century-old pact that bound generations of tribal communities to the patronage and protections of the Hashemite throne. The gradually rising, though still moderate, level of tribal dissent attests to the mutual dependencies engendered by this bargain, as well as the intensity to which these coalitional members essentially *need* a monarchical state to exist. The economic shock of 1989 still looms large.

Second, the Jordanian case reveals how exogenous factors can shape coalitional strategies. Throughout its development, foreign aid rents were inextricably intertwined with the economic and political institutions created to bind tribal preferences to monarchical power. However, it also rendered the coalitional arrangement vulnerable to financial difficulties. External aid and assistance have always flowed from foreign patrons like the United States, who see political stability in Jordan as integral to grander geopolitical schemes in the Middle East. Such reliance upon exogenous capital amplified the economic crisis of the late 1980s by exposing the regime's lethargic capacity for domestic taxation. As ramping up its extractive power would require revisiting its rentier social contract, the Jordanian autocracy instead chose to narrow its coalition to a smaller base while gambling that the old tribal foundation would not abandon it wholesale. This is a logical decision, but time will tell whether it is the wisest one.

REFERENCES

Abu Jaber, Kamel, and Schirin Fathi. 1990. "The 1989 Jordanian Parliamentary Elections." *Orient* 31 (1): 67–86.

Abu Nowar, Maan. 2006. *The Development of Trans-Jordan 1929–1939*. Reading, UK: Ithaca Press.

Abu Odeh, Adnan. 1999. *Jordanians, Palestinians, and the Hashemite Kingdom in the Middle East Peace Process*. Washington, DC: United States Institute of Peace.

Adely, Fida. 2012. "The Emergence of a New Labor Movement in Jordan." *Middle East Report* 264: 34–37.

Alon, Yoav. 2007. *The Making of Jordan: Tribes, Colonialism, and the Modern State*. London: I.B. Tauris.

Al-Shraah, Ibrahim. 2012. "Al-Ittihad al-watani al-'arabi 'al-urduni' baina 'ami 1971–1974: Dirasa ta'rikhiyyah tahliliyyah." *Al-Najah University Journal of Research in the Humane Sciences* 26 (3): 731–66.

Amawi, Abla. 1994. "The Consolidation of the Merchant Class in Transjordan during the Second World War." In *Village, Steppe, and State: The Social Origins of Modern Jordan*, ed. Eugene Rogan and Tariq Tell. London: British Academic Press.

Amer, Mona. 2014. "The School to Work Transition of Jordanian Youth." In *The Jordanian Labor Market in the New Millennium*, ed. Ragui Assaad. Oxford: Oxford University Press.

Anderson, Betty. 2005. *Nationalist Voices in Jordan: The Street and the State*. Austin: University of Texas Press.

Aruri, Nasser. 1972. *Jordan: A Study in Political Development, 1921–1965*. The Hague: Martinus Nijhoff.

Axelrod, Lawrence. 1978. "Tribesmen in Uniform: The Demise of the Fida'iyyun in Jordan, 1970–71." *Muslim World* 68 (1): 25–45.

Bank, André, and Oliver Schlumberger. 2004. "Jordan: Between Regime Survival and Economic Reform." In *Arab Elites: Negotiating the Politics of Change*, ed. Volker Perthes. Boulder, CO: Lynne Rienner.

Brand, Laurie. 1995. *Jordan's Inter-Arab Relations: The Political Economy of Alliance Making*. New York: Columbia University Press.

Brumberg, Dan. 2002. "Democratization in the Arab World? The Trap of Liberalized Autocracy." *Journal of Democracy* 13 (4): 56–68.

Carroll, Katherine Blue. 2003. *Business as Usual? Economic Reform in Jordan*. Lanham, MD: Lexington Books.

Central Bank of Jordan. Serial. *Annual Statistical Yearbook*. Amman: Department of Statistics.

El-Edroos, Syed Ali. 1980. *The Hashemite Arab Army, 1908–1979: An Appreciation and Analysis of Military Operations*. Amman: Publishing Committee.

Greenwood, Scott. 2003. "Jordan's 'New Bargain': The Political Economy of Regime Security." *Middle East Journal* 57 (2): 248–68.

Hammad, Khalil. 1987. "The Role of Foreign Aid in the Jordanian Economy, 1959–1983." In *The Economic Development of Jordan*, ed. Bichara Khader and Adnan Badran. London: Croom Helm.

Harrigan, Jane, Hamed Al-Said, and Chengang Wang. 2006. "The IMF and the World Bank in Jordan: A Case of Over Optimism and Elusive Growth." *Review of International Organizations* 1 (3): 263–92.

Heydemann, Steven. 1999. *Authoritarianism in Syria: Institutions and Social Conflict, 1946–1970*. Ithaca: Cornell University Press.

Joyce, Miriam. 2008. *Anglo-American Support for Jordan: The Career of King Hussein.* London: Palgrave Macmillan.

Kanaan, Taher. 1995. "Relative Roles of the Public and Private Sectors." In *The Jordanian Economy*, ed. Tejinder Minhas, Taher Kanaan, Said Mammamy, and Ali Kassay. Amman: Steering Committee.

Kanovsky, Eliyahu. 1989. *Jordan's Economy: From Prosperity to Crisis.* Tel Aviv: Moshe Dayan Center for Middle Eastern and African Studies.

Knowles, Warwick. 2005. *Jordan since 1989: A Study in Political Economy.* London: I.B. Tauris.

Layne, Linda. 1994. *Home and Homeland: The Dialogics of Tribal and National Identities in Jordan.* Princeton: Princeton University Press.

Le Troquer, Yann, and Rozenn Hommery Al-Oudat. 1999. "From Kuwait to Jordan: The Palestinians' Third Exodus." *Journal of Palestine Studies* 28 (3): 37–51.

Lucas, Russell. 2005. *Institutions and the Politics of Survival in Jordan: Domestic Responses to External Challenges, 1988–2001.* Albany: SUNY Press.

Lynch, Marc. 1999. *State Interests and Public Spheres: The International Politics of Jordan's Identity.* New York: Columbia University Press.

Mazur, Michael. 1979. *Economic Growth and Development in Jordan.* London: Croom Helm.

Moss, Dana. 2014. "Repression, Response, and Contained Escalation under 'Liberalized' Authoritarianism in Jordan." *Mobilization* 19 (3): 261–86.

Musa, Sulayman. 1989. *Ta'sis al-imarah al-urduniyyah, 1921–1925.* Amman: Maktabat al-muhtasib.

Peters, Anne Mariel, and Pete Moore. 2009. "Beyond Boom and Bust: External Rents, Durable Authoritarianism, and Institutional Adaptation in the Hashemite Kingdom of Jordan." *Studies in Comparative International Development* 44 (3): 256–85.

Pillai, Vel. 1982. "External Economic Dependence and Fiscal Policy Imbalances in Developing Countries: A Case Study of Jordan." *Journal of Development Studies* 19 (1): 5–18.

Piro, Timothy. 1998. *The Political Economy of Market Reform in Jordan.* Lanham, MD: Rowman & Littlefield.

Reiter, Yitzhak. 2004. "The Palestinian-Transjordanian Rift: Economic Might and Political Power in Jordan." *Middle East Journal* 58 (1): 72–92.

Ryan, Curtis. 2002. *Jordan in Transition: From Hussein to Abdullah.* Boulder, CO: Lynne Rienner.

Ryan, Curtis. 2010. "We Are All Jordan . . . But Who Is We?" *Middle East Report Online*, July 13. https://www.merip.org/mero/mero071310

Slater, Dan. 2010. *Ordering Power: Contentious Politics and Authoritarian Leviathans in Southeast Asia.* Cambridge: Cambridge University Press.

Susser, Asher. 1994. *On Both Banks of the Jordan: A Political Biography of Wasfi Al-Tall.* Portland, OR: Cass.

Tal, Lawrence. 2002. *Politics, the Military, and National Security in Jordan: 1955–1967.* London: Palgrave Macmillan.

Tell, Tariq Moraiwed. 2013. *The Social and Economic Origins of Monarchy in Jordan.* London: Palgrave Macmillan.

US Agency for International Development (USAID). 2018. *Greenbook: U.S. Overseas Loans and Grants*. Washington, DC: USAID.

Vatikiotis, P. J. 1967. *Politics and the Military in Jordan: A Study of the Arab Legion, 1921–1957*. London: Cass.

Wright, Esmond. 1951. "Abdallah's Jordan: 1947–1951." *Middle East Journal* 5 (4): 439–60.

Yom, Sean L. 2014. "Tribal Politics in Contemporary Jordan: The Case of the Hirak Movement." *Middle East Journal* 68 (1): 229–47.

Yom, Sean L. 2015. "The New Landscape of Jordanian Politics: Social Opposition, Fiscal Crisis, and the Arab Spring." *British Journal of Middle East Studies* 42 (2): 284–300.

Yom, Sean L. 2016. *From Resilience to Revolution: How Foreign Interventions Destabilize the Middle East*. New York: Columbia University Press.

Zakharova, Daria. 2004. "Development of Social Protection Institutions." In *Jordan: Selected Issues and Statistical Appendix*, ed. Mohsin Khan. Washington, DC: International Monetary Fund.

Conclusion

Victor C. Shih

In an era of slowing global growth, volatile commodities prices, and rising authoritarianism, both authoritarian regimes and advanced democracies that interact with them will need to confront the possibility of unstable politics in autocracies, as well as autocracies' responses to potential instability. Within highly integrated global trade and financial systems, instability in major autocracies will impact the economies and politics even in high-income, established democracies. Likewise, reactions by authoritarian leaders to major economic shocks also will impact neighboring countries and even certain sectors in both advanced and developing democracies. For example, China's role as the largest global commodities buyer means that economic outcomes in the country will affect growth in Brazil, Chile, and Australia in substantial ways. This book begins an exploration of the complex interaction between economic shocks and authoritarian stability and hopes to inspire future research in this direction.

The chapters of this book show that when confronted with major external economic shocks, authoritarian regimes react in different ways with varying consequences. As the extant literature suggests, strong single-party institutions, especially when coupled with confident control over financial institutions, very likely would immunize regimes from political risks during shorter economic crises. The longer time horizon provided by political institutions coupled with continuity in the flow of fiscal and financial resources likely would negate the need to cut off benefits to key supporters of the impacted regimes. Thus, status quo coalitions, perhaps with some degree of reduction in benefits to members of the ruling coalitions, likely would persist without disturbance. This was seen in the case of Taiwan during the oil crisis, as the Wong contribution documents. Likewise, Malaysia in 1998 and China in 2008–9 also handled their respective shocks with ease through these mechanisms.

As the duration of crises lengthens, however, the effectiveness of regime control over financial institutions degenerates, and even political control may become brittle. Even in regimes with strong party systems and administrative control over the financial sector, long-term reduction in resources caused by structural changes in commodities prices or prolonged sanctions would force the regime to reduce promised welfare provision to the population or benefits to the elite. As the Dimitrov chapter on Eastern Europe communist regimes suggests, a prolonged shortfall in promised benefits to the urban constituencies made these regimes extremely vulnerable to political shocks. As China faces increasing budget constraints due to years of leveraging and the anticorruption campaign, the Chinese Communist Party also may enter a period of brittle rule, with a large segment of mid- and low-level officials latently dissatisfied, as the Shih chapter suggests. To be sure, even when faced with prolonged contraction in resources, some regimes adapted by shrinking the share of the ruling coalition that enjoyed extraordinary level of welfare and monetary compensation. Although such reduction increased political risks, as the cases of Iraq and Jordan show, the incumbents hung on to power for quite some time because the austerity allowed these regimes to shift resources toward core supporters or even a new support base. In regimes where political or financial control is weaker to begin with, longer crises may compel autocratic leaders to shrink the support coalitions, but weaker political control may precipitate mass defection by the elite at the moment of austerity. This arguably was the case in Indonesia after the Asian Financial Crisis.

The major contributions of this book are numerous. First and foremost, going beyond the binary outcomes of "authoritarian resilience" and democratization, the authors in this book also consider revisions in the ruling coalition as a major outcome of interest. For theorists of democratization, revising the ruling coalition has not been considered as an outcome different from the status quo (O'Donnell, Schmitter, and Whitehead 1986; Przeworski 1991; Diamond 1996; Huntington 1991). Upon revisiting well-known cases and observing new cases of economic shocks, however, the contributors of this volume see revision in the ruling coalition as an important outcome because it has implications for how regimes govern henceforth, as well as the medium-term stability of these regimes. Analogous to the rich literature investigating the coalition lineup that made democratization more likely (O'Donnell, Schmitter, and Whitehead 1986;

Huber, Rueschemeyer, and Stephens 1993; Bellin 2000; Przeworski 1991), the cases in this volume suggest that even during economic hardship, autocrats can make new pacts to *prolong* authoritarian rule.

The cases in this volume do not suggest any generalizable rule for these pacts for resilience, as dictators seem to make different new coalitions contingent on a host of factors. Future research, both in-depth case studies and cross-national comparisons, will be needed to clarify this issue. Iraq, Jordan, Malaysia, and even China show that revisions in the ruling coalition may undermine the political stability and financial viability of major autocracies in the medium term and may serve as precursors to greater changes.

Moreover, the ways in which regimes compensated for dwindling resources available to ruling coalitions potentially have important implications. For example, although Putin has faced dwindling resources due to lower energy prices and US sanctions, he thus far has maintained his popular support by saturating both the traditional and new media with propaganda messages, according to the Treisman and Lamberova contribution. In China, censorship and insertion of subtly pro-government messages in social media platforms likewise have maintained the apparent popularity of the central government in the midst of an economic slowdown (King, Pan, and Roberts 2017). High popularity helps the incumbent in reducing the probability of major urban protests and in deterring potential elite challengers from openly confronting the incumbent (Magaloni 2006). Like corporations around the world, autocracies have borrowed new technologies to reduce the costs of operation. Can these regimes endlessly exploit the technological frontiers for their own benefit, or is there a limit to bolstering support with media messaging alone when faced with economic hardship? The cases in this volume suggest that this is a fruitful avenue for future research.

Second, this volume adds to the literature on politics during economic crises and recognizes that the sudden diminution of resources to authoritarian regimes may well necessitate important changes, either voluntary or involuntary (Haggard and Kaufman 1995; Haggard 2000; Gourevitch 1986). As the extant literature points out, economic hard times often require politicians to adjust policies, which bring about welfare consequences on key constituencies (Gourevitch 1986). Other works suggest that during economic crises, nondemocratic regimes gain the incentive to liberalize policies to placate the disaffected population (Acemoglu and Robinson 2006; Desai, Olofsgård, and Yousef 2009). The need to adjust runs up against the concept of minimum winning coalitions in authoritarian regimes, which predicts that dictators will only buy support from the minimum number of actors required to stay in power (Bueno de Mesquita et al. 2003; Egorov and Sonin 2011). The cases in this volume show that many autocracies were able to drastically reduce the number of beneficiaries during economic crises, and even among the remaining beneficiaries, their payoffs have been cut drastically. Contrary to the expectation of the literature, dictators facing economic hardship rarely liberalized and often imposed even greater repression on the population. How was this possible if these dictators' coalitions had been "minimum"?

One possible interpretation was that the coalitions had not been "minimum" but had been "surplus" coalitions, as Magaloni's work on the PRI in Mexico suggests (Magaloni 2006). Surplus coalitions, support coalitions greater than the minimum necessary to maintain dictators' power, may have been motivated by a combination of the desire to credibly show strength to deter challenges and risk aversion. Because successful coups lead to very negative outcomes for dictators, if they have the resources, they may prefer to pay off core members of their regimes to disincentivize them from plotting against the incumbents.

Alternatively, the minimum winning coalition theory still applies in the cases in this volume. During economic hardship, both the dictator and potential rivals faced tighter budget constraints, thus allowing the dictators to reduce benefits to their support coalitions without the fear of defection. There were no better alternatives for the suffering members of these coalitions. Simultaneously, a tighter budget constraint during a crisis incentivized dictators to "innovate" more cost-effective measures of staying in power, such as saturating the airwaves with propaganda or increasing the deployment of the secret police or even invading a neighboring country to firm up domestic support, as the Russia case shows (Treisman and Guriev 2015). During crises, especially those accompanied by less commercial interactions with the rest of the world, the relative costs of intense propaganda and repression also diminished, thus making these tools of staying in power more worthwhile. With these "sharper" tools of staying in power, perhaps the minimum winning coalition could be reduced, compared to when softer tools were used. Also, instead of liberalizing, economic hardship may have spurred regimes to innovate and deploy repressive and propaganda tools. The cases in the volume suggest the fruitfulness of further theoretical and empirical research on minimum winning and surplus coalitions in authoritarian regimes.

Furthermore, there is a dynamic element to adjustments during hard times. In Iraq, Iran, and Jordan, adjustments in the ruling coalitions made these regimes more brittle to further political shocks. Although these regimes have not so far fallen from power due to internal dissent, our contributors, who are all experts in these countries, suggest that coalitional adjustments have increased the potential for internal splits. These splits manifested as protests and even assassination attempts against the incumbents in both Iran and Iraq after their respective economic shocks. In China and Malaysia, the regimes successfully mobilized financial resources and administrative control at their disposal to smooth the impact of the crises. However, in both cases, the response to the crises left lasting legacies of high government deficit and government and corporate debt, as well as, in the case of Malaysia, general dissatisfaction with an increasingly repressive environment. This contributed to the incumbent's defeat a few years later, as the Slater contribution shows. In China, there has not been any regime change as of 2019, but the Chinese government now struggles with nonfinancial debt to the tune of 300 percent of GDP.

Implications of Authoritarian Survival Strategies for Policies in Democracies

Beyond academic interests, insights on how authoritarian regimes respond to economic shocks have profound implications for policymakers in advanced democracies. First of all, as emphasized by the authoritarian resilience literature already, autocracies have turned out to be much more durable than scholars had hoped during the brief post–Cold War euphoria (Fukuyama 1992; Huntington 1991). Events in subsequent decades have shown that autocracies are much more resilient than previously believed. More recent scholarship has identified institutional and technological reasons for their resilience. The flexibility to reshape support coalitions at a time of crisis constitutes yet another reason for authoritarian resilience. This volume adds to the torrent of literature that suggests to policy makers that absent very compelling reasons to think otherwise, policies toward an incumbent autocratic regime should not assume its imminent demise. To go one step further, policies toward authoritarian regimes should try to avoid vague objectives such as undermining or changing a particular regime, unless all-out war has commenced between countries. The ability of autocratic regimes to survive most economic sanctions likely will disappoint policymakers who hope to use nonmilitary means to overthrow regimes.

The application of economic sanctions against authoritarian regimes, which include the withholding of aid, trade sanctions, and sanctions on financial transactions, should instead aim at specific behavioral changes and with consideration for the coalition makeup of the target regime. As Kirshner (1997, 42) points out, economic sanctions often disappoint policymakers because of the failure of the economic impact of sanctions "to translate into the desired political outcome." Again, Kirshner points out that sanctions should target the government as well as "core groups" of key supporters for the regime, who indirectly bring about pressure on the leadership (Kirshner 1997). This is an insight shared by Brooks (2002). The more recent literature on authoritarian resilience, which includes this volume, suggests that sanctions should not aim at regime change. Instead, sanctions should have a clearly stated compliance standard and should aim at the payoff structures of authoritarian leaders and their core supporters, as well as the payoffs of any new coalition that may emerge in the midst of an economic crisis caused by the sanctions.

The simplest hypothetical example is the withdrawal of substantial military aid from a military dictatorship that has a powerful secret police organization. Obviously, this would cause a problem for the regime because both the dictator and his core constituency would suffer significant income losses, compelling the dictator to change behavior in compliance with the demands of the originator. As long as sanctions do not aim at regime change, the dictator can partially expect that changing behavior will result in a resumption of aid and a more stable equilibrium. If the dictator can change his coalition to include only the secret police, the originator of the sanction may fruitfully consider imposing additional sanctions on all business interests related to the secret police. This would put intense pressure on the dictator to comply with sanction demands. The findings of this book suggest that originators should incorporate dynamic targeting of sanctions toward the dictator's shifting coalitions.

Furthermore, given the limited impact of short-term shocks for many surviving autocracies today, sanctions that, at least in principle, can be enacted over the long term are more likely to be effective. As our cases show, longer-duration economic shocks forced dictators to change the calculus of governance, which introduced substantial political risks to their continual rule. This may compel them to comply with the demands of the sanctions. Domestically, this means that countries imposing sanctions on dictatorships should obtain as wide a consensus across the political spectrum as possible and should codify the sanctions into law. To be sure, this will increase the time it takes to impose sanctions and quite possibly water down the provisions of sanctions to appease various domestic interests, but after implementation, the target countries also will know that electoral swings will not lead to the lifting of sanctions. Again, knowing the heightened political risks of prolonged sanctions, dictators in most circumstances would entertain compliance with greater probability.

As a torrent of literature on international institutions suggests, policies that are institutionalized and have multilateral participation create incentives for participants to adhere to them in the medium term due to side payments, information advantages, and punishment for defection (Keohane 1984; Martin 1992). Accordingly, economic sanctions that are adopted by well-established international organizations such as the UN at least signal to the target countries the potential pervasiveness and persistence of sanction policies, thus incentivizing them to comply. In both the domestic and the international cases, obtaining wider consensus for durable sanctions will lead to delays in imposing sanctions as the various originators of sanctions each seek to maximize their own utility (Fearon 1998). However, our cases show that prolonged economic shocks introduce fundamental uncertainties even to established authoritarian regimes, thus raising the prospects of compliance. In the case of Iran in the Harris chapter, UN-backed sanctions ultimately led to an agreement, at least in principle, of compliance to the demands of the UN.

Coalition Making with Actors in Democracies

The cases in this book also help make sense of recent election meddling in established democracies by major autocracies such as Russia and China and longer-term lobbying by other autocracies (Mayer 2018; Brady 2017). The cases in this volume show that authoritarian leaders responded with remarkable flexibility in the face of sharp drops in available resources. Saddam Hussein, as described in the Blaydes contribution, reduced the subsidies going to the Sunni community in favor of tribes closest to him around Tikrit. Likewise, in Jordon, support was cut from the traditional tribal supporters of the monarchy in favor of the globalized elites who could help the monarchy secure greater international financing.

Such institutional and legal flexibility is inherent in authoritarian regimes (Acemoglu, Egorov, and Sonin 2008). Dictators, far more so than democratic politicians, do not need to pass laws or to disclose to the public any changes in coalition strategies. Although this freedom has trade-offs in the long run, in the short run it can be an advantage in that they can adopt new strategies and find new and useful supporters without internal hindrance. Given the substantial financial clout and global reach of some non-democracies, it would be tempting if not expected for autocracies facing an ongoing or potential crisis to redeploy resources toward acquiring international figures to join their support coalitions, even actors in advanced democracies.

Through both economic and security policies, the United States and to a lesser extent the European Union and the United Kingdom have exerted important influence on the economic well-being of many autocracies. Most obviously, economic sanctions imposed by the United States and its allies can literally bar authoritarian regimes from receiving payments for exported goods and services. This type of sanction introduces an immediate economic shock. Economic sanctions also can prevent key goods and technologies from being sold to autocracies, thus impacting the welfare of the political elite and the general population. Less severely, the United States and other advanced democracies can impose tariffs or nontariff barriers on goods exported by autocracies, worsening their balance of payments. Historically, the United States and other countries also have provided substantial aid to authoritarian regimes deemed as allies or strategic partners (Yom and Al-Momani 2008).

In the financial arena, because most of the largest banks in terms of the volume of international transactions still reside in advanced democracies, the flow of international credit mainly originates from banks domiciled in the United States, UK, EU, or Japan (Bank for International Settlement 2018). Depending on the existing debt level of authoritarian regimes, a "sudden stop" in the flow of international credit can immediately lead to a financial crisis (Reinhart and Rogoff 2009). Finally, the IMF, an organization traditionally dominated by the United States and Europe, can exert important influence over a country's access to international credit via its Article IV evaluation and inclusion of countries in its various programs (Gelos, Sahay, and Sandleris 2004).

Given that authoritarian regimes face many vulnerabilities from advanced democracies and international organizations controlled by them, it is not surprising that they try to influence policymaking in these entities. An autocracy facing prolonged downturns due to lower energy prices and US sanctions, such as Russia, may well fall victim to an elite revolt if the payoffs to the elite continue to shrink. If autocrats can exercise influence to shorten the duration or to reduce the severity of economic sanctions, the effort can make for a handsome payoff both economically and politically. Autocrats do not face much domestic opposition to overseas influence activities, and the threat of additional sanctions lacks credibility if a regime already faced substantial sanctions or international ostracism.

Besides the minimal funds required to carry out an overseas campaign, a desperate autocracy has almost nothing to lose in trying to buy political influence in advanced democracies. According to the framework of this book, autocrats merely would be reacting to crises by redeploying limited funds from domestic constituencies toward acquiring international coalition partners. To the extent that the international community has already imposed sanctions on a regime, the additional costs of angering the public in advanced democracies may be minimal, while the expected payoffs may be high, even if the probability of success is modest. In short, trying to buy influence in advanced democracy is a perfectly sensible strategy for autocrats to pursue.

What can advanced democracies do in the face of overt or subtle influence activities from autocracies? Democracies need to play to their strengths in order to weaken the incentives of autocrats and their agents to exert influence overseas. The core strengths of democracies include institutions and transparency. First and foremost, law enforcement in democracies will need to police outright attempts to interfere with elections. Whereas police forces in authoritarian regimes do the bidding of their leaders, police forces in democracies are sworn to defend a set of institutions and their integrity. Democracies should put in place legislation and a sufficient budget to enable their police forces to ensure the integrity of the democratic process from foreign autocratic influence. Clear laws and consistent policing also will disincentivize domestic political actors from receiving benefits from authoritarian governments for electoral purposes.

Moreover, transparency at the international level on the influence activities of authoritarian governments also will reduce the effectiveness of their efforts and deter agents from doing the bidding of these regimes. For example, the media and NGOs in advanced democracies can pool their resources in monitoring and disclosing to their public the overseas political activities of institutions and individuals closely linked to adversarial autocracies. After all, there are only so many billionaires in major authoritarian regimes who can serve as a front for their government. If well-documented, multilateral lists of these individuals can be derived and disclosed to the public, the effectiveness of their attempts to exert influences, though such activity is legal in many democracies, would be reduced. In general, greater transparency decreases the incentives of billionaires to aid the influence activities of these regimes because negative publicity decreases the commercial opportunities of the sympathetic billionaires and puts them at risk of legal actions.

Democracies, however, would still need to grapple with whether former officials and relatives of current and former officials can work for institutions and individuals close to adversarial autocracies. In a world of growing inequality, lobbying for autocrats seems increasingly an acceptable post-government career. Ultimately, voters and their elected officials need to have a conversation on what modes of authoritarian influence constitute threats to the healthy functioning of their democracy.

REFERENCES

Acemoglu, Daron, Georgy Egorov, and Konstantin Sonin. 2008. "Coalition Formation in Non-democracies." *Review of Economic Studies* 75 (4): 987–1009.

Acemoglu, Daron, and James A. Robinson. 2006. *Economic Origins of Dictatorship and Democracy*. New York: Cambridge University Press.

Bank for International Settlement. 2018. "Summary of Consolidated Statistics, by Nationality of Reporting Bank." In *Consolidated Statistics*. Basel: BIS.

Bellin, Eva. 2000. "Contingent Democrats: Industrialists, Labor, and Democratization in Late-Developing Countries." *World Politics* 52 (2): 175–205.

Brady, Anne-Marie. 2017. "Magic Weapons: China's Political Influence Activities under Xi Jinping." In *Kissinger Institute for the US and China Report*. Washington, DC: Wilson Center.

Brooks, Risa. 2002. "Sanctions and Regime Type: What Works, and When?" *Security Studies* 11 (4): 1–50.

Bueno de Mesquita, Bruce, Alastair Smith, Randolph M. Siverson, and James D. Morrow. 2003. *The Logic of Political Survival*. Cambridge, MA: MIT Press.

Desai, Raj M., Anders Olofsgård, and Tarik Yousef. 2009. "The Logic of Authoritarian Bargains." *Economics & Politics* 21 (1): 93–125,.

Diamond, Larry. 1996. "Is the Third Wave Over?" *Journal of Democracy* 7 (3): 20–37.

Egorov, Georgy, and Konstantin Sonin. 2011. "Dictators and Their Viziers: Endogenizing the Loyalty-Competence Trade-off." *Journal of the European Economic Association* 9 (5): 903–30.

Fearon, James. 1998. "Bargaining, Enforcement, and International Cooperation." *International Organization* 52 (2): 269–305.

Fukuyama, Francis. 1992. *The End of History and the Last Man*. New York: Free Press; Toronto: Maxwell Macmillan Canada.

Gelos, R. Gaston, Ratna Sahay, and Guido Sandleris. 2004. "Sovereign Borrowing by Developing Countries: What Determines Market Access?" IMF Working Paper No. WP/04/221. Washington, DC: IMF.

Gourevitch, Peter Alexis. 1986. *Politics in Hard Times: Comparative Responses to International Economic Crises*. Ithaca: Cornell University Press.

Haggard, Stephan. 2000. *The Political Economy of the Asian Financial Crisis*. Washington, DC: Institute for International Economics.

Haggard, Stephan, and Robert R. Kaufman. 1995. *The Political Economy of Democratic Transitions*. Princeton: Princeton University Press.

Huber, Evelyne, Dietrich Rueschemeyer, and John Stephens. 1993. "The Impact of Economic Development on Democracy." *Journal of Economic Perspectives* 7 (3): 71–86.

Huntington, Samuel P. 1991. *The Third Wave: Democratization in the Late Twentieth Century*. Norman: University of Oklahoma Press.

Keohane, Robert O. 1984. *After Hegemony: Cooperation and Discord in the World Political Economy*. Princeton: Princeton University Press.

King, Gary, Jennifer Pan, and Margaret E. Roberts. 2017. "How the Chinese Government Fabricates Social Media Posts for Strategic Distraction, Not Engaged Argument." *American Political Science Review* 111 (3): 484–501.

Kirshner, Jonathan. 1997. "The Microfoundations of Economic Sanctions." *Security Studies* 6 (3): 32–64.

Magaloni, Beatriz. 2006. *Voting for Autocracy: Hegemonic Party Survival and Its Demise in Mexico*. New York: Cambridge University Press.

Martin, Lisa. 1992. "Interests, Power, and Multilateralism." *International Organization* 46 (4): 765–92.

Mayer, Jane. 2018. "How Russia Helped Swing the Election for Trump." *New Yorker*, October 1.

O'Donnell, Guillermo A., Philippe C. Schmitter, and Laurence Whitehead. 1986. *Transitions from Authoritarian Rule*. Baltimore: Johns Hopkins University Press.

Przeworski, Adam. 1991. *Democracy and the Market: Political and Economic Reforms in Eastern Europe and Latin America*. New York: Cambridge University Press.

Reinhart, Carmen M., and Kenneth S. Rogoff. 2009. *This Time Is Different: Eight Centuries of Financial Folly*. Princeton: Princeton University Press.

Treisman, Daniel, and Sergei Guriev. 2015. "How Modern Dictators Survive: An Informational Theory of the New Authoritarianism." NBER Working Paper No. 21136. Cambridge, MA: NBER.

Yom, Sean L., and Muhammad H. Al-Momani. 2008. "The International Dimensions of Authoritarian Regime Stability: Jordan in the Post–Cold War Era." *Arab Studies Quarterly* 30 (1): 9–60.

Contributors

Lisa Blaydes is Professor of Political Science at Stanford University and a Senior Fellow at the Freeman Spogli Institute for International Studies. She is the author of *Elections and Distributive Politics in Mubarak's Egypt* (Cambridge University Press, 2011) and *State of Repression: Iraq under Saddam Hussein* (Princeton University Press, 2018). Her articles have appeared in the *American Political Science Review*, *International Studies Quarterly*, *International Organization*, *Journal of Theoretical Politics*, *Middle East Journal*, and *World Politics*.

Martin K. Dimitrov is Professor of Political Science at Tulane University. He is interested in the origins and evolution of authoritarian regimes. He has conducted fieldwork in China, Taiwan, Russia, Bulgaria, France, Germany, the Czech Republic, and Cuba.

Kevan Harris is Assistant Professor of Sociology at the University of California, Los Angeles. He is the author of *A Social Revolution: Politics and the Welfare State in Iran* (2017, University of California Press). His current research focuses on state-business relations in postrevolutionary Iran.

Natalia Lamberova is a PhD candidate in the Department of Political Science, University of California, Los Angeles.

Thomas Pepinsky is Professor of Government at Cornell University and Nonresident Senior Fellow at the Brookings Institution. His current research focuses on identity and political economy in Southeast Asia and around the world. His most recent book is *Piety and Public Opinion: Understanding Indonesian Islam* (Oxford University Press, 2018, with R. William Liddle and Saiful Mujani).

Victor C. Shih is Associate Professor at the School of Global Policy and Strategy at the University of California, San Diego, specializing in China. He is the author of *Factions and Finance in China: Elite Conflict and Inflation* (Cambridge University Press, 2008). He is further the author of numerous articles appearing in academic and business journals, including the *American Political Science Review*, *Comparative Political Studies*, *Journal of Politics*, and the *Wall Street Journal*.

Dan Slater is Professor of Political Science and the Ronald and Eileen Weiser Professor of Emerging Democracies and Director of the Weiser Center for Emerging Democracies at the University of Michigan. He is the author of *Ordering Power: Contentious Politics and Authoritarian Leviathans in Southeast Asia* (Cambridge Studies in Comparative Politics, 2010) and coauthor of *Coercive Distribution* (Cambridge Elements Series on the Politics of Development, 2018), and has published articles in journals such as the *American Journal of Political Science*, *American Journal of Sociology*, *Comparative Politics*, *Comparative Political Studies*, *International Organization*, *Journal of Democracy*, *Perspectives on Politics*, and *World Politics*. He was Professor of Political Science and Sociology at the University of Chicago from 2005, when he received his PhD from Emory University, until 2017.

Daniel Treisman is Professor of Political Science at the University of California, Los Angeles, and a research associate of the National Bureau of Economic Research. His work focuses on Russian politics and economics as well as comparative political economy, including the analysis of democratization, authoritarian states, political decentralization, and corruption. He is the editor of *The New Autocracy: Information, Politics, and Policy in Putin's Russia* (Brookings Institution Press, 2018).

Joseph Wong is Professor of Political Science at the University of Toronto, where he is also the Ralph and Roz Halbert Professor of Innovation at the Munk School of Global Affairs and Public Policy.

Sean Yom is Associate Professor of Political Science at Temple University. He is a specialist on governance, repression, and foreign policy in the Middle East, especially in Arab monarchies like Jordan, Kuwait, and Morocco. His publications include *From Resilience to Revolution: How Foreign Interventions Destabilize the Middle East* (Columbia University Press, 2016) and various academic journal, syndicated, and policy articles.

Index

Abdullah, King of Jordan, 226, 229–30
Abdullah I bin Al-Hussein, 214
Afghanistan, 94n3
Ahmadinejad, Mahmoud, 74, 76, 80, 82–86, 90–91, 93
Albania, 83
al-Dulaimi, Turki, 34
al-Majid clan, 33
al-Samarrai, Wafiq, 34
Anbar governorate, 27–29, 33–35
Anis tribe, 34
anti-regime protests. *See* protests
Anwar Ibrahim, 169, 175–80, 182–84, 186
Arab-Israeli War (1948), 216
Arab League, 220
Arab Legion, 215
Arab nationalism, 216–17
Arab Nationalist party (Jordan), 216
Arab Spring uprisings, 77, 108, 211, 228, 229–30
Ascherio, Alberto, 26
Asian Financial Crisis (1997), 10, 16, 81, 119–21, 123–27, 135–39, 145, 167–70, 173–86, 237
Asian Wall Street Journal, 187n10
austerity: China, 155–61, 237; Indonesia, 237; Iraq, 155, 237; Jordan, 237

authoritarian regimes: cases and future research, 15–18; causal mechanisms for regime outcomes, 4, 8–9, 15, 41, 72, 76, 135, 139; collapse of (*see* regime change; regime collapse); construction of, 78, 83 (*see also* post-revolutionary authoritarian regimes); repression in (*see* repression); support for (*see* coalitions); surviving economic shocks, 1–15 (*see also* regime stability/survival); uprisings against (*see* protests). *See also* communist regimes; single-party regimes; *individual countries*
authoritarian resilience, 3–8, 16, 18, 237–38, 240–42

Baathist party (Jordan), 216
Baathist regime (Iraq), 23, 26–27, 30, 33, 36. *See also* Hussein, Saddam; Iraq
Badawi, Abdullah, 181–82, 184, 186
Baghdad, 26–27, 31, 32–33
Bakr clan, 33
Bank Moskva, 103
Bank Negara (Malaysia), 177
Bank of Korea, 198
Bank Rossia, 102–3
Baram, Amatzia, 26

Barisan Nasional (BN) regime (Malaysia): Asian Financial Crisis and, 135, 168, 174–86; Chinese community support for, 169, 171–73, 187n3; elections and, 140, 181–82, 184; factionalism in, 182; military/police and, 140n4; overview of, 128–32; regime survival, 170, 213
Basra governorate, 27, 28
Bastrykin, Aleksandr, 108
Bawazier, Fuad, 140n4
Bay of Pigs invasion, 60
Bedouins, 214–15, 221
Benin, 83
Berezovsky, Boris, 103
Black September conflict (Jordan), 218–23, 225
Blaydes, Lisa, 7, 10, 13, 15, 17, 33, 121, 213, 242
Blyth, Mark, 75
BN. *See* Barisan Nasional (BN) regime (Malaysia)
Bordia, Prashant, 30
Boston Consulting Group, 148
Brazil, 74
Brooks, Risa, 241
Brumberg, Daniel, 79
Brzezinski, Zbigniew K., 46
Bulgaria: citizen complaints, 54–56; debt, 57; external funds, 8, 15, 16; information gathering, 48; protests in, 55–56, 63; regime collapse, 12, 16, 41–44, 57; repression in, 65n3; social spending, 45, 53–57; trade with Soviet Union, 16, 41–44, 50, 56–57, 63; welfare dictatorship, 16, 45, 53–57
Bulgarian Communist Party: Central Committee, 54; Politburo, 53–54, 57; State Security, 48, 55
Bush, George W., 74, 85

capital flight, 10, 13, 73, 136, 177, 223
Carothers, Thomas, 79
Castro, Fidel, 78, 98
Castro, Raúl, 61, 62
censorship, 4, 100; China, 238; Russia, 17–18, 100, 111–15. *See also* internet control; media control
Central Bank of China, 198

Central Bank of Iran (CBI), 75, 86–87, 89, 91
Central Committee Opinion Research Institute (GDR), 51
Central Electoral Commission (Russia), 114
Central European communist regimes. *See* Eastern and Central European communist regimes
Central Evaluation and Information Group (ZAIG), 51
Chechnya, 103
Cheng, Tun-jen, 194, 201
Chiang Ching-kuo, 204
Chiang Kai-shek, 192–93
China: austerity, 155–61, 237; balance of payments, 146; capital flight, 10; citizen complaints, 59; coalitions, 6, 237–38; construction projects, 153–54, 157; corruption and anticorruption measures, 150, 155, 158, 160–61; currency, 152, 162; debt, 146, 240; democracies and, 236; economic slowdown, 1, 145, 155–61; famine, 57–59; foreign exchange inflows, 152–53, 155–56, 161–62; global financial crisis (2008–9) and, 145–46, 151–55; inflation, 59, 157, 162; information gathering, 47, 49, 58–60; instability, 161–63; KMT and, 193; latent discontent, 59–60; media control, 15, 109, 238; monetary policy, 156–57, 161; overt discontent, 58; political institutions, 149–51; as postrevolutionary regime, 83, 151; protests in, 42, 47, 60, 64, 162; regime stability/survival, 5, 41–44, 145–46, 151, 161–63; repression in, 60, 162; resource mobilization, 145; shortsighted policies in, 18, 239; social spending, 60; state-owned enterprises (SOEs), 146, 152, 156; trade with Iran, 86, 93; trade with Soviet Union, 41–44, 50, 57; US embargo on, 57; wealthy elites in, 147–49, 163. *See also* Chinese Communist Party (CCP)
China Petroleum Corporation, 195
Chinese capital: in Indonesia, 136–37; in Malaysia, 132

Chinese Communist Party (CCP): Central Committee, 147, 158–60; Central Discipline and Inspection Commission (CDIC), 158; Central Law and Politics Committee, 148; control over financial system, 8, 13, 16, 145–46, 151–52, 195; "Eight Regulations," 158; Leading Group on Reform, 160; People's Armed Police, 147–48; People's Liberation Army, 147; Politburo, 147, 158, 160; Politburo Standing Committee (PSC), 147, 158–60, 163; promotion and rent-seeking opportunities, 3, 149–51, 153–55, 157–58, 161, 163; selectorate, 145–49, 159, 161–63; State Council Standing Committee, 160; strength of, 14, 237
Chua, Tian, 181
Churov, Vladimir, 114
citizen complaints: Bulgaria, 54–56; China, 59; consumption preferences and, 43; Cuba, 62–63; GDR, 50–53; information gathering and, 49. *See also* discontent
cleavages. *See* coalitions
Clinton, Hillary, 82
coalitions, 1–3; median-voter theory, 170, 185; minimum winning coalition theory, 238–39; regime outcomes and, 119–20; revisions in, 237–38; selectorate theory, 171, 185. *See also* patronage networks; protection pacts; ruling party strength; support coalitions; surplus coalitions; *individual countries and coalitions*
coercive institutions, 77; Jordan, 216, 220, 228, 231; Malaysia, 172–73, 177, 183, 185. *See also* repression
COMECON (Council for Mutual Economic Assistance), 41–42, 52, 56, 60
commodities prices, changes in, 2, 7. *See also* oil price shocks
Communist Party (Jordan), 216
communist regimes, single-party: loyalty in, 49; strength of, 146–47; trade with Soviet Union, 41–44, 63–64; welfare dictatorships, 44–64. *See also* Bulgaria; China; Eastern and Central European communist regimes; German Democratic Republic (GDR); Russia; Soviet Union
competence, 99–100
consumption preferences, 43–47; Bulgaria, 53–57; China, 57–60; Cuba, 60–63; East Germany, 50–53; information-gathering on, 48–50
co-optation, 97, 100–101; in Middle Eastern countries, 77, 214; Russia, 112–15
corruption: China, 150, 155, 158, 160–61; economic shocks and, 101; Indonesia, 134; Jordan, 220, 226; Russia, 104; South Korea, 191
Council for Economic Planning and Development (Taiwan), 203
coups: attempts against Saddam Hussein, 23, 29–30, 34–36; regimes originating in, 83, 191–92
Crimea, 110, 113
Crouch, Harold, 172
Cuba: citizen complaints, 62–63; debt, 61; economic reform, 61–62; elite cohesion, 78; information gathering, 48; oil price shocks and, 1; regime survival, 41–44, 83, 98; repression in, 62; social spending, 45; trade with Soviet Union, 41–44, 50, 60–63; US sanctions on, 60–61; welfare dictatorship, 60–64

Davis, Eric, 33
debt, 6–8, 12, 14–15, 41–42, 50, 243; Bulgaria, 57; China, 146, 154–57, 161–62, 240; Cuba, 61; GDR, 52; Jordan, 223, 225, 227; Korea, 190, 197–99; Latin America, 81; Malaysia, 172, 174–75, 177, 240; Mexico, 79; Russia, 101–2, 104, 110
defamation, 108
Delikat/Exquisit shops, 51
Demetry, David, 123
Demetry, Lionel, 123
democracies, 7, 236; foreign autocratic influence in, 242–45; regime change policies and, 240–42
Democratic Action Party (DAP), 179, 181, 183

democratization, 77, 94n2, 237–38; "democracy through strength," 178, 182, 185–86, 207–8. *See also* political liberalization
Deripaska, Oleg, 105
developmentalist regimes, 130–31, 189, 191–92, 199, 205
Dewan Rakyat (Malaysia), 128
Dhi Qar (Iraq), 28, 31
Díaz-Canel, Miguel, 62
DiFonzo, Nicholas, 30
Dimitrov, Martin K., 9, 13, 15, 16, 237
direct investment, 2, 9, 13; China, 152; Taiwan, 203; withdrawal of, 9–10
discontent, 45–47. *See also* citizen complaints; latent discontent; opposition coalitions; overt discontent; protests
Donetsk, 110
Dozhd (Russian television), 112
Dulaim tribe, 34
durability. *See* regime stability/survival
duration of economic shocks. *See* shock duration
Durov, Pavel, 112

Eastern and Central European communist regimes: information gathering, 49; longevity of, 4–5, 237; oil price shocks and, 9; protests against, 47; state control over financial systems, 8; welfare dictatorships, 64. *See also* Bulgaria; German Democratic Republic (GDR)
Economic Planning Board (Korea), 192, 197, 204
economic sanctions: duration of economic shocks and, 241; economic crises and, 2, 7; effect versus effectiveness of, 72–76, 92–94; and elite defection from support coalitions, 14 (*see also* coalitions); imposed by democracies, 2, 10, 12, 16, 60–61, 72, 82, 86, 242, 243; regime change and, 240–42; on Russia, 110, 243. *See also* Iraq; Islamic Republic of Iran
economic shocks: defined, 2, 36n2; institutions and, 3–5, 8–18. *See also* economic sanctions; financial crises; oil price shocks; *individual countries*

Egypt, 77, 83, 214, 217
Eisenhower Doctrine, 217
el-Baradei, Mohammad, 82
elections: Indonesia, 128; Jordan, 210; Malaysia, 140, 181–82, 184, 185; Russia, 107, 114, 115n10; South Korea, 193, 199–201, 205, 207
electoral autocracies, 46–47; elite cohesion and, 79; fraud and, 115n10
elite cohesion, 78–79, 81–85. *See also* coalitions
emerging market (EM) countries, financial crises in, 9–10, 104, 119. *See also* Indonesia; Malaysia
Employees Provident Fund, 172, 174
Enloe, Cynthia H., 129
European Union (EU), 74–75, 86, 243
executions, 60
external funds, 12–14; Bulgaria, 8, 15, 16; German Democratic Republic (GDR), 8, 13, 15, 16; Iraq, 13, 23–24; Jordan, 8, 13–14; Russia, 8

factions. *See* coalitions
Falklands Island, 101
Farhi, Farideh, 79
Federal Reserve, 9–10, 161
financial crises: Asian Financial Crisis (1997), 10, 16, 81, 119–21, 123–27, 135–39, 145, 167–70, 173–86, 237; causes of, 9–10; control over financial systems and, 14; global (2008–9), 10, 98–99, 104–15, 145–46, 151–55; Indonesia and Malaysia (1980s), 119–23, 132–35, 138–40
financial institutions, regime control over, 2; authoritarian durability and, 205–8; China, 8, 145–46, 151–52; duration of financial crises and, 10; Eastern and Central European communist regimes, 8; external funds and, 12–14; Indonesia, 8, 16; Iran, 73, 88–91; Malaysia, 13, 16, 172; regime outcomes and, 7–12, 236–37; Russia, 13; South Korea, 205–8; Soviet Union, 8; Taiwan, 8, 13, 16, 195, 205–8; UMNO, 16
First Gulf War (1990–91), 25–26
Food and Agricultural Organization (FAO), 26

France, 93
Frantz, Erica, 129
Freedom House, 109
Friedrich, Carl J., 46
funds, external. *See* external funds

Gaddhafi, Mu'ammar, 38n43, 98
Galtieri, Leopoldo, 101
Geddes, Barbara, 3, 129
German Democratic Republic (GDR): citizen complaints, 50–53; debt, 52; external funds, 8, 13, 15, 16; information gathering, 58; protests in, 5, 50, 52–53, 63–64; regime collapse, 12, 16, 41–44; repression in, 50, 60, 65n3; secret police in, 5; social spending, 45, 50–53; Stasi, 48, 51, 58, 65n3; trade with Soviet Union, 16, 41–44, 50, 52, 63; welfare dictatorship, 16, 45, 50–53
Germany, 72, 93
Golkar (Indonesia), 127–29, 136, 138–39
Gorbachev, Mikhail, 53
Granma (Cuban newspaper), 62–63
Great Leap Forward (China), 57, 58
Green Movement (Iran), 76, 80, 82
Greenpeace (organization), 108
Gref, German, 103
Gulf War, 223
Guriev, Sergei, 99–100, 114
Gusinsky, Vladimir, 103

Habibie, B. J., 137
Haggard, Stephan, 75, 148, 203
Harmoko, 136, 139
Harris, Kevan, 15, 16, 36n2, 242
Hasan, Bob, 140n4
Hashemi-Rafsanjani, 80
Hashemite monarchy, 210–32
Havel, Václav, 44
Herb, Michael, 77
Heryanto, Ariel, 179
Hirschman, Albert O., 49
Hishamuddin Hussein, 183–84
Honecker, Erich, 52–53
Housing Bank (Iran), 91
Huang Guangyu, 148
Hu Jintao, 148, 154–55, 159–60
Huntington, Sam, 83
Hussein, King of Jordan, 216, 220–21

Hussein, Saddam: coup and assassination attempts against, 23, 29–30, 34–36; regime survival, 12, 98; secret police and, 5; spending by, 38n40; support coalitions and, 7, 17, 29–36, 121, 242. *See also* Baathist regime (Iraq); Iraq
Hussein, Uday, 30
Hussein Onn, 183

Ibrahim clan, 33
import substitution industrialization (ISI), 192
Indonesia: Asian Financial Crisis (1997) and, 119–21, 123–27, 135–39, 174, 177; austerity, 237; capital flight, 10; Chinese capital in, 136–37; deregulation, 132–35; elections, 128; elite splits in, 78; employment, 123, 125–26; ethnic violence, 179–80; exchange rate, 124–25, 135; financial crisis (1980s), 119–23, 132–35, 138–39; financial management of open economy, 124–25; government expenditures, 123, 125–27, 132; liberalization, 120–21, 123; political structures, 127–32; privatization, 120–21, 123, 132–35; protests in, 136–37, 181; regime collapse, 12, 83, 135–38; repression in, 137; revenues, 123, 125–26; state control over financial system, 8, 16; support coalitions, 127–32, 134, 139–40; veto players, 131; widespread directed credit, 124
Indonesian Bank Restructuring Agency, 136
Indonesian Democratic Party, 128
inflation, 13; China, 59, 157, 162; Iran, 73, 87, 89, 91; Iraq, 30–31; Jordan, 221; Korea, 193–94, 197; Malaysia, 183, 185; Taiwan, 190, 193–97, 199, 205
information control. *See* censorship; media control; propaganda
information-gathering institutions, 46–50, 58–60, 64
Information-Sociological Center, 54, 56
Institute of Collective Action, 105
institutional strength, 5–6, 138–40, 168–70. *See also* ruling party strength

institutions, political and financial, interactions between, 1–3, 6–18
Integrated Public Use Microdata Series (IPUMS), 26
interest groups. *See* coalitions
Internal Security Act (ISA), 173, 183, 184
International Atomic Energy Agency (IAEA), 82
international credit, 243. *See also* external funds
International Monetary Fund (IMF): Asian Financial Crisis and, 174; influence of, 243; Iranian economy and, 75, 90; Jordan and, 223–25, 228; Soviet Union and, 53
internet control, 4; Russia, 17–18, 108–9, 111–12. *See also* censorship; media control
Intershop/Genex shops, 51
investments. *See* direct investment; portfolio investments
Iran-Iraq War, 16, 83, 87
Iraq: austerity, 155, 237; childhood stunting, 22, 28; child mortality, 22, 25–27, 35, 36n8, 37n9; citizen petitions, 37n10; coalitional adjustments, 238–40; co-optation in, 214; economic sanctions on, 7, 10, 13, 16–17, 22–36, 121; external funds and imports, 13, 23–24; food-rationing system, 24–25, 29, 36n3; inflation, 30–31; malnutrition, 22, 24–25, 28, 36n4; protests in, 32–35; regime survival, 35–36, 213; rumors and political dissent, 23, 30–32, 36, 37n31, 38n40, 38n43; trade with Iran, 94n3. *See also* Baathist regime (Iraq); Hussein, Saddam; Iran-Iraq War
Islamic Republic of Iran: balance-of-payments surplus, 15; coalitional adjustments, 239–40; currency crises, 86–87; diffuse political institutions, 73, 76–85, 93–94, 94n1; economic sanctions on, 10, 16–17, 72–76, 85–94, 242; economy, 75, 85–91, 94n3; elites, 73; inflation, 73, 87, 89, 91; and Joint Comprehensive Plan of Action (JCPOA), 72–74, 77–79, 83–85, 89, 92–93; monetary policy, 89, 91; nuclear enrichment program, 72–76, 80–82, 92–93; oil and, 91; postrevolutionary origins, 91, 93; protests in, 1, 76, 80, 82; state control over financial system, 73, 88–91; trade with China, 86, 93; trade with Iraq, 94n3; trade with Russia, 93. *See also* Iran-Iraq War
Israel, 216; Jordan and, 220, 227
Israeli-Palestinian conflict, 225

Jervis, Robert, 75
Jiang Zemin, 159
Joint Comprehensive Plan of Action (JCPOA), 72–74, 77–79, 83–85, 89, 92–93
Jordan: austerity, 237; British colonial rule, 214–15; business elites, 211, 213–14, 226–32; capital flight, 223; civil society, 210, 224; conflict between Palestinians and tribal Jordanians, 212–14, 223, 225; corruption in, 220, 226; debt, 223, 225, 227; democratic reforms, 224, 228; domestic revenue, 220–21, 224; economic crisis in, 1, 223–26, 232; elections, 210; ethnocracy, 218–22; external funds, 8, 13–14; foreign aid, 212–13, 217–18, 220–21, 223, 225, 227–28, 232; inflation, 221; Iraqi rumors about, 31–32; martial law, 224, 231; monarchy, institutional nature of, 212–13, 231–32; neoliberal economics, 210–12, 214, 226–32; oil price shocks and, 9, 121, 223; opposition movements, 210, 216–17; Palestinians in, 216–23, 226, 228–30; patronage networks, 210–32; political liberalization, 6–7, 210–11, 224–26, 228; political parties in, 231; private sector, 222, 226–27; privatization, 226–27; protests in, 223–24, 229–30; public sector, 222, 224, 227; regime survival, 12; repression, 211–12, 216–17, 219, 229–30; shortsighted policies in, 18; strikes in, 229; structural adjustment, 225; support coalition, changes in, 210–32, 238; tribal-state compact, 210–32; Western states and, 217–18, 220, 227–28, 232

Juburi tribe, 34
Jumailat tribe, 34

Karbala (Iraq), 28
Kasparov, Garry, 109
Kaufman, Robert, 75, 148
Keadilan (Malaysian multiracial party), 180, 182, 183
Kedah (Malaysia), 183
Kerry, John, 92
Khamenei, Ali, 81, 83–84, 93
Khaskovo, Bulgaria, 53
Khatami, Mohammad, 80, 85
Khodorkovsy, Mikhail, 102, 103, 108
Khomeini, 80
Kim, Eun Mee, 203
Kim Dae-jung, 191, 193, 200, 201
Kim Jong-il, 98
Kirshner, Jonathan, 241
Kiselyov, Dmitri, 111
KMT. *See* Kuomintang (KMT)
Korea. *See* Republic of Korea
Kostin, Andrei, 103
Kovalchuk, Yuri, 102–3, 106
KPB (Konsortium Perkapalan Berhad), 175
Krenz, Egon, 53
Kuala Lumpur Stock Exchange, 173
Kubaysis tribe, 34
Kudrin, Aleksey, 104, 105
Kuomintang (KMT): arrival in Taiwan, 192; international derecognition of, 193; oil price shock (1973) and, 14, 194–200; prevention of opposition coalition, 200–204; regime survival, 190–91
Kurdish areas of Iraq, 26, 28, 32–33
Kuwait, 77, 223

Lacy, Dean, 10
Lamberova, Natalia, 9, 13, 15, 17, 213, 238
Lankina, Tomila, 105
latent discontent, 45–47; East Germany, 52–53; information on, 48; social spending and, 49, 63–64. *See also* overt discontent
Latin America, 4, 81
Lebanon, 213

Lee, Jonghyuk, 158
legitimacy, 4, 192; dynastic, 212; economic development and, 189, 191–92, 200, 204; in Iran, 84; of KMT regime, 193, 201–2; welfare dictatorships and, 42, 50, 61
Lehman Brothers (US bank), 104
Leninist party structures, 4
Levada Center, 111
Levitsky, Steven, 83
Liddle, R. William, 137
Liu Han, 149
Liu Yandong, 159
Loke, Anthony, 179–80
longevity. *See* regime stability/survival
loyalty, 49, 101; of tribal communities in Jordan, 211, 213, 214, 222–26
Lugansk, 110

Magaloni, Beatriz, 239
Mahathir Mohamad, 4, 129–30, 134, 138–39, 169, 170, 173–78, 181, 186
Malaysia: adjustment policies, 168; Asian Financial Crisis (1997) and, 119–21, 123–27, 135–39, 145, 167–70, 173–76; capital controls, 176–78, 180, 187n10; capital flight, 10, 13, 177; Chinese capital in, 132, 187n3; Chinese minority population, 168–70, 178–81; crisis quiescence, 168; debt, 172, 174–75, 177, 240; democratization, 178, 182, 185–86; deregulation, 132–35; economic growth, 183; employment, 123, 125–26; ethnic conflicts, 172, 179–80; ethnic Malay population, 168–70, 178–81; exchange rate, 124–25, 135; financial crisis (1980s), 119–23, 132–35, 138–40; financial management of open economy, 124–25; government expenditures, 123, 125–27, 132, 174–75, 182, 184, 185; inflation, 183, 185; liberalization, 120–21, 123; maladjustment, 176–85; media control, 15; opposition coalition, 178–81, 184, 186; patronage networks, 184; political structures, 128–32; privatization, 120–21, 123, 132–35; protection pact, 170, 178–82; protest delay, 168–69, 178–81; protests in, 169, 178–81,

Malaysia (*continued*)
  187n3; pump-priming, 170, 175, 180, 182; regime survival, 5, 83; repression in, 170, 172–73, 180, 182–84, 186; revenues, 123, 125–26; ruling party strength, 14, 168–73, 178–82, 185–86; shortsighted policies in, 18, 239; state control over financial system, 13, 16, 172; support coalitions, 6, 134, 139–40, 168–69, 178–81, 201, 237, 238; veto players, 131, 173; widespread directed credit, 124
Malaysian Chinese Association (MCA), 128, 171, 180, 183, 187n3
Malaysian Indian Congress (MIC), 128
Malaysian Islamic Party (PAS), 180, 182
Mamontov, Arkady, 109
Mandal, Sumit, 179
Mao Zedong, 57–60, 76
Maysan (Iraq), 31
Mazaheri, Nimah, 35
Mazlum, Mohammed, 34
MCA. *See* Malaysian Chinese Association (MCA)
media control: China, 15, 109, 238; Malaysia, 15; Russia, 15, 17–18, 103–4, 108–9, 111–14, 238; strong one-party states, 14–15, 100. *See also* censorship; internet control
median-voter theory, 170, 185
Medvedev, Dmitri, 107, 108
Mehr program (Iran), 91
Memorial (human rights organization), 108
Mexico, 79, 239
Meyer, David, 158
MIC. *See* Malaysian Indian Congress (MIC)
Middle East, 4; authoritarianism in, 77; postrevolutionary states in, 83. *See also* Israel; Jordan
military conflicts, 101, 111, 113–14
minimum winning coalition theory, 238–39
Ministry of State Security (China), 59
Mirzan Mahathir, 175
monarchies, 5, 212–13, 231–32. *See also* Jordan

monetary policies, 6–7; China, 156–57, 161; Iran, 89, 91; Korea, 196
Mousavi, Mir-Hossein, 82
Muslim Brotherhood, 225
Muthanna (Iraq), 28

Nahavandian, Mohammad, 92
National Consultative Council (Jordan), 221
National Iranian Oil Company, 86
National Union (Jordan), 221
Navalny, Alexei, 108, 112, 114
neoliberal economics, 210–12, 214, 226–32
Nephew, Richard, 75
New Economic Policy (Malaysia), 130, 171
New Order regime (Indonesia), 16, 120, 127–32, 135, 139
Niou, Emerson M. S., 10
nongovernmental organizations (NGOs), 107–8, 244
Non-Proliferation Treaty, 85
North Korea, 83

Obama, Barack, 85–86, 92–93
Oil-for-Food program (Iraq), 24, 26, 32
oil price shocks, 9, 14, 102, 121–22, 132; 1973 energy crisis, 189–90, 193–208
one-party regimes. *See* single-party regimes
Onn Jaafar, 183
OPEC crisis (1973), 189–90, 193–208
opinion polling, 48, 59, 62
opposition coalitions: in Jordan, 210, 216–17; in Malaysia, 120, 178–81, 184, 186; in South Korea, 201; in Soviet Union, 4; in Taiwan, 191, 200–204. *See also* discontent; protests; regime collapse
Organisation for Economic Co-operation and Development (OECD), 2, 162
overt discontent, 45–47; social spending and, 49; welfare dictatorships and, 63–64. *See also* discontent; protests

Palestinian Liberation Organization, 220
Palestinians: and Israeli-Palestinian con-

flict, 225; in Jordan, 212–14, 216–23, 225–26, 228–30
Pamfilova, Ella, 114
Pancasila (Indonesian ideology), 128
Paris Club, 61
Park Chung-hee, 190–93, 197–205
Partido Revolucionario Institucional (PRI), 79, 239
PAS. *See* Malaysian Islamic Party (PAS)
patronage networks, 78, 82, 182; Iran, 80; Jordan, 210–32; Korea, 203; Malaysia, 184. *See also* coalitions
Penang (Malaysia), 183
People's Bank of China (PBOC), 152, 156–57
People's Congress, 148
People's Consultative Assembly (MPR), 128
Pepinsky, Thomas, 13, 15, 16, 187n3
Petronas (Malaysian oil company), 174–75
Philippines, 181
Pikalyovo, Russia, 104–5
Plovdiv, Bulgaria, 53
Poland, 47, 55
Political Consultative Conference, 148
political liberalization, 238–39; Indonesia, 120–21, 123; Jordan, 6–7, 210–11, 224–26, 228; Malaysia, 120–21, 123. *See also* democratization
popularity of leaders, 99–100, 114, 238
portfolio investments, 2, 9–10, 131, 174
postrevolutionary authoritarian regimes, 78; diffuse ruling institutions, 78–81; elite cohesion in, 81–85; ruling coalitions, 78
preference falsification, 46, 48, 49
propaganda, 15, 18, 239; Russian, 100, 107, 109, 111–15
protection pacts, 82; in Malaysia, 170, 178–82
protests: in Bulgaria, 55–56, 63; in China, 42, 47, 60, 64, 162; in Eastern and Central European communist regimes, 47; in German Democratic Republic (GDR), 5, 50, 52–53, 63–64; in Indonesia, 136–37, 181; in Iran, 1, 76, 80, 82; in Iraq, 32–35; in Jordan, 223–24, 229–30; in Malaysia, 168–69, 178–81, 187n3; in Russia, 105–9, 111–12; in Taiwan, 202. *See also* discontent; opposition coalitions; regime collapse; uprisings
provision pacts, 78
Pussy Riot (performance artists), 108, 109
Putin, Vladimir, 11, 17, 98–99, 102–15, 213, 238

Rania, Queen of Jordan, 229
Rawis tribe, 34
Razak, Najib, 139, 184, 186
rebellions. *See* protests; uprisings
regime change, 2, 8; economic sanctions and, 240–42
regime collapse, 6, 8–12; competitive elections and, 47; institutions and, 5; prolonged economic shocks and, 15; welfare dictatorships and, 64. *See also individual countries*
regime stability/survival, 1–6, 168, 236–45; Iraq, 29; key variables, 2–3 (*see also* financial institutions, regime control over; ruling party strength; shock duration); single-party regimes, 3, 150, 236–37; statistics on regime type, 65n2; strategies for, 99–101; welfare dictatorships and, 63. *See also individual countries*
repression, 4–5, 46–47, 185, 239; Bulgaria, 65n3; China, 60, 162; Cuba, 62; German Democratic Republic (GDR), 50, 60, 65n3; Indonesia, 137; Jordan, 211–12, 216–17, 219, 229–30; Malaysia, 170, 172–73, 180, 182–84, 186; Russia, 107–15, 239
Republic of Korea: Asian Financial Crisis and, 177; chaebol sector, 197–98, 200; corruption in, 191; debt, 190, 197–99; democratization, 207–8; developmental state regime, 189, 191–92, 199, 205; economic growth, 189–90, 192; elections, 193, 199–201, 205, 207; Emergency Decree for Economic Stability, 198; export drive, 190–91, 193, 197–99, 204; heavy and chemical industries, 193, 197, 204; inflation, 193–94, 197; land reform, 192;

Republic of Korea (*continued*)
  monetary policy, 196; oil price shock (1973) and, 189–90, 193–94, 197–208; opposition parties, 201; patronage networks, 203; political legitimacy, 192; regime survival, 190–91, 199–207; state control over financial system, 205–8; strength of ruling party, 205–8; support coalitions, 191, 200–204; trade with Iran, 86
RIA Novosti (Russian news agency), 111
Robertson, Graeme, 105
Roh Tae-woo, 207
Rosmolodezh (agency), 109
Rosneft (Russian oil company), 102
Rotenberg, Arkady and Boris, 106
Rouhani, Hassan, 80, 85–86, 89, 91–93
Rozenas, Arturas, 100
ruling coalitions. *See* coalitions
ruling party strength, 2, 8–12, 14–15, 17–18, 185–86; authoritarian durability and, 205–8; broad coalitions and, 170–71; "democracy through strength," 178, 182, 185–86, 207–8. *See also individual countries and coalitions*
rumors: in Bulgaria, 48; in Iraq, 23, 30–32, 36, 37n31, 38n40, 38n43
RusAl (company), 105
Russia: capital flight, 10; censorship in, 17–18, 100, 111–15; co-optation in, 112–15; corruption in, 104; debt, 101–2, 104, 110; economic rebound in, 101–4; economic sanctions on, 110, 243; elections, 107, 114, 115n10; emergency management, 105, 112–13; external funds, 8; global financial crisis (2008) and, 98–99, 104–15; media control, 15, 17–18, 103–4, 108–9, 111–14, 238; military interventions, 110, 111, 113–14; oil prices and, 1, 9; propaganda in, 100, 107, 109, 111–15, 238; protests in, 105–9, 111–12; regime survival, 12; repression in, 107–15, 239; selectorate, 101, 113; social spending, 106; state control over financial system, 13; strength of ruling party, 17; support coalition, changes in, 11; trade account, 116n31; trade with Iran, 93; wages in, 105, 109. *See also* Soviet Union
Russia Today (news agency), 111

Sadli's Law, 132, 140n3
Salah al-Din (Iraq), 28, 33
sanctions. *See* economic sanctions
Sassoon, Joseph, 24, 35
Saudi Arabia, 1, 215, 220, 228
Sberbank (Russian bank), 103
Schürer, Gerhard, 52
Scitovsky, Tibor, 196
Seabrooke, Leonard, 75
secret police, 4–5, 239, 241
Selangor (Malaysia), 183
selectorate, 43, 63; rewards for, 44, 101, 113. *See also* patronage networks
selectorate theory, 171, 185
Shanghai, 58
Shanghai Municipal Party Committee, 59
Shia areas of Iraq, 27
Shih, Victor C., 13, 15, 16, 36n2, 158, 200, 237
Shiite-majority areas of Iraq, 28, 29
shock duration, 2–3, 6–12, 14–15; economic sanctions and, 241, 243; regime control over financial institutions and, 237. *See also individual countries*
shortsighted policies, 8, 18, 185, 195, 239
Siang, Lim Kit, 181
single-party regimes: stability of, 3, 150, 236–37; strength of, 5, 14, 79. *See also* communist regimes, single-party
slander, 108
Slater, Dan, 15, 16, 78, 81–82, 145, 147, 201, 207, 213, 219, 240
socialist consumption, 44–50
social media, 17–18. *See also* internet control
social spending, 42–43; discontent and, 44–49, 63–64; information gathering and, 48–50; regime collapse and, 64. *See also* welfare dictatorships
Soeharto, 127–31, 134–39
Sokolov, Sergei, 108
South Korea. *See* Republic of Korea
Soviet Union: collapse of, 77, 78; media liberalization, 47; one-party regime,

147; opposition to, 4; perestroika, 47, 48; state control over financial system, 8; trade with, 16, 41–44, 50, 52, 56–57, 60–64; welfare dictatorship, 45. *See also* Russia

Springer, Axel, 111–12

Stalin, Joseph, 50

status quo coalitions, 8–12, 236–37

strikes, 50, 53, 229

Suharto, 78, 148

Sukarno, 127

Sunnis (in Iraq), 17, 27–29, 33–35, 121, 242

support coalitions, 2; broad, 170–71; changes in, 8–12; duration of economic shock and, 6–7; economic sanctions and, 240–42; elite defection from, 14; reducing benefits to, 7, 17, 237–39, 237–39; regime outcomes and, 5–7. *See also* coalitions; *individual countries and coalitions*

surplus coalitions, 7, 43, 239

Svolik, Milan, 149

SWIFT (Society of Worldwide Interbank Financial Telecommunications), 86, 89

Syarwan Hamid, 136

Syngman Rhee, 191

Syria, 1, 113–14, 213, 214, 217, 220

Taiwan: coalitions, 236–37; democratization, 207–8; developmental state regime, 189, 191–92, 199, 201–2, 205; distributive politics, 201–2; economic growth, 189–90, 192; foreign assets, 198; industrial organization, 202; inflation, 190, 193–97, 199, 205; land reform, 192, 201–2; oil price shocks and, 9, 14, 16, 189–90, 193–208; as one-party state, 200; opposition coalitions, 191, 200–204; political legitimacy, 192; private sector, 203; protests in, 202; regime survival, 190–91, 199–207; resource mobilization, 145; Six-Year Plan, 196; stabilization measures, 190–91, 194–99; state control over financial system, 8, 13, 16, 195, 205–8; state-owned enterprises (SOEs), 195–96; strength of ruling party, 14, 205–8; tax schemes, 196; Ten Major Projects, 196

Taiwan Power (SOE), 195

Talfah clan, 33

Teske, Werner, 60

Thailand, 125, 173, 177

Thorbecke, Erik, 123

Tiananmen protests, 42, 47, 60

Timchenko, Gennady, 106

Transjordanians, 210–32

transparency, 244

Treisman, Daniel, 9, 13, 15, 17, 99–100, 114, 213, 238

Tunisia, 77

Turkey, 74, 83

Tutut (Soeharto's daughter), 140n4

Ukraine, 83, 110–11, 113–14

Union for Solidarity with Political Prisoners (USPP), 108

United Arab Emirates, 77

United Development Party, 128

United Kingdom, 243

United Malays National Organization (UMNO), 4, 13, 128, 130–31, 134, 138–40; Asian Financial Crisis (1997) and, 168, 174–86; control over financial system, 16; elections and, 181–82, 184; ethnic Malay support for, 169, 171; factionalism in, 182, 183; MCA and, 187n3; regime survival, 170, 213. *See also* Barisan Nasional (BN) regime (Malaysia)

United Nations (UN): economic sanctions imposed by, 22–24, 72, 82, 86, 242; Inter-Agency Humanitarian Programme for Iraq, 26; Relief and Works Agency, 218; Taiwan and, 193

United Russia (UR) party, 114

United States (US): aid to Jordan, 217–18, 225, 232; dollar rates, 161; economic sanctions imposed by, 2, 10, 12, 16, 60–61, 243; global financial crisis (2008) and, 104, 106–7; Iranian nuclear program negotiations, 74, 80–81, 91, 92

United States-Jordan Free Trade Agreement (2001), 226

uprisings, 1, 12, 32–33, 97–98; Arab Spring, 77, 108, 211, 228, 229–30. *See also* discontent; protests
VKontakte (social media), 112
VTB (Russian bank), 103

Wade, Robert, 195, 203
Walder, Andrew G., 147
Walter, Alissa, 37n10
Wang Qishan, 158–59
Way, Lucan, 83
welfare dictatorships, 16, 42–50; information on consumption preferences, 48–50; latent discontent and, 63–64; political logic of, 45–47. *See also* social spending
Wen Jiabao, 154–55, 160
West Bank, 225
Widmaier, Wesley, 75
Wiranto, 137
Wong, Joseph, 9, 13, 15, 16, 145, 237
Woo, Jung-en, 197, 204
Worker-Peasant Inspection, 51

World Bank, 223–25, 228
World Economic Forum, 226
World Trade Organization (WTO), 152, 226
Wright, Joseph, 129

Xi Jinping, 146, 150, 158–63
Xi Zhongxun, 59
Xu Caihou, 158

Yeltsin, Boris, 11, 104
Yom, Sean L., 6–7, 13–15, 18, 121
Yukos (Russian oil company), 102
Yushin constitution (Korea), 193, 197, 201, 204

Zahid Hamidi, Ahmad, 175–76
Zainuddin, Daim, 139
Zambia, 83
Zarif, Javad, 73, 81, 84, 85–86
Zhivkov, Todor, 57
Zhou Youngkang, 148–49, 158
Zimbabwe, 83
Zyuganov, Gennady, 104